英语专业系列教材

A COURSE IN
CHINESE-ENGLISH TRANSLATION

汉英语篇翻译

李运兴　编著

清华大学出版社
北　京

内容简介

本书参照互文性理论，确立了通过阅读英语原创语篇获取语言资源、通过分析汉英对照语篇领悟翻译技能，以及通过翻译试笔体会翻译过程的三环相扣的汉译英教学模式。教程本着以读促译、"以渔代鱼"的原则，着意引导学生以教材为起始点，因人制宜，自我探索、丰富和完善。本书结构新颖，语料充实，极具启示性。通过学习本书，学习者可提高英语表达能力，掌握不同体裁汉语语篇的英译要领，进而独立承担实际翻译任务。

本书可作为英语专业高年级或翻译专业汉译英课程教材，也可供水平相当的英语学习者阅读使用。

版权所有，侵权必究。举报：010-62782989，beiqinquan@tup.tsinghua.edu.cn。

图书在版编目（CIP）数据

汉英语篇翻译 / 李运兴编著. —北京：清华大学出版社，2015（2021.8重印）
英语专业系列教材
ISBN 978-7-302-41666-1

Ⅰ.①汉⋯ Ⅱ.①李⋯ Ⅲ.①英语-翻译-高等学校-教材 Ⅳ.①H315.9

中国版本图书馆CIP数据核字（2015）第233624号

责任编辑：曹诗悦
封面设计：李双双
责任校对：王荣静
责任印制：沈　露

出版发行：清华大学出版社
网　　址：http://www.tup.com.cn，http://www.wqbook.com
地　　址：北京清华大学学研大厦A座　　邮　　编：100084
社 总 机：010-62770175　　　　　　　　邮　　购：010-62786544
投稿与读者服务：010-62776969，c-service@tup.tsinghua.edu.cn
质量反馈：010-62772015，zhiliang@tup.tsinghua.edu.cn

印 装 者：涿州市京南印刷厂
经　　销：全国新华书店
开　　本：170mm×230mm　　印　张：20.75　　字　数：357千字
版　　次：2015年9月第1版　　　　　　　　印　次：2021年8月第5次印刷
定　　价：78.00元

产品编号：063538-04

Preface 前言

> **语篇翻译、互文关系、因袭性**

对于翻译教学，我们自 20 世纪 90 年代以来一直在进行认真的求索。

在 1998 年出版的《英汉语篇翻译》（李运兴，1998）中，我们提出了语篇翻译的三个"强调"，即"强调语篇的整体性及层次性""强调翻译是一个动态的译者的思维和决策过程""强调语篇由于文体不同在翻译策略及方法上造成的差异"（见该书前言），初步确立了以语篇为基点的教学思路。八年后（2006 年），该书修订版秉持第一版的教学原则，进一步凸显了"语篇是翻译操作的最终决策级层"以及"语篇在一定的语境中发挥交际功能"等教学思想（见该书第二版前言）。又过了五年（2011 年），该书又进行了增删，着力培养学生的"五种意识"，其中除了"培养职业伦理意识"和"强化交际意识"之外，特别提出了"互文意识"的重要性（见该书第三版前言）。

不论是原文还是译文，它们都是各自语篇世界中的一员，都与其他语篇有着种种联系。这种联系存在于语篇所属的语言体系中，也可能是跨语言的。译文的构建既受到原文的制约，也受到译语中其他语篇，特别是在体裁和题材上相似、相近的语篇的制约。原文是译文之源，但原文也可能和目标语（及其他语言）中业已存在的语篇具有某些关联。

互文关系可表现为不同的层面。就语言范畴而言，包括引用、典故（allusion）、模仿（parody）、套语（cliché）、修辞方法等。比如，美国民主党国会议员、1984 年副总统候选人 Geraldine Ferraro 在当年民主党代表大会上的发言中说："The issue is not what America can do for women but what women can do for America."显然这是在仿照肯尼迪就职演说中的"Ask not what your country can do for you but what you can do for your country."一句的所谓交错配列修辞法（chiasmus）。就交际方式而言，互文性可表现为对其他语篇的回应、颂扬、支持、反驳等互动关系。而就语篇结构而言，则可包括对固有成篇模式、叙述结构、体例等的依循或反叛关系。

语篇和语篇间的联系不仅仅是语言的，还必然是文化的。"在后现代时代，理论家们经常声言，已很难谈论一件艺术品的原创性或独特性，不管是绘画还是小说，因为每一件艺术品都显然是由已经存在的艺术品的片段组装而成的"（In the Postmodern epoch, theorists often claim, it is not possible any longer to speak of originality or the uniqueness of the artistic object, be it a painting or novel, since every artistic object is so clearly assembled from bits and pieces of already existent art.）（Allen, 2000）。互文关系实际上为人类的语言交际编织了一个无所不在的大网。

在本人 2006 年出版的《汉英翻译教程》（李运兴，2006）中，我们同样遵循互文性原则，针对以外语为目标语的翻译的特点，提出"汉译英不同于英译汉的是，译者会更倚重于英语写作中所固有的因袭成分"。也就是说，英语业已存在的语篇的行文、措辞、搭配、句式等，都是译者构建英语译文的导向性参照。没有对英语成篇规范的了解和把握，译者将无从组词成句，连句成章。

翻译语篇较之原创语篇具有较少创新性，而有更多的因袭性，这得到了语料库资料的印证。首先，语料库研究表明了语言使用中创造性和因袭性的关系：

语言的创造性是毋庸置疑的，但语料库的索引强有力地提醒我们，在大部分话语中，我们都是被习惯驱使的生物，我们的话语有很大一部分是可预知的，不论谈论什么我们都一直在重复着同样的陈旧词语和套话。如果不是这样，语言就无法发挥功能。人类不能容忍太多的创造性（The creative potential of language is undeniable, but the concordances to a corpus remind us forcibly that in most of our utterances we are creatures of habit, immensely predictable, rehearsing the same old platitudes and the same old clichés in almost everything we say. If it were not so, language would become unworkable. Humankind cannot bear very much creativity.）（Hanks, 1995）。

其次，译文的语言一般倾向于规范化（normalization）。Vanderauwera 在她的荷兰语—英语翻译小说语料库研究中发现，大量的标点、选词、文体、句子结构、谋篇布局等方面的转换都指向一个明显的倾向：对"显然被目标语读者所认可的语篇规范"的倚重（"tendency towards textual conventionality" apparently approved of by the target audience）（Baker, 1998）。翻译语篇的这个特点，如果放在目标语为外语的翻译培训和实践中，会更加凸显其启发和导向意义。因为如果按语言使用的因袭性的程度来排列，原创语篇最弱，以母语为目标语的译文居中，以外语为目标语的译文则最甚（Stewart，2000）。既然我们将母语译为英语时须特别倚重对英语成文规范的了解，那么翻译学习的重要一环就是，必须借助大量英语语料的研读，使自己尽量具备以英语为母语人士的语感（native speaker intuitions）。

› 不同的目的，不同的阅读

英语阅读与英语写作的密切关系是不言而喻的。英语学习听说读写译这五种基本技能中，听和读是输入，说和写是输出，没有输入何以谈输出。而汉译英就是一种特殊形式的英语写作。一些学者（Chesterman & Arrojo，2000）指出，"翻译理论用于翻译教学，要特别重视翻译作为一种写作形式的种种启示和导向"（Applications of translation theory in translator training should emphasize a reflection of the many implications and consequences of translation as a form of writing.），要特别"强化译者的写作意识，因为这关乎他们在不同文化间建立种种联系的重大责任"（Raise their conscience as writers concerning the responsibility they will face in the seminal role they will play in the establishment of all sorts of relationships between cultures.）。

英语阅读有不同的目的：为获取信息，只需快速浏览，抓住感兴趣的内容即可；为学习英语，要放慢速度，理解内容，关注词语、搭配、句式等，以期牢记、运用，丰富自己的表达。为提高英译汉能力，要更加精密地解读其内容，特别要关注英语和汉语在表达同一意义时的区别。而为了学习汉译英所进行的英语阅读，是要获取构建英语译文的各种参照模式，这既包括词语层面，也包括文体层面。我们的注意力要聚焦于英文中对表达我国社会、文化事件有参照价值的词语和句式上，聚焦于对应汉语原文信息的英文语义和结构框架。没有这个框架，汉英翻译就只能产生机械对译的中国式英语（Chinglish）。把翻译试笔与汉英对照阅读，特别是与目标语阅读结合起来，是学习汉译英过程中的追本溯源之举，只有这样才能保证汉译英水平有实质性地稳步提升。

以阅读促翻译的教学模式

我们认识到,汉译英就是一种特殊形式的英语写作,而要运用作为外语的英语进行写作,必须到相关英语语料中寻找和汲取语言资源(linguistic resources)。那么,怎样构建起以英语阅读为引导和支撑的汉译英教学模式呢?

我们摸索出的教学模式是:先建立两个相互交叉关联的语篇类型范畴:体裁(genre)和题材(topic),分别构成两个阶段的教学内容*。根据当下英语专业学生汉译英的实践情况,翻译活动大量集中在小说、散文、时政文献、旅游景点介绍等几类体裁上。而题材则可包括社会、经贸、文化、教育、卫生、科技、体育等常见话题。

本书按语篇的体裁分类,分为三篇,供一学期使用。第一篇讨论小说、散文等文学语篇的翻译;第二篇讨论领导人讲话、官方文件等时政语篇的翻译;第三篇则是景点介绍、博物馆解说词等旅游相关的应用性语篇翻译。每篇又分三章:第一章,基于大量英语语料,用实例说明此类英语语篇在用词、句式、文体上的特点,以引导学生充分阅读相关语篇,强化语感,为汉译英积累有用的词语、搭配、句式和修辞手段。第一章讲解体现的是"译文是译语语篇世界的一员,其构建要参照同类语篇"的互文性原则。第二章关注的是汉译英平行语篇(即汉语原文及其英译文),讨论此类体裁译文的行文规律,在总体上和上一章形成呼应之势。大家可以将第一章当做是对某类体裁的某些语篇特点的归纳和概括,把第二章当做翻译技巧阅读,就像学习其他翻译教材那样。但我们更倾向于把这两章视为阅读导向:现在你看到的只是一部分教师和学生总结出来的阅读体会和感受,在他们阅读经验的基础上你可以自己去阅读,对已有经验或补充,或修正,将我们称之为"互文阅读"的过程延续下去,总结出可和他人共享的丰富的心得。第三章是翻译试笔,包括短文和长篇节选,目的是将读者进一步拉近翻译操作实际,启发他们对实践中常见的问题进行独立思考,并自己动脑动笔进行更多的翻译练习。这一章所提供的双语语篇,我们建议作为翻译实践处理,先写出译文,然后和提供的参照译文进行对照、比较、分析和思考。

---

* 我们将语料划分为不同的体裁和题材,当然并不是说每个体裁/题材各自都有一套语言操作机制,不同体裁/题材所用的语言都遵循着同样的英语规范,共享远远大于独有。我们常常讲的科技英语、医学英语、新闻英语之类,只是为了表明学习英语时在体裁或题材上的侧重点,为了教学的方便。

新闻语篇的对外传播有其不同于上述几种体裁的特殊之处，极少见与汉语新闻句、段相应的英译文。对外新闻稿基本都是针对同一事件用某一外语的重新表述，它可能参照了一篇或几篇汉语原稿，但只是对其内容的综述或重述，而非狭义上的翻译，这称为编译。编译与用外语写作更是密不可分，不会用英语写新闻稿，那还谈何编译。新闻写作自有其规律，需要用时用心专门训练，英语专业的翻译课尚无力涵盖。故此，本书只将新闻编译作为附录，对英语新闻语篇的特点、编译的一般要领只作简要介绍。

本书所彰显的是一条 3R 学习路径：Read—Remember—Re-contextualize。Read 指目标语语篇阅读，Remember 指以翻译为目的对相关词语、搭配和句式的记忆，Re-contextualize 则指将记忆的语言资源在当下的语境中使用。在 3R 链条中，Read 是基础，要广泛；Remember 是累进，要坚持；Re-contextualize 是活用，量大才能出经验。在学习每篇的第一章时，一定鼓励和督促学生充分阅读相应体裁的英语语篇，以期帮助学生建立起挖掘和获取语言资源的兴趣和能力。章节中所讲"语篇特点"旨在帮助学生更好、更快地抓住要领，加深对目标语成篇特点的理解和把握。英语写作能力的提高，离不开阅读中所获得的从用词到句法再到修辞等一系列知识和技能，没有阅读时的吸纳就没有写作时的输出。汉译英归根到底就是用英语写作，就是译者用英语重述他所理解的原文信息。第二章的教学同样强调充分阅读，只不过这里要阅读的是汉英对照语篇。本章所列"翻译要略"也同样是为了帮助学生阅读时形成有效的关注和讨论焦点，以借鉴他人的翻译经验，为我所用。供学生阅读的英语语篇以及双语语篇可由教师随时提供，比如美国每年都选编出版的 The Best American Series 就有大量可用于教学的材料，尤其是 The Best American Short Stories 和 The Best American Essays 两个选集。同时教师也要要求学生自己查找阅读材料，并与同学共享。第三章试笔实际上只是提供了有限的几个典型的语篇翻译练习，学生可自行阅读，独立思考。至于学生的其他翻译练习，还须教师精心选择、布置、批阅，并细心讲评。整个教学过程应该采用工作坊模式，即课上教师启发学生集思广益，课下学生自主阅读和练笔。

总之，学习汉译英不能从汉语词句如何转换成英语入手，而必须从阅读英语开始，厚积（读）薄发（译），起码也要边读边译。不这样做我们的译文就只能是一厢情愿的汉式英语。也许我们尽可孤芳自赏，而真正的目标语读者却未必买账。一句话，必须"读起来"，才能"译得顺"。

教材的局限性和学习的主动性

　　教学和教材都具有很大局限性。教学中所涉及的目标语的体裁及体裁特点只能是提示性的（indicative），所涉及的翻译问题也只能是典型化的；教学中讨论的译例只是社会生活中发生的翻译交际活动的九牛一毛，所布置的作业更是远远不能满足培养一个合格翻译所需要的翻译量。所以，教给学生如何自学翻译，告诉他们翻译学习的有效路径，激发他们自主学习的能动性，就显得十分重要了。

　　教材的内容也是有局限性的，但一本好的教材所展示的学习路径和策略能够使学习者终身受益，其作用和意义可以不断延伸、扩展。一个会学习的人，不仅读教材的内容，还能领悟其中所蕴含的学习方略，结合自身学习条件和目标，因人制宜，因时制宜，探索出最适合自己的学习途径。教材和课堂教学不是学习的全部，甚至不是大部，充其量只能指明某种学习路径，演示某种学习方法，"授之以渔"说是也。Stewart（2000）在讨论电子语料库和翻译培训的关系时说："必须把运用自身的大脑软件置于比运用计算机软件更重要的位置上"（Making good use of one's mental software must take precedence over exploiting computer software.）。收集了大量语料，不用心阅读熟记，指望临时抱佛脚现查现用，是难有进步的。发掘自身的智力潜势，强化自己的学习动机，永远是学习的关键。再次提醒大家，读完本书只是学习汉译英的开始。这本书能帮你找到有效的学习路径和方法，唯有沿着这个路径走下去，步步为营，坚持不懈，才真正能有大的收获。书不尽言，言不尽意，不断求索，方可悟透。

　　本教材呈现一种独特的三篇中各有同名三章的"三三"格局，意在以这种形式强调"目的语阅读—双语阅读—翻译试笔"之间环环相扣的紧密联系。翻译质量的提高，归根结底要从目的语中汲取营养和能量。目的语阅读是战略性的，双语阅读是战术性的，翻译试笔是实用性的。为方便教材的使用，我们在每篇的开始都以列表的形式提供了一个课时分配建议，仅供教学参考。课时以一个学期18周计，也可按比例延长至一个学年。当然就按教材的章节顺序学习也是可以的，请教师和同学们根据自己的情况灵活掌握安排。

　　网络时代提供给我们的学习资源实在是太丰富了。不患没材料，患来之太易而不知珍惜，不去利用。在当下的网络时代，任何出版的教材，不管多么新，都是落后的。积极的学习者应当充分利用网络，收集语料，分类储存，共享共用，以备检索。有用的网站很多很多，从有关政府部门的网站到著名景点、景区的官网，从各个英语新闻媒体网站到文学网站，不一而足。大家只需经常浏览自己最感兴趣的几个，不断积累资料，定期回顾整理，就会有意想不到的收获。

参考文献

李运兴 . 1998. 英汉语篇翻译 . 北京：清华大学出版社 .

李运兴 . 2003. 英汉语篇翻译 . 2 版 . 北京：清华大学出版社 .

李运兴 . 2006. 汉英翻译教程 . 北京：新华出版社 .

李运兴 . 2011. 英汉语篇翻译 . 3 版 . 北京：清华大学出版社 .

Allen, G. (2000). *Intertextuality*. London: Routledge.

Baker, M. (Ed.). (1998). *Routledge encyclopedia of translation studies*. London: Routledge.

Chesterman, A. & Arrojo, R. (2000). Shared ground in translation studies. *Target, 12*(1), 51-160.

Hanks, P. (1995). Contextual dependency and lexical sets. *International Journal of Corpus Linguistics, 1* (1), 75-98.

Stewart, D. (2000). Conventionality, creativity and translated text: The implications of electronic corpora. In M. Olohan (Ed.), *Intercultural faultlines* (pp. 73-91). Manchester: St. Jerome.

Contents 目录

第一篇　文学语篇：小说、散文等

课时安排建议 1

第一章　目标语语篇导读 2
　　第一节　叙述 2
　　第二节　描写 6
　　第三节　说明 15
　　第四节　对话 19

第二章　双语语篇导读及翻译要略 22
　　第一节　叙述 22
　　第二节　描写 30
　　第三节　说明 35
　　第四节　对话 39
　　第五节　时态 46
　　第六节　话题—主语转换 50
　　第七节　省略成分的翻译 51
　　第八节　流水句和词组堆叠句 56
　　第九节　拆句 60
　　第十节　人称—物称转换 64
　　第十一节　名物化 67
　　第十二节　连贯 70

     第十三节　修辞手段的翻译 76

     第十四节　信息的调适 82

第三章　翻译试笔和思考 86

     第一节　叙事语篇 86

     第二节　描写语篇 101

     第三节　说明语篇 109

第二篇　时政语篇：官方文件、讲话等

课时安排建议 117

第一章　目标语语篇导读 118

     第一节　词语 118

     第二节　习语和搭配 128

     第三节　动词 131

     第四节　句式和从句 138

     第五节　语篇连贯 144

第二章　双语语篇导读及翻译要略 147

     第一节　词语 147

     第二节　主语的确立 163

     第三节　拆译和主语安排 168

     第四节　行文视角的变化 175

     第五节　逻辑显性化 181

     第六节　拆句和逻辑安排 193

     第七节　信息的衍化：意译和释义 201

	第八节	合译	206
	第九节	构句的关键词语和句式	209
	第十节	名物化	212

第三章　翻译试笔和思考 216
  第一节　拆句练习 216
  第二节　确立主语练习 220
  第三节　逻辑连贯练习 225
  第四节　数字表达练习 232

第三篇　旅游语篇：导游解说词、景点介绍等

课时安排建议 237

第一章　目标语语篇导读 238
  第一节　词语 238
  第二节　句式 243
  第三节　从属成分的运用 248
  第四节　连贯 252

第二章　双语语篇导读及翻译要略 255
  第一节　词语和句式 255
  第二节　主语的确立 259
  第三节　主从的识别 261
  第四节　拆句 265
  第五节　合句 270
  第六节　信息的调整 271

　　　　第七节　重写 274
第三章　**翻译试笔和思考** 278
　　　　第一节　信息功能——词语、句式练习 278
　　　　第二节　行事功能——祈使句练习 284

附录　新闻语篇编译

英语新闻语篇导读 290
新闻编译 304

第一篇

文学语篇：小说、散文等

› 课时安排建议

本篇第一章与第二章的一至四节内容一一相对，学习时可以分别配对，共占用四周时间（以每周两课时计）。这一部分的教学目的是凸显目标语阅读与汉英翻译之间的紧密联系，在学习者头脑中树立英语阅读是英语写作的语言源泉的观念。第二章五至八节可占用两周时间，重点认识由汉英之间的差异而导致的翻译操作问题。第二章九至十二节也占用两周时间，从认知角度探讨翻译技能。最后的十三和十四两节则分别聚焦修辞和行文两个方面，只占一周时间。这一篇约需九周时间教学。

周次	内 容 提 要	英语及双语阅读	翻译试笔和思考
1	英语阅读和汉英对照阅读：叙述	第一章第一节，第二章第一节	第三章第一节《哲学》
2	英语阅读和汉英对照阅读：描写	第一章第二节，第二章第二节	第三章第一节《第六只羊》
3	英语阅读和汉英对照阅读：说明	第一章第三节，第二章第三节	第三章第一节《第六只羊》
4	英语阅读和汉英对照阅读：对话	第一章第四节，第二章第四节	第三章第一节《我和锁三儿的编年史》
5	汉英差异与翻译要领：时态、话题—主语转换	第二章第五节、第六节	第三章第一节《我和锁三儿的编年史》
6	汉英差异与翻译要领：省略成分的翻译、流水句和词组堆叠句	第二章第七节、第八节	第三章第二节《写给生命》
7	心理情景—语言框架：拆句、人称—物称转换	第二章第九节、第十节	第三章第二节《离太阳最近的树》
8	心理情景—语言框架：名物化、连贯	第二章第十一节、第十二节	第三章第三节《杞人忧天》
9	修辞和谋篇	第二章第十三节、第十四节	第三章第三节《家在途中》

第一章
目标语语篇导读

本章按叙述、描写、说明和对话四个范畴，摘录英语语篇中典型的句子或段落，并分别从选词、搭配、句式和修辞等方面进行点评和分析，凸显此类英语语篇的行文特点，引导读者在目标语阅读中加深对英语行文的理解和把握。

第一节 叙 述

本节选录的是小说和散文中叙述动作、活动、事件的典型段落。

叙述就是要讲清一件事情的发展过程，这其中当然少不了动词的选择和恰当运用。阅读中，要留心观察简单句、并列句、从句等动词句式以及过去分词、现在分词、动名词短语和动词不定式结构是如何被组织成连贯的叙述语篇的。

阅读英语叙述语篇时，建议从以下几个方面留心观察。

第一，要注意各种句式、结构的灵活运用。我们常常看到下面这样简短而流畅的段落，既有简单句也有复合句，还有修饰结构（分词短语、插入语），各类结构长短相间，相互配合，层层展开。

干旱之年，黎巴嫩的一个小村庄。村妇们等在一条小溪旁取水，于是：

Sometimes, amid the long wait and the heat and the flies and the smell of goat dung, tempers flared, and the younger women, anxious about their babies, argued over whose turn it was to fill up her jar. And sometimes the arguments escalated into full-blown, knockdown-dragout fights; the women would grab each other by the hair and curse and scream and spit and call each other names that made my ears tingle.

这个段落中，动词的运用值得注意，尤其是 grab... and curse and scream and spit and call each other names 等并列动词结构的运用，将妇人的口舌之战表述得活灵活现。

再阅读下面段落,特别注意简单句、各种从句、分词结构以及省略句的配合运用,体味长短相间、结构多样、错落有致的叙述模式。

It was dark when Maureen left the Hundred Club. She stopped just outside the door, a little thrown by the sudden cold, the change from daylight to night. A gusting breeze chilled her face. Lights burned over the storefronts, gleaming in patches of ice along the sidewalk. She reached in her pockets for her gloves, then hopelessly searched her purse. She'd left them in the club…

…

She had gone almost a block when she realized that she was walking in the wrong direction. Easy mistake—the lot where she and the others usually parked had been full. She headed back, crossing the street to avoid the club. Her fingers had gone stiff. She put her hands in her coat pockets, but then yanked them out when her right foot took a skid on the ice. After that she kept them poised at the sides.

再比如下面段落,它叙述了一个落后的黎巴嫩村落是如何在没有现代时间观念的状态下日复一日、年复一年地生活的。

In those days, there was no real need for a calendar or a watch to keep track of the hours, days, months, and years. We knew what to do and when to do it, just as the Iraqi geese knew when to fly north, driven by the hot wind that blew in from the desert, and the ewes knew when to give birth to wet lambs that stood on long, shaky legs in the chilly March wind and baaed hesitantly, because they were small and cold and did not know where they were or what to do now that they were here. //The only timepiece we had need of then was the sun. It rose and set, and the seasons rolled by, and we sowed seed and harvested and ate and played and married our cousins and had babies who got whooping cough and chickenpox—and those children who survived grew up and married their cousins and had babies who got whooping cough and chickenpox. We lived and loved and toiled and died without ever needing to know what year it was, or even the time of day.

我们用双斜线将这一段落分为两部分。前一部分的第二句是一个很长的复合句,句子虽长,但层次分明,读来十分顺畅;后一部分的突出特点是并列句中多

3

个谓语动词的并列使用，极力渲染人们一天天、一季季、一代代周而复始的古老生活方式。

我们还可以看到十分口语化的叙述段落，句子结构更趋简短。下面选段写的是作者当建筑工人时邂逅电视明星 Victoria 的往事。

She sat down a yard from me. Maybe less when I think of it. Yes, less. Expert with a carpenter's tape, I assure you, reconsidering it now, it was less. Her precious hips were between sixteen and twenty inches from mine once she sat down. I saw her coming before she sat. It seemed like a mirage at first, bad eyesight. And I didn't want to stare while she sat there. I was eating. I can't remember what I was eating. Tacos? Yogurt? I think both when I strain to remember. I said hi. She turned and said hi back. Victoria. She was very pleasant about saying hi, not self-conscious or worried in the unnatural heat about sitting next to me, a sweaty, dirty construction worker.

段落中用了许多简短的结构，表现出作者当时意外、惊喜、不知所措的神态。

同时我们看到，英语叙述语篇中也会出现结构繁复的复合句。

比如下面一个长句就叙述了安保人员引导客人穿过玻璃门，乘上电梯，穿过走廊，最后来到接见厅，又宣布接见等一连串事件。

Castro's security guards, <u>who</u> know in advance the names of all the bus passengers, guide Ali and the others through the glass doors and then into a pair of waiting elevators for a brief ride <u>that</u> is followed by a short walk through a corridor and finally into a large white-walled reception room, <u>where</u> it is announced that Fidel Castro will soon join them.

句中的三个关系代/副词使句子结构不断延展，看来复杂，但层次很清楚。这类结构与汉语用流水短句叙事的格局形成鲜明的对照。虽然将汉语译为英语时使用这种结构的机会不会很多，但阅读英语时仍要注意体味这种长句的语流和文气，以增强我们的语感和运用英语的能力。

第二，要留意英语中如何用介词短语、分词、动名词等非谓语形式来表示动作或动态。比如，She scanned the faces as she walked by, helplessly <u>on the watch for her daughter</u>. 这一句中表述了三个动作：扫视—走过—搜寻（女儿）。这最后一个动作就是用 on the watch 来表述的。类似的短语还有：at war/work, in use, on fire/sale/show, under discussion/investigation, 等等。

动词还常和介词搭配使用，以叙述一连串的动作，如下面段落中的 drove past 后的四个并列句（..., past..., past..., past..., on past...）。

She drove <u>past</u> the Toll House Inn, <u>past</u> the bankrupt development with its unfinished, skeletal houses open to the weather, <u>past</u> the road to the bridge that would take her home, <u>past</u> the burned-out house with the trailer beside it, <u>on past</u> the brickworks and the quarry and a line of dairy farms and the farm her grandparents had worked as tenants…

下面一段则用动词 led 和 to、through、into 等介词搭配完成了对一系列动作的叙述。

A few nights later he led us <u>to</u> a warren of rundown apartment blocks, <u>through</u> an open front door and <u>into</u> a brightly lit side-room just big enough for a TV, a fish tank, and a gold plastic love seat.

下面的五个动名词短语结构罗列了作者少年时无忧无虑、漫无目标的活动。

Stuff like that—<u>throwing</u> rocks at a fresh mudflat to make craters, <u>shooting</u> frogs with slingshots, <u>making</u> forts, <u>picking</u> blackberries, <u>digging</u> in what we were briefly persuaded was an Indian burial mound—occupied much of our time in the woods. Our purpose there was a higher sort of un-purpose, a free-form aimlessness that would be beyond me now.

第三，阅读中还要注意针对某些特定活动或事件（如驾车、骑马、演奏、表演、赌博等）所用的动词以及有关词语。比如下面段落就描述了雪后道路尚未清扫，一辆汽车在夜色中行驶的情景。

The side road was unplowed, covered with crusty snow that <u>scraped against the undercarriage of the car</u>. She hit a deep dip; <u>the front end clanged</u>, <u>the wheels spun wild</u> for a moment, then they <u>caught</u> and <u>car shot forward</u> again, <u>headlights jumping giddily</u>.

阅读中会遇到西方作者描述我国事物的文字，这对汉译英颇具参照价值，比如下面文字描述我国斗蟋蟀赌博的情景。

Their motions were slow and deliberate. They <u>pulled on white cotton gloves</u> supplied by the house, <u>lifted</u> the lids from the pots to examine their animals, <u>stirred</u> them with <u>long straws of yard grass</u>, and <u>delicately transferred them to opposite sides of the arena</u>. One of trainers was clumsier than the other; he <u>faltered as he eased his fighter</u>

5

out of the transfer case, nervous in the knowledge that <u>most of the bets are placed before the animals were even visible</u>, that many people <u>wager on</u> the trainers more than on the insects. As the crickets <u>emerged</u> under the lights, everyone <u>leaned in</u>, eager for that moment when the animal's spirit, power, and discipline would be revealed.

你看，蟋蟀主人如何慢条斯理地戴上白手套，小心翼翼地从罐里取出蟋蟀，如何用小草棍儿撩拨，人们又如何俯首引颈，一睹小斗士的风采，都一一在作者笔下展现出来。翻译中遇到类似事物岂不是大可借鉴吗？

第二节 描 写

本节选录了小说和散文中描写人物、景物或事物的句子和片段，提醒大家在阅读时特别留意以下几点。

第一，要留心词语的选择，包括形容词和副词，也包括动词和名词，因为后两者同样有表示事物性质和状态的作用。

一位女教师被莫名劫持，一个男人将她逼进汽车，自己坐进后排，并命她开车。她一回头，看到劫匪的模样：

He was leaning back into the corner, <u>hunched</u> into a <u>puffy</u> coat of the vivid orange color worn by highway crews. In the reflected glare of the headlights, his dark eyes had <u>a blurred, liquid brightness</u>. Above the <u>straight line of his eyebrows</u> the bald dome of his head <u>gleamed dully</u>. He wore a short beard. <u>A few thin patches</u> of it grew high on his cheeks, to just below his eyes.

寥寥数行，劫持者形象已跃然纸上。是什么在起作用？当然是所有词句的整体效果，而划线词语起到了关键的作用。这些词语并非生僻罕见，如果以了解故事情节为最终目的，并不会引起我们多大关注。但以学习汉译英为目的的阅读则要求读者务必留心这些常见词语是如何组合起来达到描写效果的。hunched into a puffy coat 是怎样一副形象， a blurred, liquid brightness 又呈现了怎样的眼神？这些我们都要用心琢磨，以备在自己的翻译中模仿（甚至照搬）。

再比如描写色彩时有这样的语句：

My memories of life in Paterson during those first few years are all in shades of gray. Maybe I was too young to absorb vivid colors and details, or to discriminate between the slate blue of the winter sky and the darker hues of the snow-bearing clouds, but that single color washes over the whole period. The building we lived in was gray, as were the streets, filled with slush the first few months of my life there. The coat my father had bought for me was similar in color and too big; it sat heavily on my thin frame.

在 Paterson 市度过的童年留给作者一片灰色的记忆：all in shades of gray/that single color washes over the whole period。还要注意描写不同色调的词语：the slate blue/darker hues。最后两句说就连她的衣服也是灰乎乎的，别别扭扭地罩在她瘦小的身体上：sat heavily on my thin frame。

描写声音可以说：

I do remember the way the heater pipes banged and rattled, startling all of us out of sleep until we got so used to the sound that we automatically shut it out or raised our voices above the racket. The hiss from the valve punctuated my sleep (which has always been fitful) like a nonhuman presence in the room—a dragon sleeping at the entrance of my childhood.

这一段描写供暖管道的噪音，注意描写声音的词 banged/rattled/racket/hiss，吵得睡不着觉是 startling… out of sleep/punctuated my sleep，习以为常以致充耳不闻是 shut it out，作者把阀门的嘶嘶声还比做西方文化中口喷烈焰、邪恶凶狠的 dragon。

描写衣着又可以说：

One New Year's Eve we were dressed up like child models in the Sears catalogue: my brother in a miniature man's suit and bow tie, and I in black patent-leather shoes and a frilly dress with several layers of crinoline underneath. My mother wore a bright-red dress that night, I remember, and spike heels; her long black hair hung to her waist. Father, who usually wore his Navy uniform during his short visits home, had put on a dark civilian suit for the occasion: we had been invited to his uncle's house for a big celebration.

这里有许多表达穿着的词语，值得特别留意，比如 patent-leather shoes（漆革皮鞋），frilly dress（带花边的裙子），spike heels（细高跟鞋）等。

阅读英语时不妨按描写类型对相关表达进行积累。除了上面所说色彩、声音、衣着，还可包括相貌、举止、各种场景/情景等，可粗分也可细分，只要适合自己的记忆和查找习惯即可。

另外必须提及的是，英语中常用合成词作定语，比如 barrel-chested man。请注意观察下面例句中该类词语的运用。

- She passed a hunched, foot-stamping crowd waiting to get into Harrigan's, where she herself had once gone to hear the local bands.
- He was wearing hip, dark-framed glasses and a dog tag around his neck with a Chinese dragon on it.
- There she is, done up as a white-haired, dewlapped, thick-waisted, thick-lensed hag, seriously myopic.
- …and she is a girlishly petite olive-skinned woman of twenty-three who, standing next to her husband in the lobby, rises barely higher than the mid-section of his embroidered guayabera—a tightly tailored, short-sleeved shirt that accentuated his tapered torso, his broad shoulders, and the length of his dark, muscular arms, which once prevented his opponents from doing any injustice to his winning Latin looks.

第二，要留心观察描写语篇中常常出现的句子结构，分析、记忆，并在翻译练习中模仿使用。

看下面两句对拳王阿里第四任妻子 Yolanda 的描写：

She is a large and pretty woman of thirty-eight, with a radiant smile and a freckled, fair complexion that reflects her interracial ancestry. A scarf is loosely draped over her head and shoulders, her arms are covered by long sleeves, and her well-designed dress in vivid hues hangs below her knees.

这段文字在读者脑海里引发的是一个体态丰盈健硕、衣着宽松的中年女人形象。而究其句法，第一句是复合句，划线部分是句中的从属成分：with 短语中含有一个 that 从句（双划线）。第二句是由三个小句构成的并列句，分别描写 scarf、arms 和 dress。这好像并不能揭示什么，无非是英语中两大主要句式——复合句和并列句。问题是，我们在汉译英中能否灵活得体地使用它们？这就需要多多阅读此类语篇，加深印象，并在翻译实践中模仿。

再看下面景物描写中从句的运用（划线部分）：

We have a nine-acre lake on our ranch and a warm spring that feeds it all winter. By mid-March the lake ice begins to melt where the spring feeds in, and every year the same pair of mallards come ahead of the others and wait. Though there is very little open water they seem content. They glide back and forth through a thin estuary, brushing watercress with their elegant folded wings, then tip end-up to eat and, after, clamber onto the lip of ice that retreats, hardens forward, and retreats again.

此例中第三句由 Though 引导，单独一句，更强化了和前句的让步关系。

下面段落描写牧场和小马。注意第一句中的定语从句（单划线）和过去分词短语（双划线），以及第二句中现在分词短语（波浪线）的运用。

Our ranch faces south down a long treeless valley whose vanishing point is two gray hills, folded one in front of the other like two hands, and after that—space, cerulean air, clouds like pleated skirts, and red mesas standing up like breaching whales in a valley three thousand feet below. Afternoons, our young horses played, rearing up on back legs and pawing oh so carefully at each other, reaching around, ears flat back, nipping manes and withers. One of those times falsetto squeals looped across the pasture and hung on frozen currents of air.

下面一个描写段落出现了两个动词 +-ing 的短语结构，第一个是状语，第二个是动名词短语作主语。

The diminutive and delicate-boned Fraymari has painted her lips scarlet and has pulled back her hair in a matronly manner, hoping no doubt to appear more mature than her twenty-three years suggest, but standing next to the three much older and heavier and taller men transforms her image closer to that of an anorexic teenager.

下面是一个存在句（there is... Teofilo Stevenson...），其中在主语 Stevenson 前面有分词短语构成的状语，其后又有两个由 who 引导的定语从句，分别说明他所获的荣誉和身份。

...and there is also in the crowd, standing taller than the rest, the forty-three-year-old, six-foot five-inch Cuban heavyweight hero Teofilo Stevenson, who was a three-time Olympic gold medalist, in 1972, 1976, and 1980, and who, on this island at least, is every bit as renowned as Lit or Castro.

正确熟练地使用从句、介词短语和分词短语，是构建英语描写语篇的基本技能。除此之外，还要学会使用同位语、独立主格、后置定语、插入成分等，以便在主干结构外添加更多细节。

- …the men of the village used to gather regularly at the house of Im Kaleem, <u>a short, middle-aged widow with jet-black hair and a raspy voice</u> that could be heard all over the village, even when she was only whispering.

- She wears black, <u>a suitable choice</u> for one who should be unobtrusive. Yet the arresting manner in which her black clothes shelter her flesh, <u>flesh</u> that seems molded like clay and yields to the fabric with a certain playful, even droll resistance, defies unobtrusiveness. Her black long-sleeved knit shirt reaches just below her waist, and the fabric of her perfectly fitting black slacks stirs gently around her narrow hips and thighs. Beyond the hem of her slacks can be glimpsed her shiny, but not too conspicuously shiny, black boots with a thick two-inch heel. Her face is heart-shaped, like the illustrations of princesses in fairy tales. The skin of her face and neck and hands, <u>the only visible skin</u>, is pale, and off-white like heavy cream or the best butter. Her lips are painted magenta.

- Two prostitutes are smoking and talking privately on the corner of a dimly lit street bordering the manicured lawns of Havana's five-star Hotel National. They are copper-colored women in their early twenties wearing faded miniskirts and halters, and as they chat, they are watching attentively while two men—<u>one white, the other black</u>—huddle over the raised trunk of a parked red Toyota arguing about the prices of the boxes of black-market Havana cigars that are stacked within.

- Maureen could see his face clearly now, <u>the full, finely molded, almost feminine lips, the long thin nose, the dark unexpected freckles across the bridge of his nose and under his eyes</u>, vanishing into the beard.

以上几个段落都出现了同位语结构，或添加细节，或评论抒发，挥洒自如，勾勒出一幅幅生动的画面。

再有，排比结构的运用也可构成信息密集的段落，达到言简而意赅的效果。

With her back straight, her seated body making a slender black L shape, once again she waits with hands folded, and very soon rises, quite silently, to perform the same set of movements. Soon this becomes a ritual, <u>expected and hypnotic, changeless and evocative</u>.

作者描写的是钢琴演奏会上一位翻乐谱的姑娘，她虽然重复着同样的动作，但既在预料之中又令人神驰，既单调又耐人回味。划线部分用排比的后置定语刻画了这一精妙形象。

独立主格结构也是值得观察和模仿的构句手段。比如：

He leaned back again, <u>lips pursed, cheeks working out and back, out and back like a fish's</u>.

有时还会见到如汉语一样的名词性短语堆叠架构，比如：

The red mountains thrusting up, the basins between them <u>flat as glass</u>, <u>salt everywhere</u>.

也会见到用事件罗列的方式描述过去经历的段落：

Of my preschool years I have only impressions: <u>the sharp bite of the wind in December as we walked with our parents towards the brightly lit stores downtown; how I felt like a stuffed doll in my heavy coat, boots, and mittens; how good it was to walk into the five-and-dime and sit at the counter drinking hot chocolate</u>. On Saturdays our whole family would walk downtown to shop at the big department stores on Broadway.

上面段落中划线部分是由 the sharp bite of…; how…; how… 构成的类平行句式，浓缩了以往的事件和感受，是一种又简洁又便于模仿的结构。

第三，要注意观察和学习各种修辞技巧，特别是比喻的运用。比如：

Hand's eyebrows writhed on his face <u>like two huge caterpillars</u>.

眉毛成了毛毛虫。

That night <u>a luscious, creamy fog</u> rolled in, <u>like a roll of fat</u>, hugging me, but it was snow.

此句中，雪被比喻成一团脂肪的浓雾。

Im Khalil came by to welcome my father home and to take a long, myopic look at his foreign-born wife, my mother. Im Khalil was so old that the skin of <u>her cheeks</u>

looked like my father's grimy tobacco pouch, and when I kissed her, it was like kissing a soft suede glove that had been soaked with sweat and then left in a dark closet for a season. Im Khalil's face got me to wondering how old one had to be to look and tasted the way she did.

老妇人的面颊看上去像油乎乎的装烟丝的皮袋子，亲上去像绒面革手套。

Mornings, a transparent pane of ice lies over the meltwater. I peer through and see some kind of water bug—perhaps a leech—paddling like a sea turtle between green ladders of lake weed. Cattails and sweetgrass from the previous summer are bone dry, marked with black mold spots, and bend like elbows into the ice. They are swords that cut away the hard tenancy of winter. At the wide end a mat of dead water plants has rolled back into a thick impregnable breakwater. Near it, bubbles trapped under the ice are lenses focused straight up to catch the coming season.

香蒲和甜味草像插入冰中的臂肘，又像刺破严冬的利剑。

He was like a potato that had been worn down by cooking. Everything on him—his eyes, his teeth, his legs and torso—seemed like it had been sloughed away. What he had been was mostly gone now and I was looking at the nub of a man. In a wheelchair, he grasped my hands and tugged on them—violently. His hands were still thick and, I believed, strong enough to lift me out of my own seat into his lap.

这里，患早期老年痴呆症的祖父被比喻为煮烂的土豆。在欣赏英语中这一类新颖的比喻时，要思考汉译英过程中如何将汉语比喻译为可接受的英语。

The guide who explained the exhibits was a small young woman who in between speeches conversed in a perfectly normal relaxed manner. But when she went into her speeches she lifted herself on to her toes and her chest swelled out like a bullfrog's; her words swooped down from peak to peak, and nearly took the plaster off the walls with their reverberation. The speeches were a mixture of rhapsody, rant, and rodomontade. At the end of each speech she deflated, and returned to normal.

这个段落描写一位解说员做作的语调和姿态，使用的修辞手法还有夸张的意味。

I'll even blame the heat for my inability to remember which year it was—1986, give or take. It was hot like never before, my skin so porous it was hard to distinguish

<u>which side of it I was on. Like I could sweat and become a puddle. A dirty puddle,
because I'd absorbed that construction site. And because this was Los Angeles, and it
was smoggy too.</u> But you know what, it wasn't the smog or the dirt or the cement dust,
it was the <u>heat</u> that seemed to drain all the color into an overexposed gauze. It was so
<u>hot</u>. I'm talking about three digits, so don't think I'm exaggerating. It was so <u>hot</u>. It
was so <u>hot</u> everybody had to say it again and again. So <u>hot</u> I don't remember if the <u>heat</u>
lasted three weeks, a month, two three. It was day and night <u>hot</u>, as forever and endless
as boredom.

这一段中 hot/heat 重复使用八次（双划线部分），不厌其烦，强调天气之炎热。单划线一句更是用类比法极力描写出天气在"我"身上的效果。

第四，要观察英语中对方位、布局等的描写。

- On the bus, as always, Ali is sitting alone, spread out across the two front seats in the left aisle directly behind the Cuban driver. Yolanda sits a few feet ahead of him to the right; she is adjacent to the driver and within inches of the windshield. The seats behind her are occupied by Teofilo Stevenson, Fraymari, and the photographer Bingham. <u>Seated behind Ali, and also occupying two seats is an American screenwriter</u> named Greg Howard, who weighs more than three hundred pounds.

- The room has high ceilings and potted palms in every corner and is sparsely furnished with modern tan leather furniture. <u>Next to a sofa is a table with two telephones</u>, one gray and the other red. <u>Overlooking the sofa is an oil painting of the Vinales valley</u>, which lies west of Havana; and <u>among the primitive art displayed on a circular table in front of the sofa is a grotesque tribal figure</u> similar to the one Ali had examined earlier in the week at a trinket stand while touring with the group in Havana's Old Square.

注意上述两个例段中的倒装结构（下划线部分）在此类描写段落中的衔接作用。另外注意对空间关系的描写要清楚有序。

第五，还要注意动态描写，即对动作的描写。

- ...and as he walks through the lobby of the Hotel Nacional toward the bus, wearing a gray sharkskin suit and a white cotton shirt buttoned at the neck

without a tie, several guests approach him and request his autograph. It takes him about thirty seconds to write "Muhammad Ali," so shaky are his hands from the effects of Parkinson's syndrome.

- She [Yolanda] knows that he [Ali] is enjoying himself. There is a slight twinkle in his eyes, not much expression on his face, and no words forthcoming from this once most talkative of champions. But the mind behind his Parkinson's mask is functioning normally, and he is characteristically committed to what he is doing: he is spelling out his full name on whatever cards or scraps of paper his admirers are handing him. "Muhammad Ali." He does not settle for a time-saving "Ali" or his mere initials. He has never shortchanged his audience.

以上两段描写拳王阿里在饭店中为粉丝签名的情景：由于患帕金森症，他的手不住发抖，但他诚心诚意对待粉丝的请求，一丝不苟地写下自己的全名。发抖的手和认真的态度形成了鲜明对比，彰显出他的独特人格魅力。

The page turner listens attentively but appears, fittingly, unmoved by the music itself; her body is focused entirely on her task, which is a demanding one, not simply <u>turning</u> the pages at the proper moments but <u>dimming</u> her presence, <u>suppressing</u> everything of herself except her attentiveness. But as able as she proves to be at turning pages—never a split second late, never <u>fumbling</u> with the corners or <u>making</u> an excessive gesture—she cannot, in her helpless radiance, keep from absorbing all the visual energy in the concert hall.

这一段描写的是一个乐谱员的动作，现在分词状语的运用，更是把人物动作勾勒得淋漓尽致、细致入微。一个动作低调而娴熟，无意彰显而又引人注目的形象呈现在了读者眼前。

As the weeks went by I realized that they never looked at anything in their immediate vicinity—not at me or their stand or anybody who might come within ten or fifteen feet. They did not look at approaching customers once they were inside the perimeter. Save for the instant it took to discern the color of the shoes, they did not even look at what they were doing while they worked, but rubbed in polish, brushed, and buffed by feel while looking over their shoulders, into the distance, as if awaiting the arrival of an important person. Of course there wasn't all that much distance in the underground station, but their behavior was so focused and consistent they seemed somehow to transcend the physical. A powerful mood was created, and I came almost to believe that these men could see through walls, through girders, and around corners to whatever hyperspace it was where whoever it was they were waiting and watching for would finally emerge.

上面一个段落描写纽约地铁擦皮鞋黑人总是凝望远方的眼神：身处阴暗狭窄的地铁站角落，仍心存对摆脱卑微地位的渴望。

第三节 说　明

　　说明语篇常用来说明和解释想法、概念、观点。阅读这类语篇的关键，在于识别语篇的逻辑脉络。观察英语说明段落的逻辑模式，有助于提升逻辑思维意识，加深对英语说明文行文模式的认识，这为行文逻辑不如英语那么彰显的汉语语篇的英译，提供十分必要的思维导向。

　　试读下面一段：

The transition from exterior vocalizing to silent but perceptible lip movement to an interiority indicated outwardly only by the back and forth shuttling of the eyes signifies a considerable augmentation of the power of the reading act. <u>So long as</u> there are still lip motions, there exists a bridge between the world conjured on the page and the exterior realm. <u>But</u> when those motions cease, then the reader simultaneously represents two opposed kinds of presence. One is the physical, the actual—<u>that which occupies space and can be located</u>; the other is the invisible, the unreal—<u>that which happens vividly in the imagination and cannot be fathomed or legislated by any other person</u>. Silent reading, <u>then</u>, is the very signature—the emblem—of the subjectivity. The act of reading creates for us a world within a world—indeed, a world within a hollow sphere, the two of them moving not only at different rates, but also, perhaps, counter to one another.

首句点明观点——从"出声朗读"到"有嘴唇运动的默读"再到"只见眼睛在动的完全默读",标志着阅读力度的提升。接着以让步的语气(so long as…)指出只要还有嘴唇的动作,外部世界和语篇世界之间就仍存有联系;而(but)当嘴唇也不动时,读者就代表着完全不同的两个世界了;于是(then)可以得出结论说:默读是主体性的标志。

那么,以上步步为营的逻辑结构是如何构建的呢?首先 so long as, but, then 等连词起着导向作用,其次"同位语(that)+ which 定语从句"、插入语、同位语等结构在说明观点、构建逻辑层次上也起了重要作用。

表示逻辑关系的连接词语,在说明文中就像路标一样向读者指示着文章的发展脉络和行文走向。再看下面一个例子:

If the human mind were a strictly logical device like a calculating machine, it would deal with words simply as names of categories, and with categories as essential tools for imposing order and system on a universe which otherwise presents itself as an unsorted chaos of sense stimuli. But human reaction to words, like much other human behavior, is also motivated by irrational impulses such as those we label *love*, *hate*, *joy*, *sorrow*, *fear*, *awe*, and so forth; and, whenever the users of a language evince a fairly uniform emotional response to a given word, that response becomes part of the connotation, therefore part of the standard meaning of the word in that language. While the bulk of the vocabulary doubtless consists of words that carry little or no perceptible emotional charge, there are nevertheless a good many that produce reactions of various colors and shades, with voltages ranging from mild to knockout force.

本段从"人脑如机器"的假设(if)开始,接着语气一转(but)——可是"人对词语是有情感的",从而(and)赋予了它们附加意义,于是(therefore)也就成为那些词语的标准意义的一部分。最后一句将这一结论进一步阐发:尽管(while)大部分词语不带什么感情色彩,但不少词语还是或多或少带有某些情感色彩。

阅读英语说明语篇时,要有意识地体会英语的行文逻辑,以提高自己的逻辑分析和组词谋篇能力。下面我们参照英语写作教程中经常提到的几种逻辑模式,为大家提供阅读此类语篇时可行的观察视角和关注焦点。

第一,说明段落常常对一个概念进行精确的定义,比如:

Although the difference between the qualities of intelligence and intellect is more often assumed than defined, the context of popular usage makes it possible to extract the nub of the distinction, which seems to be almost universally understood: ① <u>intelligence is an excellence of mind that is employed within a fairly narrow, immediate, and predictable range;</u> ② <u>it is a manipulative, adjustive, unfailingly practical quality—one of the most eminent and endearing of the animal virtues.</u> ③ <u>Intelligence works within the framework of limited but clearly stated goals, and may be quick to shear away questions of thought that do not seem to help in reaching them.</u> ④ <u>Finally, it is of such universal use that it can daily be seen at work and admired alike by simple or complex minds.</u>

此段落对 intelligence 这一概念进行界定。作者首先指出 intelligence 的含义可以从其具体使用语境中得以体现，接着便分四个句子对其从不同角度加以定义（见划线部分及标号）。阅读时注意形容词的运用，以及定语从句、同位语等结构。

第二，说明某个过程、某种变化、演变等。

Several things happen when we move via the first string of words from our quotidian world into the realm of the written. We experience almost immediately a transposition—<u>perhaps an expansion, perhaps a condensation</u>—of our customary perception of reality. We shift our sense of time from our ordinary, sequential, clockface awareness to a quasi-timeless sense of suspension, <u>that sublime forgetting of the grid sometimes called duration.</u> Finally and no less significantly, we find ourselves instantly and implicitly changing our apprehension of the meaning structure of the world.

这一段落清晰地陈述了人们阅读书籍时从日常生活世界进入到文字世界的转化过程：先是 immediately a transposition，然后 shift our sense of time，最后 changing our apprehension of the meaning structure。同时要注意插入语（单划线）、同位语（波浪线）等的运用。

第三，将两种事物进行比较或对照。

The cardinal difference between gift and commodity exchange is that a gift establishes a feeling-bond between two people, whereas the sale of a commodity leaves no necessary connection. <u>I go into a hardware store, pay the man for a hacksaw blade, and walk out. I may never see him again.</u> The disconnectedness is, in fact, a virtue of the commodity mode. <u>We don't want to be bothered, and if the clerk always</u>

wants to chat about the family, I'll shop elsewhere. I just want a hacksaw blade. But a gift makes a connection. There are many examples, the candy or cigarette offered to a stranger who shares a seat on the plane, the few words that indicate goodwill between passengers on the late-night bus. These tokens establish the simplest bonds of social life, but the model they offer may be extended to the most complicated of unions—marriage, parenthood, mentorship. If a value is placed on these (often essentially unequal) exchanges, they degenerate into something else.

这一段解释了礼品和商品之间的区别，划线部分也用实例对二者的区别进行了生动的说明。

第四，举例说明。

The male sense of space must differ from that of the female, who has such interesting, active, and significant inner space. The space that interests men is outer. The fly ball high against the sky, the long pass spiraling overhead, the jet fighter like a scarcely visible pinpoint nozzle laying down its vapor trail at forty thousand feet, the gazelle haunch flickering just beyond arrow-reach, the uncountable stars sprinkled on their great black wheel, the horizon, the mountaintop, the quasar—these bring portents with them, and awaken a sense of relation with the invisible, with the empty. The ideal male body is taut with lines of potential force, a diagram extending outward; the ideal female body curves around centers of repose.

此段将男人和女人的空间感进行比较，其中大部分篇幅都是说明男人只对外部空间感兴趣的实际例子。

第五，说明段落还可以用比喻或类比的方法构建。

... In effect, we have applied the modular principle to human relationships. We have created the disposable person: Modular Man.

Rather than entangling ourselves with the whole man, we plug into a module of his personality. Each personality can be imagined as a unique configuration of thousands of such modules. Thus no whole person is interchangeable with any other. But certain modules are. Since we are seeking only to buy a pair of shoes, and not the friendship, love or hate of the salesman, it is not necessary for us to tap into or engage with all the other modules that form his personality.

以上段落中，人格被比做一个个模块构成的 Modular Man，并按此思路展开其观点：只需接触一个人的某个模块即可，就像购物时只买一个商品而非售货员整个人的情感一样。

第六，先提问再分析解答也是构建说明段落常用的方式。

But why has New York become a boomtown for hustlers? Not because of the increased use of drugs, as most people assume. It began with a change in New York's penal code four years ago. Loitering for the purpose of prostitution was reduced by former Police Commissioner Leary from a misdemeanor to a violation. Even girls found guilty on the more serious "pross collar" rarely go to jail. Most judges let them go for a twenty-five to fifty dollar fine—and a week to pay. It amounts to a license.

上面段落先提出问题——为何当下纽约妓女成患。然后将其归因于 penal code 的变化：prostitution 不再是 misdemeanor（轻罪）而只是 violation（违规）而已。

第四节 对 话

对话在小说和叙事散文中都很常见。将汉语作品中的对话译成英语并非易事，因为我们在汉语为母语的环境中学习英语，对英语口语的熟悉程度和把握往往还不如书面语。要克服这个弱点，可以采取多种措施。比如观看英语电影学习口语，多和母语为英语人士面对面交谈。当然也可以在英语小说、散文阅读中注意观察和积累，以备将汉语对话译为英语时仿用或参照。

下面段落叙述了作者幼时不愿吃午饭，百般应付，而最终未能逃过母亲监视的往事，读来颇有兴味。请特别注意对话的一般特点：用词简单，结构简洁，省略频现。

We lived only a few blocks from the elementary school and routinely ate lunch at home. It is reported that the following dialogue and ensuing action occurred on January 22, 1941:

"Eat your sandwich."

"I don't want to eat my sandwich."

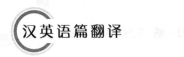

"I made that sandwich, and you are going to eat it, Mister Man. You filled yourself up on penny candy on the way home, and now you're not hungry."

"I'm late. I have to go. I'll eat the sandwich on the way back to school."

"Promise?"

"Promise."

Allegedly, I went up the street with sandwich in my hand and buried it in a snowbank in front of Dr. Wright's house. My mother, holding back the curtain in the window of the side door, was watching. She came out in the bitter cold, wearing only a light dress, ran to the snowbank, dug out the sandwich, chased me up Nassau Street, and rammed the sandwich down my throat, snow and all.

小说、散文中对话在叙事中进行，靠描写加以烘托。要注意观察叙事、描写和对话如何共同构成叙事段落。下面一段文字叙述的是哈瓦那街头一个白人与倒卖雪茄的黑人烟贩子讨价还价的情景。

The white man is a squared-jawed Hungarian in his mid-thirties, wearing a beige tropical suit and a wide yellow tie, and he is one of Havana's leading entrepreneurs in the thriving illegal business of selling top-quality hand-rolled Cuban cigars below the local and international market price. The black man behind the car is a well-built, baldish, gray-bearded individual in his mid-fifties from Los Angeles named Howard Bingham; and no matter what price the Hungarian quotes, Bingham shakes his head and says, "NO, no—that's too much!"

"You're crazy!" cries the Hungarian in slightly accented English, taking one of the boxes from the trunk and waving it in Howard Bingham's face. "These are Cohiba Esplendidos! The best in the world! You will pay one thousand dollars for a box like this in the States."

"Not me," says Bingham, who wears a Hawaiian shirt with a camera strapped around his neck. He is a professional photographer, and he is staying at the Hotel Nacional with his friend Muhammad Ali. "I wouldn't give you more than fifty dollars."

"You really are crazy," says the Hungarian, slicing through the box's paper seal with his fingernail, opening the lid to reveal a gleaming row of labeled Esplendidos.

"Fifty dollars," says Bingham.

"A hundred dollars," insists the Hungarian. "And hurry! The police could be driving around."

在这个语篇片段中，每个人说的话以及相关叙述和描写构成一个单独的自然段，有人物话语也有相关描述，共同推进故事情节的展开，口语表达符合人物的身份和当时的情景场合。

本章前三节分别讨论了叙述、描写和说明三类段落的阅读聚焦点——用词和构句是叙述和描写的关键，而逻辑连贯则是说明段落的灵魂。第四节则提醒大家注意人物对话中用词简约、语气合于情景的特点。依照这样的思路，在阅读中留心有助于提升英语表达能力的词语和段落，用心分析，反复诵读，甚至熟记，培养自己的英语行文的感觉，从而对英语写作产生示范和导向作用。

第二章
双语语篇导读及翻译要略

本章与第一章一样,也是导读性章节。第一章是对英语作为目的语阅读的导读,本章是对汉英对照语篇的导读。所谓导读,就如同一个景点的导游图,它是有游览经历的人标出的可行路径,可驻足留步、细细体味的看点,对后来的游者大有参考价值。但导游图绝对代替不了身临其境的游览。每一个用心的游者都可以根据自己的经历进一步丰富、校正手中的导游图,甚至重新绘制自己的游览图。本章的各个小节是有经验的师生阅读感受的总结,这就像一个个路标,大家顺着这些路标走,就可能会收到事半功倍的效果。

全章分为十四节。一至四节与第一章的一至四节相对应,分别讨论叙述、描写、说明和对话的翻译问题;五至八节主要涉及由于语言差异而导致的翻译操作规律;九至十二节从心理情景—语言框架角度讨论和认识翻译操作的认知属性;而最后的十三、十四两节则分别从修辞和谋篇两个层面考察译文语篇的构建规律。

第一节 叙 述

我们对事物的叙述,是以动词为中心进行的。表达事态(goings-on)的动词,辅之以表达时间、地点、方式等的副词,就构成了一幅幅动态的画面。叙事句的英译特别强调动词的运用,这包括动词的选择及其应用形式(表现为主句、从句、分词、动名词等)。

下文是《鹿鼎记》第一回中一段动态的场景描述:

那书生微笑不答,迈步踏进船舱。刀光闪动,两柄单刀分从左右劈落。那书生闪身避过,随即欺向瓜管带,挥掌拍向他头顶。瓜管带忙伸左臂挡格,右手成拳,猛力击出。那书生左脚反踢,踹中了一名亲兵胸口,那亲兵大叫一声,登时鲜血狂喷。另外三名亲兵举刀或削或剁。船舱中地形狭窄,那书生施展擒拿功夫,劈击勾打,咯的一声响,一名亲兵给他掌缘劈断了颈骨。瓜管带右掌拍出,击向那书生的后脑。那书生反过左掌,砰的一声,双掌相交,瓜管带背心重重撞上船舱,船舱登时塌了一片。那书生连出两掌,拍在余下两名亲兵的胸口,咯咯声响,二人肋骨齐断。

The scholar made no reply but continued to smile as he stepped inside the cabin. Immediately, to left and right of him, two cutlasses flashed out and would have cut him down; but already he had dodged and was lunging towards Major Gua with arm upraised to slice down on his head. The Major parried the blow with his left hand, simultaneously striking out with his right fist. Ducking the blow, the scholar kicked backwards with his left foot at the nearest of the guardsman, catching him in the pit of the stomach. The man let out a great cry and began vomiting blood. The other three guardsmen had their cutlasses up and were cutting and slashing at the scholar, who, because of the lack of space in the cabin, was now bringing into play his advanced "grappling" skills. One blow, made with the edge of the hand, landed with a cracking sound on one of the guardsmen, breaking his neck. Major Gua swung a blow with his right palm towards the back of the scholar's head, but the scholar had already whirled about, bringing his own left palm round to catch the blow. He did this with such force that the two palms met in a mighty clap, throwing the Major off his balance, so that he fell against the cabin wall, hitting it heavily with his back and causing the whole structure to lean towards one side. In quick succession the scholar now aimed two chopping blows at the midriffs of the two remaining guardsmen. There were sickening thumps as they landed and both men collapsed with broken ribs. (translated by John Minford)

可以说,译文将动词的作用发挥得淋漓尽致。不妨先来个汉英对照:(刀光)闪动—flashed out,闪身避过—dodged,欺向— lunging towards,拍向— slice down,挡格—parried,猛力击出— striking out,反踢— kicked backwards,或削或剁— cutting and slashing,(右掌)拍出— swung a blow。译者的选词十分精当。

汉语的动词串联如珠,依次叠加,没有限定和非限定之分。但译为英语有了主从之分,结构上必须作出相应的变化。除了"那亲兵大叫一声,登时鲜血狂喷"

（The man let out a great cry and began vomiting blood）一句的译文仍保持多个动词谓语并行的并列句形式以外，其他句子都变成了主从结构，尤其是运用了非限定动词短语。比如，"瓜管带忙伸左臂挡格，右手成拳，猛力击出"译为 The Major parried the blow with his left hand, simultaneously striking out with his right fist。

只关注译文在词和句子结构上与原文的对应，还远远不能揭示译者的功力所在。通观全篇，可以看到译者的着眼点实则不在字句，而在情景：译者活灵活现地再现了原文的情景。译者叙述视角时有转换，比如"那书生施展擒拿功夫，劈击勾打，咯的一声响，一名亲兵给他掌缘劈断了颈骨"一句，叙述视角从"书生"起，而后转至"亲兵"。译文将其分为两个句子，第一句始于 who，第二句转为以 One blow 起句，从"击""打"落到亲兵身上的视角展开描述。

另外，译文还在适当的地方补充了某些动作，使描述更趋完整、连贯。如"Ducking the blow"和"the scholar had already whirled about"等处就添加了原文字面没有但实际上应存在于情景中的动作，而"would have cut him down"则是添加了一个逻辑环节。

下面是朱自清《背影》中叙述父亲越过铁道去买橘子的经典片段：

我看见他戴着黑布小帽，穿着黑布大马褂，深青布棉袍，蹒跚地走到铁道边，慢慢探身下去，尚不大难。可是他穿过铁道，要爬上那边月台，就不容易了。他用两手攀着上面，两脚再向上缩；他肥胖的身子向左微倾，显出努力的样子。这时我看见他的背影，我眼泪很快地流下来了。我赶紧拭干了泪，怕他看见，也怕别人看见。我再向外看时，他已抱了朱红的橘子往回走了。过铁道时，他先将橘子散放在地上，自己慢慢爬下，再抱起橘子走。到这边时，我赶紧去搀他。他和我走到车上，将橘子一股脑儿放在我的皮大衣上。于是扑扑衣上泥土，心里很轻松似的，过了一会说，"我走了；到那边来信！"我望着他走出去。他走了几步，回过头看见我，说，"进去吧，里边没人。"等他的背影混入来来往往的人里，再找不着了，我便进来坐下，我的眼泪又来了。

译文 1：So I watched him in his black cloth cap and jacket and dark blue cotton-padded gown, as he waddled to the tracks and climbed slowly down—not so difficult after all. But when he had crossed the lines he had trouble clambering up the other side. He clutched the platform with both hands and tried to heave his legs up, straining to the left. At the sight of his burly back tears started to my eyes, but I wiped them hastily so that neither he nor anyone else might see them. When next I looked out he was on his way back with some ruddy tangerines. He put these on the platform before climbing slowly down to cross the lines, which he did after picking the fruit up. When he reached my side I was there to help him up. We boarded the train together and he plumped the tangerines down on my coat. Then he brushed the dust from his clothes, as if that was a weight off his mind.

"I'll be going now, son," he said presently. "Write to me once you get there."

I watched him walk away. After a few steps he turned back to look at me.

"Go on in!" he called. "There's no one in the compartment."

When his back disappeared among the bustling crowd I went in and sat down, and my eyes were wet again.

译文 2：I watched him waddle over to the tracks, dressed in his black mandarin jacket and dark blue padded gown, with his black skullcap on his head. He slowly lowered himself down, which didn't prove too difficult. But climbing onto the other platform was a different matter. Supporting himself with both hands on the edge of the platform, he drew his feet up; then he inclined his body to the left and appeared to be making a strenuous effort. As I watched him from behind, my tears gushed out. I hurriedly wiped my face dry, afraid that he would see, afraid that others would see. When I looked up again he was already on his way back with an armful of bright red oranges. To cross the tracks he first placed the oranges on the ground, then slowly climbed down, then picked the oranges up again. I hurried to help him up when he got to my side of the track. He walked with me onto the train, plonked all the oranges down on my fur coat, and dusted himself off. Now seeming very relaxed, he said after a while, "I'll be off, then. Write to me when you get there." I watched him leave. After taking a few steps, he turned his head and saw me. He said, "You'd better go in, there's no one looking after your things." I waited until his retreating figure had been swallowed up in the throng before taking my seat. Then my tears came again.

以上两种译文分别出自杨宪益和 David E. Pollard 之手，请仔细对比体味，加强选词意识。不妨选出两组动作，对两种译文进行对比。

- 他用两手攀着上面，两脚再向上缩；他肥胖的身子向左微倾，显出努力的样子。

    译文 1：He clutched the platform with both hands and tried to heave his legs up, straining to the left.

译文2：Supporting himself with both hands on the edge of the platform, he drew his feet up; then he inclined his body to the left and appeared to be making a strenuous effort.

- 他和我走到车上，将橘子一股脑儿放在我的皮大衣上。于是扑扑衣上泥土，心里很轻松似的，……

译文1：We boarded the train together and he plumped the tangerines down on my coat. Then he brushed the dust from his clothes, as if that was a weight off his mind.

译文2：He walked with me onto the train, plonked all the oranges down on my fur coat, and dusted himself off. Now seeming very relaxed, …

可以取两个观察点比较两种译文。一是两种译文对动词限定形式（谓语动词）和非限定形式（分词）的运用：译文1配合使用，构句通达；而译文2用非谓语动词稍多。第二个观察点是对同一动作的不同传译，如"两脚再向上缩"，译文1为 heave his legs up，而译文2为 drew his feet up；"身子向左微倾，显出努力的样子"，译文2为 he inclined his body to the left and appeared to be making a strenuous effort，而译文1简略地译为 straining to the left；"将橘子一股脑儿放在我的皮大衣上"，译文1用 plumped… down on…，而译文2用 plonked… down on…。这样的观察有助于丰富我们的词汇储备。

下面是摘自鲁迅《风筝》中的一个段落：

有一天，我忽然想起，似乎多日不很看见他了，但记得曾见他在后园拾枯竹。我恍然大悟似的，便跑向少有人去的一间堆积杂物的小屋去，推开门，果然就在尘封的什物堆中发现了他。他向着大方凳，坐在小凳上；便很惊惶地站了起来，失了色瑟缩着。大方凳旁靠着一个蝴蝶风筝的竹骨，还没有糊上纸，凳上是一对做眼睛用的小风轮，正用红纸条装饰着，将要完工了。我在破获秘密的满足中，又很愤怒他的瞒了我的眼睛，这样苦心孤诣地来偷做没出息孩子的玩艺。我即刻伸手折断了蝴蝶的一支翅骨，又将风轮掷在地下，踏扁了。论长幼，论力气，他是都敌不过我的，我当然得到完全的胜利，于是傲然走出，留他绝望地站在小屋里。后来他怎样，我不知道，也没有留心。

One day it occurred to me I had not seen much of him lately, but I had noticed him picking up bamboo sticks in the backyard. The truth dawned on me in a flash. I ran to a small deserted store-room and, sure enough, as I pushed open the door, I discovered him there in the midst of the dusty debris. He had been sitting on a footstool in front of a big square stool; but now, standing up in confusion, he <u>changed colour and shrank back</u>. Propped up against the big stool was the bamboo framework of a butterfly-kite, not pasted yet with paper; while on the stool lay two small wind-wheels for the butterfly's eyes, which had just been beautifying with red paper. This work was nearly done. I was pleased to have found out his secret; but furious that he could deceive me so long, while he <u>toiled so single-heartedly</u> to make the toy of a good-for-nothing child. I <u>seized</u> the framework at once, <u>broke</u> one of its wings, then <u>swept</u> the wheels to the ground and <u>trampled on</u> them. In size and strength he was no match for me; so of course I came off completely victorious. Then I <u>stalked out</u> proudly, leaving him standing in despair in that little room. What he did after that I neither knew nor cared.

这一段叙述了"我"发现弟弟偷偷做风筝，继而大怒，将其扯坏扬长而去的故事。先注意谓语动词的选择：恍然大悟——dawn on，失了色瑟缩着——changed colour and shrank back，苦心孤诣地来偷做——toiled so single-heartedly，伸手折断……掷……踏扁……傲然走出——seized... broke... swept... trampled on... stalked out。也注意分词结构、插入成分以及倒装句的运用。

为节省篇幅，下面列出一些较简短的例子。细心观察译文是如何依照英语的行文需要，选择恰当的英语动词来再现原文的词义和神韵的。

- 松涛如吼，霜月当窗，饥鼠吱吱在承尘上奔窜。
  The wind <u>roared</u> down from the pine-clad hills like a wild beast, frosty moonlight <u>framed</u> the window, hungry mice <u>scurried</u> squeaking over the ceiling.
- 他明知道辩不清的，每次替人受过之后，总只张大了两眼，滴落几滴大眼泪，摸摸头上的痛处就了事。
  He knew his protestations would not be believed, and did no more on being punished in another's stead than <u>bulge out his eyes</u>, <u>let fall some big tear drops</u>, <u>rub his head where it hurt</u>, and <u>forget it</u>.
- 而各个账房先生，又都一样地板起了脸，放大了喉咙，说是赊欠不来。
  And each cashier in turn <u>set his features forbiddingly</u>, <u>raised his voice an</u>

27

octave, and <u>declared</u> that no credit sales were allowed.

以上三例，汉语中的并列动词大都一对一地译为英语的谓语动词，呈并列句形式。而下列例句中汉语连串动词中的一个或几个动词，在英语译文中被处理为非限定动词或介词短语。

- 趁着酒兴，剔亮了油灯，取张花笺，打开墨盒，抽出笔试了试，也还趁手，兴致就越发好了。

  <u>Taking advantage of</u> the mood created by the wine, he turned up the oil lamp, took out a piece of flower-patterned paper, opened his ink pot, selected a brush that was responsive to his touch and the mood waxed in him.

- 众多的上海人处于第二线，观看着，比较着，追随着，参谋着，担心着，庆幸着，来反复品尝第二线的乐趣和风险。

  The bulk of the Shanghainese occupied the second line, <u>observing, comparing, following, advising, worrying, congratulating</u> themselves, <u>tasting</u> over and over the pleasures and risks of the second line.

- 我从小就喜欢听戏，常看见有人坐在戏园子的边厢下面，靠着柱子，闭着眼睛，凝神危坐，微微的摇晃着脑袋，手在轻轻的敲着板眼，聚精会神的欣赏那台上的歌唱，……

  I got a liking for listening to plays when I was young. Many a time I have seen men sitting under the gallery at a playhouse, <u>sitting</u> bolt upright against a pillar, <u>with eyes shut, head wagging slightly, hand lightly marking the beat, concentrating</u> with every nerve on the singer's rendition.

- 费妈和她丈夫，在外面做工糊口，到晚来回郑家操持家务。每天一早背着郑板桥出门，先用一文钱买个烧饼放在他手里，找个安静地方把他安顿好了，才去做自己的事。

  Mother Fei and her husband found work outside to help make ends meet, and <u>returning</u> in the evening they would attend to the household responsibilities. Every day early in the morning, <u>with Zheng Banqiao on her back</u> Mother Fei went out to work. She would first buy a sesame-seed cake for one cash and <u>putting it in his hand</u>, she would then settle him in a quiet spot before <u>going off to her own work</u>.

- 但一听到了要赊欠的时候，却同样地都白了眼，作一脸苦笑，说要去问账房先生的。
  But <u>at the mention of</u> buying on credit they all turned their nose up, put on a cold smile, and said we'd have to ask the cashier.
- 郑板桥不知道他们吵些什么，只见费妈无缘无故流泪不止，……
  Zheng Banqiao had no idea what they were quarrelling about. What he could see was that Mother Fei was constantly <u>in tears</u> for no apparent reason.

当汉语重复使用同一个动词的时候，翻译为英语时既可简约为一个动词，亦可译成不同的英语动词。例如：

它展着笔直的翅膀，<u>掠过</u>苍老的树枝，<u>掠过</u>寂静的瓦房，<u>掠过</u>皇家的御湖，环绕灿烂的琉璃瓦，<u>飞着</u>，<u>飞着</u>。

With its straight wings spread out, it <u>swept past</u> sturdy old trees, quiet tile-roofed dwellings and lakes of imperial gardens, and circled over dazzling glazed tiles. It kept flying and flying.

汉语中的"掠过"一词出现三次，英语只用了 swept past 一个短语动词，而"环绕……飞着，飞着"则一分为二，先说"circled over…"，再用一个单立的短句强化了飞机盘旋不去的景象。

于是——洗手的时候，日子从水盆里过去；吃饭的时候，日子从饭碗里过去；默默时，便从凝然的双眼前过去。

Thus, the day <u>flows away</u> through the sink when I wash my hands, <u>wears away</u> in the bowl when I eat my meal, <u>passes away</u> before my day-dreaming gaze as I reflect in silence.

译者用了不同动词以呼应不同的比喻形象。

本节我们以动词的运用为切入点对一些典型译例进行了分析，很明显，选对、选好动词是译好叙事句/段的关键。回想与本节相对应的第一章第一节，同样提到了动词的运用，但那是以结构为切入点请大家关注动词的。这其实是一个重要的阅读方略：读英语语篇从结构入手带动对动词的关注，读汉英对照语篇则从动词的选择切入，兼顾组词、构句的技能。将合适的动词纳入合适的结构，这就是叙事的关键。

第二节 描 写

描写句的翻译重在词语的选择。说到词语,首先想到的当然是具有状物功能的形容词,但同时也不要忽视英语介词短语和动词,因为汉语形容词可翻译为英语介词短语结构,而英语中的动词对动作的状态也具有描写作用。除此之外,描写语篇的英译也较多使用名词。

以张洁的《爱,是不能忘记的》中的一段文字为例,说明翻译描写语篇时选词的重要性。

一辆黑色的小轿车悄无声息地停在人行道旁边。从车上走下来一个满头白发、穿着一套黑色毛呢中山装的、上了年纪的男人。那头白发生得堂皇而又气派!他给人一种严谨的、一丝不苟的、脱俗的、明澄得像水晶一样的印象。特别是他的眼睛,十分冷峻地闪着寒光,当他急速地瞥向什么东西的时候,会让人联想起闪电或是舞动着的剑影。要使这样一对冰冷的眼睛充满柔情,那必定得是特别强大的爱情,而且得为了一个确实值得爱的女人才行。

A black limousine pulled up silently by the pavement. Out stepped an elderly man with white hair in a black serge tunic-suit. What a striking shock of white hair! <u>Strict, scrupulous, distinguished, transparently honest</u>—that was my impression of him. The cold glint of his flashing eyes reminded me of lightning or swordplay. Only ardent love for a woman really deserving his love could fill cold eyes like those with tenderness.

上段中"严谨的、一丝不苟的、脱俗的、明澄得像水晶一样的印象"译为 Strict, scrupulous, distinguished, transparently honest—that was my impression of him。前两个形容词翻译成英语时次序颠倒,因为英语中较短的形容词往往放在较长的形容词前面;"明澄得像水晶一样的"译为"副词+形容词"短语;原文的偏正结构译为一个句子。另外注意第二句译文的倒装结构。

又如陆文夫《小贩世家》的开篇部分:

我推开临街的长窗往下看,见巷子的尽头有一团亮光,光晕映在两壁的白粉墙上,嗖嗖地向前,好像夜神在巡游。渐渐地清楚了,原来是一副油漆亮堂的馄饨担子,担子上冒着水汽,红泥锅膛里燃烧着柴火。那挑担子的便是朱源达,当年十七八岁,高而精瘦。担子的旁边走着一个头发斑白、步履蹒跚的老头,那是朱源达的父亲。他再也挑不动了,正在把担子向儿子交付,敲着竹梆子走在前面,向儿子指明他一生所走过的、能够卖掉馄饨而又坎坷不平的小路。

  I opened the long window facing the street, and looking down I spotted a light at the other end of the alley. The light wavered on the white chalk walls, whizzing along like a spirit on night patrol. Gradually it became more distinct. It was a brightly lacquered wonton carrying pole. Steam was rising above the pole, while sticks of firewood burned in a stove. The pole carrier was Zhu Yuanda. At that time he was perhaps seventeen or eighteen, tall and thin. Beside him shuffled an old grey-haired fellow—his father. His carrying days were over. He'd very recently passed the carrying on to his son. Now he went on ahead striking the bamboo clapper, leading his son along the bumpy road he'd followed in his life that had enabled him to sell enough wonton.

  动词的选择，如"见巷子的尽头有一团亮光"译为 spotted a light，"光晕映在两壁的白粉墙上"译为 The light wavered on the white chalk walls，"好像夜神在巡游"译为 whizzing along like a spirit on night patrol 等；形容词的翻译，如"油漆亮堂"为 brightly lacquered，"高而精瘦"为 thin and tall 等，精准传神。构句上，注意倒装句 Beside him shuffled… 以及诸多分词短语的运用。

  下面摘自夏丏尊《白马湖之冬》的句段描写严冬景色，几个色彩形容词——"惨白、紫而黯、深蓝"——被巧妙地译为动词短语，十分传神。

  在平常的日子，风来大概在下午快要傍晚的时候，半夜即息。至于大寒风，那是整日夜狂吼要二三日才止的。最严寒的几天，泥地看去惨白如水门汀，山色冻得发紫而黯，湖波泛深蓝色。

  Normally the wind would get up towards dusk and die down again about midnight, though when a winter monsoon set in, it would rage all day and night, and not let up for two or three days. When the cold was most extreme, the earth would be blanched grey like cement, the mountains would purple into somberness, and the waves of the lake be shot with deep blue.

  语言的使用是群体行为，但词语的选择则是在群体行为所形成的规范和制约下的个体行为，每个人都会有自己选词的风格、自己的偏好或用词习惯。不同译者对原文语句的翻译会体现出个体差异和不同的选词风格，这就需要我们对同一原文的不同译文多加体味，借以扩充自己的选词思路，提高选词技巧。词语的选择归根结底不仅仅是对词语本身的选择，而是对某种搭配和句式的选择。

  看下面《荷塘月色》中的一段描述及三种译文：

沿着荷塘，是一条曲折的小煤屑路。这是一条僻静的路；白天也少人走，夜晚更加寂寞。荷塘四面，长着许多树，蓊蓊郁郁的。路的一旁，是些杨树，和一些不知道名字的树。没有月光的晚上，这路上阴森森的，有些怕人。今晚却很好，虽然月光也还是淡淡的。

译文1：A cinder-path <u>winds</u> along by the side of the pool. It is <u>off the beaten track</u> and few pass this way even by day, so at night it is still more <u>quiet</u>. Trees grow <u>thick and bosky</u> all around the pool, with willows and other trees I cannot name by the path. On nights when there is no moon the track is almost <u>terrifyingly dark</u>, but tonight it was quite clear, though the moonlight was <u>pale</u>.

译文2：At the edge of the pond is a <u>winding narrow</u> cinder path. This path, being <u>out of the way</u>, is little used even in the daytime, and at night is all the more <u>deserted</u>. All around the pond grow many trees, <u>lush and dense</u>, while on one side of the path there are some willows, and other trees whose names are unknown to me. On moonless nights the path is <u>overcast and gloomy</u>, somewhat <u>eerie</u>. But tonight all was <u>well</u>, even though the moonlight was only <u>dim</u>.

译文3: Along the Lotus Pond runs a small cinder footpath. It is <u>beautiful and secluded</u> here, a place not frequented by pedestrians even in the daytime; now at night, it looks more <u>solitary</u>, in a <u>lush, shady</u> ambience of trees all around the pond. On the side where the path is, there are willows, interlaced with some others whose names I do not know. The foliage, which, in a moonless night, would loom somewhat <u>frighteningly dark</u>, looks very nice tonight, although the moonlight is not more than <u>a thin, grayish veil</u>.

"曲折的"一词，译文1和译文2分别处理为动词（winds）和形容词(winding narrow)，译文3则没有译出。再比如"寂寞"一词，三位译者分别译作了 quiet, deserted 和 solitary 三个不同的形容词，quiet 意在"静"，而 deserted 和 solitary 则分别强调"荒凉"和"无人"。"阴森森的"译为 terrifyingly dark、overcast and gloomy, and somewhat eerie 和 frighteningly dark。何以如此？译者的个人选择使然。译文3在处理某些形容词结构的时候，将其译成了名词短语，比如"蓊蓊郁郁的"译为 a lush, shady ambience of trees，"淡淡的"译为 a thin, grayish veil。

说到形容词可以译为名词，再从《荷塘月色》中选一个句子，观察译者是如何处理名词的。

这是独处的<u>妙处</u>，我且受用这<u>无边</u>的荷香月色好了。

译文 1：That was the advantage of solitude: I could savour to the full that expanse of fragrant lotus and the moonlight.

译文 2：This was the beauty of solitude. I resolved to make the best of this abundance of lotus and moonlight.

译文 3: That is the beauty of being alone. For the moment, just let me indulge in this profusion of moonlight and lotus fragrance.

"妙处"译为 advantage 和 beauty，"无边的"转换为名词 expanse、abundance 和 profusion。这里可以特别体会到名词的描述功能。

下面一例中的名词短语更能突出名词的描写功能：

因为我家城里那个向来很著名的湖上，满生了芦苇和满浮了无数的大船，分外显得逼仄、湫隘、喧嚷，所以我也不高兴常去游逛。有时几个友人约着荡桨湖中，每每到了晚上，各种杂乱的声音一齐并作，锣鼓声、尖利的胡琴声、不很好听的歌声、男人的居心喊闹与粉面光头的女人调笑，更夹杂上小舟卖物的叫声，几乎把静静的湖水掀起了"大波"。

I seldom cared to visit the famous lake although I lived in a city along its shore. Filled with reeds and large craft, it seemed exceptionally narrow and cramped and noisy. Sometimes I went rowing with a few friends in the evening, but every night it was the same bedlam. The clash of cymbals, the high-pitched squeal of fiddles, the unpleasant singing, the men's raucous shouts, the seductive laughter of painted women with sleekly oiled hair, the cries of the vendors on the little peddler boats… swept the placid surface of the lake like a huge wave.

下面译例也显示译者选择名词的用心。余秋雨在《上海人》中谈上海人的特点用了"心理品性""实际效益"等名词，且看译者是如何依照上下文和作者的意向选用英语词语的：

上海文明的又一心理品性，是对实际效益的精明估算。也许是徐光启的《几何原本》余脉尚存，也许是急速变化的周围现实塑造成了一种本领，上海人历来比较讲究科学实效，看不惯慢吞木讷的傻样子。

Another feature of the Shanghai temperament is astute calculation of practical advantage. Perhaps this is a throwback to Xu Guangqi's mathematical achievements, perhaps it is a competence shaped by a rapidly changing environment, but in any case the Shanghainese have always been interested in provable benefits, and have no patience with doddering and slow-wittedness.

上文集中讨论词语的运用，与此同时也要关注句子结构的安排。汉语中会出现动宾词组构成的定语，有时还比较长，这时可用英语的宾语从句对译。

引入曲曲的深院，在烨烨的红烛照耀之下，他无论如何不能相信，眼前这位丰腴的盛装丽人，就是当年胭脂点额，惯做男孩儿装束的远房表妹。视线所及，没有一样略微熟悉的东西，可以为他唤起比较生动清晰的回忆。朦胧的不仅是往日，也是此刻！

Led into a quiet winding hall, Zheng Banqiao, under the light of the radiant red candles, simply could not believe that this plump and regally attired elegant lady with the full figure standing before his eyes was the same distant cousin who, in the old days, used to put rouge on her forehead and dress like a boy. Nothing within sight had even the most remote familiarity to summon up a vivid memory of the past. But not only were those past days in a haze, so was the present moment.

另外，句子的节奏也会影响描写的效果。比如下面的两种译文：

有一天，我伏案写作时，它居然落到我的肩上。我手中的笔不觉停了，生怕惊跑它。呆一会儿，扭头看，这小家伙竟扒在我的肩头睡着了，银灰色的眼睑盖住眸子，小红脚刚好给胸脯上长长的绒毛盖住。我轻轻抬一抬肩，它没醒，睡得好熟！还呷呷嘴，难道在做梦？

译文1：One day it landed on my shoulder while I was hunched over the desk writing. I automatically halted my pen, for fear of scaring it away. I froze for a moment, and when I turned my head the little chap had gone to sleep perched on my shoulder, its eyes lidded silver-grey and its little red feet covered by the long down on its breast. I gently shrugged my shoulder without waking it. It was sound asleep, its beak still working. Was it dreaming?

译文2：One day I was working at the desk when the small bird flew over and rested on my shoulder. I stopped writing for fear that it would fly off. After a moment when I turned and looked at it, I found it had fallen asleep there, its silver eye-lids covering its eye-balls, its red claws buried in its fluffy chest. I slightly lifted my shoulder, but it did not awake. It was having a fast sleep. Once it opened its beak a bit—obviously it was enjoying itself in a dream.

很明显，译文1的句子结构较简洁，描写效果也更好，尤其结尾部分十分传神。

第三节　说　明

在本篇第一章第三节中，我们关注了英语说明语篇中的逻辑模式。本节对比分析英译者对汉语中各种常见逻辑模式的处理方式。

第一，可以以定义某个概念的方式展开一个段落。如巴金在《做一个战士》中给"战士"下了定义：

战士是永远追求光明的。他并不躺在晴空下享受阳光，却在暗夜里燃起火炬，给人们照亮道路，使他们走向黎明。驱散黑暗，这是战士的任务。他不躲避黑暗，却要面对黑暗，跟躲藏在阴影里的魑魅、魍魉搏斗。他要消灭它们而取得光明。战士是不知道妥协的。他得不到光明便不会停止战斗。

A fighter is always in pursuit of light. Instead of basking in the sunshine under a clear sky, he holds a burning torch in the darkness of night to illuminate people's way so that they can continue their journey till they see the dawn of a new day. It is the task of a fighter to dispel darkness. Instead of shirking darkness, he braves it and fights the hidden demons and monsters therein. He is determined to wipe them out and win light. He knows no compromise. He will keep on fighting until he wins light.

原文几乎每句都以"战士"/"他"作主语，从战士的行为界定他的品质。译文构句紧随原文，但英语的逻辑标识要更形式化一些，第二句中的 ...so that... till... 将"使他们走向黎明"中的逻辑关系外化出来。另外，两个 instead of 状语重现了原文"不……却……"的逻辑关系。

第二，说明行为或进展过程的句段。如下面夏丏尊在《我之于书》中谈他读书的习惯：

书籍到了我的手里，我的习惯是先看序文，次看目录。页数不多的往往立刻通读，篇幅大的，只把正文任择一二章节略加翻阅，就插在书架上。除小说外，我少有全体读完的大部的书，只凭了购入当时的记忆，知道某册书是何种性质，其中大概有些什么可取的材料而已。什么书在什么时候再去读再去翻，连我自己也无把握，完全要看一个时期一个时期的兴趣。

As soon as a new book comes to hand, I always read the preface first and then the table of contents. If it happens to be a thin one, I often finish reading it in one sitting. Otherwise, I often browse through one or two chapters or sections before putting it

onto my bookshelf. I seldom read a thick book from cover to cover unless it is a novel. By dint of the first impression it made on me at the time of buying, I have a rough idea of what a book is about and what useful materials in it are available to me. But I have little idea which book is to be read or looked over again at what time. It is completely subject to the whims of the moment.

请观察两点。第一,译者增加了 If...,Otherwise... 和 But... 三个连词,将原文的逻辑关系显化;第二,注意学习译者的断句技巧:原文第二句是个长句,按其逻辑和语义关系被译成四个句子。

第三,含有比较或对照的段落。

就伦敦,巴黎,罗马来说,巴黎更近似北平——虽然"近似"两字都拉扯得很远——不过,假使让我"家住巴黎",我一定会和没有家一样的感到寂苦。巴黎,据我看,还太热闹。自然,那里也有空旷静寂的地方,可是又未免太旷;不像北平那样复杂而又有个边际,使我能摸着——那长着红酸枣的老城墙!面向着积水潭,背后是城墙,坐在石上看水中的小蝌蚪或苇叶上嫩蜻蜓,我可以快乐的坐一天,// 心中完全安适,无所求也无可怕,像小儿安睡在摇篮里。是的,北平也有热闹的地方,但是它和太极拳相似,动中有静。巴黎有许多地方使人疲乏,所以咖啡与酒是必要的,以便刺激;在北平,有温和的香片茶就够了。

Of all these cities, Paris has the closest affinity with Peiping (The word "affinity" may perhaps sound a bit farfetched). Nevertheless, if should make my home in Paris, I would feel very lonely as if I had no home at all. As far as I know, Paris is too much of a bustling town. It does have quiet open spaces, but they smack of mere expanses of vacancy. Peiping is complicated and yet tangible. I can feel it by touch. I can feel the red wild jujubes growing on its ancient city wall! I can spend a whole day enjoying myself sitting on a rock to observe tiny tadpoles in the water or tender dragonflies on reeds while facing me lies Ji Shui Tan Pond and right behind me rises the high city wall. I can thus enjoy a perfect inner clam, free from any desire or fear, like a child sleeping peacefully in the cradle. There are also bustling places in Peiping, to be sure, but like the traditional Chinese shadow boxing Tai Ji Quan, the city retains its stillness in the midst of motion. While Parisians have to turn to coffee or wine for the relief of boredom caused by so many wearisome places in their city, the mild beverage of jasmine tea will be more than adequate for dwellers of Peiping.

对比阅读时注意以下要点：第一，全段出现了四个连词（划线部分），表明了四层对照关系，其中最后的 While... 一句表达的对照关系在原文中并无显性标示（explicitly marked）；第二，译文用加括号的方式对译原文的插入语；第三，注意"面向着积水潭……"一句在"//"号处被断为两个句子，学习译文中各种从属成分的运用。

第四，运用举例的方法构建的段落。余秋雨在《上海人》中举例说明现代上海人所面对的种种"闹腾"：

徐光启的后代既有心理准备，又仍然未免吃惊的一下子陷入了这种闹腾之中。一方面，殖民者、冒险家、暴发户、流氓、地痞、妓女、帮会一起涌现；另一方面，大学、医院、邮局、银行、电车、学者、诗人、科学家也汇集其间。黄浦江汽笛声声，霓虹灯夜夜闪烁，西装革履与长袍马褂摩肩接踵，四方土语与欧美语言交相斑驳，你来我往，此胜彼败，以最迅捷的频率日夜更替。

The descendants of Xu Guangqi were both psychologically prepared for and surprised by the uproar that overwhelmed them. On the one hand there was an invasion of colonizers, adventurers, upstarts, gangsters, hooligans, prostitutes and triads; on the other hand there was a forgathering of colleges, hospitals, post offices, banks, trams, scholars, poets and scientists. Against the background of the sound of steam whistles on the Huangpu River, the nightly flashing of the neon lights, Western suits and leather shoes jostling with long gowns and mandarin jackets, the babel of Chinese dialects and European languages, and the comings and goings, there was constant turnover, things replacing each other with the highest frequency.

原文先是用"一方面……另一方面……"句式，罗列了一系列名词，然后举出几种典型的景象，说明这个大都市里各色人等聚集，嘈嘈杂杂，瞬息万变。译文主要句构是三个 there be 句式，并用 on the one hand 和 on the other hand 与原文的逻辑层次相对应。但最后 there was 句则进行了逻辑重组：首先加了 Against the background of 引导的长长的状语，句末又使用了独立主格结构 things replacing...。于是，原文平铺的意合句式译成了有主有从的复合句。

第五，借助类比方法写成的段落。矛盾在《白杨礼赞》中将北方农民比做白杨树：

汉英语篇翻译

白杨不是平凡的树。它在西北极普遍，不被人重视，就跟北方农民相似；它有极强的生命力，磨折不了，压迫不倒，也跟北方的农民相似。我赞美白杨树，就因为它不但象征了北方的农民，尤其象征了今天我们民族解放斗争中所不可缺的朴质，坚强，以及力求上进的精神。

White poplars are no ordinary trees. But these common trees in Northwest China are as much ignored as our peasants in the North. However, like our peasants in the North, they are bursting with vitality and capable of surviving any hardship or oppression. I pay tribute to them because they symbolize our peasants in the North and, in particular, the spirit of honesty, tenacity and forging ahead—a spirit central to our struggle for national liberation.

对照汉语与英译文，首先，注意译文中逻辑关系的显性化趋势（划线连词表达的逻辑转折关系在原文中是隐含的）；其次，注意"我们民族解放斗争中所不可缺的朴质"在译文中被处理成同位语，这也是对原文逻辑关系的一种调整和重组。

人类在历史上的生活正如旅行一样。旅途上的征人所经过的地方，有时是坦荡平原，有时是崎岖险路。志于旅途的人，走到平坦的地方，固是高高兴兴地向前走，走到崎岖的境界，愈是奇趣横生，觉得在此奇绝壮绝的境界，愈能感到一种冒险的美趣。

The historical course of man's life is just like a journey. A traveler on a long journey passes through now a broad, level plain, now a rugged, hazardous road. While a determined traveler cheerfully continues his journey upon reaching a safe and smooth place, he finds it still more fascinating to come to a rugged place, the enormously magnificent spectacle of which, he feels, is better able to generate in him a wonderful sensation of adventure.

此段以一个明喻开始，继而将喻体"旅行"的寓意进一步挖掘，扩展为类比。注意译文第二句主语由原文的物"historical course"，转换成了人"a traveler"。另外，While引出的长句使原文的逻辑层次得以显化。

第六，以问答形式组织的段落。

究竟是结婚的好呢，还是不结婚的好？这问题似乎同先有鸡还是先有鸡蛋一样，常常有人提起，而也常常没有人解决过的问题。照大体看来，想租房子的时候，是无眷莫问的，想做官的时候，又是朝里无裙莫做官的，想写文章的时候，是独身者不能写我的妻的，凡此种种似乎都是结婚的好。

Marriage or no marriage, which is more desirable? That sounds like the chicken-and-egg question, which, though often discussed, remains a perpetual puzzle. Generally speaking, one who has no family dependants is not supposed to rent a house, one who has no petticoat influence in the government should refrain from becoming an official, an unmarried male writer is in no position to write about "my wife." All these seem to hint at the advantage of marriage.

以上段落先是提出问题，并用一个类比强调其难解之处，然后例举数个可资类比的事物，推论出结婚为好。注意译文以 one who…, one who…, an unmarried male writer… 句对译"想……的时候，是……的，想……的时候，又是……的，想……的时候，是……的"的巧妙转换，这种以重建的英语框架容纳汉语原文信息的技巧值得借鉴。

汉语语篇的逻辑常处于隐性状态，而英语的语篇逻辑呈显性化。本节对照第一章的第三节，力图将注意力导向英语行文的逻辑层次，强化汉译英时构建英语语篇的逻辑感，增强解决语篇逻辑问题的能力。

第四节　对　话

对话是口语体，这不言而喻，但这也正是汉译英的难点所在。要多多留意英语人士的日常对话，细心阅读英语小说中的对话，琢磨汉译英作品中对话翻译的特点，积累语料，以备使用。

大家在阅读双语语篇的对话部分时应留意以下几方面。

第一，口语句式简练，常常省略句中某些成分，常用缩略形式。翻译时，对话中的迟疑、结巴等语气要反映出来。比如下面王统照的《湖畔儿语》中"我"偶遇一个熟识的小孩，便问起家里近况，小孩回答迟疑、断断续续。请看译文是如何处理的。

"你的爸爸现在在哪里？"

"算在家里。……"小顺迟疑地答我。我从他呆呆的目光中,看得出他对于我这老朋友有点奇怪。

"你爸爸还给人家作活吗?"

"什么?……他每天只是不在家,却也没有一次,……带钱回来,……作活……吗?……不知道。"

"Where is your papa now?"

"At home, you might say…" Little Shun replied hesitantly. From his expression I could see that he thought this old friend was rather peculiar.

"Is he still working?"

"What? … He goes out every day, but he never… brings home any money… Working? … I don't know."

第二,对话在推进故事情节发展和表现人物性格方面起着非常重要的作用。对话和叙述、描写结合起来就可以将人物活脱脱地塑造出来。阅读时要留意译者是如何再现原文中人物的语气和神态的。《孔乙己》中有许多经典范例,如下面一段:

孔乙己着了慌,伸开五指将碟子罩住,弯下腰去说道,"不多了,我已经不多了。"直起身又看一看豆,自己摇头说,"不多不多!多乎哉?不多也。"于是这一群孩子都在笑声中走散了。

Growing flustered, he would cover it with his hand and bending forward from the waist would say, "There aren't many left, not many at all." Straightening up to look at the peas again, he would shake his head and reiterate, "Not many, I do assure you. Not many, nay, not many at all." Then the children would scamper off, shouting with laughter.

再如《小二黑结婚》中二诸葛这个人物。他满脑子封建迷信的婚姻观,见了区上的干部一口一个"恩典恩典":

……二诸葛道:"那也可以,不过还得请区长恩典恩典,不能叫他跟于福这闺女订婚!"区长说:"这你就管不着了!"二诸葛发急道:"千万请区长恩典恩典,命相不对,这是一辈子的事!"又向小二黑道:"二黑!你不要糊涂了!这是你一辈子的事!"……

"I don't object to that at all," said Kong Ming the Second. "But please Your Honour, be more merciful; don't let Little Erhei marry Yu Fu's daughter."

"Now that's none of your business!"

"Please be more merciful, more merciful! Their horoscopes don't agree. If they marry, they'll be unhappy all their lives!" Turning to his son, he said, "Erhei, don't be so pigheaded. The happiness of your whole life is at stake!"

译文中用 Your Honour、be merciful 再现了二诸葛一脸谦卑的可怜相。另外译文的段落格式有所调整。

第三，对话中常出现方言、习语和土语，翻译时多采取规范化的方法，即用规范的英语再现其意，并确保上下文的连贯。比如郁达夫的《春风沉醉的晚上》写的是沪上的故事，"我"在过马路时被电车司机骂了一通：

……我抬起头来一看，我的面前正冲来一乘无轨电车，车头上站着的那肥胖的机器手，伏出了半身，怒目的大声骂我说：

"猪头三！侬（你）艾（眼）睛勿散（生）咯！跌杀时，叫旺（黄）够（狗）抵侬（命）噢！"

I looked up and saw that a trolley-bus was rushing towards me and the fat driver, leaning out, was glaring at me angrily. "Swine, have you no eyes? Serve you right if you get killed. Your life's worth no more than a yellow dog, anyway."

原文是上海话，英译倾向于规范化，并没用英语的方言，只有 have you no eyes 一句不大合乎语法。

对话中出现的一些习语、土语，可用英语中意义相同或相近的成语代替，也可以采取直译的方法。如艾芜《石青嫂子》中，石青嫂子和催债人的对话：

石青嫂子痛苦地叹气：

"他简直要叫人家的鸡下金蛋哪！"

老头子感慨地说：

"他老人家也太想钱了，儿子在外头带兵，一年要寄多少回来，这点押金就算了嘛！"

石青嫂子在痛苦的脸色上又露出鄙夷的神情，冷冷地说：

"他要能够这样想，那他就长命百岁了！"

老头子现出为难的样子，边走边叹气：

"这叫我咋个去回话嘛？简直捏红炭圆！"

石青嫂子赶在后面说：

"你老人家就这样告诉好了！你说，他们干竹榨不出油的！"

"He's asking for the impossible!" Mrs. Shi sighed in distress.

"He is too grasping," the old man agreed, experiencing a wave of righteous indignation. "His son's an officer in the army and sends him plenty of money every year. It wouldn't hurt him in the least to cancel the deposit."

"If he could only see it that way!" she exclaimed.

Disconcerted, the *jia zhang* began to move off, sighing, "What am I to say to the landlord? I've really got a hard nut to crack."

"Just tell him you can't squeeze oil out of a bamboo," Mrs. Shi shouted after him.

对话中"下金蛋"和"捏红炭圆"两个俗语译为意义相近的英语习语,而"干竹榨不出油"采用了直译的方法。原文中的"那他就长命百岁了",当然不是字面意义,而是"他要是那样想,可就好了"的意思,所以用 If he could only… 译出其意。

第四,英语中对话体的行文,往往是换一个人说话便另起一段,而汉语中有时是不分段的,因此汉英翻译时需要作相应的段落调整。如赵树理的《小二黑结婚》中小芹正在一个大窑里和小二黑诉说她母亲如何不同意他们婚事,却被金旺等人"捉了奸":

说到这里,听见外边有脚步声,小二黑伸出头来一看,黑影里站着四五个人,有一个说:"拿双拿双!"他俩人都听出是金旺的声音,小二黑起了火,大叫道:"拿?没有犯了法!"兴旺也来了,下命令道:"捉住捉住!我就看你犯法不犯法,给你操了好几天心了!"小二黑说:"你说去哪里咱就去哪里,到边区政府你也不能把谁怎么样!走!"兴旺说:"走?便宜了你!把他捆起来!"小二黑挣扎了一会,无奈没有他们人多,终于被他们七手八脚打了一顿捆起来了。兴旺说:"里边还有个女的,也捆起来!捉奸要双,这是她自己说的!"说着就把小芹也捆起来了。

Hearing footsteps, Blacky put his head out and looked. Four or five men were standing in the shadows. One of them shouted:

"Arrest them both." It was the voice of Wang.

Blacky grew angry. "Arrest who?" he cried. "Nobody's broken any law."

Xing was there too. He ordered his men: "Nab him. We'll see whether he's broken any law or not. That fellow's been giving me trouble for a long time."

"I'll go wherever you say," Blacky retorted, "even to the Border Region government. You've got nothing on me."

"Go?" sneered Xing. "We're not going to let you stroll there. That would be letting you off too easy. Tie him up."

Blacky fought valiantly, but he was outnumbered. In the end, they tied his hands behind his back.

"There's a girl in there too," said Xing. "Tie her up also. You need two culprits to prove this kind of thing. She said so herself."

汉语原文的一大段，英译分成了 8 个自然段。

还有一种情况，汉语中某些表示对话轮回的词语，如"某某说"之类，在英译中可酌情省略，只要读者清楚说话人是谁即可。比如孙犁的《荷花淀》中，水生到区上开会回来，他女人问道：

"今天怎么回来的这么晚？"站起来要去端饭。水生坐在台阶上说：

"吃过饭了，你不要去拿。"

女人又坐在席子上。她望着丈夫的脸，她看出他的脸有些红涨，说话也有些气喘。她问：

"他们几个哩？"

水生说：

"还在区上。爹哩？"

女人说：

"睡了。"

"小华哩？"

"和他爷爷去收了半天虾篓，早就睡了。他们几个为什么还不回来？"

水生笑了一下。女人看出他笑的不像平常。

"怎么了，你？"

水生小声说：

"明天我就到大部队上去了。"

"What kept you so long today?"

She stood up to fetch him some food. Shuisheng sat on the steps.

"Never mind about that—I've eaten."

She sat down on the mat again. Her husband's face was rather flushed and he seemed out of breath.

"Where are the others?" she asked.

"Still in town. How's dad?"

"Asleep."

"And Xiaohua?"

"He was out half the day with his granddad shrimping and went to bed hours ago. Why haven't the others come back?"

Shuisheng gave a forced laugh.

"What's wrong with you?"

"I'm joining the army tomorrow," he said softly.

原文中划线部分，前两个译文省去了，后一个也未单独成段。

有时候汉语对话夹在叙事之中，并不加引号。英译时也可这样处理：不加引号，不分行，但对话中的基准时态是一般现在时，句首字母要大写。如：

打电话的是李。李是吴所长从光屁股一块儿玩大的伙伴，别看后来连个中专都没有考上，可是现在人家腰包里钞票多得装不了，时不时地还让吴所长等老伙计跟着沾沾光。他说大所长啊这么些年了我可没有求你办过什么事儿吧？吴所长打个哈哈说你小子兜里装满了能让鬼推磨的玩艺儿你会瞧得上我这小芝麻官？李说你先别这样说，现在还真有一件事儿恐怕非你帮忙不行。吴所长就问天塌下来了你说得这么严重？李说你们那儿是不是刚刚有一个发廊妹去报案？吴所长说什么报案不报案的只不过是一个发廊妹与老板娘分赃不均相互咬了一下，我正准备各打五十大板打发她们走人。李说这就是你的不对了，中国是法制的国家，想打人就打人，那她把你手中握着的法律当什么玩艺儿了？发廊妹也是人啊，是不是？打人的人那她就得受到法律的制裁，是不是？

It was Li, his childhood playmate. You'd be wrong to dismiss Li just because he couldn't even get into a vocational school. Now having money to burn, he occasionally shared his wealth with old pals like Chief Wu. He was saying, Chief, in all these years I've never bothered you with anything, have I? Chief Wu replied, jokingly, You son of a gun, with your pockets stuffed with money, when did you ever give a thought to a petty government official like me? Li said, Don't talk like that. At the moment there's something I'm afraid only you can help with. Chief Wu said, You make it sound like the sky is falling. Li asked, Is there a hairdresser who's come to you to lodge a complaint?

Lodge a complaint? Chief Wu replied. It was just a cat fight between a hairdresser and her proprietress over ill-gotten gains. I was just about to fine them each fifty and let them go. Li said, That's not the way to do it. China is a country of laws, and if people go around hitting each other, what do the laws amount to? Hairdressers are people, too, aren't they? If someone has slapped her, she should be punished, shouldn't she?

第五，汉语原文中的内心独白，英译时可以处理成直接引语的形式。例如：

现在，他正衔着旱烟管，扒在洞窟随手捡翻。他当然看不懂这些东西，只觉得事情有点蹊跷。<u>为何正好我在这儿时墙壁裂了缝呢？或许是神对我的酬劳。趁下次到县城，捡几个经卷给县长看看，顺便说说这桩奇事。</u>

上述句群中，作者在叙述一个世纪前莫高窟的王道士偶然发现藏于石壁中的珍贵文物的情况。前两句依循的是第三人称叙述者的思路："他"如何，如何。但从画线部分开始，思路转入王道士的思维轨迹："我"如何，如何。这种转换不会破坏语篇的连贯性，因为在汉语读者看来这十分自然，读者会构想出有关情节，跟上作者思路的转换，形成一种心理脚本（mental scenario）。那么，这一句群是如何译成英语的呢？请看：

With a pipe in his mouth, Taoist Wang jumbled through his new discoveries in the cave. Of course, he didn't know their value. He just felt it strange, <u>thinking to himself,</u> "Why did the wall break while I was here? It might be a reward for me from Heaven. Next time I go to the county town, I'll show some of these to the county magistrate and tell him about this strange event."

他对洞窟壁画有点不满，暗乎乎的，看着有点眼花。<u>亮堂一点多好呢</u>，他找了两个帮手，拎来一桶石灰。

"亮堂一点多好呢"实际是"他"的所想，英译文把它译为直接引语：

He was not quite satisfied with the frescoes he saw in the caves, because they were in the dark and hard to see. "How nice it would be if I make the caves brighter!" he thought to himself. He found two helpers and a pail of lime white.

上例划线部分即人物独白，译文处理为直接引语，但要注意直接引语中时态的运用。

第五节 时 态

英语的谓语动词因时态不同会有形式变化。叙事用什么时态,要有一个时间参照系,这个参照系以文章写作时(或那个时段)为基点,语篇生成时就是"现在"。以此为准,则所叙述的多为"过去"发生的事情,故翻译时多用过去时态(包括一般过去时、过去进行时、过去完成时、过去将来时等),但下列情况可以用现在时。

1. 作者在叙事或描写时会夹杂着议论或评述,这是作者写作时的所感所想,英译时可使用一般现在时。如钱钟书《围城》中的一段文字:

三闾大学校长高松年是位老科学家。这"老"字的位置非常为难,可以形容科学,也可以形容科学家。不幸的是,科学家跟科学大不相同,科学家像酒,愈老愈可贵,而科学像女人,老了便不值钱。

Kao Sung-nien, the president of San Lu University, was an "old science scholar." The word "old" here is quite bothersome. It could describe science or it could just as well be describing a scientist. Unfortunately, there is a world of difference between a scientist and science. A scientist is like wine. The older he gets, the more valuable he is. Science is like a woman. When she gets old, she's worthless.

又如张行健的《婆娘们》,粗线条勾勒出山西妇女的群像,开篇便议论道:

我们这方土地生长五谷杂粮,生长击壤歌,生长古老的传说,也生长着一群群和男人们一样野性十足的婆娘们。

Our home soil grows all the cereals, grew the "Song of the Simple Life", grew the ancient legends, and also grows a tribe of goodwives every bit as wild as men.

译文的四个小句中,中间两个用了过去时,因为"生长击壤歌,生长古老的传说"显然都是"过去"的事,而"生长五谷杂粮""生长着……野性十足的婆娘们"则"现在"仍是事实。

我从此便整天的站在柜台里,专管我的职务。虽然没有什么失职,但总觉有些单调,有些无聊。掌柜是一副凶脸孔,主顾也没有好声气,教人活泼不得;只有孔乙己到店,才可以笑几声,所以至今还记得。

Thenceforward I stood all day behind the counter, fully engaged with my duties. Although I gave satisfaction at this work, I found it monotonous and futile. Our employer was a fierce-looking individual, and the customers were a morose lot, so that it was impossible to be gay. Only when Kung I-chi came to the tavern could I laugh a little. That is why I still remember him.

原文最后一句"至今还记得",说的是"我"写作时的心理状态,所以用了现在时。

2. 为了叙述或描写的生动,可在过去时为基调的叙述中转而使用现在时。如陆文夫的《小贩世家》中描写冬夜朱源达和父亲卖馄饨的情景,译文在以过去时为主调的叙述中,有整整一个自然段都转为现在时。

如果有谁熬过冬天的长夜,身上衣衫单薄,室内没有火炉,那窗外朔风像尖刀似的刺透窗棂,那飘洒的夜雨变成了在瓦垄上跳动的雪珠;十二点钟以后,世界成了一座冰窟,人冻僵了,只有那紧缩着的心在一阵阵地颤抖。这时候,五分钱一碗的小馄饨,热气腾腾,可以添汤,可以加辣,那是多么巨大的引诱,多么美好的享受!

Whoever works through the long winter nights dressed only in a thin shirt becomes frozen stiff with only his shrunken heart continuing to beat. Inside the room there is no stove, while outside the north wind cuts through the window lattice like a sharp knife. The swirling night rain is turned into ice crystals which dance on the roof tiles. After midnight the whole world becomes an icehouse. At that hour, a steaming hot bowl of wonton dumplings for five fen with which you can have extra helpings of soup and hot sauce is a powerful temptation and a delightful pleasure!

下面一例出自叶圣陶的《三种船》,描述了一系列的动作:

当推出橹柄去的时候,他们的上身也冲了出去,似乎要跌到河里去的模样。接着把橹柄挽回来,他们的身子就往后顿,仿佛要坐下来似的。五把橹在水里这样强力地划动,船身就飞快地前进了。

译文1:The men's bodies thrust forward as they pushed the handles of the oars away from them, almost in the attitude of one about to rumble into the water, then as they hauled back fell into a squatting position as if they were about to sit down. The hull flew forward to the mighty strokes of the oars… (translated by Simon Johnstone)

译文2:When the oarsman pushes out the sweep handle, the upper half of his body pitches outwards, as if he is going to fall into the water. Then when he drags the handle back again, he stoops on his heels, as if he is going to sit down. With five sweeps pulling energetically in the water like this, the boat is propelled forward at flying speed. (translated

by David E. Pollard)

  原文记叙作者的经历,译文1用过去时理所应当,而译文2为突出描述的"现实"感,用了现在时。纵观《三种船》整篇文章的翻译,第一位译者通篇以过去时为基调,而第二位译者则以现在时为基调,只有原文的第一段用过去时译出。另外,译文2将原文的"他们"(船夫)译为单数(oarsman),似乎也是为了将船夫的形象作为一种典型化的画面呈现。这是译者以一己之笔重新书写原文形象的译者主体意识的体现。

  3. 小说、散文中的人物对话的译文一般使用现在时,对话是直接引语,它的时间参照系与叙述不同。对话的参照系是故事或事件中的"彼时彼地",决定直接引语中的时态的参照点是"那个时候"。比如郁达夫的《春风沉醉的晚上》中的一段对话:

  她又沉默了一会,便断断续续的问我说:"我……我……早想问你了,这几天晚上,你每晚在外边,可在与坏人做伙友么?"

  我听了她这话,倒吃了一惊,她好像在疑我天天晚上在外面与小窃恶棍混在一块。她看我呆不作答,便以为我的行为真的被她看破了,所以就柔柔和和的连续着说:

  "你何苦要吃这样好的东西,要穿这样好的衣服?你可知道这事情是靠不住的。万一被人家捉了去,你还有什么面目做人。过去的事情不必去说它,以后我请你改过了吧。……"

  我尽是张大了眼睛,张大了嘴,呆呆的在看她,因为她的思想太奇突了,使我无从辩解起。她沉默了数秒钟,又接着说:

  "就以你吸的烟而论,每天若戒绝了不吸,岂不可省几个铜子。我早就劝你不要吸烟,尤其是不要吸那我所痛恨的 N 工厂的烟,你总是不听。"

  There was an awkward pause and then she started, falteringly, "I've been… er… wanting to ask you something for a long time. Recently you have been going out every night. Have you been mixing with bad men?"

  I was very surprised at this idea of hers. She had been suspecting me, of mixing with thieves and gangsters since I had been going out at night, it seemed. When she saw that her words had startled me, she thought her suspicion was right and that she had found me out. She went on talking to me, her voice friendly but pleading. "Do you have to eat such rich food and wear new clothes? Don't you know what you are doing is very risky? What if you are caught? How would you be able to face people? Let's not bother about what has already happened, though. I just want you to reform from now on…"

I couldn't say a word, but stared at her with my mouth agape. Her thoughts were so strange and unexpected that I didn't know how to explain. She was silent for only a few seconds and then went on, "Now take your smoking, for instance. If you cut that you'd be able to save a few coppers. I've already told you you shouldn't smoke, and particularly not the cigarettes made in my factory. But you won't listen."

在以上选段中，作品叙述所用的时态以一般过去时为基调时态，包括过去完成时和过去完成进行时；而在人物对话中，则用一般现在时、现在完成时、现在完成进行时等，这是因为叙述中的"彼时"却是对话中的"此时"。

另外，小说中人物的独白是自说自话，也可以用现在时态。比如老舍《骆驼祥子》中的一段文字：

不敢过去敲门，恐怕又被人捉住。左右看，没人，他的心跳起来，<u>试试看吧，反正也无家可归，被人逮住就逮住吧</u>。

He didn't dare push at the door; he was afraid someone would grab him again. He looked around and saw no one. His heart began to thump. <u>Try taking a look. There's no other house to go to. Anyway, if someone arrests me, then I'm arrested.</u>

原文划线部分从第三人称叙述转为人物心理独白，译文转用现在时。

再如沈从文《边城》中的原文和译文：

那青年走去后，祖父温习着那些出于一个男子口中的真话，实在又愁又喜。/ <u>翠翠若应当交把一个人，这个人是不是适宜于照料翠翠？当真交把了他，翠翠是不是愿意？</u>

译文1：After Tianbao's departure, the old man, both worried and pleased, chewed over the young fellow's frank declaration. <u>He must find Emerald a husband who will care for her. But will the girl agree?</u>

译文2：When the boy had disappeared, Grandfather mused over the truth of his words, and was alternately gladdened and made melancholy; for <u>he wondered whether he was the best man for her, and whether Green Jade would accept him</u>.

这一段也是从叙述事件转而描述人物心理活动。但两个译文有不同的处理，译文1转用现在时为基调，而译文2仍然以过去时为基调。

第六节　话题—主语转换

赵元任在《汉语口语语法》中说：

"主语和谓语的关系可以是动作者和动作的关系。但在汉语里这种句子（即使把被动的动作也算进去，把'是'也算进去）的比例是不大的，也许比50%大不了多少。因此，在汉语里，把主语、谓语当做话题和说明来看待，比较适合。"

赵元任提出的汉语"话题＋说明"的分析方法，已被不少学者进一步论述过。他们提出，语言可分为"主语突出型"和"话题突出型"两种，前者如英语，后者如汉语。据此，汉语中的"主语"在概念和术语上与英语句法中的主语概念有所区别。例如下面两个句子：

（1）<u>零花钱</u>我买了个笔记本。

（2）<u>新方案</u>他们不认账。

这类句子的谓语部分，汉语语法称之为主谓结构。句1中的"买"和"零花钱"没有动作和动作者的关系；句2中的"认账"与"方案"也没有直接语法关系。"零花钱"和"新方案"都应被称为话题，而非主语。

对已收集到的语料进行分析整理，我们发现汉译英中话题句向主语句的转换是一个很值得关注的现象。比如：

<u>每日点心钱</u>，他也不买了吃，聚到一两个月，便偷个空，走到村学堂里，见那闯学堂的书客，就买几本旧书。

He also saved the coppers he was given each day to buy a snack with, and every month or so would seize an opportunity to go to the village school to buy some old books from the book vendor making his rounds.

此例汉语句中的"每日点心钱"显然是统辖全句的话题，而英语译文则须转而用 he 来充当主语，重构主谓宾句式。

下面几例情况类似：

- 以前的功课也许有一大部分是为了这张毕业文凭，不得已而做的，从今以后，你们可以依自己的心愿去自由研究了。
  You have perhaps finished your college courses mostly for obtaining the diploma, that is, out of sheer necessity. However, from now on you are free to follow your personal bent in the choice of studies.

- 这以后的路，卢进勇走得特别快。天黑的时候，他追上了后卫部队。
  Lu finished the rest of the journey quickly. He caught up with the rear-guard before dark.
- 对于大自然的爱好，我是多方面的，我爱山，但更爱海。
  I love diverse aspects of Mother Nature, but I love the sea more than the mountain.
- 上海也流行过"读书无用论"，但情况与外地略有不同，……
  The doctrine that "education is useless" had its day in Shanghai, but the situation was rather different from elsewhere.

以上译例，汉语的话题部分都未译成英语的主语，而是译成了宾语（college courses, the rest of the journey）、融入宾语中（love… Mother Nature）或放入状语（in Shanghai）。

下面一例中的话题"这种死亡"仍放在句首，译作主语，但全句结构有所调整。

这种死亡他自己感到很痛苦，别人看了心里也很难受。
This kind of death causes not only much pain to the writer himself, but much sadness to other people as well.

汉语中的话题，有时可以统辖很长的一个段落，英译时要分成几句来处理。

一排留宿的小店，没有名号，只有标记，有的门口挂一支笊篱，有的窗口放着一对鹦鹉，有的是一根棒槌，有的是一条金牛，地方宽敞的摆着茶桌，地方窄小的只有炕几，后墙紧贴着峥嵘的山石，前脸正对着万丈的深渊。
The small lodging houses bore no name but displayed different signs: a broom over the door, a couple of parrots in the window, a baton, or a golden ox. The larger lodging houses had tea-tables set out, the smaller ones nothing but a kang. This row of buildings backed on the steep mountainside and overlooked the abyss.

第七节　省略成分的翻译

英、汉语中都有省略。英语的省略发生在句法层面，可在紧邻的上文中明确地追寻到，是一个词语或结构；而汉语的省略不仅发生在句法层面，它更像是对

某些语境成分的隐性化处理。英语的省略就限定性小句而言都是承前省略，而汉语语篇中除了大量的承前省略外还有蒙后省略。下面分三种类型分别讨论汉译英中如何应对汉语省略成分，即承前省略、蒙后省略和情景成分省略及其翻译技巧。

1. 承前省略

承前省略在汉语中很常用。吕叔湘在《中国文法要略》中指出，这是汉语句法的常态，是与西方语言的一个重要区别。汉语中被省略的主语成分具有充当全句话题的功能。汉语的省略与其说是句法上的，倒不如说是对语篇可激发出的情景中的某个成分的省略。读者自知，无需言明。这样的汉语句子译成英语，就要根据英语构句的需要，把省略的情景成分补充进来。请看下面例子：

这些书，都是在全国解放以后，来到我家的。最初 / 零零碎碎，中间 / 成套成批。/ 有的来自京沪，/ 有的来自苏杭。最初，囊中羞涩，也曾交臂相失。中间也曾一掷百金，稍有豪气。总之，时历三十余年，我同他们，可称故旧。

<u>The books</u> had arrived at my home since 1949, the year the country was liberated (from KMT rule). At first <u>they</u> came piecemeal and, later, in set or in bulk, some from Beijing and Shanghai, some from Suzhou and Hangzhou. During the first years, as <u>I</u> was financially embarrassed, sometimes <u>I</u> had to turn from the books that I would have liked to give everything in exchange for. However, there were occasions on which <u>I</u> threw my money on books with quite a sense of lavish generosity. In short, having kept each other company for over 30 years, <u>I</u> felt lifelong intimacy with them all

汉语原文各句均围绕"这些书"展开，原文中加"/"的地方显然隐去了"这些书"，而第四句中的"交臂相失"和"一掷百金"自然也是指"这些书"中的某一些，直到末尾一句才出现了代词"他们"，回指"这些书"。"这些书"是全段信息的起始点，是整个句群的话题。相比之下，英语译文则没有这样一个全段的话题统辖，而是由多个名词和代词构成的主谓结构：The books… they… I… I… I…。

这几年我没写什么杂文。20世纪30年代末期和40年代写得多些，那时办报纸，经常值夜班，写了不少。编集子时，自己也感到吃惊，竟写了这么多，有的自己都记不得了。

In recent years, I have seldom written essays. During the late 1930s and throughout the 1940s, however, I wrote more. In those days, as a newspaper editor, I often worked on the night shift and wrote a great many essays, so that, when compiling

52

a collection of my works, I was astonished to find myself to have authored so many essays, some of which I could not even remember.

汉语中"我"只出现一次，而英语译文中"I"出现五次。

我的父亲曾为我苦了一生，把我养大，送我进学校，为我造屋子，买了几亩田地。六十岁那一年，还到汉口去做生意，怕人家嫌他年老，只说五十几岁。

Father went through untold hardships for me all his life. He brought me up, sent me to school, had a house built for me and bought me a few mu of land. He went to Hankou to engage in trade the year when he was already sixty. And he tried to make out that he was still in his fifties lest people should consider him too old to be of much use.

此句中，句首的"我的父亲"是整个句群的话题，英语须用数个主语 Father—He—He—he 表达。

上文汉语例句和英语中的省略尚可相比，下文的省略现象就很难和英语比附了。

他跳上岸，爱姑跟着，/①经过魁星阁下，/②向着慰老爷家走。/③朝南走过三十家门面，/④再转一个弯，/⑤就到了，/⑥早望见门口一列地泊着四只乌篷船。

此例选择鲁迅的《离婚》，文中"他"指爱姑的父亲庄木三。原文"/"处显然省略了"他们"而不是"他"或"爱姑"，这和英语中的省略完全不同。译文要把省略的代词补上。

Chuang jumped ashore, and Ai-ku followed him. They passed the pavilion and headed for Mr. Wei's house. After passing thirty houses on their way south, they turned a corner and reached their destination. Four boats with black awnings were moored in a row at the gate.

2. 蒙后省略

蒙后省略的成分要到下文中去追寻。比如高阳短篇小说《藕丝莲心》开篇头一段是：

①展开一幅画，②是墨竹，③枝叶披离，占了大半张纸；右上角一片空白题着字，——题词是一篇小品，④写的篇幅不够了，就写向枝叶间的空隙。⑤一眼望去，⑥满纸糊涂，王一姐就懒得多看了。

Unrolled, it was an ink painting of bamboo, with branches and leaves spreading out in all directions, occupying more than half of the entire sheet of paper. At the upper righthand corner was an empty space where a poem was written. There not being enough room, the inscription was continued into the gaps between the branches and leaves. Wang Yijie on a first glance found the painting such a mess that she was inclined not to give it a second glance.

故事第一部分出场的只有两个人物：王一姐和她丈夫于少棠。汉语读者在阅读这一段的时候，会很自然地把数字处省略的语义成分填充进去：①于少棠，抑或是两个人一起；②画；③墨竹；④小品；⑤王一姐；⑥王一姐看到。其中②、③、④承接前文的语义，而①、⑤和⑥则要依后文填充。读者何以能够这样做，因为这些语义成分存在于语篇所展示的情景之中。对照原文可以看出，译文采取了另起炉灶、重构主谓的方法，和汉语是两个不同的结构模式。

3. 情景成分省略

汉语中有些省略不但在紧邻的上文中追溯不到，紧邻的下文也没有。省略的成分存在于更远的上下文或语篇所描述的情景之中。例如，冰心在《笑》里回想起"五年前的一个印象——一条很长的古道"：

驴脚下的泥，兀自滑滑的。田沟里的水，潺潺的流着。近村的绿树，都笼在湿烟里。弓儿似的新月，挂在树梢。// 一边走着，似乎道旁有一个孩子，抱着一堆灿白的东西。驴儿过去了，无意中回头一看。——他抱着花儿，赤着脚儿，向着我微微的笑。

前四句可与英语比照，但"//"处以后的结构就与英语大相径庭了。汉语的语义结构是：（我）一边走着，（我注意到）似乎道旁有一个孩子，（这孩子）抱着一堆灿白的东西。驴儿过去了，（我）无意中回头一看……也就是说，这几句中有两个略去的情景成分——"我"和"孩子"，甚至连心理活动"注意到"也省去了。而省略成分"我"在同一自然段中从未出现过，只能从更远的上文——整个语篇的语境中搜寻。英译文中，省略成分"我"大都以主位"I"的形式得以显现，心理活动"sensed the presence of"也得以添加。

The ground under my donkey's feet was slippery with mud. The water in the field ditches was murmuring. The green trees in the neighboring village were shrouded in a mist. The crescent new moon looked as if hanging on the tips of the trees. As <u>I</u> passed along, <u>I</u> somewhat sensed the presence of a child by the roadside carrying something snow white in his arms. After the donkey had gone by, <u>I</u> happened to look back and saw the child, who was barefoot, looking at me smilingly with a bunch of flowers in his arms.

总之,汉语中的省略比英语更常见,对语境的依赖性也更强。这就需要译者依照语篇所描述的情景,整体把握,摆脱汉语表层结构,将所述情景重新纳入英语以主谓宾结构为本的形合构架之中。仔细分析上面例句可以看出,这大致包括三个主要环节:划分意群——确立主句的主谓和句式——安排从属结构。如下例:

①那是忽忽若有所失的感觉,/②心里有莫名的烦躁,书看不下去,酒也喝不出味道;/③草草敷衍了一顿夜饭,回到自己屋里,兀坐在灯下,/④仿佛置身于大海孤舟,四面黑茫茫一片,/不知自己到明朝是何光景。

He suddenly felt as though there was something missing. He seemed for no reason to be on tenterhooks—he couldn't read and found no pleasure in his wine. Hastily disposing of dinner, he returned to his room and sat down alone under the lamp. It was as though he was adrift in a solitary boat in a wide ocean, with darkness closing in on him from all sides. He didn't know what was to become of him on the morrow.

译文将原文分为五个意群(斜线所示),几乎都依上下文需要补充了主语 he,第四个意群用 It was as though... 句式翻译,汉语中下划线部分被译为从属成分。

①路是迂环的,岩峰也有高低。因此月亮总是时隐时现。/②虽说长天如练,但山、路、树、草却是明一段,暗一段。/③走到明处,像饮着沁凉的酒;行到暗处,又觉得身在魔魅之中。/④就这样饮着,魔着,在不知名的夏虫如铜簧一般的鸣叫中,不觉已走了十几二十里山路。

As we strolled along the winding path, hills rose unevenly on either side, and the moon occasionally dipped from view. Despite the moon-lit sky, the hills, path, trees and grass, brilliantly illuminated one moment, were plunged into darkness the next; and while the bright spots filled us with an intoxicating joy, the dark ones filled us with a nightmarish sense of foreboding. Alternating between these emotional extremes, and accompanied by the incessant drone of a chorus of insects, we covered roughly ten kilometers before being aware of it.

原文被断为四个意群。①句并没有"人"的参与,译文加进了 we;③句的译文有视角上的转换:由"(我们)走到……饮着……行到……觉得……"变为 bright spots filled us with..., dark ones filled us with...;④句的译文加入了主语 we,划线部分译为从属成分。

第八节 流水句和词组堆叠句

"流水句"是汉语有别于英语的一大特点。吕叔湘在《汉语语法分析问题》中提出:"汉语口语里特多流水句,一个小句接一个小句,很多地方可断可连。"其实,书面语,特别是文学语言中,此类句式也很多。《水浒传》第四十二回有这么一段:"李逵恰待要赶,只见就树边卷起一阵狂风,吹得败叶树木如雨一般打将下来。自古道:'云生从龙,风生从虎。'<u>那一阵风起处,星月光辉之下,大吼了一声,忽地跳出一只吊睛白额虎来。那大虫望李逵势猛一扑。</u>" 其中下划线部分显然和英语的"主谓宾"句法大相径庭,如果将其按英语语法"理顺",恐怕应该是:星光月辉之下,一头吊睛白额虎忽然大吼一声,带着一阵风,跳了出来。当然,这个"理顺"了的汉语句子已大大减色。Sidney Shapiro 的译文将原文信息进行梳理,重写为:"From the place where the wind blew, a roaring tiger leaped out. It had upward-slanting eyes and a white forehead and it charged directly at Li Kui."

"流水句"只是个形象的比喻,后来虽有语法学家进一步从语调、结构等方面对其进行过界定,但它仍然是一个虽广为认可却比较模糊的概念。

从汉英翻译学习的角度出发,我们可以对"流水句"作出如下较为明确的界定:

(1)语义连贯,句段(指小句或短语)或长短相间,或短语堆叠,或疾,或徐,段段推进,直至意尽;

(2)形散而意合,不用或很少用关联词语,貌似无主无从,句段间逻辑关系自在语境中;

(3)主语常隐于语境中,许多语境因素也被省略,无法对应英语语法的"主谓"句法框架和复合句类型;

(4)通常由三个或三个以上句段组成复合句,句段以逗号或分号分隔。
如下面例句:

- 老黄老了,人称"黄老"。老啦,没办法,吃过晚饭,看了点电视新闻,有些迷糊了,打算洗个脸、泡泡脚,上床寻梦去。
  Being old, he easily got tired and could not help it. After supper, having watched *News Today* on TV, he began to feel sleepy, so he went about

washing his face and feet before going to bed.

- 什么也没有了，唐代的笑容，宋代的衣冠，洞中成了一片净白。
  Thus everything in the cave, from the Tang dynasty smiles to the Song dynasty dresses, disappeared into a world of white emptiness.

- 这下是一姐的脸色大变，一双眼泪光隐隐，望着他不断眨动，无限自怜怜人的痛惜怨悔，尽在无声之中。
  At this Yijie turned pale. Her eyes glistened. Holding back the tears, she stared at him. And in the silence was the profound regret and pain of a person who was sorry for both herself and the other person.

- 他画鸡冠花，也画牡丹，但他和人家的画法不一样，大红花，笔触很粗，叶子用黑墨只几点。
  His way of painting cockscombs and peonies was quite different from that of other artists. He would paint large blossoms with thick brush strokes while leaves were only indicated by only a few dots of black ink.

- 我曾多次见他画小鸡，毛茸茸，很可爱；也见过他画的鱼鹰，水是绿的，钻进水里的，很生动。
  On several occasions I watched him paint fluffy little chicks and vivid cormorants with their heads in clear green water.

- 絮絮叮咛，说又说得在情理上，尤其那略带命令的语气，郑板桥的感觉中，一姐应该是表姐而不是表妹，不由得就点头答应。
  The persistent urgings made good sense, especially when spoken with such a tone of authority. It made Zheng Banqiao feel as though she were his elder rather than younger cousin, and all he could do was to nod in assent.

有些流水句先点出话题，然后围绕话题展开。例如：

- 还有寂寞的瓦片风筝，没有风轮，又放得很低，伶仃地显出憔悴可怜的模样。
  Or there may be a solitary tile-kite, without a wind-wheel and flown too low, looking pathetically lonely and forlorn.

- 酒取来了，淡红的玫瑰露，斟在白瓷酒杯中，色香的诱惑，都叫本来贪杯的郑板桥无法抗拒；忍不住说了句："你也来一杯！"
  Wine was brought in. The pale red wine called "rose dew" was poured into

white china cups, and the allure of both colour and fragrance was well-nigh irresistible for Zheng Banqiao, who liked his wine. He couldn't help coming out with the words, "Why don't you join me for a cup?"

- 志于路途的人，走到平坦的地方，固是高高兴兴地向前走，走到崎岖的境界，愈是奇趣横生，觉得在此奇绝壮绝的境界，愈能感到一种冒险的美趣。

译文1：While a determined traveler cheerfully continues his journey upon reaching a safe and smooth place, he finds it still more fascinating to come to a rugged place, the enormously magnificent spectacle of which, he feels, is better able to generate in him a wonderful sensation of adventure.

译文2：Walking on a flat and level road, an experienced traveler certainly feels delighted. However, walking in a rugged and rough terrain, one can enjoy more wits and humor. Walking in such an area of wonderful and magnificent scenes, one can savor more tastes of adventure.

流水句如按英语语法审视，可能是缺少某些成分的。这些成分存在于其所触发的语境之中，中文读者不会觉得缺乏连贯，但译为英语则需将原文意义重新纳入英语语法构架之中。比如：

你去了解吧，原来姓王的他家女人下岗，儿子残疾，<u>政府头头访贫问苦，去过他家，景象惨不忍睹，希望有关部门予以照顾。</u>

此句中"政府头头"和"景象惨不忍睹"之间显然缺少了"看到"或"发现"之类的动词。翻译要根据英语行文的需要加以补足。

If you take a little trouble to find out, you will understand why. What happened was that the Wangs had a disabled son with them and, to make things worse, the woman of the family was out of work. When the local government officials went to see them, they were touched by the domestic plight of the family, so they arranged for the department concerned to do something to help.

一箱子，又一箱子。一大车，又一大车。都装好了，扎紧了，吁——车队出发了。

One box after another was removed from the grottoes, and one cart after another was loaded. The caravan thus started out of Dunhuang.

译文根据上文补足了动作（was removed）和地点（from the grottoes, out of Dunhuang）等语境成分。

<u>女友轻轻跨进花园，东闻闻，西嗅嗅，神采飞扬，就是不肯采摘。我说没关系，多的是</u>，我又不是花店的老板，不会靠玫瑰赚钱的。

句中划线部分显然是我"说"的内容，其中的"没关系，多的是"按英语思维应该说：花多的是，所以你采花没有关系。译文就作了相应的补足。

That girl friend of mine, tiptoeing into the garden in high spirits, sniffed here and smelt there, but in the end she didn't pick a single rose. I said there were so many of them that she could pick as many as she'd like to; I told her that I was not a florist and didn't make a living out of them.

词组堆叠句或许可看做流水句的一种特例。全句由简短的尤其是四字词语组成，指代省略和情景成分的省略现象十分突出。

- 潇潇秋雨，宜寻好梦。
  The chilly autumn rain made it a time for sweet dreams.
- 五日新婚，七日守灵，阴间阳界，聚首十二天。
  Counting the five days of marriage and seven days of deathwatch, Li Duicheng and her husband had been together for merely twelve days.

汉语中既无主语，也未明示四个词组间的逻辑关系。读者只是借助上下文所建立起来的语境得知，这里说的是李兑承和她为抗日而捐躯的丈夫，他们新婚仅五日丈夫便以身殉国，她守灵七日，所以连同生时和死后，他们一共也才相处了十二天。译文则参照这些信息将原句意义形合化了。

又如：

长发长袜，飘来跳去，三点泳装，耀眼生辉。
Then the long-haired and the long-stocked shake their legs as if adrift, sandwiched by the radiating bikinied.

原文谈看电视的感受，屏幕上忽古忽今，节目缤纷，场景变换无穷。作者并未说明"长发长袜"者和"三点泳装"者的相对位置，而其英译则用一个"sandwiched by..."将空间关系加以明示，应属于译者的想象。

再如，同一篇文章的另一句话，谈的是老年生活：

- 偶尔有人来，不论男女老少认识不认识，天南地北，天上地下，天

文地理，谈天说地，百无禁忌。
Occasionally I had some visitors, male or female, old or young, acquainted and unacquainted. We could chat about everything in the north or in the south, in the space or at the core, related to astronomy or geography, in the Heaven or in the Hell and there were no taboos for us at all.

- 昏昏的灯焰，沉沉的长夜；如果不能寻得好梦，便会寻得烦恼。
If dim lights and long nights don't inspire sweet dreams, they inspire troubles.

可以看出，各种流水句的英译特别凸显具有形合结构意识的必要性。提取汉语的信息、淡出汉语结构、重塑英语形合句式，这应该是译者在处理流水句与词组堆叠句时须经历的三个步骤。

第九节 拆 句

本节到第十二节讨论语言使用者的心理情景和语言框架之间的关系，以及由此而引发的翻译问题。

如第八节所讨论的，在翻译流水句和词组堆叠句的过程中，译者为构建符合英语句法规范的语句而酌情添加某些情景成分，是很关键的一环。也就是说，语篇所激发的是相对完整的"情景"，而表达为语言时，某些情景成分可能被显化，而某些情景成分有可能被隐化。Fillmore 曾经提出，人们在学习语言时，会将情景和语言框架联系在一起。这里的"情景"含义很宽泛，不仅包括视觉景象，还包括典型的场景、陈设、机构设置、人体形象，以及人们的信念、行为、经验或想象的连贯片段。换言之，"情景"即人们对自身和外部世界的各种印象和感悟，或人们大脑中所储存的对周围世界的各种连贯信息，而"语言框架"则指和这种种"情景"相对应的从词语到句式等的各种语言选择。他还认为，情景和框架相互触发，也就是说，语言框架可以在人的头脑中引发相应的情景，而情景也可引发人们对某种语言框架的选择。另外，在人的大脑中情景是相互联系的，语言框架也是相互联系的。

Fillmore 的这种"情景和框架语义理论"对翻译，特别是流水句的翻译，颇具启示意义。面对一系列连贯的语言符号，大脑中相关的知识或经验会被激活，浮现出相应的情景。当这些情景被纳入另一种语言的框架时，翻译活动便发生了。汉英翻译中，如何将长长的、结构相对松散的汉语流水句拆分成符合英语句法框架的语段，是必须掌握的技巧。比如冰心《小橘灯》里的一句话：

我赞赏地接过，谢了她，/ 她送我出到门外，/ 我不知道说什么好，/ 她又像安慰我似地说：……

这句汉语用一连串的小句表述一连串的活动，构成人物行为的连贯片段。汉语的语言框架是一个接一个的小句，用逗号分隔，依自然时间顺序展开。译为英语时，要将这一行为片段纳入可行的英语表达框架，但英语中可构建出这种"一逗到底"的长句吗？英语句法容得下这么多并列的谓语动词吗？英语语言框架可提供的选择，显然有别于汉语。译者必须学会顺应英语的表达框架，而英语表达框架的来源当然是英语阅读，读得越多，积累越多，英语表达才可能游刃有余，灵活自如。

一般说来，英译时须把这样的汉语表达框架切割成多个句子。如何切割，要在实践中一点点体会，积累经验。下面译文将原文断为四节，构建了四个英语句子。

I accepted the lamp with admiration, and thanked her. / She came out to see me off. / I did not know what to say. / Again, as if to console me, she spoke....

再观察下面几个相似的译例，原文中用斜线标出了译者断句的地方。

- 不知哪一年春天，我和两个同伴，摇着小船到十里外一个镇上看社戏，/ 完场已是午夜，归途遇雨，/ 穿在河塘中缓缓前进，灯火暗到辨不出人面，/ 船身擦着河岸新生的茅草，发出沙沙的声音。
  One spring, together with two companions, I rowed a small boat to a townlet ten li away to see a village opera. At midnight, after the performance was over, we got caught in a rain on the way home. The boat made its way slowly and our faces were hardly distinguishable by the dim light of the lantern. Rustles were heard as the boat rubbed its body against the newly grown green grass by the river bank.

- （小玉……背那定情之夕，李益亲笔所写的誓约。）背不到一半，突然一阵抽搐，整个脸都歪曲了，/ 浣沙和桂子大惊，李益更是慌张得

- 手足发抖。/就这一转眼间，小玉的头一歪，倒在李益胸前，双手垂落，/呛啷一声，酒杯掉在地上，打得粉碎。

  Half way through, she had a sudden convulsion, which distorted her entire face. Huansha and Guizi were shocked, and Li Yi was so terrified that his hands and feet began to shake. Then Xiaoyu's head dropped and she fell into Li Yi's arms, her hands falling to her sides. With a crash, the wine cup fell to the floor and broke into pieces.

- 我掀开帘子，看见一个小姑娘，只有八九岁光景，/瘦瘦的苍白的脸，冻得发紫的嘴唇，/头发很短，穿一身很破旧的衣裤，/光脚穿一双草鞋，/正在登上竹凳想去摘墙上的听话器，/看见我似乎吃了一惊，把手缩了回来。

  I lifted the curtain and looked, only to find a small girl of about eight or nine. She had a pale thin face, and her lips were frozen purple because of the cold. Her hair was cut short and she was dressed in worn-out clothes. She wore no socks, only a pair of straw sandals. She was climbing onto the bamboo stool, trying to get hold of the receiver; but she quickly withdrew her hand as if startled at the sight of me.

- 和我相反的是我的小兄弟，/他那时大概十岁内外罢，多病，瘦得不堪，然而最喜欢风筝，/自己买不起，我又不许放，他只得张着小嘴，呆看着空中出神，有时竟至于小半日。

  My young brother was just the reverse. He must then have been about ten, often fell ill and was fearfully thin, but his greatest delight was kites. Unable to buy one and forbidden by me to fly one, he would stand for hours at a time, his small lips parted in longing, gazing raptly at the sky.

翻译的过程历经"源语语言框架—激发心里景象—再激发译语语言框架"三个过程。心理景象是一种深层结构，而语言框架是表层结构。同样的深层结构，可表达为不同的表层结构。

下面两例中，译文和原文所表达的景象的线性排列便有所不同（变动部分由下划线标出）。

- 庄校长奎章，虽然是师大的同学，我们却并不认识，/是抵厦门的第二天，我便随便到厦中去参观，看见校舍建筑在高高的山坡上，面临着海，风景非常幽美，于是就信步走去，无意中会到了庄校长，随便谈起来，/ 他就要请我去教国文；然而我当时不能决定，因为我还需要去游历闽西。

Zhuang Kuizhang, headmaster of the school, was a stranger to me when we first met though he has been a schoolmate of mine at Beijing Normal University. The middle school is located high up on a mountain slope facing the sea. On the second day after my arrival at Xiamen, I was so struck by the beauty of the school environment that I went sauntering into the campus where Zhuang and I met by accident and started chatting. He asked me if I would like to be a teacher of Chinese at his school, but, as I was to go on a tour to western Fujian, I could not say yes or no immediately.

- 原来我生平没有看见人家游泳过，只在画报上看到一些游泳的照片，既然来到了海滨，而且天气这么热，自然我想下水去练习练习；没想到海浪是这么可怕的，/ 它突然袭来，我被卷去了丈多远，/ 口里灌进去很多海水，咸得我大声叫喊"救命呀！救命呀！" / 他们连忙把我的膀子捉住，又是一个大浪打来，把我们卷去了丈多远。

As I had never in my life seen people swim except in some pictorials and as the weather was so hot, I, being at the seaside and not knowing how dreadful the sea could become, naturally felt like having a go at dabbling in the water. Suddenly the violent waves came upon me and carried me quite a few metres away. "Help! Help!" I cried out with lots of salty seawater in my mouth. They rushed to my rescue. But no sooner had they seized me by the arm than the surging waves returned to carry all of us quite a few metres away.

译文 They rushed to my rescue 在原文中并没有相应的句子，译者加上这样一个句子，显然是为了和下一句构成连贯的陈述，没有这一句下一句就显得突兀了。但必须认识到，这一句所表达的动作其实是业已存在于读者心理情景中的。下面译例中的 (When) she had done all this 也是这种情况。

我站起来要走，/ 她拉住我，一面极其敏捷地拿过穿着麻线的大针，/ 把那小橘碗四周相对地穿起来，像一个小筐似的，用一根小竹棍挑着，/ 又从窗台上拿起一段短短的蜡头，放在里面点起来，/ 递给我说："天黑了，路滑，/ 这盏小橘灯照你上山吧！"

I stood up to go. The little girl held me back, quickly and deftly took out a big needle with a linen thread and worked at the bowl-shaped orange peel. She linked the opposite corners in such a way as to a small basket, which she hung on a thin bamboo stick. She then took the stub of a candle from the windowsill, placed it in the orange peel basket, and lit it. <u>When she had done all this,</u> she handed the lamp to me, saying, "It's dark now, and the road is slippery. Let this little orange lamp light the way for you up the mountain."

第十节　人称—物称转换

　　同一个事物，拍照可以选不同的角度，用语言描述同样可以有不同的视角。叙述一件事情要有一个切入点，或者说起始点，然后顺着这个思路展开，这反映了说话人对信息的选择和组合的方式。这就是叙述视角，是运用不同语言框架表达同一心理情景的一种选择。《水浒传》第十回有下面的句子：

　　　　忽一日，李小二正在门前安排菜蔬下饭，只见一个人闪将进来，
　　酒店里坐下，随后又一人入来。看时，前面那个人是军官打扮，后
　　面这个走卒模样。跟着也来坐下。

　　金圣叹评论道："'看时'二字妙，是李小二眼中事。一个小二看来是军官，一个小二看来是走卒，先看他跟着，却又看他一齐坐下，写得狐疑之极，妙妙。"这里点评所涉及的，实际就是叙述视角：从作者视角到小说中某个人物的视角的转换。不过 Shapiro 的译文并未再现这种转换，而一直保持了第三人称视角。

　　One day, while Xiaoer was cooking in the entry, a man slipped in and sat down inside at one of the tables. Then another fellow furtively entered. The first man was an army officer, by the looks of him. The second seemed more like an attendant. He also hurried in and sat down.

　　将一句汉语译为英语，译者可以有不同的视角选择。比如沈从文的小说《丈夫》中头一句说："落了春雨，一共有七天，河水涨大了。"将这句译成英语恐怕至少有以下三种译法：

译文 1：That spring, it rained for 7 days and the river rose.

译文 2：That spring, after a whole week's rain, the river rose.

译文 3：Seven days of spring rains have left the river swollen.

这句汉语的信息中心在"河水涨了"，译文 1 和 2 的视角和汉语一样，而译文 3 则从 rain 着眼，体现了另一种信息序列切入角度。再如：

路途上的征人所经过的地方，有时是坦荡平原，有时是崎岖险路。

译文 1：The places the travelers have traversed are open and flat here, but craggy and risky there.

译文 2：A traveler on a long journey passes through now a broad, level plain, now a rugged, dangerous road.

这句汉语以物（"地方"）为着眼点。译文 1 的视角没有变化，译文 2 则将"地方"换成了 traveler（"征人"），即从物称视角转换为人称视角。

"有过这样的事么？"他惊异地笑着说，就像旁听着别人的故事一样。他什么也记不得了。

"Did that really happen?" he smiled incredulously, as if he were hearing a tale about someone else. It had slipped his mind completely.

最后一句的视角由"他"换成 It，是人称视角换成了物称视角。

汉英翻译中，人称/物称视角间的转换比较常见。比如：

只要稍稍具有现代世界地理眼光的人，都会看中上海。

From a modern geographical perspective, Shanghai is a good proposition.

汉语中还常有这样的情况：虽然采用了人称视角，但表述中并无明确标示，这也就是流水句中主语隐于情景中的情况了。如下面一例：

经过三十余年的岁月，把当时的痛苦，一层层地摩擦干净，现在回想起来，这书塾里的生活，实在是快活得很。

这句叙事句显然是从"我"出发并展开的：是"我"把痛苦摩擦干净，是"我"回想起来如何如何。但这个"我"（代词）并未在原句中出现。译文于是把这个"我"字推到背景上，以物称视角组织英语译文。

The thirty-odd years that have elapsed since then have soothed away all the pains suffered at that time; life in the village school, as I remember it now, was really very happy.

有时候，这种隐性的人称视角未必都转换成物称视角，如下例：

遇到一声韵味十足的唱，便像是骚着了痒处一般，从丹田里吼出一声"好！"若是发现唱出了错，便毫不容情的来一声倒好。

这句话是人称视角，说的是听戏人的一系列举止。译文有物化视角的转换：a roar—came...，但更值得注意的是不同人称的调整：从"听戏人""遇到……发现……"变为 singer（"唱戏人"）。

When the singer hit a perfect note, it was to them like scratching an itch: a roar of "bravo!" came from deep within them. If the singer hit a wrong note, they would equally forthrightly come out with a catcall.

怕只怕三杯酒下肚，豪情大发，嘟嘟嘟，来个瓶底朝天，而且一顿喝不上便情绪不高，颇有怨言，甚至会到处去找酒喝。

The pity is after three cups of alcohol he gets wild and unrestrained and ends in gulping down a whole bottle. One meal without liquor will upset him and set him complaining and searching around for a drink.

原文取人称视角，译文第一句加上主语，第二句则改为物称视角。

人称视角和物称视角间的转换往往不是强制性的，而只是译者的一种选择。选择的依据自然是行文的需要，即看译者如何构句。看下面一个译例：

船家一听说要过石湖就抬起头来看天，看有没有起风的意思。到进了石湖的时候，脸色不免紧张起来，说笑都停止了。<u>听得船头略有汩汩的声音，就轻轻互相警戒，"浪头！浪头！"</u>

译文 1：The crew, on being told that I wished to cross it, scanned the heavens for traces of wind, and as we entered the lake their features tensed and laughter ceased as faint gurglings from the bows elicited casual warnings to each other of "Waves, waves!"

译文 2：As soon as the boatmen hear you say you want to go across Stone Lake they look up at the sky to see if there is any sign a wind might blow up. When they put out onto the lake, the tension shows on their faces, and all cheerful talk ceases. At the first sound of water lapping against the prow of the boat they warn each other in hushed voices: "Waves! Waves!"

译文 1 构句较译文 2 紧凑，将原文划线部分处理为从句，这就解释了为什么会出现物称转换从"（船家）听得……警戒……"变为 gurglings—elicit warnings... 的现象：因为译者已无法安排像译文 2（At the sound... they warn... in hushed voices "Waves!")那样的复杂结构了。

一家人都坐在庭间曝日，甚至于吃午饭也在屋外，像夏天的晚饭一样。日光晒到哪里，就把椅凳移到哪里，忽然寒风来了，只好逃难似地各自带了椅凳逃入室中，急急把门关上。

The whole family would sit sunning themselves in the yard, and even take lunch outdoors, in the same way as we had supper in summer. Chairs and stools were moved around to catch the best of the sunlight. But then if the wind blew up we were forced to beat a hasty retreat indoors, carrying our chairs with us like a lot of refugees.

原文是以"一家人"为视角展开叙述的，译文第二句改用物称视角，增加了整段句子结构的变化。

第十一节 名 物 化

功能语法中，动宾或系表结构向名词短语的转换称为名物化。也就是说，同一心理情景既可用动词短语表达，也可用名词短语表达，这也体现了心理情景和语言框架之间的选择关系。比如：

(1) If we add or remove heat, the state of matter may change.

(2) The addition or removal of heat may change the state of matter.

上面句（1）中的小句结构 we add or remove heat 在句（2）中被改写成了名词短语 the addition or removal of heat，完成了名物化。汉译英中，将动词结构译为名词结构也可称为名物化，这是一种跨语言的名物化操作。一个小句被压缩成一个名词性词组，可以简化结构，便于构句。比如：

有几位是要天天打照面的，每每超过他们，乐拓夫总还是恭敬地点点头，并且微微一笑。对方也会报之一笑，那笑容有点像十字路口的绿灯，让人感到顺畅地亮着。

Some of them he came across every day. Each time he overtook them Yue would nod respectfully and smile. Their answering smiles elated him just as a green light at a crossing.

"对方……报之一笑"名物化为"他们回报的笑"。

初冬的天,<u>灰黯而且低垂</u>,简直把人压得吁不出一口气。

It was early winter. <u>The gloomy and low sky</u> made one feel suffocating.

原文的"……天,灰黯而且低垂"是个小句结构,译文处理为名词结构 the gloomy and low sky。有趣的是,原文的"初冬的天"倒被译为一个独立的句子,名词短语变小句,似为反其道而行之。

我小时候<u>进戏园</u>,深感那是<u>另一个世界</u>,……

<u>Setting foot</u> in a playhouse was to me in my youth like <u>entering a different world</u>.

原句的"我"的叙述变成了两个动名词结构的对等比较:Setting foot… was… like entering a different world.

- 千百年没人动过这原始森林,于是整个森林长成一团。<u>树都互相躲让着,又都互相争夺着</u>,从上到下,无有闲处。

  For hundreds and thousands of years no one touched this primeval jungle—the entire forest grew into a single, tangled whole. In <u>its mutual concession and competition for growth</u>, the vegetation left no space vacant on the ground.

- 船家做的菜是菜馆比不上的,特称"船菜"。正式的船菜花样繁多,菜以外还有种种点心,一顿吃不完。非正式地做几样也还是精,船家训练有素,出手总不脱船菜的风格。折穿了说,船菜所以好就在于只准备一席,小镬小锅,做一样是一样,汤水不混合,材料不马虎,自然每样有它的真味,叫人吃完了还觉得馋涎欲滴。倘若船家进了菜馆里的大厨房,大镬炒虾,大锅煮鸡,那也一定会有坍台的时候的。话得说回来,船菜既然好,坐在船里又安舒,可以眺望,可以谈笑,玩它个夜以继日,于是快船常有求过于供的情形。

  译文1:The food served by boatmen, "boat food" as it was designated, was unrivalled in any eating house, and no one meal could exhaust the elaborations of the real thing, from its dishes proper to its varied snacks. Even specialties outside its usual range had a refinement due to <u>the strict training of the boatmen</u>, nothing to which they applied their skill ever escaping the style of boat food, the mystery of whose excellence lay in individual <u>preparation</u> with small pots and pans, so that everything was different, with no <u>mixing of sauces</u> or adulteration of ingredients, and everything tasted as it should, leaving the mouth still watering after all had been consumed. Had a boatman fried his prawns or boiled his chicken in the capacious utensils of a large restaurant kitchen, there would no doubt have been falls from grace. Be that as it may, given the excellence of the boat food, the added relaxation of the journey with its opportunities for sightseeing, light banter and night-long indulgence generally created a demand in excess of supply.

译文 2: The meals prepared on the boat are in a different class from meals in restaurants, and have earned the special name of "boat fare". Proper boat meals include a wide variety of dishes, plus all sorts of snacks: there is always more than one can finish. Occasionally, ordered dishes will still be good, for the cook will have had long training, and will not produce anything that is not in the authentic boat fare style. To expose their secret, the reason why boat fare is good is that they cater for one table at a time: with their little pans and woks, they cook the dishes one by one, each in its own juice, and with picked ingredients. Naturally every dish will have its true taste, and will make you greedy for more. Supposing the boat cooks were to operate in a restaurant kitchen, frying big woks of shrimps and stewing big pans of chicken, they would certainly be taken down a peg. To get back to our subject, since the boat fare was good, and traveling was comfortable, allowing you to look out on the scenery, laugh and talk, and play mahjong or amuse yourself with girls, the fast boats used to be in great demand, more than they could meet.

这一例选自叶圣陶的散文名篇《三种船》，描述船上独特的菜肴。两位译者风格各异，各有千秋，我们这里不去评说。我们关注的，只是两种译文在名物化处理上的差异，和由此而导致的整体风格的差异。仔细对比两段译文中的划线部分，很明显，译文 1 中划线的名词结构和译文 2 中划线的小句结构形成了鲜明的对照：译文 1 多名物化，译文 2 则依原文结构多以小句译小句。这样一来，译文 1 多从属结构，句子较为冗长繁复，译文 2 多简短小句，跳跃简明。

第十二节 连 贯

  语篇的连贯性是语篇构建问题，也是交际参与者的认知问题。首先必须把心理情景用适当的语言框架表达出来，才可达到与他人交流的目的；而同时，交际的参与者彼此之间必须在一定程度上共享某些相关知识和经验，才能相互理解，即在自己头脑中构建起相应的心理情景。

  阅读汉语语篇时，我们对母语的词汇、修辞的了解，对中国社会、文化的了解，一般能够保证我们与语篇建立有效的沟通。而一篇汉语文章被译为英语，它所面对的信息接受者是处于迥异的社会文化环境中的群体，他们不懂汉语，不了解中国文化；汉语文本中和汉语读者的知识结构相吻合的信息，在英译文中一下子失去了产生其应有意义的根基。作为译者必须设身处地，从英语读者的认知角度构建译文，以使英译文在新的语境中发挥与其原文在汉语语境中相应的交际功能。

  先谈由于英汉两种语言本身差异所造成的译文连贯性问题。

  风在路另侧的小树林中呼啸，忽高忽低，如泣如诉，仿佛从废墟上漂来了"留——留——"的声音。

  ……风又从废墟上吹过，依然发出"留——留——"的声音。我忽然醒悟了。它是在召唤！召唤人们留下来，改造这凝固的历史。

  上面段落引自宗璞的散文《废墟的召唤》。汉语"留"字可用来模拟风的声音，本身又自有其意，行文是连贯的。但英语译文怎么处理呢？看下面两种翻译方法：

  译文1：A wind is whistling through the small forest on the other side of the road. I seem to hear the words "Stay—Stay—" drifting from the ruins.

  … The wind is blowing through the ruins again, and is again making human sounds "Stay—Stay—". Suddenly I realize what it is saying. It is calling! It is calling people to stay and to transform this solidified history.

  译文2：The wind whistled through the copse on the other side of the path, rising and falling, plaintive and sorrowful. The wind seemed to float the sound "*liu… liu…*" over from the ruins.

  The wind blew across the ruins again, as before making the sound of "*liu… liu…*" I suddenly realize: it was a summons! Summoning people to stay and remake this frozen history.

译文 1 用 stay 直接译出"留"字的意义,但 stay 的发音恐怕很难引发英语读者对风声的联想,译文接着又说 "Suddenly I realize what it is saying. It is calling!" 这会使译文读者更不知所云。译文 2 的译者 David Pollard 充分意识到了这个拟声词的不可译性,只译其音,并在评论中向英语读者解释道:The "*liu... liu...*" sound that the wind seems to make in the ruins means "stay". Unfortunately, neither "stay" nor any of its synonyms in English sounds anything like a wind, so "*liu*" had to be retained, and here explained.

一个大生日蛋糕在两位领导的手中以"人"字形被切开,"人"字需要相互的支撑,这也许正说明海滨浴场是多方鼎力相助的结果。

Two officials cut a large birthday cake, their knives tracing the strokes of the Chinese character *ren*—"people," implying that the success of the resort comes from the unfailing support from many people.

这一例原文的连贯是建立在汉字"人"本身的象征意义上的,这种意义在英语中无从表达,所以译文采取了意译的方法,自成一体地达到了连贯:没有涉及"人"字具体笔画结构,只强调了切蛋糕方式的寓意。

看书和看电视共享一个"看"字,好像它们是兄弟。但这实在是一个冤案,细细比较起来,这两个"看"是大不一样的。

Reading a book and watching television, they both involve the use of the eye. But this is only superficially true. A careful comparison will reveal that they actually represent two distinctive uses of the same organ.

汉语"看书"和"看电视"同用一个动词,但英语则不可。译文顺应英语的搭配,转而表达为"这两种活动都要使用眼睛,但用法不同"的意思,这样便重新构建了译文的语义连贯。

汉译英中还会遇到一些具有特定文化内涵的词语,如果直译,可能使译文读者不知所云或产生误解,也可能会与读者的知识结构相冲突,译文失去连贯。一个解决办法是,用相应英语词语替换。如下面译例:

- 要全方位地开拓国际市场,市场多元化是立于不败之地的关键。俗话说:"不能在一棵树上吊死。"

    It is important to tap the market potential around the world. And geographical market diversification is the key to surviving the unsteady world market. In common parlance, it is unwise to "put all our eggs in one basket".

- 是夜半，是女人声音，先是摇铃随后是喊"小姐"，然后一声铃间一声喊，由元板到流水板，越来越促，越来越高，我想医院里的人除了住了太平间的之外大概谁都听到了，然而没有人送给她所需要的那件东西。

  It was the middle of the night, and the voice was a woman's. First the bell rang, then came a call of "Nurse!" Thereafter a ring, followed after an interval by a call, the tempo rising from largo to allegro, the tone becoming more and more urgent, the pitch more and more shrill. Everyone in the hospital, apart from those resting in the mortuary, must have heard, but no one brought her what she wanted.

"不能在一棵树上吊死"换成了 it is unwise to put all our eggs in one basket，"元板"换成了 largo（风格缓慢、庄严的广板），"流水板"换成了 allegro（快板），这样便顺应了译文读者的认知语境。译者必须考虑译文所处的文化语境，迎合译文读者的知识结构和心理预期。

为使译文与读者的经验、知识结构相契合，除可以用相应英语词语替换外，还可以在译文中增加释义性文字，或在译文外加上译者注解。释义可以针对熟语、成语等语言方面的问题，比如 Pollard 译周作人的《哑巴礼赞》，原作一开篇便用了两个俗语：

俗语云，"哑巴吃黄连"，谓有苦说不出也。但又云，"黄连树下弹琴"，则苦中作乐，亦是常有的事，哑巴虽苦于说不出话，盖亦自有其乐，或者且在吾辈有嘴巴人之上，未可知也。

There is a proverb which runs: "The dumb man chews on yellow rue", <u>the point of which lies in the matching line</u>, "Bitter as gall, but he can't tell you." But another proverb says, "Under the rue bush strumming a tune", which indicates that making merry when things look black is common enough too. Though the mute is afflicted by not being able to express himself, doubtless he has his own private pleasures, which may be superior to those of us who can wag our tongues; how are we to say?

译文划线部分是译者添加的信息，译者还另加注释说：

"Yellow rue": the plant *huanglian* is not actually rue, but to English speakers, rue is about the only plant proverbially associated with bitterness.

第一篇 文学语篇：小说、散文等

- 虽然是明媒正娶，而且于少棠也从未有过花钱买了个老婆的想法；但他知道，一姐总是觉得是她老子卖了女儿！
  <u>It was a proper marriage arranged by a go-between with all the ceremonials observed</u>, and it never entered Yu Shaotang's head that he had bought his wife with money. But he knew that Yijie always felt that her father had sold his daughter.
- 那两年闹灾荒，郑板桥的父亲又宦游在外，不能按时接济家用。
  There were those two years of famine. Zheng Banqiao's father was away <u>wherever his official duties took him</u>, and could not always get money to them at regular intervals.

以上两例中，"明媒正娶"按《现代汉语词典》意为：旧时指有媒人说合，按传统结婚仪式迎娶的婚姻。"宦游"按《新华词典》的解释是：为求做官而四方奔走，也指在外做官。译文划线部分简直就像是该词典的英语翻译。当然，添加的释义部分必须连贯而流畅地融入上下文中。

旧式讣闻喜用"寿终正寝"字样，不是没有道理的。在家里养病，除了病不容易治好之外，不会为病以外的事情着急。如果病重不治必须寿终，则寿终正寝是值得提出来傲人的一件事，表示死者死得舒服。

The old style notice of bereavement liked to use the phrase "passed away at the end of his/her allotted span in the bosom of his/her family", not without reason. If you nurse an illness at home you may not get the best of treatment, but you won't be bothered by extraneous irritations. Supposing the illness were incurable and you had to slip this mortal coil, to do so in the bosom of your family is something that may justifiably be mentioned with pride, for it means the death would have been a comfortable one.

"正寝"是全段连贯的基础，强调"在家里养病"，在亲人关爱下死去。如译为 die peacefully, die of old age, die a natural death 等便会使译文失去连贯，所以译文特别凸显了"正寝"的意思：in the bosom of his/her family.

除解释有特定含义的词语外，译文增加的释义也可以针对历史、典故、风俗等文化方面的问题。

它的成为假山，原由于我的利用，本身只是一块粗糙的钢铁片，非但不是什么"吉金乐石",说出来一定会叫人发指,是"一·二八之役"日人所掷的炸弹的裂块。

It is an ornamental mountain because that is the way it serves my use. In itself it is just a crude lump of iron. It is none of your lucky talismans, in fact to say what it is will only evoke outage, for it is a fragment of a bomb dropped by the Japanese <u>when they attacked the Chinese city of Shanghai in 1932.</u>

"一·二八之役"指1932年1月28日夜间日本侵略军由上海租界向闸北一带进攻的事件。文章发表于1935年,语境自然为当时读者所熟悉,现译为英语便添加了有关历史信息。

有些住在离城十余里的乡下的学生,于文课作完后回家的包裹里,往往将这两个肉馒头包得好好,带回乡下去送给邻里尊长,并非想学颖叔考的纯孝,却因为这肉馒头是学堂里的东西,而又出于知县官之所赐,……

Some of them who lived miles away in the country wrapped up these buns carefully and put them in their satchels to take home after class. When they got home they presented them to the local elders, not in imitation of the "pure piety" of Ying Kaoshu <u>who put aside some of the food Duke Yin gave him to take back to his mother</u>, but because the buns were from the academy, and besides were the gift of the county magistrate.

译文中划线部分便是对"颖考叔的纯孝"的释义。

应对文化词语的翻译,除了替换和释义,还可以采取"去文化"的方法,即将文化词语译为一般词语,去其文化、历史内涵,只表其意。

- 有这种标准横亘在心里,便容易兴起"除却巫山不是云"之感。
  They set permanent standards for me, and it is easy for me to slip into <u>thinking no one will ever compare with them</u>.
- 像春香闹学似的把戏,总是由他发起,由许多虾兵蟹将来演出的,……
  <u>All the japes and pranks</u> were instigated by him and carried out by his <u>lieutenants and underlings</u>, …

以上译文中,对元稹的"除却巫山不是云"诗句、汤显祖的"春香闹学"故事、"虾兵蟹将"的神话的联想已荡然无存。但译文自身是连贯的,因为它已无须调动读者的特定有关知识来理解译文。

最后，还要强调的是，不同的译者对文化词语的翻译方法是不一样的，但不管采用什么译法，译文自身必须连贯，译文所传递的信息必须顺应读者的心理预期，换言之，译文和读者的认知环境必须是连贯的。

河中涨了水，平常时节泊在河滩的烟船妓船，离岸极近，船皆系在吊脚楼下的支柱上。

译文1：Rising waters submerge the sandbanks where floating opium dens and brothel boats are used to mooring. They are close in to shore now, lashed to the support piers of houses hanging over water on stilts, the "balconies with hanging feet."

译文2：(…the river rose.) Whenever this happened, the opium boats and boat brothels moored by the bank came so close to the shore that they were tied to the pillars of the stilt buildings.

译文1把汉语中"吊脚"的形象再现了出来，译文2则只译其意，同样是连贯的。

而且乱石衰草中间，仿佛应该有着妲己、褒姒的窈窕身影，若隐若现，迷离扑朔。

译文1：I feel as if fluttering among the jumbled mass of ruins could be seen the graceful figures of Daji, imperial concubine of King Zhou, last ruler of the Shang Dynasty, and of Baosi, queen-consort of King You, last ruler of the Western Zhou Dynasty.

译文2：It would have been fitting too if the lissome figures of the fabled concubines of ill-fated ancient Chinese emperors could have been glimpsed flitting like phantoms among the litter of stones and jungle of grass.

译文1将文化内涵具体化，增加了"商纣王""周幽王"等历史信息；译文2则将之抽象化，进行了笼统的解释。可以说前者趋于异化，后者趋于归化。前一位译者似有较深的源语文化情结，而后者显然站在了目的语读者的立场。

汉英语篇翻译

第十三节　修辞手段的翻译

排比、比喻、象声等修辞手段的使用使语篇能够超越纯粹的信息传达功能，进而增强语篇的感染力，打动读者的情感，激发读者的美感。翻译过程中，要力求把汉语语篇中所蕴含的感染力充分再现出来；构建译文的时候，不能只注重基本信息的传译，还必须培养强烈的修辞意识。译文中可以运用与原文同样或类似的修辞手段，也可异曲同工，力求同等效果。比如朱纯深翻译朱自清的《匆匆》，有下面一句：

去的尽管去了，来的尽管来着，去来的中间，又怎样地匆匆呢？
Those that have gone have gone for good, those to come keep coming; yet in between, how swift is the shift, in such a rush?

据译者说（见《中国翻译》1994，4：63），原句以排比加设问引出整段对时光匆匆的具体描述，译文选用了 swift, shift, such rush 这些短元音和爆破音、摩擦音的集中重复，以表达匆匆中的纷扰。这样，虽然译文没有再现原文的工整排比句式，却用另一种修辞方法进行了弥补。

翻译的关键在于译者要具备敏锐的修辞鉴别力，并善于运用译语中相应的修辞手段。再看同一篇文章的另一排比句：

燕子去了，有再来的时候；杨柳枯了，有再青的时候；桃花谢了，有再开的时候。
Swallows may have gone, but there is a time of return; willow trees may have died back, but there is a time of regreening; peach blossoms may have fallen, but they will bloom again.

关于这一句的译文，译者说：文章一开头就用了三个排比句，具有很强的气势。英译时采用了相应的句式，但为了避免重复过多而显得单调，最后一句作了调整，没用 there is a time of reblooming。

同样是排比结构，英语中有不同的表达方式。下面一句的汉语排比结构，就可再现为三种不同的英语排比结构。

我爱热闹，也爱冷静；爱群居，也爱独处。

译文1：I like both excitement and stillness, enjoy both a crowd and solitude.

译文2：I like excitement, and also like calm; I love to be in crowds, and also love to be on my own.

译文 3：I like a serene and peaceful life, as much as a busy and active one; I like being in solitude, as much as in company.

但不是所有排比结构都要在英译中再现。英语有自己的修辞原则，下面一句中的"即使……，即使……，即使……"结构如果以相应的"even if... even if... even if..."来译，则会臃肿不堪，反而失去感染力。

江南的紫砂壶玲珑剔透，泥人张的彩塑令人拍案叫绝，它们不都是泥土的微笑吗？弥足珍贵。即使曾丑陋，即使曾卑微，即使曾朴素，同样让人肃然起敬。

Both the exquisiteness of the boccaro teapots made in south China, and the shockingly beautiful sculptures by Clay Sculptor Zhang of Tianjin—aren't they all smiles of the earth? They are such exquisite treasures that—even if they look ugly, humble, plain, or whatsoever—they no doubt deserve respect and veneration.

如果说排比、重复等修辞手法是超越纯粹的句法手段，用以调动读者对语言形式的审美认同，增加记忆的深度，那么比喻，包括明喻、暗喻、拟人等，就是超越单纯的词汇搭配，而刻意激发读者形象思维能力，让读者融入作者所创造的意境当中。

这时节，你环顾四周，全是一扇扇的肉屏风，不由你不随着大家而肉袒。前后左右都是肉，白晳晳的，黄澄澄的，黑黝黝的，置身其间如入肉林。这虽颇富肉感，但绝不能给人以愉快。戏一演就是四五个钟头，中间如果想要如厕，需要在肉林中挤出一条出路，挤出后那条路便翕然而阖，回来时需要重新另挤出一条进路。

You looked round you then, and on all four sides there was <u>screen after screen of flesh</u>, so you had no choice but to divest yourself like the others. In front and behind, left and right, it was all flesh, mild white, lemon yellow and berry brown. It was like being surrounded by <u>sides of meat in a cold store</u>. Though any appetite for carnality would have been satisfied, there was absolutely no pleasure in it. Plays lasted for four or five hours and if you needed to go to the lavatory in the middle you had to force a way through the <u>phalanx of flesh</u>, a way which immediately closed seamlessly after you; on your return you had to force open a passage all over again.

下面一例选自梁实秋的《听戏》，讲的是旧时戏园子里观众们赤膊听戏的场景。一排排光膀子被比喻为"一扇扇的肉屏风""肉林",起身如厕要穿过"肉林",挤出一条通道,可谓生动淋漓。英译文中,这些形象未必都能照样直译,"肉屏风"可说 screen of flesh,而肉林就分别用了 sides of meat in a cold store 和 phalanx of flesh 来应对,这里"林"的形象已经没有,取而代之的是"冷藏库里一片片的肉"和"肉的方阵",同样可调动读者的感知经验,达到和读者互动的目的。

下面译例把人过三十比为"张了一顶阳伞"和"日历上撕过了立秋的一页",这一类比手法在英译中基本照译,只是加进了英语读者熟悉的比喻——一个人最后的行动或作品的 swan song。

我的年岁上冠用了"三十"二字,至今已两年了。不解达观的我,从这两个字上受到了不少的暗示与影响。虽然明明觉得自己的体格与精力比二十九岁时全然没有什么差异,但"三十"这一个观念笼在头上,犹之张了一顶阳伞,使我的全身蒙了一个灰暗色的阴影,又仿佛在日历上撕过了立秋的一页以后,虽然太阳的炎威依然没有减却,寒暑表上的热度依然没有降低,然而只当得余威与残暑,或霜降木落的先驱,大地的节候已从今移交于秋了。

It is now two years since my year of age carried the prefix "thirty". Never one to take things philosophically, I have felt the influence and intimations of this word in several ways. Though I am fully aware that in health and spirits I am in no way different from what I was at the age of twenty-nine, this notion of "thirty" hangs over my head. It is the opening of a parasol that casts one in dark shade, or like the tearing off of the page that marks the first day of autumn from the calendar: although the sun's power has not diminished, and the thermometer's reading has not dropped, one thinks of it only as fading strength or swan song, or as the prelude to frost and leaf-fall; from now on the natural world has shifted to the autumn season.

对于汉语中的同一个比喻形象,不同的译者,构想是不会完全相同的,细节有差异,整体形象也会有差异。这是因为他们的个人经历不同,构想的方式和审美角度也会不同,比如下面选自朱自清的《荷塘月色》的译例:

曲曲折折的荷塘上面,弥望的是田田的叶子。叶子出水很高,像亭亭的舞女的裙。层层的叶子中间,零星地点缀着些白花,有袅娜地开着的,有羞涩地打着朵儿的;正如一粒粒的明珠,又如碧天里的星星,又如刚出浴的美人。

译文 1: All over this winding stretch of water, what meets the eye is a silken field of leaves, reaching rather high above the surface, like the skirts of dancing girls in all their grace. Here and there, layers of leaves are dotted with white lotus blossoms, some in demure bloom, others in shy bud, like scattering pearls, or twinkling stars, our beauties just out of the bath.

译文 2: As far as eye could see, the pool with its winding margin was covered with trim leaves, which rose high out of the water like the flared skirts of dancing girls. And starring these tiers of leaves were white lotus flowers, alluringly open or bashfully in bud, like glimmering pearls, stars in an azure sky, or beauties fresh from the bath.

译文 3: On the surface of the serpentine lotus pond all one could see was fields of leaves. The leaves stood high above the water, splayed out like the skirts of a tall slim ballerina. Here and there among the layers of leaves were sown shining white flowers, some blooming glamourously, some in shy bud, just like unstrung pearls, or stars against a blue sky.

"舞女的裙"前两种译文大致相同,译文 3 则用了更为鲜明的芭蕾舞演员的形象;"明珠""星星"三种译文大致相同,但译文 3 略去了"出浴的美人"这一比喻。

月光如流水一般,静静地泻在这一片叶子和花上。薄薄的青雾浮起在荷塘里。叶子和花仿佛在牛乳中洗过一样;又像笼罩着轻纱的梦。虽然是满月,天上却有一层淡淡的云,所以不能朗照;但我以为这恰是到了好处——酣眠固不可少,小睡也别有风味的。月光是隔了树照过来的,高处丛生的灌木,落下参差的斑驳的黑影,峭楞楞如鬼一般;弯弯的杨柳的稀疏的倩影,却又像是画在荷叶上。塘中的月色并不均匀;但光与影有着和谐的旋律,如梵婀玲上奏着的名曲。

译文 1: Moonlight cascaded like water over the lotus leaves and flowers, and a light blue mist floating up from the pool made them seem washed in milk or caught in a gauzy dream. Though the moon was full, a film of pale clouds in the sky would not allow its rays to shine through brightly; but I felt this was all to the good—though refreshing sleep is indispensable, short naps have a charm all their own. As the moon shone from behind them, the dense trees on the hills threw checkered shadows, dark forms loomed like devils, and the sparse, graceful shadows of willows seemed painted on the lotus leaves. The moonlight on the pool was not uniform, but light and shadow made up a harmonious rhythm like a beautiful tune on a violin.

译文 2：The moonbeams spilled placidly onto this expanse of leaves and flowers like living water. A thin mist floated up from the lotus pond. The leaves and flowers seemed to be washed in milk, and at the same time trapped in a dream of flimsy gauze. Although the moon was full, there was a veil of light cloud, which prevented it from shining brightly; but to me this was just right—we cannot do without deep sleep, admitted, but a quiet doze also has its pleasures. The moonlight was filtered through the trees, while the clumps of bushes on the high ground cast heavy irregular mottled shadows. The spare silhouettes of the arching willows appeared to be painted on the lotus leaves. The moonlight on the pond was not all smooth and even, but the rhythm of light and shade was harmonious, like a musical masterpiece played on a violin.

译文 3：The moon sheds her liquid light silently over the leaves and flowers, which, in the floating transparency of a bluish haze from the pond, look as if they had just been bathed in milk, or like a dream wrapped in a gauzy hood. Although it is a full moon, shining through a film of clouds, the light is not at its brightest; it is, however, just right for me—a profound sleep is indispensable, yet a snatched doze also has a savour of its own. The moonlight is streaming down through the foliage, casting bushy shadows on the ground from high above, dark and checkered, like an army of ghosts; whereas the benign figures of the drooping willows, here and there, look like paintings on the lotus leaves. The moonlight is not spread evenly over the pond, but rather in a harmonious rhythm of light and shade, like a famous melody played on a violin.

上面三种译文都在对原文中的比喻形象进行精心的再创造，请细心观察他们所运用的词汇、语法手段的异同。比如，对"（月光如）流水（一般），（静静地）泻（在这一片叶子和花上）"这一形象，三种译文分别是：

Moonlight cascaded like water over the lotus leaves and flowers.

The moonbeams spilled placidly onto this expanse of leaves and flowers like living water.

The moon sheds her liquid light silently over the leaves and flowers.

前两个译文着意刻画月光的充盈，最后一个译文的 shed her light 似乎更着笔于月光的自然流泻。另外，译文2将"如鬼一般"略去未译，似乎是担心"鬼"

的形象会破坏了月下荷塘的柔美景象。

总之，在阅读译作，特别是同一原文的不同译本时，不但要体味原作者的修辞意图，也要体味译者的用心，从而提高自己运用修辞手段调动读者的感官、经验和情感，吸引读者、打动读者的能力。比如下面这句选自宗璞的《废墟的召唤》一文接近尾声时的一句感叹：

我们仍望着落照。通红的火球消失了，剩下的远山显出一层层深浅不同的紫色。浓处如酒，淡处如梦。那不浓不淡处使我想起春日的紫藤萝，这铺天的霞锦，需要多少藤萝花瓣啊。

译文1：We are still looking at the setting sun; the red ball of the fire gradually disappears, leaving the distant hills in different shades of purple. The dark purple is like liquor, and light purple like a dream. The shade in-between reminds me of wisteria in spring. How many wisterias would be needed to form these rose-tinted clouds which cover the sky?

译文2：We continued to watch the sunset. The fiery ball sank out of sight, leaving the distant hills clothed in purple bands of different intensity. The dense bands were like wine, the pale bands like a dream. The in-between bands reminded me of the wisteria in spring. That sunset tapestry spread across the sky could have done with more wisteria petals!

作者看着晚霞，联想起紫藤萝，她说要铺就这漫天的晚霞需要多少花瓣，实则在感叹"文革"大劫后的祖国建设需要多少人才呀。两位译者对作者意图的理解和再现，各有自己的视角：译文1似在直接呼唤年轻人像花瓣一样融入这锦霞当中，而译文2则似乎在感叹本应有更多的花瓣投身晚霞的辉煌。

象声词也是常用的修辞手段，英译时一般要使用英语中惯用的象声词。比如：莫言《天堂蒜薹之歌》中狗的叫声：

小伙子咳嗽了一声。清了清嗓子，狗叫起来，他学得惟妙惟肖："汪汪——汪汪汪——汪汪汪汪汪汪汪汪、汪、汪汪、汪汪汪汪汪汪汪！——这是小狗叫，一共二十六声。

The young beggar coughed and cleared his throat, then began to bark, sounding remarkably doglike: Arf arf—arf arf arf—arf arf arf arf arf arf arf arf arf, arf, arf, arf arf, arf arf arf arf arf arf arf! That was a little dog. Twenty-six barks.

再比如该书中的另一句：

他的耳朵里都灌满了蒜薹汤，它们呼噜呼噜响着，呼噜呼噜翻腾着，呼噜呼噜地对耳膜、对膀胱、对尿道施加着压力。

His ears filled with garlicky soup sounds: slurping and tumbling inside his eardrums, straining against the walls of his bladder, swelling his urethra.

句中的呼噜声对译为英语中的 slurp。

有时也见到译文中用汉语拼音来模仿声音的：

只记得三十二年前，我到这条巷子里来定居时，头一天黄昏以后，便听见远处传来一阵阵敲竹梆子的声音，那声音很有节奏：笃笃笃、笃笃、嘀嘀嘀笃；嘀嘀嘀、笃笃、嘀嘀笃。虽然只有两个音符，可那轻重疾徐、抑扬顿挫的变化很多，在夜暗的笼罩之中，总觉得是在呼唤着、叙说着什么。

All I remember is that, thirty-two years ago, the day after I moved to this lane, just after dusk, I heard the sound of a bamboo clapper approaching from a distance. The rhythm was very marked. "Duo duo duo, duo duo, di di di duo, di di di, duo duo, di di duo." Although there were only two notes, there were many variations in modulation and in the strength of the tapping. Under the cover of night it seemed as though someone were calling or relating something.

第十四节　信息的调适

汉英翻译中，对原文信息顺序加以调整以适应英语行文需要的情况很普遍，这反映了英汉在组句谋篇时信息安排的差异，即行文思路上的差异。英语和汉语在句法层面上信息分布不同，信息重心也会有所不同。学习汉英翻译时，必须仔细观察有经验的译者在英语谋篇布局上的策略和方法，并在实践中逐步摸索和体会。请看下面一例：

北京的冬季，地上还有积雪，灰黑色的秃树枝丫叉于晴朗的天空中，而远处有一二风筝浮动，在我是一种惊异和悲哀。

A Peking winter dismays and depresses me: the thick snow on the ground and the bare trees' ashen branches thrusting up towards the clear blue sky, while in the distance one or two kites are floating.

第一篇　文学语篇：小说、散文等

译文将原文最后的信息放在句首，先说自己的感受，然后才将具体景物一一陈述出来。

她（母亲）从不教训我，不过常如朋友那样，与我坦诚地追忆、探讨她的人生。<u>过失居多，成功居少</u>。我往往便沉迷在她那没有多少女性温存，噪音低沉的叙述中。

She never lectured me, just told me quietly in her deep, unwomanly voice about her successes and failures, so that I could learn from her experience. She had evidently not had many successes—her life was full of failures.

我们不妨先将译文回译为汉语：她从不教训我，只是以她低沉、非女人的声音静静地告诉我有关她的成功和失败，以便我能够学习她的经验。她显然没多少成功—— 她的人生充满失败。

可以清楚地看出，原句中间的划线部分被移到译文最后，而其前后两个句子的信息被融合在一起，有取有舍地被重新构句。

汉译英时也常出现将原文信息加以简化或压缩的情况，这主要是为了迎合英语行文的需要。比如：

每当他在台上作报告，她坐在台下，<u>隔着距离、烟雾、昏暗的灯光、窜动的人头，看着他那模糊不清的面孔</u>，她便觉得心里好像有什么东西凝固了，泪水会不由地充满她的眼眶。

Whenever he made a speech, she sat at the back of the hall watching his face rendered hazy by cigarette smoke and poor lighting. Her eyes would brim with tears.

句中划线部分的信息在译文中被删减和压缩。

没准儿，他这个不相信爱情的人，到了头发都白了的时候才意识到他心里也有那种可以称为爱情的东西存在，到了他已经没有权力去爱的时候，却发生了这足以使他献出全部生命的爱情。<u>这可真够凄惨的</u>。<u>也许不只是凄惨，也许还要深刻得多</u>。

Maybe, this man, who didn't believe in love, realized by the time his hair was white that in his heart was something which could be called love. By the time he no longer had the right to love, he made the tragic discovery of this love for which he would have given his life. Or did it go deeper even than that?

原句中有关"真够凄惨的"这个信息被淡化，也被移位，只体现在 the tragic discovery of 这样的字眼里。

83

我和乔林相处将近两年了，可直到现在我还摸不透他那缄默的习惯到底是因为不爱讲话，还是因为讲不出来什么？逢到我起意要对他来点智力测验，一定逼着他说出对某事或某物的看法时，他也只能说出托儿所里常用的那种词藻："好！"或"不好！"<u>就这么两挡，再也不能换换别的花样儿了</u>。

<u>当我问起："乔林，你为什么爱我"的时候，他认真地思索了好一阵子。对他来说，那段时间实在够长了</u>。凭着他那宽阔的额头上难得出现的皱纹，我知道，他那美丽的脑壳里面的组织细胞，一定在进行着紧张的思维活动。<u>我不由地对他生出一种怜悯和一种歉意，好像我用这个问题习难了他</u>。

I have known Qiao Lin for nearly two years, yet still cannot fathom whether he keeps so quiet from aversion to talking or from having nothing to say. When, by way of a small intelligence test, I demand his opinion of this or that, he says "good" or "bad" like a child in kindergarten.

Once I asked, "Qiao Lin, why do you love me?" He thought the question over seriously for what seemed an age. I could see from his normally smooth but now wrinkled forehead that the little grey cells in his handsome head were hard cogitating. I felt ashamed to have put him on the spot.

显然原文划线部分在译文中被简化了。

下面一例则连段落也进行了重组。

倒是我自己拿不准主意要不要嫁给他。因为我闹不清楚我究竟爱他的什么，而他又爱我的什么？

我知道，已经有人在背地里说长道短："凭她那些条件，还想找个什么样的？"

在他们的想象中，我不过是一头劣种的牲畜，却变着法儿想要混个肯出大价钱的冤大头。这使他们感到气恼，好像我真的干了什么伤天害理的、冒犯了众人的事情。

我不能对于他们过于苛求。在商品生产还存在的社会里，婚姻，也像其他许多问题一样，难免不带着商品交换的烙印。

But I can't make up my mind to marry him. I'm not clear what attracts me to him, or him to me. I know people are gossiping behind my back, "Who does she think she is, to be so choosy?" To them, I'm a nobody playing hard to get. They take offense at such preposterous behaviour.

Of course, I shouldn't be captious. In a society where commercial production still exists, marriage like most other transactions is still a form of barter.

译文中多有对原文信息的缩减，而原文引语则是以不同的表达方式译出来的——"她以为她是谁？这么挑剔。"

我不由地想：当他成为我的丈夫，我也成为他的妻子的时候，我们能不能把妻子和丈夫的责任和义务承担到底呢？也许能够。因为法律和道义已经紧紧地把我们拴在一起。而如果我们仅仅是遵从着法律和道义来承担彼此的责任和义务，那又是多么悲哀啊！那么，有没有比法律和道义更牢固、更坚实的东西把我们联系在一起呢？

I couldn't help wondering, if we were to marry, whether we could discharge our duties to each other as husband and wife. Maybe, because law and morality would have bound us together. But how tragic simply to comply with law and morality! Was there no stronger bond to link us?

译文将原文的信息进行了流线化处理，叙述简约了许多，但基本信息都已传达出来。

本章提出了双语阅读时十四个可行的关注点，意在帮助大家带着问题去阅读更多的双语对照语料，能动地寻找和理解不同译者的翻译思路和具体处理方法，不断积累，并结合自己的翻译实践，为我所用，化为己有。翻译方法不一定是一些条条框框或具体步骤，翻译学习也不是求得一个金科玉律。翻译学习强调以读带译——读英语原创语篇，读双语对照语篇，在阅读过程中悟出对自己有用的东西。这其中，宜于意会难于言传的东西还是不少的，更多的需要大家自己在实践中去体味。

第三章
翻译试笔和思考

本章按语篇的功能分叙事、描写和说明三节，包含七篇散文和小说，以供读者翻译练习之用，每篇文章后附有参考译文、简明注释和思考，可与前两章内容配合使用。建议大家先阅读原文，然后自己动笔翻译，至少要打个腹稿；归纳自己遇到的难题和拿捏不定的语句，思考片刻，再对照参考译文逐段阅读；联系自己在英语阅读和双语阅读中的心得，思考翻译难点，借鉴他人翻译经验，找出自己改进的方向。

第一节 叙事语篇

【练习一】

哲　学

秦志刚

阿呆人如其名[1]，在校时成绩一直徘徊在中下游，后来实在混不下去了[2]，就退学回家。阿呆有个理想，他想成为哲学家。他有个老师亲戚在县中学任教，亲戚委婉地告诉他实现理想之不易，但阿呆不为所动。

一天，阿呆在一本杂志上看到一则逸闻，说是大哲学家苏格拉底十分惧内，所以当有人向他请教怎样才能成为哲学家时他深有感触地说："娶一个像我妻子一样的女人做老婆！"亲戚还告诉他，苏格拉底的妻子是个出了名的悍妇，常做河东狮吼，因此苏格拉底才有此一说的[3]。

阿呆认为找到了捷径，决定依法仿效。几经艰苦寻觅，终于如愿。

阿呆等着成为哲学家。

不曾想[4]，老婆太过凶悍，以至于几次"交战"后阿呆服服帖帖甘拜下风！老婆说："你也不撒泼尿照照自己，凭你也想成为哲学家？现在吃饭都成了问题还不醒悟？想成为哲学家？做梦去吧！"[5]

从此，阿呆真的在梦中才能想起哲学了，因为一天的时间被老婆安排得满满当当，哪还有闲时间啊。不过，苦是苦了点[6]，但几年下来也发家致富了，小日子过得滋滋润润的，和以前的穷酸相比真有天壤之别[7]！

阿呆不再想成为哲学家了。

又有一天，那个老师亲戚到阿呆家中做客，才又勾起他的回忆。趁老婆不在家[8]，他偷偷地问："为什么苏格拉底娶悍妇可以成为大名鼎鼎的哲学家而我不能？"

老师亲戚意味深长地说："这就是哲学啊！"

参考译文

A Would-be Philosopher

Qin Zhigang

Mr. Dull was dull-witted indeed. At school he never achieved above the average in his studies, and seeing no hope for better performance he quitted school to idle around at home. Nevertheless, he was always obsessed with a fantasy that he would make a great philosopher someday. He went to seek advice from a relative, a high school teacher in town, who warned him tactfully that the road to his dream would be strewn with difficulties, but he didn't take him seriously.

One day, Mr. Dull read an anecdote in a magazine about the great philosopher Socrates, who was so henpecked that when asked about the quick way to become a philosopher he answered thoughtfully, "Find a woman like my wife, and marry her!" This story was later echoed by his teacher-relative, who added that Socrates' wife was every inch a shrew, that it was amid her deafening roars of abuse that Socrates emerged

as a great thinker, and that Socrates' words were, therefore, well-founded.

Mr. Dull believed he had found a short-cut and decided to follow Socrates' example. Through much hunting and screening he picked out the right woman and married her as he had wished.

Mr. Dull waited for his dream to come true.

Alas, he had never imagined that a woman could be so ferocious and ruthless! After fighting a few "battles" with his wife, he had to admit defeat in utter subjugation to her. His wife taunted him, "You want to be a philosopher? Piss on the ground and see if you look like one in the puddle! Don't you realize the plight we're in? We're starving, and daydreaming won't put rice in our bowls!"

From then on, Dull could only dream of being a philosopher at night, because he was ordered around by his wife all day, unable to give even a fleeting thought to philosophy. His ambition was suppressed, his every waking hour packed with work. Meanwhile however, their family prospered. Their purse bulging, they began to lead a decent and comfortable life, a world of difference from their earlier state of poverty.

The idea of being a philosopher was forgotten about for the time being.

One day, his teacher-relative paid him a visit and this rekindled his interest in philosophy. When his wife happened to be out of the way, Dull asked him furtively, "Socrates became a great philosopher by marrying a shrew, so why did I fail in copying him?"

His relative replied profoundly, "Isn't this what philosophy studies?"

思考

1. 也可译为：Mr. Dull was as dull-witted as his name suggests.
2. "成绩一直徘徊在中下游"意译为"从未高于平均成绩"，其中 achieve 一词的用法可再参见下面两个例句：（1）This school achieved above the national average in this year's *gaokao*. 这所学校今年高考好于全国平均成绩。（2）He has achieved his TEM 8 qualification. 他英语8级过关了。"混不下去"意译为"看不到学习成绩提高的希望"，其中 performance 意为"学习表现"，如：Her students' performance has brought back her confidence. 学生们的学习成绩让她找回了自信。

3. 译文用了三个并列的宾语从句表达阿呆的"亲戚"对苏格拉底逸事所做的进一步说明。
4. "不曾想"的语气用感叹词 alas 译出。
5. 这里将老婆数落阿呆的话在语义上进行了重新组合安排，目的是使英译文更像一个泼妇的口气。其中对汉语俗语"撒泡尿照照自己"采取了直译的方法，以求增加中国色彩。put rice in our bowls 也是一种异化的译法，按英语习惯应说 put food on our plates。
6. 译文将"苦"具体化，重复了上文的有关内容，以两个短句的形式加强了叙述的力度。
7. a world of difference 意为"差别很大"。如：There's a world of difference between coastal cities and inland towns. 沿海城市和内陆城镇有天壤之别。Work out half an hour in the gym every day, and it will make a world of difference in the long run. 每天在健身房锻炼半小时，时间长了就会大有裨益。
8. "不在家"译为 out of the way 不碍事、不在场。

【练习二】

第六只羊

心 仪

秋后山区的深夜，干冷干冷的。抬头看不见星星，低头看不见自己的脚面，山是黑的，树是黑的，蜿蜒起伏的山路是黑的。¹ 一辆机动三轮车刺眼的车灯如一道流星从山间公路划过，很快又被身后的夜色愈合。

车上坐着两个人，大黑和小亮。

小亮坐在副驾驶上双手使劲抱着蜷缩的身体。但即便把身体蜷缩得再小，寒冷还是无孔不入。出来前他就曾劝他大："这么冷、这么黑，大，咱可别去了！"大黑兴冲冲开着自己的车，心想：都说初生牛犊不怕虎，这小子，他怎么就不随我呢？黑怕什么？冷怕什么？这样才更安全，不容易被人发现。²

小亮还小，才 15 岁，他还不敢不听他大的，因为他还得吃他的喝他的。再过几年，他才可以去他向往的城市打工；也只有到了那时候，他才不用被他大牵着鼻子走，跟他一样偷鸡摸狗。

想到从今以后再也不用和别人搭伙了，大黑就压制不住自己的兴奋。打仗还得亲兄弟，上阵还得父子兵。这样不光安全可靠，成果也全都归自己家了。[3] 至于小亮，他想他一回生两回熟，历练历练就胆大了[4]。

白天早踩好点了。到了地方，大黑在僻静处把三轮车停好，嘱咐小亮说，儿子，你的活儿挺简单，一会儿我把那家的石头墙掏好窟窿，你只负责把那六只羊赶出来就行了[5]！记住，六只。

小亮蹲在父亲的身边，静静地听着父亲掏墙的声音。声音很轻，只有他们俩能听见。尽管声音很轻，可那一块块沉重的石头，还是把小亮的心敲得有些疼[6]。六只羊啊，明天早晨，主人突然看不见了自己一天天喂大的羊，还不心疼死啊！[7] 小时候，他家养的羊卖了或者杀了，他都会急哭的。他轻轻拉了下大黑说，大，我们回家吧！石头是沉重的，大黑扒开石头的动作却很轻，轻车熟路了，他的心里也感觉越来越轻快，他每扒开一块石头，那六只肥羊就离他近一步[8]。

"傻小子，你怕啥？这种鬼天气，谁也发现不了咱们的！"大黑用只有小亮能听到的声音说。

"好了！进去吧。" 大黑用手护住小亮的头和后背，把小亮推进去，最后还轻轻拍了拍小亮的屁股。

其实他根本不用那么仔细护住儿子的身体，为了让每只羊能够顺利钻出来，他掏的这个洞已足够大，爬着进去的小亮是没有那些站着走出来的羊高的。

一股冷风顺着小亮的屁股跟进来。他很快摸到了那六只羊，因为冷，它们都紧紧挤在一起。小亮轻轻摸着一只羊的头、后背和屁股，就像他大摸他一样。他也和这些羊们一起挤成一堆，挤在墙角，羊们温暖着他。

他有些忘了自己是来偷羊的，他，似乎也成了其中的一员。他不忍心，一点儿也不忍心下手。

"找到了吧？快点啊！"他大的声音顺着窟窿钻进来，也像一股冷风一样。

这么温暖的羊群，很快就会变成他大斧头下的冤死鬼，太残忍太残酷了。就这一次，就这一次吧，下次就是大把自己打死，也不来了！小亮开始一只一只向外赶羊。他知道，每只羊被赶出去的时候，还来不及叫一声，就会被他大的斧头照准羊头用力一劈，奔赴黄泉了。

他抚摸着每一只羊的头、背、屁股，甚至尾巴。每一只羊离开他的时候，也把贴近他身体的那份温暖一起带走了。

一只，两只，三只，四只，五只，已经到了最后一只。小亮刚一摸到墙角，没有了依靠的第六只羊就主动把身体靠向他。

小亮心软[9]了，喃喃出声说，你这畜生什么都不懂啊，唉。你肯定还是一只和我一样年轻的羊啊[10]，如果你知道是我祸害了你的伙伴们，你还不得用你的角顶死我啊！小亮紧紧抱着第六只羊的脖子，半蹲着，他的另一只手几乎摸遍了羊的全身。这只羊用脸轻轻摩挲着小亮稚嫩的脸，痒痒的、暖暖的，小亮有泪水顺着这两张脸的夹缝落下。

快点啊，还没摸着啊？大黑在细声唤小亮。

"没有啊，大，等我再找找……"小亮不由得骗了父亲。

他准备爬出去，他想告诉父亲，无论怎么找也找不到第六只羊了。这样想着，小亮就开始向外面爬。他爬出洞口，正准备抬起头和父亲讲话的当儿，父亲的斧头迎头向他砸来。

小亮也像那五只羊一样，还没来得及叫一声，甚至还没来得及抬起他的头，就一头扑倒在地上。

参考译文

The Sixth Sheep

Xin Yi

It was midnight in autumn, and the air in the mountains was dry and cold. The mountains, trees and serpentine roads were all shrouded in darkness. Looking up one could barely discern a single star; looking down one could hardly even see his own feet. A motorized tricycle was running along the mountain road, its dazzling headlights shooting past like a stream of meteors and then being swallowed up by the night.

On the tricycle were two men: Dahei and his son Xiaoliang.

Sitting beside his father, Xiaoliang curled himself up for warmth. But no matter how hard he tried to wrap himself up with his arms, the cold still found its way to his bones through every penetrable space. Before they set out, he had tried to stop his father, saying: "Dad, it's so dark and cold, let's not go!"

Driving the car excitedly, Dahei thought to himself: How come my son doesn't

take after me? Why does he fear the dark and the cold? The darker and colder it is, the safer we'll be. Nobody will notice us.

Xiaoliang was only 15, too young to say no to his father, the provider of his food and clothing all these years. He had to wait a few more years till he could go out to earn his own bread in the city he had dreamed of. Only then would he become strong enough to free himself of his father's control and thus no longer be driven into theft.

The thought that he no longer needed to partner with an outsider made Dahei flutter with joy. To hunt a tiger, we need a team of blood brothers; and to go into a battle, better let a father fight side by side with his own son. This not only ensures trust and loyalty, but also means that they don't have to share the spoils with anyone else. Speaking of his son, he thought, practice would in time make him bolder and more skillful.

Having thoroughly spied it out during the day, Dahei knew the location very well. He parked his car in a hidden corner, and then told his son: "Son, I'll make a hole in the stone wall of the sheepfold. Your job is simple, to drive out the sheep, one at a time. There are altogether six of them. Remember, six."

Silently, Xiaoliang squatted down beside his father, listening to him prizing out the stones. The noise was kept to a minimum, only discernable by the two of them. Yet, the stones thus taken off fell heavily on Xiaoliang's tensed-up nerves, sending spasms of pain to his heart. "Altogether six sheep! When their master wakes up tomorrow morning only to discover his carefully-tended sheep are all missing, how will he cry!" When he was younger, he recalled, he used to cry over every sheep his parents sold out or butchered. Now he pulled at his father, murmuring, "Dad, let's go home!"

Though the stones were quite heavy, Dahei handled them with ease and skill: after all, he was an old hand at this kind of thing. With each piece of stone pulled out of the wall, he was an inch closer to the six sheep. He felt a surge of gleeful satisfaction.

"Son, what are you so afraid of? No one's going to see us in such wretched weather!" Dahei whispered, loud enough only to let his son hear.

"OK, now get in there!" Dahei urged, shielding Xiaoliang's head and back with his hands, and finally giving him a few encouraging pats on his buttocks.

However, his protection was not at all necessary, for the hole was large enough for a sheep to walk through, and Xiaoliang in a crawling position was no higher than a sheep standing.

A gust of cold wind followed in the wake of Xiaoliang. He groped for the sheep, and soon found them, huddling together in a corner to keep out the bitter cold. He caressed the head, back and rump of a sheep, the way his father did to him. He moved even closer and joined their circle, his body warmed up by theirs.

At this moment, he forgot what he was there for, as if he had become one of the sheep. How could he be so cruel to do any harm to them!

"Have you found them? Quickly!" his father's voice came in through the hole, like another gust of cold wind.

The sheep, which now gave him so much warmth, would soon become the helpless victims of his father's axe. That would be too cruel, too inhuman! "This is the first and the last time I'll do it, I won't do it again even if he kills me!" he said to himself. Xiaoliang began to drive the sheep out one by one, knowing that when their heads popped out of the hole, his father's axe would fall down before they could even let out a final cry.

He tenderly caressed the sheep, their heads, backs, rumps and even their tails. With each of them being pushed out of the hole, the part of warmth it had given him through body contact was also gone.

One, two, three, four, five, until there remained only the last one. Before he reached out for the corner, the sixth sheep, in utter despair, had already moved toward him.

Xiaoliang became more sympathetic, murmuring, "You don't know what's happening, do you? Ah, you must be quite young, as innocent as I am. If you knew it was me who helped murder your fellows, you'd probably kill me with your horns!" Half squatted, Xiaoliang held the sheep's neck with one hand, and with his other hand stroked it all over, which it responded to by rubbing its face against his. He felt an itchy and warm sensation on his face, while at the same time tears ran down the gap between their faces.

"Quickly! Haven't you found the last one yet?" Dahei pressed him.

"Not yet, I'm looking, just wait…" Xiaoliang had no choice but to lie.

He wanted to crawl out and tell his father that he couldn't find the sixth sheep. With this thought, he began to move toward the hole. Just as he was about to put his head out and utter something, his father's axe dropped down upon his neck.

Like the other five sheep, Xiaoliang flopped onto the ground without so much as a cry, not even having the chance to look up at his father.

思考

1. 这部分信息的顺序在译文中有所颠倒。
2. 这一段心里活动在译文中另起一段，用一般现在时译出。
3. 这一部分译作一般现在时，其中的汉语熟语采用直译法。
4. 译文对这句话的语义有所变通。
5. 这句话的译文强调了一个细节，一次赶出一只羊，以和下文的故事情节发展更好地呼应。
6. 译文根据语境对有关细节作了增译，即增加了 fell heavily on Xiaoliang's tensed-up nerves 这部分信息。
7. 这里的心里活动译作直接引语。
8. 原文信息在译文中有所颠倒，"心里也感觉越来越轻快"不宜译作 his heart lightened 或 he felt relaxed 之类。译文根据故事情节，将其译为"心中顿生一种损人利己的满足感"之意。
9. "心软"不宜译作 his heart softened。此处要根据上下文理解和确定词义。
10. "和我一样年轻"不宜译作 as young as I am。

【练习三】

我和锁三儿的编年史

罗永常

我和锁三儿出生在牛蹄凸，是同年同月不同日的同庚。我们打小在一起玩耍，就如一对不脱坨的连体油盐罐儿。[1]

4岁那年,老天爷非要和锁三儿过不去:他年轻力壮的爹在一次排除哑炮[2]的事故中丢了命,不久,他那漂亮的妈妈又改嫁他人,把他扔给年迈的爷爷彻底抛了野,基本上是吃了上顿愁下顿。而我,爸是乡里的干部,妈妈是乡村教师,从小衣食无忧,而且受到良好教育。

6岁那年我和锁三儿一起入小学。妈妈把我打扮得干净整洁,而且能熟背唐宋诗词三百首,会做一千以内的加减法,口齿清晰,思维敏捷,[3]老师拍着我的头笑着对妈妈说:"这伢子今后肯定有出息呢。"而锁三儿呢,从头到脚脏兮兮的,老师提问他是一问三摇头,神情木然,语无伦次。老师的眉头,看着看着就皱了起来。

11岁那年,我的作文《一个好学生》在全省小学生作文大赛中获奖,老师陪我上省城领奖,还奖赏我游览了动物园和海底世界。也就在那一天,锁三儿趁老师外出逃了学,翻墙进入某阀门厂偷窃废铜废铁,当场被抓,挨了保安一顿饱揍。

13岁那年,我爸在文苑宾馆为我设宴,庆贺我在中学生奥数比赛中喜获大奖。而此时,锁三儿那年迈的爷爷,却正跪在一位同学的家长面前,乞求饶恕他那年幼不懂事的孙子。因锁三打群架,把一位同学的左眼睑打伤,缝了6针。

14岁那年,或许是女生早熟吧,校花白云朵悄悄给我递纸条,读得我脸上火辣辣的,心里甜滋滋的。但我还是口不对心地劝她:"我们还小,正是学习的大好时光咧。"羞得白云朵脸蛋儿红得如那醉了酒的桃花瓣儿。可笑的是,锁三儿也狗胆包天地给白云朵递条子,白云朵毫不客气地送他俩卫生球:"咯讨厌的癞蛤蟆!"当场把纸条交给了老师。校长看了那狗屁不通而又令人肉麻的纸条,简直气炸了肺,很坚决地说:别让一粒老鼠屎搅坏一锅汤!于是,锁三儿被赶出了校门。

19岁那年,我和白云朵考上了同一所大学。我不仅被选为班长、学生会主席,而且还和白云朵谈上了恋爱。真是才子配佳人,花前月下,情深深,意浓浓啊。[4]锁三儿呢,先是倒腾廉价衣服、走私电子手表,后来竟然承包起工程来了。当然,他承包的尽是些维修厕所、粪池、烟囱一类没人干的脏活儿或险活儿。

25岁我大学毕业,揣着文凭和个人简历,穿梭于各个人才市场拼命地推销自己。白云朵见我穷得连买碗米线的钱都没有,便悄然离去。金钱是基础,没有金钱,什么狗屁爱情也没有!

同年七月,我从晚报上发现一则消息,金锁房地产公司招聘一名高管。僧多粥少，我本不报多少希望，但最后抱着去试试的心态，还是去了。当我跨进大厅，见一肥头阔耳的胖家伙正在那儿指指戳戳，我眼前不禁陡然一亮：他不是小时候和咱连体的那只油盐罐吗？锁三儿那阔绰潇洒的劲儿给人一种脱胎换骨的感觉[5]！我急忙奔过去，紧紧攥住他的手——就像溺水人抓住了一根救命稻草，迭声道："锁……不、不，邓……邓总！""林子，你就叫咱小名吧，还亲切些呢。"锁三儿望着我看了又看，便说："如果林子不嫌弃，就来金锁公司咱们一起干吧！"这样，我就成了金锁的一名高管。锁三儿对我不薄，给我开了五千的月薪。而且后来我才知道，白云朵离开我后，就悄然投奔[6]锁三儿来了。锁三儿还算仗义，说，"朋友之妻不可夺！"白云朵没脸再回到我身边，就蒙羞去了深圳……

　　27岁春，由于我面对兴旺发达的锁三儿无地自容，嗟来之食的自卑感时不时地折磨着我，工作起来也挺别扭，[7]所以我毅然辞职。之后，找了半年的工作，几乎碰得头破血流。人活在世上总要吃饭穿衣吧，出于万般无奈，我先是推销婴儿奶粉和高山云雾茶。三氯氰胺事件后，我只好改行推销洗发水、洗发膏之类的妇女用品，为满足最低的生活需求，我成天蹬着破三轮满大街疯跑[8]。而腰包鼓了的锁三儿呢，竟然行起了善事，资助贫困学生呀，给孤寡老人拜年呀，慷慨解囊支援办学呀[9]，很快成为民营企业家的楷模，被推为省政协委员，本届政协又安排他做了常委……于是，他开着香车宝马，经常出入党政首脑机关和高档娱乐场所。

　　30岁秋，家乡的中学举办校庆。我和锁三儿应邀回校。我被安排在一个极不显眼的角落里，而锁三儿却在县长、校长的陪同下，端坐在主席台前排，昂首挺胸，神气活现。而且他当场表态：为支持家乡的教育事业，捐款一百万！一时，台上台下欢声雷动。一位大爷指着台上的锁三儿教育小孙子说："你要向台上那位伯伯学习，白手起家，富甲一方，连咱们学校都跟着沾光咧。"继而，又指着蜷缩在角落里的我："千万莫学那个人，读了那么多的书，连自己都养不活哩。"

　　这狗日的命运[10]！我望着台上志得意满的锁三儿，心里恶狠狠地骂：你别太得意，哼，说不定一过三十咱也会时来运转呢！

参考译文

A Chronicle of Suosan and Me

Luo Yongchang

We were born in the same month of the same year in the same village. In our childhood we were intimate playmates, and we resembled each other as much as twin brothers.

When he was 4, misfortune struck. His father, young and robust, was killed in an attempt to clear dud explosives. And later his mother, pretty and charming, got remarried, leaving him to his old grandfather, who barely managed to scrape by from meal to meal, to say nothing of giving him much care. In contrast, my father was a township official, and my mother a village teacher, so I was well-fed and clothed, and received a good family education.

At the age of 6, we went to the same primary school. My mother dressed me up decently and brought me to the teacher. Young as I was, I could already recite poems of the Tang and Song dynasties and do addition and subtraction of numbers under 1,000, clear proof that I was exceptionally articulate and quick-minded for my age. The teacher patted me on the head and said to my mother, smiling, "What a promising child!" But look at Suosan! Covered with dirt from head to toe, he was such a miserable sight. In response to the teacher's questions, he either shook his head perplexedly or murmured something incoherent. Fixing him with a long gaze, the teacher knitted his eyebrows.

At the age of 11, I entered my name for the provincial primary school essay writing contest with an article entitled *A Good Student*, and won a prize. My teacher took me to the provincial capital to attend the prize-giving ceremony, also taking me to the zoo and the oceanarium as a special treat. The same day, taking advantage of the teacher's absence from school, Suosan played truant. He jumped over the wall of a valve factory and stole some iron and copper scraps. Caught red-handed, he was beaten black and blue by the factory guards.

Then, when I was 13, my father hosted a banquet at the Wenyuan Hotel in

celebration of a big prize I'd won in the Olympic Maths Contest, while at the same time, Suosan's grandfather was kneeling before the parents of one of our classmates, begging them to forgive his good-for-nothing grandson, who had been involved in a brawl and badly hurt the boy on his left eyelid, leaving a wound sewed up with 6 stitches.

When we reached the age of 14, our school beauty White Cloud, perhaps because girls mature earlier than boys, slipped me a love note. Reading the words on it, I felt my cheeks glowing and a sweetness in my heart. But I hypocritically answered her, "We're still young, best to concentrate on our studies." White Cloud blushed, her cheeks as red as drunk peach flower petals. Ridiculously, Suosan was even brazen enough to try handing a note to the girl. Staring at him in disdain, she jeered, "You dirty toad! " and handed the note straight to the teacher, who submitted it to the headmaster. Reading through the lines of nauseating drivel, the headmaster was enraged, proclaiming decisively, "We cannot let one obnoxious little brat spoil the good name of the whole school!" And thus Suosan was expelled.

When we were 19, White Cloud and I enrolled into the same university. Soon afterwards I was elected monitor of the class and chairman of the Students' Union, and we fell in love. You see, I was a rising scholar and she a classical beauty. What a perfect match! Many a moonlit night saw us sauntering along the flower-flanked paths, exchanging words of love and affection. During the same period, Suosan began to trade in cheap garments and smuggle electronic watches. Later he even went so far as to undertake small-scale construction projects, of course, only those messy and risky ones like refitting a public latrine, a manure pit, or a chimney.

At the age of 25 I graduated and began to search for work. With my diploma and CV, I ran around from one job market to another, doing my best to sell myself. For a while, I was so hard up I couldn't even afford a bowl of rice noodles. Seeing my plight, White Cloud left me without so much as a word of goodbye. Money is the basis of love, without money any talk of love is just bullshit!

In July the same year, I saw an ad in an evening newspaper: The Jinsuo Real Estate Company was seeking a senior manager. I knew it would be a much-coveted job and my chances were slim. But with an attitude of just trying my luck, I finally decided to go for it. In the lobby a fat man was ordering people around with dramatic gestures. My eyes brightened up. Wasn't this my childhood companion Suosan? He had completely changed: so confident, so dignified! I hastened my steps toward him, taking his hands in mine as a drowning man might grab at a straw. I blurted out, "Suosan, no, sorry…Manager Deng…" "Better to call me by my pet name. That will sound more intimate." He looked me up and down and continued, "If you can put up with me, join my company. We can work together." So I became a manager under Suosan, and he generously paid me 5,000 yuan per month. Later I learned that White Cloud, after leaving me, went to Suosan for emotional comfort but was given the cold shoulder. Suosan adhered to the traditional principle that a gentleman should never covet the woman of his friend. Crestfallen, White Cloud went to Shenzhen alone.

Through the spring when we were both 27, Suosan's business continued to prosper, while my sense of shame and inferiority grew ever stronger: the high-salaried job was obviously a handout and I always felt out of place in the office. Eventually, I resolved to resign, and my second round of job hunting began. In the following six months, I met with rebuffs everywhere I went. Bogged down with financial troubles, I had no choice but to start to peddle such products as baby milk powder and Mountain Cloud green tea, which after the Sanlu poisonous milk powder scandal were replaced by women's products such as shampoo and cosmetics. Barely eking out a living, each day I loaded my goods onto a tricycle and spent hour after hour slogging around the streets of the town. In the meantime, however, Suosan, having money to burn, began to donate to charity. His donations went to needy students, old people and schools. Held up as a model example for private business owners, he was first elected as a member of the provincial Political Consultative Committee and then swiftly appointed to its standing committee. Driving his luxurious limousine, he frequented the leading organs of the Party and government, and could be found at all the top-end clubs.

Once we reached 30, the middle school in our hometown invited both of us to its anniversary celebration. I was arranged to sit in an inconspicuous corner, while Suosan, accompanied by the county magistrate and the headmaster, sat in the front row on the platform, his head held high and his eyes shining. He declared then and there that to promote the educational development of his hometown he would donate a million yuan to the school. Immediately there was a burst of applause and cheers. An old man, pointing at Suosan, instructed his grandson, "That uncle there has set you a fine example. He started from scratch and now is the wealthiest man in our county, even our school benefits from his success." He then turned to look at me and continued, "Don't be like him. He can't even support himself despite all the books he's read."

What had I done to deserve such a fate? Staring at the triumphant Suosan, I cursed viciously under my breath, "Ha! Don't be so arrogant! Who's to say that my luck will not change now I've turned 30?"

思考

1. 地名"牛蹄凸"似无特别含义，略去未译。比喻"一对不脱砣的连体油盐罐儿"略去形象，只保留其意。
2. 军事上的哑炮可译作 unexploded munitions/mines 之类，此处应指工程中使用的炸药。
3. 此处译文加进了 and brought me to the teacher 和 clear proof that… 等词语，以使文气连贯。
4. 译文对此句信息进行了重新组合，句式按行文需要灵活安排。
5. 注意译文对英语句式的灵活运用。
6. "投奔"一词译得更为具体——"寻找感情上的慰藉"。
7. 译文对原文信息进行了重新梳理，按英语行文需要构句。
8. 译文补充了语境中存在的细节。
9. 这几件善事在译文中的表述有所简化。
10. 译文表达视角有所变通。

第二节 描写语篇

【练习一】

写给生命

席慕蓉

我站在月亮底下画铅笔速写。

月亮好亮,我就站在田野的中间用黑色和褐色的铅笔交替地描绘着。

最先要画下的是远处那一排参差的树影,用极重极深的黑来画出它们浓密的枝叶。

在树下是慢慢绵延过来的阡陌,田里种的是番薯,在月光下有着一种浅淡而又细致的光泽[1]。整个天空没有一片云,只有月色和星斗。我能认出来的是猎人星座[2],就在我的前方,在月亮下面闪耀着,天空的颜色透明又洁净,一如这夜里整个田野的气息。

月亮好亮,在我的速写本上反映出一层柔白的光辉来,所有粗略和精密的线条都因此能看得更加清楚,我站在田里[3],慢慢地一笔一笔地画着,心里很安定也很安静。

家就在十几二十步之外,孩子们都已经做完了功课上床睡觉了,丈夫正在他的灯下写他永远写不完的功课,而我呢?我决定我今天晚上的功课要在月亮底下做。[4]

邻家的狗过来看一看,知道是我之后也就释然了,在周围巡视了几圈之后,干脆就在我的脚旁睡了下来。我家的小狗反倒[5]很不安,不明白我为什么不肯回家,所以它就一会儿跑回去一会儿又跑过来的,在番薯的茎叶间不停地拨弄出细细碎碎的声音。乡间的夜出奇的安静,邻居们都习惯早睡,偶尔有夜归的行人也只是从田野旁边那条小路远远经过,有时候会咳嗽一声,声音从月色里传过来也变得比较轻柔。

多好的月色啊!满月的光辉浸润着整块土地,土地上一切的生命都有了一种在白昼时从来也想象不出的颜色。这样美丽的世界就在我的眼前,既不虚幻也非

梦境，只是让人无法置信⁶。

所以，我想，等我把这些速写的稿子整理好，在画布上画出了这种月色⁷之后，恐怕也有一些人会认为我所描绘的是一种虚无的美吧。

我一面画一面禁不住微笑了起来。风从田野那头吹过，在竹林间来回穿梭，月是更高更圆了，整个夜空澄澈无比⁸。

生命里也应该有这样一种澄澈的时刻吧？可以什么也不想什么也不希望，只是一笔一笔慢慢地描摹，在月亮底下，安静地做我自己该做的功课⁹。

参考译文

Notes to Life

Xi Murong

I was standing in the moonlight, to make a pencil sketch.

The moon shone brightly. I took my position in the fields and began by using my black and brown pencils alternately.

First, I drew the distant trees, a row of dark shadows, jagged and uneven. I used heavy black shades to depict their dense foliage.

From under the trees a footpath meandered its way to where I was standing, and here around my feet grew patches of sweet potatoes, their leaves glossed with a delicate silvery hue in the moonlight. Without a single wisp of cloud in the sky, the world was filled with the light of the moon and stars. Among them I could easily identify Orion the Hunter, which was twinkling just in front of my eyes. The color of the sky was as clear and crisp as the smell of the country at night.

The moon shone brightly. It cast a film of soft white light over my sketch book, enabling me to see the strokes, both bold and subtle, more clearly. I sketched leisurely, one stroke and then another, feeling quiet and calm.

Ten or twenty yards away was my house, where the children had gone to bed after finishing their homework while under a lamp my husband was doing his work which, it seemed to me, he would never finish. And here in the fields, I had decided to do my job in the company of the moon.

My neighbor's dog trotted along to have a look. Having recognized me, he relaxed his vigilance, but still continued to make a few rounds of patrol before finally settling down at my feet. Strange enough, it was our own dog who was the more upset, perhaps wondering why I was reluctant to go home. She shuttled back and forth between me and my house, her legs rustling through the potato stems and leaves in the fields. The rustic scene was exceptionally quiet: the neighbors were already in bed as usual, and although a shadowy figure or two might be seen hurrying homeward, they were quite a distance from me on the path across the field; even their occasional coughs took on a hushed tone.

Oh, what a full moon! Her brilliance spilled over the vast expanse of ground, giving everything living on the land a different color unimaginable in daytime. A world of charm presented itself before my eyes, neither a hallucination nor a dream, yet still beyond description.

Thus, I think, when I have finished sorting out my sketches and captured the moonlit country scene on my canvas, might not someone also view my painting as depicting a sort of illusory beauty?

A smile spread involuntarily across my face as I drew. A breath of wind rose from the other side of the field and whistled through in the bamboo grove. The moon was now higher and looked fuller, transforming the night sky into a world as limpid as living water.

Shouldn't every life have moments of clarity like this? Moments in which you don't have to think of or hope for anything, but only concentrate on penciling a sketch, stroke by stroke, under the moon, doing what you are supposed to do in utter tranquility.

思考

1. "光泽"翻译为 gloss，意为 to put a substance on something to make it look shiny。
2. "猎人星座"或只译作 Orion。
3. 此处略去未译，以免重复。
4. 此句有三个"功课"，英语中不宜都译为 homework。

103

5. "反倒"的语气通过 strange enough, it was... 再现。
6. 此处未译作 unbelievable 或 beyond belief，而是译为 beyond description，即无法用语言描述，恐怕只能用画笔来再现了。
7. 译文 capture something on canvas，即在画布上画下来的意思。
8. 此处译文添加了 living water 的比喻形象，意在使译文更生动。
9. 译文用了第二人称，有助于营造一种与读者交流的氛围。

【练习二】

离太阳最近的树

毕淑敏

30年前，我在西藏阿里当兵。

这是世界的第三极，平均海拔5000米，冰峰林立，雪原寥寂。不知是神灵的佑护还是大自然的疏忽[1]，在荒漠的褶皱里，有时会不可思议地生存着一片红柳丛。它们有着铁一样锈红的枝干，凤羽般纷披的碎叶，偶尔会开出穗样细密的花，对着高原的酷热和缺氧微笑。这高原的精灵，是离太阳最近的绿树，百年才能长成小小的一蓬。在藏区巡回医疗，我骑马穿行于略带苍蓝色调的红柳丛中，竟以为它必与雪域永在。

一天，司务长布置任务——全体打柴去！

我以为自己听错[2]了，高原之上，哪里有柴？！

原来是[3]驱车上百公里，把红柳挖出来，当柴火烧。

我大惊，说红柳挖了，高原上仅有的树不就绝了吗？

司务长回答，你要吃饭，对不对？饭要烧熟，对不对？烧熟要用柴火，对不对？柴火就是红柳，对不对？[4]

我说，红柳不是柴火，它是活的，它有生命。做饭可以用汽油，可以用焦炭，为什么要用高原上唯一的绿色！

司务长说，拉一车汽油上山，路上就要耗掉两车汽油。焦灰炭运上来，一斤的价钱等于六斤白面。红柳[5]是不要钱的，你算算这个账吧！

挖红柳的队伍，带着铁锹、镐头和斧，浩浩荡荡地出发了。

红柳通常都是长在沙丘上的。一座结实的沙丘顶上，昂然立着一株红柳。它的根像巨大的章鱼的无数脚爪，缠附到沙丘逶迤的边缘。

我很奇怪，红柳为什么不找个背风的地方猫着呢？生存中也好少些艰辛。老兵说，你本末倒置了，不是红柳在沙丘上，是因为了这红柳，才固住了流沙。[6] 随着红柳渐渐长大，流沙被固住的越来越多，最后便聚成了一座沙山。红柳的根有多广，那沙山就有多大。

啊，红柳如同冰山。露在沙上的部分只有十分之一，伟大的力量[7]埋在地下。

红柳的枝叶算不得好柴薪，真正顽强的是红柳强大的根系，它们与沙子黏结得如同钢筋混凝土。一旦燃烧起来，持续而稳定地吐出熊熊的热量，好像把千万年来，从太阳那里索得的光芒，压缩后爆裂出来[8]。金红的火焰中，每一块红柳根，都弥久地维持着盘根错节的形状，好像傲然不屈的英魂。

把红柳根从沙丘中掘出，蓄含着很可怕的工作量。红柳与土地生死相依，人们要先费几天的时间，将大半个沙山掏净。这样，红柳就枝丫遒劲地腾越在旷野之上，好似一副镂空的恐龙骨架。这里需请来最有气力的男子汉[9]，用利斧，将这活着的巨型根雕与大地最后的联系一一斩断。整个红柳丛就訇然倒下了。

一年年过去，易挖的红柳绝迹了，只剩那些最古老的树精了。

掏挖沙山的工期越来越长，最健硕有力的小伙子，也折不断红柳苍老的手臂了[10]。于是人们想出了高技术的法子——用炸药！

只需在红柳根部，挖一条深深的巷子，用架子把火药放进去，人伏得远远的，将长长的药捻点燃。深远的寂静之后，只听轰的一声，再幽深[11]的树怪，也尸骸散地了。

我们餐风宿露。今年可以看到去年被掘走红柳的沙丘，好像眼球摘除术的伤员，依然大睁着空洞的眼睑，怒向苍穹。但这触目惊心的景象不会持续太久，待到第三年，那沙丘已烟消云散，好像此地从来不曾生存过什么千年古木，不曾堆聚过亿万颗沙砾。

听最近到过阿里的人讲，红柳林早已掘净烧光，连根须都烟消灰灭了。

有时深夜，我会突然想起那些高原上的原住民，它们的魂魄，如今栖息在何处云端？会想到那些曾经被固住的黄沙，是否已飘洒在世界各处？从屋子顶上扬起的尘沙，通常会飞得十分遥远。

参考译文

The Trees Closest to the Sun

Bi Shumin

Thirty years ago I served in the army in Ali, Tibet.

With an average elevation of 5,000 meters, this area is known as the Third Pole of the earth. Here, ice-covered peaks rise like forests above a vast stretch of deserted snow fields. Either blessed by God or spared by Nature, clusters of Chinese tamarisk trees had impossibly managed to survive in the folds of the valley, their stems and branches having the color of rusty iron and their leaves spreading out like soft feathers. Occasionally they produce dense tiny flowers crowded into the shape of rice ears, beaming in spite of the heat and thin air on the plateau. Symbolizing the spirit of the plateau, they are the closest to the sun of all green tree species. It takes a whole century for them to grow into a small cluster. Riding on my horse through the grayish tamarisk trees on my medical-service rounds, I was even convinced that they would exist as long as the snow-covered plateau itself.

One day, our company quartermaster ordered all of us to go to cut firewood.

At first I thought I'd misheard him. Where on this plateau could we find firewood?

The answer was that we would drive a hundred kilometers to some tamarisk trees, dig them out and carry them back as kitchen fuel.

I was shocked, "Aren't we going to kill off the only trees on the plateau?"

The quartermaster retorted, "You need to eat, right? Food needs to be cooked, right? To cook we need firewood, and the only firewood is tamarisk, OK?"

I said, "Tamarisk trees are not firewood. They are living. They have a life. We can use gasoline or coke. Why do we have to wipe out the only green color from the plateau?"

He explained, "To haul a truckload of oil up to our place, we burn two truckloads of oil on the road; for a jin of coke, we pay the price of 6 jin of wheat flour; and tamarisk is free of charge. You do the math!"

The soldiers took up their spades, picks and axes, and a large tamarisk-digging contingent set out.

Tamarisks usually grow on sand dunes. On top of a solid sand dune there may stand a proud tamarisk tree, whose roots, like the many tentacles of an octopus, extend all the way to the serrated edges of the dune.

I wonder why the tamarisk trees do not grow on the leeward side of the dunes to avoid the many setbacks of life. A veteran soldier said I put the cart before the horse. It is not that the trees choose to grow on top of the dunes, but that the trees fix the sand to cause a build-up of dunes. With the growth of the trees more drifting sand is fixed, and finally a big sand dune is formed. The wider their roots spread the bigger the dune can be.

Ah, the tamarisk tree is just like an iceberg. Above the sand we see only one tenth of it while a mammoth amount of strength lies underneath.

The branches and leaves of tamarisk do not make good firewood, while its roots are strong and tenacious, and can join sand grains into a cohesive whole as hard as concrete. When lit up, they burn steadily to produce a huge amount of energy, as if releasing in an eruptive manner all the radiation they've exacted from the sun over the past millennia. Even in the burning flames, the blocks of roots, like dauntless heroic spirits, still manage to stay in their intertwined shapes.

To dig out the roots called for a terrifying amount of work. The tamarisk trees and the land had long formed an inextricable relationship. We had to spend days scooping most of the sand out of a dune, thus leaving the dinosaur-skeleton frame of the tree standing there with its bare roots over the open wilderness. Then men of Herculean strength were summoned. Wielding sharp axes they hacked continuously at the roots, a living tree-root sculpture, until these last links with the earth were severed and the whole tree toppled down.

The years passed. All the tamarisk trees in sight were dug out except those most aged ones.

The digging job took even longer, for even the strongest men were no match for the unyielding stems and roots. So we resorted to a modern technique—break them with explosives!

A tunnel was dug to the root area. Having put the explosives in place, we ignited the long fuse and lay down at a safe distance. After a moment of dead silence, there was a loud bang. Even the most weather-beaten tree would be blown up into the sky and fall down in pieces.

We camped out in the open. We saw on some sand dunes large hollows, left by the sand-fixing tamarisk trees which had been pulled out the previous year. The gaping holes looked like the eyeless sockets of a wounded face staring angrily at the sky. However, this heart-rending scene would not last long: two years later even the dunes themselves would disappear. It is as if there never had been a tree that had survived the hardships over thousands of years and fixed a large heap of sand.

I was told by someone who has recently been to Ali that the tamarisk trees are no longer to be found there, their stems, roots, leaves and everything of them have vanished in fire and smoke.

Sometimes in the depth of night the images of the aboriginal inhabitants of the highlands would pop into my head: where in the clouds are their spirits anchored now? I also think of the sand dunes once fixed firmly by the trees: have they been blown to all corners of the world? Indeed, the sand grains on our roofs can be carried far and wide on the wind.

思考

1. "疏忽"在此处并非 neglect（= not to give enough attention）之意，而指严酷的自然环境似乎独独放过了红柳树，竟然使它得以存活，即 spare（= to allow sth. to escape harm, damage or death）。
2. 或译 为 my ears had deceived me。
3. "原来是"承上句起衔接作用，译文用 The answer was... 承接上文的问句，有同样作用。
4. 这一系列的反问句，译文试图用两个 right 和一个 OK 来再现原文的语气。
5. 英语中红柳树用 tamarisk 是可数的，可以说 tamarisks 或 tamarisk trees，此处用单数指砍下的红柳树木材。
6. 注意这一部分的英译使用了 it is not that..., but that... 句式。
7. 译文中 mammoth 用作形容词，意为 extremely large。

8. 译文中的 in an eruptive manner 意为"如（火山）喷发般地"，对应原文"压缩后爆裂出来"。
9. Hercules 是希腊神话中的大力神，Herculean strength 即"力大无比"之意。
10. 这部分译为 ...no match for...，即"不是……的对手"的意思。
11. "幽深"根据语境译为 weather-beaten，即"饱经风霜的"。

第三节 说 明 语 篇

【练习一】

杞 人 忧 天[1]

吴冠中

"破四旧"[2]期间，我患牙病，医生说臼齿磨损厉害，建议做套，罩住臼齿；套最好用金制，因金的硬度最适合与牙结合，且耐久。我觉得金牙太丑，医生说那是臼齿上的罩，根本看不见。于是决定用金。但哪里去找金？当时金子不是商品，且禁止买卖，"破四旧"将家家户户的金银珠宝抄尽，民间已与黄金绝缘。

幸而，我的一位入了泰国籍[3]的老同窗要返国探亲，他便特意戴了一个大大的金戒指解决了我的治牙问题[4]。感谢医生的精心设计、制作[5]，这金牙罩保护了我的病牙，让我平安度过了能吃食的几十个春秋，以为一劳永逸了。然而，竟然发现它日渐耗损，金子也衰老了！今天金子不稀罕，但那一只假牙确是我半辈子的保卫者，而它却比我先坏，令人感伤。世间没有一劳永逸的安全。但人们竭力追求永逸和永恒，筑长城、造金字塔、建地下宫……都为了保护权力及掌权者的尸身不朽，待复活。

木、石、钢铁……一切的一切都抗不住岁月的销蚀，地震、海啸，大宇宙一次次嘲弄人类的渺小。恐龙的绝灭，庞贝的遗址，早揭示了人类及任何生物

都挡不住宇宙之变幻。聪明的人类用科学来自救,为救自身却又加速毁灭自身,首先,自身的超量繁殖早已泛滥成灾。毁灭与再生是不可抗拒的规律,人类永远探不尽宇宙之谜。夏夜,满天美丽的星星,老祖母为此讲的故事依旧没变,牛郎织女永葆青春,鹊桥也永不断裂⁶。然而,老祖母不知遥远的微小星星可能是大大的太阳,或大于太阳,我们的太阳也并不因后羿⁷已死去而永远安逸。人类发觉必须保护地球的体温了,但谁又能阻止又一次冰河期或火山期的爆发。到木星去,也只才出得庭前三五步⁸。杞人真超前,他预感忧天,是神异的先知者。

一个假牙的消蚀,等同地球的变质,暗示宇宙的颤栗。人类的苦难还在后头,唯望科学救命,人之族天长地久!

参考译文

My Worries: Are They Justified?

Wu Guanzhong

During the early years of the Cultural Revolution, I had a tooth problem. The dentist told me one of my molars was badly decayed and suggested I have a crown fitted, most preferably a gold one, because the hardness of gold is similar to that of enamel and would fit in well. I was afraid it would look ugly. However, the dentist assured me that nobody would see it since it was on one of the back teeth. So gold was chosen as the material, but where to find the precious metal at that time of political turmoil? Gold transaction was then forbidden on the market. And to make things worse, gold products along with jewelry were all being searched and looted by the Red Guards in the "Destruction of the Four Olds" campaign ①. No one in mainland China had access to even a single ounce of gold.

Fortunately, an old classmate of mine, a Thai-Chinese, was planning a trip home and promised to bring me a gold ring by wearing it on his finger when going through customs. That really was an ingenious solution to my tooth crowning problem! Using the melted gold as raw material the doctor prepared the crown with great care and superb skill. Protected by the well-fit crown, I was able to eat and chew with much ease for several decades. I thought the crown would keep good forever, but, to my dismay, gold too proved to be subject to wear and tear like all other things. Now gold is no longer a rarity, but back at that time gold was very hard to get and the gold ring-turned-crown was meant to save me from dental trouble for the rest of my life, so the fact that it was aging even faster than I was actually made me quite sad and sentimental. I came to understand that nothing in this world will last for good. However, people still spare no effort to pursue ease and permanence. The Great Wall, the Pyramids, the underground palaces, all these were built in an attempt to eternalize power or to preserve corpses until they can be restored to life someday.

Wood, stone, iron and steel, none of them can resist the erosion of time; earthquakes, tsunami and other natural disasters time and again mock the insignificance of mankind. The extinction of the dinosaurs, the tragic fate of Pompeii, all these are evidence that neither men nor animals can fend off the changes of the universe. To save themselves, man cleverly resorts to science, yet in doing so they only speed up the process of self-destruction. To top it all, over-multiplication of the human species has already brought disastrous consequences. Destruction and regeneration are irresistible laws of Nature, and the universe still remains a myth to men no matter how hard they endeavor to explore into it. Looking up at the beautiful stars on a summer night, grandmothers have long been telling the same story about the Cowherd and the Weaving Maid②: their romance has always remained fresh and the magpies have never failed to build a bridge for their yearly meeting. But grandmothers don't know the tiny stars in the distant sky may turn out to be as large as or even larger than the sun, and that our sun will not shine steadily for ever, even though Houyi③ is long dead. Mankind has realized that we must keep the earth's temperature from rising, but who can prevent a volcano from erupting again or stop the coming of another glacial period? Even if we can flee to Jupiter, we're still not very far away from danger, like only being a few yards from a falling house. In a Chinese legend, someone in the State of Qi feared that the sky would someday fall. That man, to me, is a wise prophet having the presentiment that Nature may spell doom to man.

The wearing-away of my tooth crown is a warning sign equal to that of the deterioration of the earth or a tremor of the universe. Disasters we humans have to endure are yet to come. May science provide for our salvation and the human race live as long as the universe lasts!

Notes:

① The campaign to destroy the Four Olds (Old Customs, Old Culture, Old Habits, and Old Ideas) began in Beijing on August 19, 1966, shortly after the launch of the Cultural Revolution. Red Guards searched houses of famous artists, professors and other social celebrities and confiscated what they deemed belonged to the feudal or the bourgeois, including classics, works of art, jewelry, gold and so on.

② In China, Altair and Vega are known as the Star of the Cowherd and the Star of the Weaving Maid respectively. They are legendary lovers separated by the Silvery River (the Milk Way). Every year on July 7 on the Chinese lunar calendar, magpies in heaven will spread their wings to form a bridge so that the lovers can meet each other.

③ A Chinese legend says there used to be ten suns in the sky. Houyi, the god of archery, shot down nine of them and warned the last one to be dutiful.

思考

1. 杞人忧天的故事一般寓意"毫无必要的忧虑",但此文作者反其意而用之:对大自然的忧患意识并非多虑。故有此变通译法。
2. 本段两次提到"破四旧",涉及文革背景,宜作必要注释(见 Note ①)。译文中对相关历史背景亦有简明补译,以帮助读者构建连贯的认知语境。
3. 注意泰籍华人是 Thai-Chinese,而美籍华人却是 Chinese American。
4. 译文在此句后加了一句话,以补全缺失的信息。
5. 这句的译文也加上了 Using…。以上两处增译都是为了使文气更为通畅。
6. 此处也加了译注(见 Note ②)。
7. 译注见 Note ③。
8. 作者的意思是,"离正在变质的地球也没有多远",译文对此作了变通。

第一篇 文学语篇：小说、散文等

【练习二】

家在途中[1]

白岩松

对于我来说，家的概念随着年龄的变化而不断变化。

在童年的时候，家是一声声呼唤。那时的我似乎比今天的孩子拥有更多的自由，放学后不会先在父母面前露面，而是与住的相邻的同学聚在一起，天马行空，玩得天昏地暗，[2]直到炊烟散去[3]，听见父母"喂，回家了，吃饭了"的呼唤才回家，这样的声音伴着我慢慢长大，日复一日，至今仍在我的耳旁回响。

一转眼，童年过去了，当胡须慢慢从嘴角长出，家又成了一个想逃的地方。

书看多了，世界也变大了，一张床小了，父母的叮咛也显得多余了，盼望着什么时候我能拥有自己的天空[4]。后来，穿上了绿色的军装，来到了部队，家又变成了一封封信笺，每次收到信后，是最想家的时候。

走上了工作岗位之后，开始"受伤"，开始在人海中翻腾，开始知道，有些疼痛无法对人说，甚至知心的朋友。于是，重新开始想家。当受了"重伤"时，幻想着能飞到远方的家中，在推开家门的一瞬，让自己泪流满面。此刻，世界很大，而我所需要的，只是家中那种熟悉的味道，那窗前一成不变的风景……

远离母亲，在外省生存，工作之余便有无数个周末无处打发，手中的电话本很厚，从头翻到尾，却没有一个号码是为我此时准备的。这个时候，家又变成了自己要和另外一个人建立的那一个新的小家。

从相识、相恋到相拥，一个平凡的日子里，我拥有了一个平凡的家。此时，家的概念又变了，它是深夜回家时那盏为你点起的灯，是傍晚你看看书我看看电视偶尔交谈几句的那种宁静，是一桌胃口不好时也吃得下的饭菜，是得意忘形可以呼朋唤友可以张口说粗话的地方。[5]

不久前，我成了父亲，我和一个新的生命在家中相逢，一种奇妙的感受充斥我的心，小生命开始让我"玩物丧志"，想挣脱却又那么愿意沉溺其中，[6]一种用幸福来缚住你的力量。

家的概念在不停地变换着，生命在这种变换中匆匆地走着。众多的概念中，家有时也意味着悲伤，比如当年父亲的辞世[7]，便让我知道，世界对你的伤害加

113

在一起有时也不如家中的变故给你的伤害大⁸。然而在家中，你也会感受到一种坚强，比如父亲过世后，柔弱的母亲开始变得坚强，她带着我们哥儿俩，一步一步地从变故中走出，之后，家又重新"站立"了起来，又变得祥和，变得不再阴云密布。在这个过程中，家又像是一种生命力顽强的植物，野火烧不尽，春风吹又生。

生命起步虽久⁹，前路却还遥远。家的概念还会变换，然而我已经知道，家是奔波的意义，只是这家有时是自己的，有时是芸芸众生的。

参考译文

Home: A Changing Concept

Bai Yansong

To me, the concept of home changes continually along with my age.

In my childhood, home was a string of calls. It seems that I was entitled to more freedom than today's children. I didn't have to show up in front of my parents right after school, instead I would go to play with my classmates who lived in the neighborhood. We frolicked like mad until dinner was ready and our parents called "Come back! Come home for supper!" Days passed by as I grew up in the company of those calls. Even now the ringing voices are still echoing in my ears.

In a wink, my childhood was gone. When a thin layer of hair began to grow around the corners of my mouth, home became a place I tried to escape from.

As I read more and more, my world opened up, presenting a broader picture before me. The bed I used to sleep in became too small, and words of care from my parents began to sound superfluous. How I wished I could have a space of my own someday! Later I was enlisted into the army and put on the green uniform. During my service days, home was the series of letters I received one after another. My most homesick moments were when I read those letters from my family.

When I got a job, I began to get "hurt", to rise and fall in a sea of people, and to understand that you can't share all your pains with other people, even with your best friends. So again, another wave of homesickness came over me. When I was badly hurt, I imagined myself flying home on wings. Pushing open the door, I let tears flow down my face. At that moment I felt that as large as the world was, what I needed was only the familiar smell of home and the unchanged view outside the window of my old house…

Struggling for mere existence in a place far from my mother, I was often at a loss what to do after work and on the weekend. Picking up a thick telephone book, I leafed through it from cover to cover but found not a single number I could call. At this time home appeared in my mind as a cozy nest I yearned to build with another person.

From dating to engagement, we finally fell into each other's arms and decided to step into marriage. Thus on an ordinary day we formed an ordinary family. Then the concept of home changed again: it became the light left on for you when you return late at night; the peacefulness in which you occasionally exchange words, one reading a book, the other watching TV; the table of dishes that tempts the most jaded appetite; and a place where you can entertain friends and use foul language when you feel elated.

Not long ago I became a father. When I greeted into my family the birth of a new life, an odd sensation welled up in my heart. The little creature obsessed me so much that though I tried to get rid of it I only found all the more indulging myself with it. That is a kind of force that binds you with a sense of happiness.

The concept of home kept changing as my life hurried along. Among the many definitions I gave to it, there is one which relates to grief. I remember, for instance, how my father's early death led me to understand that all the injuries inflicted by the world added together are sometimes less devastating than a single misfortune in your family. However, you may also feel a kind of strength in your family. After my father's death, my mother, who used to be quiet and gentle, became strong and indomitable. She led my brother and me out of our misery and we got back on our feet again. Tranquility came back to my home, where happiness reigned as before. In retrospect, I can compare home to an unyielding plant: it may be burnt down by wildfire, but it will sprout again when the spring breeze blows.

Although I already have much life experience behind me, I know there is still a long way ahead and my concept of home will go on evolving. But already I have come to see that home is where we can find the true meaning of all the hectic rush of life. What makes the concept different is that sometimes it refers to an individual's home and sometimes to the home of many, many people.

思考

1. 看全文立意，标题的意思是"一个人一生中对家的理解是不断变化的"，故有此译。
2. 此处意译。
3. 实际上城市中已经不见"炊烟"了，估计作者亦非实指，译文对此有所变通。
4. 此句译为感叹句，以增强力度。
5. 译文用 became 引出四个排比结构和原文相应，became 为过去时，指当时的感受，后面排比结构中动词均用一般现在时，因为那是任何时候都会发生的事情。
6. 译文将这两个小句融合在一起重新表述。
7. 此处译文加上 I remember，以增强译文的连贯性。
8. 注意此句不可译为 all the injuries… are sometimes no more devastating than a single misfortune in your family。句式 X was no more devastating than Y 一般用于表达"X 并非那么严重"的意思，如 The injury was no more serious than a bee sting. 那伤也就像给蜜蜂蜇了一下似的。原则上可以用 X was NOT more devastating than Y 句式，但听上去不自然；或可用 X was not as devastating as Y…, 但意义稍有不同：此句式意在比较两者的严重程度，重心不再是 Y。
9. 如译作 Though my life started long ago 则太生硬，不可取。

第二篇

时政语篇：官方文件、讲话等

> 课时安排建议

　　本篇的目标语和双语导读聚焦以下四个方面：一是词语的运用，本篇第一章第一节和第二章第一节引导大家关注时政语篇中词语的积累和翻译。二是主语的确立，这体现在指导双语阅读的第二章第二、三、四节中。汉语主语多省略，英译时必须添加或重立主语。这一点在第一章中并未关注，因为英语的基本构架就是主谓宾，不言自明。三是语篇的连贯，这在第一章的第五节和第二章的第五、六、七节有所讨论。四是词语搭配、句式运用等构建语篇的基本技巧，这在指导英语阅读的第一章第二、三、四节有所关注，第二章的第九、十两节从汉译英角度进行了讨论。合译和拆译是相对的，翻译实践中应用较少，故放在最后一周讨论。本篇第三章为翻译试笔，可配合前两章内容同步学习。以上内容共安排五周时间教学。

周次	内 容 提 要	英语及双语阅读	翻译试笔和思考
1	时政语篇常用词语	第一章第一节，第二章第一节	第三章第四节
2	汉语信息如何纳入主语突出的英语构架，构建衔接得当的主语链	第二章第二节、第三节、第四节	第三章第一节、第二节
3	汉语信息如何纳入形合突出的英语构架，实现行文连贯	第一章第五节，第二章第五节、第六节、第七节	第三章第二节
4	英语语篇的词语搭配和句式运用	第一章第二节、第三节、第四节	第三章第三节
5	汉译英的结构安排技巧	第二章第八节、第九节、第十节	第三章第三节

第一章
目标语语篇导读

阅读国外的时政文献，可为我们的对外宣传工作提供参照和启示，在英译文的组句谋篇上也可提供有益的借鉴。以下几个研读视角可帮助大家更有效地阅读和分析英文时政语篇，为汉译英打下基础。

第一节 词 语

通过第一篇的学习，我们对英语语篇的基本特点、对汉英基本差异和汉译英的基本要点都有了概括的了解，并结合个人学习的具体情况进行了认真的思考。从文学语篇转到时政语篇，我们的注意力会更多地放在词语用法的积累上。

就词语积累而言，目标语阅读可遵循两条关注主线：其一，注意常用词语的用法；其二，留心有用的表达方式。

先谈第一条主线。阅读中要观察某些词语，特别是常用词语的用法，不仅要知道它们的词典意义，还要仔细体味它们在特定语篇中的意义，学习母语为英语人士是如何使用这些词的，以备在自己的译文中使用。请看以下几个例子：

例1：The two sides agreed to make efforts to advance exchanges and cooperation on sustainable tourism.

例2：And it is striking how closely the EU's targets mirror China's own domestic targets.

例3：Together we can show global leadership on two huge global priorities: completing the Doha Round and tackling climate change.

例4：If we are to get a deal in 2010 we need to pick up the discussions on agriculture and industrial goods where we left them in 2008, and give our negotiators the necessary flexibility to close the outstanding issues.

例 5：This is not about creating barriers but rather about sharing information on the needs of our respective markets and mapping our requirements.

例 6：The two sides welcomed and supported the convening of a EU-China High Level Energy Meeting in June, in which the two sides will have in-depth exchanges on energy security and energy science and technology, as well as China's and the EU's energy development strategies and plans, with a view to identifying the way forward and key areas for future practical cooperation. They also underlined the enhancement of cooperation in the automotive sector, aiming at the promotion of the common objectives of reduction of energy consumption and emissions, notably via the development of electro-mobility.

上述例句中划线词语的用法，我们在英语写作中可能不大会运用，如例 4 中的 close 是"结束、解决"之意，例 5 中的 map 是"讲明、提出"之意，而例 6 中的 identify 则是"确定、明确"的意思。日常阅读中一定要注意积累类似的词语表达与搭配。

阅读中我们还会发现一些词典中尚未收录的用法。如 leverage 一词，我们对它作名词的用法比较熟悉，比如：

The idea that economic sanctions are going to generate leverage over a major regional power like Russia is even more preposterous, since it has more resources and counter-strategies at its disposal.

句中的 leverage 是"影响"之意。而下面例句中 leverage 转为动词，我们可能就不大熟悉了。

例 7：The two sides welcomed the establishment of The US-China Energy Cooperation Program (ECP), a partnership between government and industry to enhance energy security and combat climate change. The ECP will leverage private sector resources and expertise to accelerate the deployment of clean energy technology.

例 8：G8 Members continue to support the Global Agriculture and Food Security Programme to finance country-owned agricultural development activities, especially those that achieve positive nutrition outcomes, and to leverage greater flows of private capital to smallholder farmers and agribusinesses in low-income countries.

例 9：In 2012, the United States leveraged its presidency of the G-8 to deepen the global commitment to food security through the establishment of the New Alliance for Food Security and Nutrition.

上述例句中，leverage 都是动词，而词典（如《牛津高阶英汉双解词典》）中并无相关释义。由此，我们应该学会依照具体语境理解词语的特定意义和用法。例 7 摘自 2009 年 11 月 17 日美中联合声明，下面是白宫新闻秘书办公室发布的译文：

双方欢迎建立美中能源合作项目（The US-China Energy Cooperation Program），这是一个旨在加强能源安全和应对气候变化的政府与产业间的伙伴关系。该项目将利用私营部门的资源和专长，加快清洁能源技术的应用。

可以看到，leverage 就是"利用"的意思，例 8 和例 9 中的 leverage 也都是"利用、使……发挥作用"的意思。

再比如 police 一词，其动词用法也比较常见：

例 10：We already expect our teachers to be social workers; child psychologists; nutritionists; child protection officers. We expect them to police the classroom, take care of our children's health; counsel our sons and daughters. Guide them, worry about them. And, on top of that, educate them too.

例 11：So we will remove statutory duties and requirements which we do not think need to be a legal requirement. Many of these requirements are "declaratory"—they have little practical force—or else cannot reasonably be policed and enforced.

两例中的 police 一个是主动，一个是被动，都是"治理、管理"之意，而且不一定表示如词典中所定义的与警力有关的意思（如例 11）。

另外，我们在阅读政要讲话稿时，常会遇到同一个措辞和结构重复使用的情况（即反复修辞法）。从修辞效果上讲，这可以增强表达力度，引起听众更多的共鸣。而从我们学习翻译的角度看，同一结构的反复出现则方便我们观察其使用的语境和技巧。比如下面摘自英国首相在 G8 Open for Growth 上讲话的四个连续段落，段落的标题如黑体所示。

Fairer Taxes, Greater Transparency and More Trade

The 3 Ts is a snappy title, but, really, why link these three together? Because they all have something in common: in each case developing countries are badly missing out.

When taxes are not collected, the poor suffer. In fact, illicit flows out of African countries exceed what they gain in aid. When companies extracting natural resources like minerals and oil are not transparent and don't publish the payments they make or when governments allow these payments to leach away into corruption people in developing countries miss out on the vital revenues they are due.

And when trade is choked by barriers and bureaucracy—developing countries miss out on the chance to grow. These issues are not just important they are ever more urgent too. Developing countries are finding new sources of natural wealth like offshore oil and gas in Ghana and Tanzania and the forces of globalisation are driving ever greater opportunities for growth and trade.

Just think what missing out on this growing income means for a country where thousands of children are dying every day because of malnutrition or where sick parents have to choose between whether to buy medicine to save their own lives, or pay for food for their hungry children.

我们看到 miss out (on) 用了四次，其基本含义不难理解，都是"失去"的意思。但既然以汉译英为目的进行阅读，就必须进一步观察该词组使用的语境：它可以指失去钱财和机会，也可以指失去某种功能或能力；还要注意跟宾语时要用介词 on。

下面是一个类似的例子，摘自布什总统的国情咨文：

On housing, we must trust Americans with the responsibility of homeownership and empower them to weather turbulent times in the housing market…

To build a future of quality health care, we must trust patients and doctors to make medical decisions and empower them with better information and better options…

On education, we must trust students to learn if given the chance and empower parents to demand results from our schools…

…

On trade, we must trust American workers to compete with anyone in the world and empower them by opening up new markets overseas…

…

To build a future of energy security, we must trust in the creative genius of

American researchers and entrepreneurs and empower them to pioneer a new generation of clean energy technology…

To keep America competitive into the future, we must trust in the skill of our scientists and engineers and empower them to pursue the breakthroughs of tomorrow…

讲演者六次使用 trust… and empower… 句式。我们看到，trust 的搭配有 trust sb. with…/trust sb. to do…/trust in…，empower 的搭配有 empower sb. to do…/empower sb. with sth。这些搭配都可作为我们翻译实践中有用的语言资源。

至于第二条主线——有用的表达方式，究竟应聚焦哪些表达方式呢？这很难明确地、机械地加以界定。可以这么说，凡是我们感兴趣的很可能就是今后汉英翻译实践中可能用到的，可以采取散在的积累方式。比如，"We have faced hard decisions about peace and war, rising competition in the world economy, and the health and welfare of our citizens."我们会注意到"日益激烈的竞争"可以译成 rising competition；"Trade that is fair and free across the Atlantic supports millions of good-paying American jobs."翻译"优质就业岗位"时也会有了参照；"We agree with him that this is a very worrying trend. At a time when fraud and e-crime is going up, the capability of the country to address it is going down."我们学到了 go up/down 的一种用法，也知道了"令人担心的倾向"的可能译法；读了"The two sides agreed to further intensify practical cooperation on issues with common concerns."就知道了"深化务实合作"的译法；"After shedding jobs for more than 10 years, our manufacturers have added about 500,000 jobs."告诉我们"裁员"不止 lay off employees 一个说法。读到下面这个句子："Too little teacher training takes place on the job, and too much professional development involves compliance with bureaucratic initiatives rather than working with other teachers to develop effective practice."原来西方的教育体系也有和我们相似的问题。谈到"学费贵，上不起学"，有哪些表达方式呢？会想到用 price 作动词吗？"让人负债累累"怎么说？会想到用 saddle 一词吗？"But today, skyrocketing costs price too many young people out of a higher education, or saddle them with unsustainable debt."再比如汉语中常说的"不能让孩子输在起跑线上"，我们想到的英语可能是"You cannot let your child lag behind at the starting point."而下面从美国总统国情咨文中选来的一段话可以借鉴：

In states that make it a priority to educate our youngest children, like Georgia or Oklahoma, studies show students grow up more likely to read and do math at grade level, graduate high school, hold a job, form more stable families of their own. We know this works. So let's do what works and make sure none of our children start the race of life already behind. Let's give our kids that chance.

凡是感兴趣的就可随时记忆，这是一种随机的、兴之所至的词语积累方式，但并非没有道理。因为引起你兴趣的东西，多半是你在一段时间里经常接触的体裁或话题，或是老师布置的作业或翻译任务所涉及的，对这些急用先学的词语，一般也最容易记牢。

除了这种随机的积累方式以外，还可以有系统地收集和记忆有用的词语。不妨以话题作为导向，留心不同体裁或语域中常用的词语，特别注意那些汉译英中可能用到的表达方式，注意它们在英语中使用的具体语境，为将来我们自己在翻译中运用这些词语做好储备。先以大家最熟悉的教育话题为例，下面这个段落摘自英国副首相 Nick Clegg 在 Southfields Community College 发表的有关教育政策的讲话。

例 12：Too often our education system ties children to their beginnings; it denies their parents choice; and it deepens social divides.

That's a problem for everyone.

It costs our economy. According to one estimate, if we could get all underachieving pupils up to the national average, by 2050 we could add 4% to our GDP.

...

And, when the best schools are concentrated in some communities but not others, poorer families get the raw deal. And all parents are faced with the well-known stresses and strains of trying to get into the right catchment area. So we need fundamental reform to break the traditional patterns of winners and losers in our schools.

例 13：Let me be clear what I want to see from free schools. I want them to be available to the whole community—open to all children and not just the privileged few. I want them to be part of a school system that releases opportunity, rather than entrenching it. They must not be the preserve of the privileged few—creaming off the best pupils while leaving the rest to fend for themselves, causing problems for and draining resources from other nearby schools. So let me give you my assurance: I would never tolerate that.

The Coalition has made it clear that our overriding social policy objective is improving social mobility. Reducing social segregation; making sure what counts in our society are ability and drive, not privilege and good connections. Free schools will only be acceptable so long as they promote those goals.

以上两个片段围绕教育公平的话题展开。例 12 谈到教育体制造成社会两极分化问题。其中划线词语就值得我们储存备用，比如 under-achieving pupils 不就是"差生、后进生"吗，"家长们争取进入某个学区"就是 All parents are faced with the well-known stresses and strains of trying to get into the right catchment area。例 13 谈了对免费学校（free school）的设想和要求：要实现教育公平，不能只为"少数特权人物"（the privileged few）服务，不能"只挑优等生而放任其他学生"（creaming off the best pupils while leaving the rest to fend for themselves），这只能给"其他学校带来麻烦，夺其生源"（causing problems for and draining resources from other nearby schools）。教育要有助于实现"社会流动"（social mobility），在我们的社会中要靠能力和努力，而不是特权和关系（what counts in our society are ability and drive, not privilege and good connections）。

网络也是我们常常谈论的话题，英国首相卡梅伦在伦敦网络空间大会（London Conference on Cyberspace）上谈到网络的作用：

And the internet has profoundly changed our economies too. Studies show it can create twice as many jobs as it destroys. It's estimated that for every 10 per cent increase in broadband penetration, global GDP will increase by an average of 1.3 per cent. So to grow our economies and get our people back to work, we've got to push harder than ever for wider access—and that's what we're doing in the UK.

卡梅伦谈到宽带普及率（broadband penetration）对国民经济的贡献，所以要发展经济（grow our economy），减少失业（get our people back to work）就必须大力推进（push）宽带普及率（wider access）。短短几句话，我们已经有所收获（特别是同一汉语概念"普及率"可能出现的不同表达方式）。

再看一段较长的文字，选自英国内务委员会（Home Affairs Committee）的一份报告，谈的是网络安全问题：

David Livingstone, Associate Fellow at the International Security Research Directorate, Chatham House, told us that the "war on cyber crime" was very serious and "getting worse". However, GCHQ's (Government Communications Headquarters) published earlier this year reported that a staggering 80% of cyber attacks could be stopped through basic information risk management. Iain Lobban, Director of GCHQ, had previously outlined how cyber crime is not just a national security or defence issue but is something which goes to the heart of our economic well-being and national interest. He stated that "good Information Assurance practice will solve 80% of Government's Cyber Security vulnerabilities. By this we mean observing basic network security disciplines like keeping patches up to date. That, combined with the necessary attention to personnel security and the 'insider' threat, will offer substantial protection for each individual network." However David Livingstone was concerned that whilst such attacks could be prevented by "getting the basics right" the public were generally unaware of what "those basics might be".

我们读到,"网络犯罪"(cyber crime)日趋严重,通过"信息风险管理"(information risk management)可以弥补大部分"网络安全漏洞"(security vulnerabilities),必须"及时更新修补程序"(keeping patches up to date),并注意"人事安全"(personnel security)和"内部威胁"(insider threat)。

经济也是一个重要话题,欧盟在2012年的一份绿皮书 Restructuring and Anticipation of Change: What Lessons from Recent Experience? 中谈到经济危机下的失业问题:

The impact of the financial crisis on the real economy started to be fully felt in 2009, when GDP declined at an unprecedented annual rate on both sides of the Atlantic. Employment proved very resilient in Europe immediately after the recession, particularly due to the strong adjustment of hours worked. Since the second half of 2009, however, job shedding became widespread and unemployment shot up in most EU countries, albeit with large differences. The recovery gained momentum in the first half of 2010 but stabilized in the remaining part of the year, also reflecting the fading of temporary factors such as the exceptional stimulus measures. Despite output recovery, employment growth did not follow until late 2010, and unemployment remained at the high levels reached in 2009.

这一段落为我们提供了不少有关失业的英语词语和表达方式。金融危机对"实体经济"（real economy）的影响自 2009 年开始充分显示出来（to be fully felt），减少"工作时间"(hours worked) 不失为一个灵活应对措施。然而，2009 下半年"裁员"（job shedding）蔓延开来，失业率飙升（shot up）。2010 上半年经济复苏初现（gain momentum），下半年持稳（stabilize），但尽管"产量恢复"（output recovery），就业却没有跟上。

下面一段摘自 2013 年 G8 Leaders Communique 的文字同样谈世界经济问题：

Global <u>economic prospects</u> remain weak, though <u>downside risks</u> have reduced thanks in part to significant policy actions taken in the US, euro area and Japan, and to the <u>resilience</u> of major developing and emerging market economies. Most financial markets have seen marked gains as a result. However, this optimism is yet <u>to be translated fully into</u> broader improvements in economic activity and employment in most advanced economies. In fact, prospects for growth in some regions have weakened since the Camp David summit. While countries have taken steps to avoid the worst of the <u>tail risks</u> that faced the world economy in 2012, vulnerabilities remain in 2013, highlighting the need for countries to <u>press ahead with</u> the necessary reforms to restore sustainable growth and jobs.

economic prospects（经济前景）、downside risks（下行风险）、tail risks（尾部风险）等词语都是经济话题中的活跃术语，而 to be translated fully into（转化成）、press ahead with（大力推进）等词语无疑可增强英文的表达能力。

以上几个实例告诉我们，以话题为主线观察和收集英文中的有用词语和表达方式，是行之有效的积累语言资源的途径。除此之外，我们还可以聚焦时政语篇中有突出特色的一些表达方式，比如外交文献中的一些固定说法，谈到经济贸易等话题时常用的数字表达方式，礼貌用语，等等。

先从外交文献中择取几个例子：

- Both sides recognized the importance of <u>accommodating each other's concerns</u>（照顾彼此关切）for furthering the overall relationship taking a strategic perspective.
- Leaders agreed that a <u>rich in substance</u>（内容丰富的）EU-China investment agreement would promote and facilitate investment in both directions.

第二篇　时政语篇：官方文件、讲话等

Negotiations towards this agreement would include all issues of interest to either side, <u>without prejudice to the final outcome</u>（不预判最终结果）.
- The two sides expressed their willingness to <u>keep the momentum of negotiation</u>（保持谈判势头）on a bilateral agreement on the protection of geographical indications.

再看下面几个有关数字表达的词语和结构。

表示"增加到/达到……"：
- Trade between the EU and China <u>reached EUR 326 billion in 2008</u>, making the EU-China trade relationship one of the most valuable in the world.
- Recent data suggests that China's economy is <u>edging closer toward 8% growth</u> again.
- As a result, we are <u>more than halfway towards the goal of $4 trillion in deficit reduction</u> that economists say we need to stabilize our finances.
- Conservative estimates suggest that a deal would <u>add around 150 billion US dollars to the world economy</u> per year, and recent study indicates that the gains could be <u>twice that</u>.

表示"减少……"：
- Over the last few years, both parties have worked together to <u>reduce the deficit by more than $2.5 trillion</u>—mostly through spending cuts, but also by raising tax rates on the wealthiest 1 percent of Americans.

表示"投资……"：
- The EU is an attractive investment destination—yet China only <u>invested EUR 2.2 billion in 2006</u> and a fraction of that in 2008. For its part, the EU <u>invested EUR 4.5 billion in China in 2008</u>, down from EUR 7 billion in 2007.

第二节 习语和搭配

阅读中要留心常用的习语和搭配,并持之以恒地进行记忆和积累。

习语即约定俗成的词语。要写好英语,尤其要留意这些习语在交际中是如何使用的。比如下面例句中的一些习语:

- People I met this morning like John Githongo—who was willing to blow the whistle on (阻止、遏止) fraud and corruption in Kenya, at real personal cost. So let's get behind (支持) President Kaberuka's work through the African Development Bank to secure the private finance that can deliver the infrastructure that is so badly needed.
- To point the finger at (指责) a particular nation is clearly not the right thing to do.
- This agreement will be effective only if it includes commitments by every major economy and gives none a free ride (搭便车).
- Many products from these nations now enter America duty-free, yet many of our products face steep tariffs in their markets. These agreements will level the playing field (创造公平的竞争环境).
- Both sides expressed their readiness to work together for constant progress on the ground (切实进展).

如何正确搭配是构建英语语篇时令人头疼的难题。解决这一难题可以求助于搭配词典,但最有效的还是自己积累的、储存在自己大脑中的语言资源。阅读中尤其应该注意动词出现的上下文,看其是如何与其他词语(介词、副词、名词等)搭配使用的。比如下面两句:

- America will continue to lead the effort to prevent the spread of the world's most dangerous weapons.
- Provocations of the sort we saw last night will only further isolate them, as we stand by our allies, strengthen our own missile defense and lead the world in taking firm action in response to these threats.

我们看到 lead 的搭配可以是 lead... to/in...。这种从阅读中积累的搭配模式,只靠查词典往往无法获得。这类动宾搭配我们在第三节动词中会单独讨论,现在让我们先关注一下其他类型的搭配问题——名词和形容词。

比如 poverty 一词的搭配:

poverty+ 名词:

- Even with the tax relief we put in place, a family with two kids that earns the minimum wage still lives below the <u>poverty line</u>.
- Authorities supported the growth of some NGOs that focused on social problems, such as <u>poverty alleviation</u> and disaster relief, but remained concerned that these organizations might emerge as a source of political opposition.
- During the year the country increased its "<u>rural poverty level</u>" to 192 RMB per month.

poverty+ 动词:

- But I believe there is an even more fundamental reason why <u>poverty has not yet been beaten</u>.
- Let me start with why the problem of <u>poverty has not gone away</u>.
- But eight years later, <u>poverty is</u> still very much <u>present</u> in many of the countries represented here today.

动词 +poverty:

- And in recent years a combination of economic growth and smart aid has helped to deliver huge advances in <u>cutting poverty</u>.
- And how I believe we can use this G8—and this meeting here today—to forge together a new agenda that will drive growth for us all and in doing so finally give us the chance to fulfil the ambition of 2005: <u>to eradicate extreme poverty from our world</u>.
- They are also vital in providing the foundations for the sustained economic growth that can <u>lift countries out of poverty</u>.

名词 + 介词 +poverty:

- Factory towns decimated from years of plants packing up. Inescapable <u>pockets of poverty</u>, urban and rural, where young adults are still fighting for their first job.

- Nelson Mandela stood in Trafalgar Square and called on humanity to "rise up" and free millions "trapped in the prison of poverty."

形容词+poverty：

- So the United States will join with our allies to eradicate such extreme poverty in the next two decades by connecting more people to the global economy.

再举一个形容词 effective 的例子：

effective+名词：

- Opportunities to observe and be observed are central to effective professional development.

更多搭配结构包括：to build effective and accountable government/ to set up a robust, impartial and effective justice system/ the effective operation of transfer pricing rules/ effective supervision and enforcement of…/encourage more effective and efficient investment/ a credible and effective way to track and report transparently on progress/ to ensure an effective transition，等等。

副词+effective+名词

- We do not have a strong enough focus on what is proven to be the most effective practice in teacher education and development.
- Third, we know that highly effective models of teacher training systematically use assessments of aptitude, personality and resilience as part of the candidate selection process.
- Teach First is a very effective third sector organisation backed by business and government which has shown what is possible.

动词+effective：

- These restructuring processes have been constructive, effective and instrumental in limiting job losses through innovative arrangements.
- The draft rules would make the Forest Rights Act more effective.
- Officials say this summer's mandatory restrictions have proven to be more effective.

effective+介词：

- It is too early to say that apps are any more effective at getting children ahead.

- While no internal control system is 100 percent effective in preventing fraud, the presence of basic internal controls can dissuade an employee from attempting a theft, since there is a perceived likelihood of their detection.

上面我们以近似词典词条的形式例举了细心阅读的收获，大家完全可以用这种方式自己独立或和他人合作编出一部小小的搭配词典。自己的词典，来自自己的阅读，用起来定会得心应手，比起买来的词典自有其优势。

第三节　动　词

动词是句子的动力所在，用好动词在汉译英中十分重要。这一点我们在学习第一篇文学语篇翻译的时候已深有体会。阅读时政语篇时同样要留意动词的搭配，短语动词、动词不定式结构等在行文中的运用。

动词的搭配主要注意其后可以搭配的宾语、介词等。

比如 drive 一词：

例1：And how I believe we can use this G8—and this meeting here today—to forge together a new agenda that will drive growth for us all and in doing so finally give us the chance to fulfil the ambition of 2005: to eradicate extreme poverty from our world.

例2：When some companies don't play by the rules, that drives more regulation and makes it harder for other businesses to turn a profit.

例3：And the UK will continue to drive a transparency revolution in every corner of the world through our leadership of the Open Government Partnership.

例4：I know some people put their hands up in the air and say this can never change. But by ending the era of tax secrecy and driving real openness over what governments and businesses do—it can change. And there are political leaders here who are making that happen.

例5：Local authorities, closer by their very nature to their community than the Secretary of State, could be more determined than distant Whitehall to drive up

attainment in their own patch—for example by setting higher standards for all schools in their area.

阅读完以上例句，我们注意到 drive 的不同词义：drive 在例 1 中有"促进、推动"之意，例 2 中有"导致"之意（drive more regulation 即"不得不制定更多规范"），而例 3 和例 4 中则有"倡导、促成"之意，至于例 5 中的 drive up 则是"提高"的意思。这些例句不仅丰富了我们原有的词汇知识，更重要的是，这样的词汇一旦连同上下文一起储存到我们大脑里，将会成为汉译英时的词汇资源。

再以 deliver 一词为例：

例 6：These are the messages I'll deliver when I travel to the Middle East next month.

例 7：It's great to see Sir John Armitt here today, and I'd like to personally congratulate him for all the work that he's done to deliver such a superb set of stadia and Games.

例 8：So let's get behind President Kaberuka's work through the African Development Bank to secure the private finance that can deliver the infrastructure that is so badly needed.

例 9：None of these steps, however, will deliver true freedom and democracy if there is not a genuine peace in the country, and it is here that I wish to speak most frankly and personally.

例 10：So that's our agenda today and for the UK's G8 Summit next week. It is about proper companies, proper taxes and proper global rules ensuring that openness delivers the benefits it should for rich and poor countries alike.

例 11：And in recent years a combination of economic growth and smart aid has helped to deliver huge advances in cutting poverty.

例 12：So, to sum up, on a day where everyone is determined to make the best of the new school year, let's set our sights even higher. Let's work together: government, schools and families to deliver the best for our children.

例 13：We have also changed the way we deliver aid by launching the Millennium Challenge Account.

例 14：We have other work to do on taxes. Unless the Congress acts, most of the tax relief we have delivered over the past 7 years will be taken away.

例 15：Since September 11, we have taken the fight to these terrorists and extremists. We will stay on the offense, we will keep up the pressure, and we will deliver justice to the enemies of America.

例 6 取"传达、发表"之意，例 7 和例 8 有"使某实体得以实现"的意思，而例 9 至例 12 则有"使某些抽象、概括的东西得以实现"的意思，例 13 和例 14 指"实施援助或财政行为"，例 15 则是习语"绳之以法"之意。

再比如动词 facilitate，我们在阅读中仔细观察发现，facilitate 的宾语所表示的大都是正面行为：

例 16：The Center will facilitate joint research and development on clean energy by teams of scientists and engineers from both countries.

例 17：In Beijing dozens of local community centers encouraged and facilitated HIV/AIDS support groups.

但也可以是负面行为：

例 18：Weak land governance and property rights systems can lead to opaque land deals, which facilitate corruption and undercut responsible actors seeking access to land for productive investment.

经常见到不定式 + 名词 +to facilitate 结构，表示某种行为的目的：

例 19：The two sides reaffirmed their strong support for a comprehensive and long-term solution to the Iranian nuclear issue through negotiations, and called on Iran to engage constructively with the P5+1 and to cooperate fully with the IAEA to facilitate a satisfactory outcome.

例 20：The two governments announced a program of joint demonstration projects in more than a dozen cities, along with work to develop common technical standards to facilitate rapid scale-up of the industry.

例 21：The United States continues to press China to facilitate a global economic environment that is consistent with "competitive neutrality" so that all firms, regardless of their form of ownership, can compete on a level playing field.

也有名词 +to facilitate，表示对名词的限定：

例 22：Short-term measures also included direct support to enterprises, such as

loans or guarantees to facilitate access to finance.

可用被动语态或过去分词短语构成后置定语：

例23：The world is witnessing the growth of a global movement <u>facilitated by technology and social media</u>

阅读时要带着汉译英实践中碰到的问题，细心观察，敏于发现，及时总结。有时会发现一个语义可能有不同的英语表达，比如以下例句中划线部分都有表示"高度评价"的意思：

- The two sides <u>commended the important role</u> of the three G-20 summits in tackling the global financial crisis.
- The United States and China <u>applauded the rich achievements</u> in scientific and technological cooperation and exchanges between the two countries over the past 30 years since the signing of the US-China Agreement on Cooperation in Science and Technology.
- Summit leaders <u>applauded the important progress</u> achieved in the development of EU-China relations in all fields and agreed that their comprehensive strategic partnership has grown both in width and in depth.

还有一些动宾搭配，也要注意积累，模仿使用。比如：

- I'm also <u>issuing a new goal</u>（设定了一个新目标）for America.
- Let's <u>streamline the process</u>（简化流程）, and help our economy grow.
- Now, as we do, we must <u>enlist our values</u>（遵循我们的价值观）in the fight.
- It also requires changing the conditions that <u>breed resentment</u>（滋生怨恨）and allow extremists to prey on despair.
- We must keep faith with all who have <u>risked life and limb</u>（冒着生命和伤残的危险）so that we might live in freedom and peace.
- Now, we know hackers <u>steal people's identities</u>（盗取个人身份信息）and <u>infiltrate private emails</u>（渗入私人邮件）. We know foreign countries and companies <u>swipe our corporate secrets</u>（偷走我们的商业机密）.
- The United States will <u>honor its relevant commitments</u>（履行有关承诺）and <u>appreciate and support the Chinese side's position</u>（理解并支持中方立场）on this issue.

- And now I believe we can use this G8—and this meeting here today—to <u>forge together a new agenda</u>（制定新的议事日程）that will drive growth for us all and in doing so finally give us the chance to fulfil the ambition of 2005: to eradicate extreme poverty from our world.
- Britain is one of the few countries in the world to have honoured its commitment to spend 0.7 per cent of its Gross National Income on aid. I urge this Congress to get together, <u>pursue a bipartisan, market-based solution to climate change</u>（达成一个两党都同意的、以市场为基础的解决全球变暖的方案）.
- President Mahama of Ghana, who has <u>opened up his country's budget</u>（公开预算）so his people can see how their money is spent. President Conde of Guinea, who has recently led the way on publishing mining contracts online. President Kikwete of Tanzania, who is working to ensure that the citizens of his country can enjoy clear and secure property rights. And President Sall of Senegal, who has simplified taxes, <u>unleashed auditors on public finances</u>（对公共财政实施审计）and set up a commission to tackle corruption.

掌握正确、地道的动宾搭配结构只能靠多看、多记，随时留心。英语不是我们的母语，要将约定俗成的搭配化为我们的英文表达习惯，只能通过持之以恒地阅读和记忆，除此以外别无捷径。比如见到了 stem the decline in global output（遏制全球产出下降）、resolutely follow the path of peaceful development and a win-win strategy of opening-up（坚决走和平发展道路，实施互利共赢的开放战略）、to adjust economic structure, raise household incomes, expand domestic demand（调整经济结构，提高家庭收入，扩大国内需求）或 cooperatively address regional and global security challenges（合作处理地区性和全球性的安全挑战），We'll engage Russia to seek further reductions in our nuclear arsenals（我们将与俄罗斯保持紧密接触，寻求进一步削减双方的核武器数量）等搭配与表达，都可以有意识地在脑子里重复一下，久而久之自然就能脱口而出了。

英语中的短语动词、动词习语，本身就是一种约定俗成的固定表达。为提高英文表达能力，必须花大力气掌握好这类动词搭配。下面例子选自英国首相讲演：

For too long the international community has <u>shied away from</u> condemning the appalling degree of corruption and mismanagement of resources and the fundamentally bad governance that is destroying lives in some developing countries, and there are always voices saying: why cause the stir; why be the one to point the finger?

句中 shy away from 是短语动词（可比较 avoid），而 cause the stir 和 point the finger at 就是我们所说的动词习语。

再比如下面这些例句中的短语动词：

- The terrorists oppose every principle of humanity and decency that we hold dear（珍惜）.
- They agreed to work towards（致力于）the start of the negotiation as soon as possible.
- None of us will get 100 percent of what we want. But the alternative will cost us jobs, hurt our economy, visit hardship on（使陷入困境）millions of hardworking Americans.
- We will keep faith with our veterans（信守对退伍军人的承诺）, investing in world-class care, including mental health care, for our wounded warriors, supporting our military families; giving our veterans the benefits and education and job opportunities that they have earned.
- So tonight, I'm announcing the launch of three more of these manufacturing hubs, where businesses will partner with（合作）the Department of Defense and Energy to turn regions left behind by globalization into global centers of high-tech jobs.

阅读中还要留心一种动词结构："动词＋不定式"或"动词＋宾语＋不定式"，这类结构出现频率高，需要大家特别加以记忆，以备在自己的翻译实践中使用。

- The two sides pledge to honor（保证履行）all commitments.
- They committed to pursue ratification（致力于尽早批准）of the Comprehensive Nuclear-Test-Ban Treaty as soon as possible.
- They also agreed to work together to strengthen the capacity（同意共同努力加强）of these institutions to prevent and respond to future crises.
- The two countries should further strengthen coordination and cooperation, work together to tackle challenges（共同应对挑战）, and promote world

peace, security and prosperity.

- The United States and China undertook to implement（开始履行）the newly signed Memorandum of Understanding Between the Department of Agriculture of the United States of America and the Ministry of Agriculture of the People's Republic of China on Cooperation in Agriculture and Related Fields.

下面是"动词+宾语+不定式"结构的例句。

- The Dialogue offers a unique forum to promote understanding, expand common ground, reduce differences, and develop solutions to common problems（对话为促进理解、扩大共识、减少分歧、寻求对共同问题的解决办法提供了独特的论坛）.

- I propose we use some of our oil and gas revenues to fund an Energy Security Trust that will drive new research and technology to shift our cars and trucks off oil for good（发展新科学技术，以让我们的汽车和卡车以后不再用石油）.

- Unfortunately, the Congress set the legislation to expire on February 1（限定这项立法于 2 月 1 日到期）.

以上三节从词语搭配和表达方式等视角讨论了阅读英语时政语篇时的关注焦点。阅读时当然会注意到词语的使用，这看来普普通通。但学生们的阅读实践告诉我们，大家阅读的时候常常是囫囵吞枣，虽然读得不慢，量也不小，但就是读后没有感觉，没有收获，结果读是读写是写，读不能促写，写也和读挂不上钩。以上三个小节中提出的关注焦点，是师生们在学习过程中逐步摸索出的行之有效的切入点。本着汉英翻译的学习目的，大家在阅读中要边读边思考，带着问题读，找到聚焦点，确立最适合自己的阅读方法。

英语阅读要和双语阅读、和汉译英对照文本的阅读紧密结合。翻译学习过程中，要留心汉英翻译与英语语篇间的互文联系。比如，embrace 作为动词，在目标语语篇中会有如下用法：

- And those of us who care deeply about programs like Medicare must embrace the need for modest reforms（接受适度的改革）—otherwise, our retirement programs will crowd out the investments we need for our children, and jeopardize the promise of a secure retirement for future generations.

- The Torch has shown the Games are not just about London, or England. Scotland, Wales and Northern Ireland have all really embraced the torch relay and the Games（承担火炬传递和奥运会工作）.

上面句中 embrace 有 to accept/include 之意，所接宾语既可以是抽象的概念，也可以是具体的事物。这样的用法可以迁移至汉英翻译实践中，下面胡锦涛讲话和李克强署名文章的英译中就用到了 embrace 一词。

- 我们要推动各方增强责任感和道义感……
  We should encourage all parties to embrace a stronger sense of responsibility and morality…
- 一个高水平的自贸协定，不仅会促进两国经贸合作全面升级，而且会向世界发出反对贸易和投资保护主义、倡导贸易自由化便利化的强有力信号。
  A high-quality free-trade agreement will not only upgrade our business and investment cooperation but also send a powerful message to the rest of the world that we reject trade and investment protectionism and instead embrace trade liberalization and facilitation.

译文一旦生成就成了译语世界的一员，目标读者是否乐于接受它，就语言层面讲，就要看译文是否符合译语的写作规范。译文要向译语原创语篇看齐，以原创语篇作为选词构句的范例和导向。

第四节　句式和从句

英语行文，特别是在官方文献、政要讲话中，各类句式，包括从句的运用就显得更为重要。阅读此类文本，务必仔细体会主句和从句以及从句之间是如何相互配合，构建出缜密、连贯的语篇的。要熟读此类段落和语句，加强用英语思维的能力，以备汉译英时处理好语义复杂的段落。

哪些英语句式或从句结构值得我们特别留意呢？一般来说，下面的句式或从句结构可能需特别关注。

第二篇 时政语篇：官方文件、讲话等

1. 带有比较结构的句式
- Today, <u>no</u> area holds <u>more promise than</u> our investments in American energy.
- Protecting our nation from the dangers of a new century requires <u>more than</u> good intelligence and a strong military.
- <u>Just as</u> in Britain people get angry when they work hard, pay their taxes and then see others not paying their fair share <u>so</u> we should demand the same justice and fairness for others in developing countries too.

2. 表示强调的句式
- <u>It is not</u> a bigger government we need, <u>but</u> a smarter government that sets priorities and invests in broad-based growth.
- <u>It is</u> this kind of prosperity—broad, shared, built on a thriving middle class— <u>that</u> has always been the source of our progress at home.

3. 倒装句式
- As long as countries like China keep going all in on clean energy, <u>so must we</u>.

4. 平行结构
- In many places, people live on little more than a dollar a day. So the United States will join with our allies to eradicate such extreme poverty in the next two decades <u>by connecting</u> more people to the global economy; <u>by empowering</u> women; <u>by giving</u> our young and brightest minds new opportunities to serve, <u>and helping</u> communities to feed, and power, and educate themselves; <u>by saving</u> the world's children from preventable deaths; and <u>by realizing</u> the promise of an AIDS-free generation, which is within our reach.

上例中五个"by+现在分词"短语将信息一层一层地延展开来。而下面一句用常用的连接词语"not only…but also…"构成的平行结构，也值得关注：

We also know that progress in the most impoverished parts of our world enriches us all—<u>not only because</u> it creates new markets, more stable order in certain regions of the world, <u>but also because</u> it's the right thing to do.

下一个例子是相连的两个自然段构成平行结构：

<u>It is our unfinished task</u> to make sure <u>that</u> this government works on behalf of

139

the many, and not just the few; that it encourages free enterprise, rewards individual initiative, and opens the doors of opportunity to every child across this great nation.

It is our unfinished task to restore the basic bargain that built this country—the idea that if you work hard and meet your responsibilities, you can get ahead, no matter where you come from, no matter what you look like, or who you love.

两个自然段均以 it 作形式主语开启；第一段包含两个 that 引导的宾语从句；第二段包括 no matter where…, no matter what…, or (no matter) who… 三个并列结构。

平行结构有利于信息的扩展和深化，而且层次清楚，易读易懂，讲演和政论文中多用。

5. 同位语和同位语从句

These initiatives in manufacturing, energy, infrastructure, housing—all these things will help entrepreneurs and small business owners expand and create new jobs. But none of it will matter unless we also equip our citizens with the skills and training to fill those jobs.

主语 all these things 复指划线部分，使信息得以强化。

同位语从句拥有更大的信息容量，它起到具体解释、添加细节的作用。比如：

- The two sides expressed the hope that the multilateral mechanism of the Six Party Talks would convene at an early date.
- They shared the view that, in an ever changing and increasingly interdependent world where their interests become more closely intertwined, they should strengthen their interaction and cooperation to better meet the opportunities and challenges in the new bilateral, multilateral and global framework.

还常见到信息承载量更大的"同位语＋定语从句"结构：

- The people's trust in their government is undermined by congressional earmarks—special interest projects that are often snuck in at the last minute, without discussion or debate.
- Our work must begin by making some basic decisions about our budget—decisions that will have a huge impact on the strength of our recovery.

- The American people deserve a tax code that helps small businesses spend less time filling out complicated forms, and more time expanding and hiring— a tax code that ensures billionaires with high-powered accountants can't work the system and pay a lower rate than their hardworking secretaries; a tax code that lowers incentives to move jobs overseas, and lowers tax rates for businesses and manufacturers that are creating jobs right here in the United States of America.

上述例句体现出"同位语 + 定语从句"结构的强大构句能力，尤其是最后一个长句，以 a tax code that… 为基本构件展开。

6. 动词后接宾语从句结构

某些动词（比如 reiterate, recognize, note, stress 等）常常后接宾语从句，这样的结构在官方文献中十分常见。

- The two sides reiterated that they are committed to building a positive, cooperative and comprehensive US-China relationship for the 21st century.
- The United States and China underlined that each country and its people have the right to choose their own path, and all countries should respect each other's choice of a development model. Both sides recognized that the United States and China have differences on the issue of human rights.
- The two sides noted that, at a time when the international environment is undergoing complex and profound changes, the United States and China share a responsibility to cooperatively address regional and global security challenges. The two sides stressed that they share broad common interests in the Asia-Pacific region and support the development and improvement of an open and inclusive regional cooperation framework that is beneficial to all.
- So in the months ahead, I will continue to engage Congress to ensure not only that our targeting, detention and prosecution of terrorists remains consistent with our laws and system of checks and balances, but that our efforts are even more transparent to the American people and to the world.

7. 非谓语动词结构

除了从句，还要留意各种非谓语动词组成的短语，特别是现在 / 过去分词短语所构成的状语、定语等。它们和从句的语义结构和功能是相当的，因而也被称为"分词从句"（participle clause）。阅读时，要特别注意观察英语中主句、从句是如何与分词短语结构相互配合，共同构建起逻辑连贯、语义明晰的语篇的。

（1）分词短语作状语结构

- Internet and other information systems have transformed our working environment, driving economic growth, connecting people and providing new ways to communicate and cooperate.
- Addressing these differences in the spirit of equality and mutual respect, as well as promoting and protecting human rights consistent with international human rights instruments, the two sides agreed to hold the next round of the official human rights dialogue in Washington D.C. by the end of February 2010.
- Recognising the significant benefits accruing from enhanced people-to-people contacts, the leaders agreed to explore the possibility of facilitating mobility for Chinese and EU citizens, and strengthening cooperation on illegal immigration.
- There are many excellent teachers, working hard and succeeding with children and young people. There are many outstanding school leaders, some of them taking the opportunity to extend their impact more widely as executive head teachers of more than one school, or as National Leaders of Education, supporting other schools to improve. There are many schools which take seriously the task of raising achievement and narrowing attainment gaps, focus sharply on the progress of every child and teach a rigorous and demanding curriculum in an inspiring way, opening up opportunity to many more young people.

（2）分词短语作定语结构

- Cyberspace is the term used to describe the internet and other information systems that form an interactive domain made up of digital networks used to store, modify and communicate information.

（3）动名词作主语、宾语等成分的情况

- Both sides agreed that deepening understanding and mutual trust between the two peoples was vital to the sustained and stable development of EU-China relations.
- Moving towards a more sustainable economic model also implies adjusting to the challenge of climate change.
- Defining e-crime has shaped the manner in which organisations such as the Police and Serious and Organised Crime Agency (SOCA) understand and respond to the evolving criminal threats presented in the digital ages.
- The honest, open relationships that the HED facilitates are the best way of tackling them and of ensuring that the EU-China economic relationship becomes ever more stable and sustainable for the long term.

本节主要关注了时政语篇中的复杂句式或结构。事实上，我们也会见到由非常简洁的短句构成的段落。比如下面摘自英国首相演讲中的一段，句式简洁，十分有力。

Corruption is wrong. It starves the poor. It poisons the system. It saps the faith of people in progress. It wrecks the case for aid. When we see it we should condemn it utterly.

长句和短句在承载信息、表达思想情感上各有所长，英语写作中讲究长短兼用，将汉语译为英语时也应如此。而汉语的时政语篇一般逻辑繁复，长句频出，致使译者一味跟进，其实完全可以长短相间，长句要层次分明，短句要用词精当。

英美等国家的官方文件的文体风格和我们有明显差别。以美国总统的国情咨文为例，它大致相当于我国的政府工作报告，但篇幅略小，文体上远没有我国的政府工作报告那样正式，句子较为简短，用词也多贴近口语，处处体现出简单英语（simple English）的倾向。如下面取自奥巴马 2013 年国情咨文中的一段：

Let's offer incentives to companies that hire Americans who've got what it takes to fill that job opening, but have been out of work so long that no one will give them a chance anymore. Let's put people back to work rebuilding vacant homes in run-down neighborhoods. And this year, my administration will begin to partner with 20 of the hardest-hit towns in America to get these communities back on their feet. We'll work with local leaders to target resources at public safety, and education, and housing.

可以看到,这里没有大词,也没有复杂句式,文体近乎口语。我们甚至还会看到近乎俚语的用词:

And tomorrow, my administration will release a new "College Scorecard" that parents and students can use to compare schools based on a simple criteria—where you can get the most bang for your educational buck.

还有生动的类比和比喻:

With all the other pressures on their finances, American families should not have to worry about the Federal government taking a bigger bite out of their paychecks.

以上举例,旨在建议大家将汉语时政文献译为英语时,切忌句式过分繁冗,力求语言简洁明快,易于普通民众阅读,以提高外宣实效。

第五节 语篇连贯

英语官方文献和政要讲话稿的逻辑层次都很清楚,读起来会感到十分顺畅。如果我们只为获取信息,往往会忽视对衔接和连贯等语篇特征的分析,而这些对汉译英的学习者来说却十分重要。阅读英语时政语篇时须细心观察,留意常见逻辑模式的构建规律,熟悉和领悟作者是如何组织和安排信息的。汉语行文的逻辑走向往往不如英语那么彰显,汉译英时往往需要将逻辑关系显性化。因此,构建英语语篇时,我们尤其要重视词语的衔接和逻辑的连贯。

1. 英译文中注意回指衔接,即用代词复指上文中的某个成分。比如:

All of us were sent to Washington to carry out the people's business. That is the purpose of this body. It is the meaning of our oath. And it remains our charge to keep.

这个段落中的衔接链是:to carry out the people's business—that... —it... — it...

In 2011, Congress passed a law saying that if both parties couldn't agree on a plan to reach our deficit goal, about a trillion dollars' worth of budget cuts would automatically go into effect this year. These sudden, harsh, arbitrary cuts would jeopardize our military readiness. They'd devastate priorities like education, and energy, and medical research. They would certainly slow our recovery, and cost us hundreds of thousands of jobs. That's why Democrats, Republicans, business leaders, and economists have already said that these cuts, known here in Washington as the sequester, are a really bad idea.

此例第二句中的 These…cuts 承接上句中的 budget cuts，第三、四两句均以 they 为主语延续同一主题 budget cuts，最后一句的宾语从句中又重现 these cuts，将主题延伸至段末。本段呈现如下衔接链：budget cuts—these cuts…—they…—they…—these cuts…

2. 借助各类关联词语构建英译文中的逻辑连贯模式。

常见的行文连贯模式有因果推进式：

Relations between the EU and China have come a long way since bilateral ties were established over thirty years ago. Our trade relationship in particular has expanded from virtually nothing to one of the most important in the world.

Inevitably, a relationship such as ours needs constant attention if we are to maintain and build confidence. We need to communicate—to speak frankly—to exchange ideas and to recognise there have been and will be some difficult moments as our relationship matures.

So, I came to Beijing this week, to continue to build the unique relationship that exists between the EU and China—a partnership that is more important than ever in the current economic turmoil, as the last few months have demonstrated.

以上三个连续自然段，前段为后段铺垫，引出后段结果。第一段说双边关系的发展迅速，由此导出第二段的"必须加以持续关注"，最后又引到北京的访问。第二、三两段段首具有连接作用的副词 inevitably 和连词 so 都起到了逻辑标志的作用。

还有转折模式：

As we meet tonight, our economy is undergoing a period of uncertainty. America has added jobs for a record of 52 straight months, but jobs are now growing at a slower pace. Wages are up, but so are prices for food and gas. Exports are rising, but the housing market has declined. And at kitchen tables across our country, there is concern about our economic future.

此段行文中 but 起到关键的承上启下作用，形成"一正一反——一正一反"的

145

转折逻辑模式。

下面一段只有一个 but，其后均为对前文内容的反驳，也构成了明显的转折推进模式。

It is true that some Chinese exports are subject to anti-dumping duties in Europe or are currently the subject of investigations, but this affects less than 1% of our imports from China. It is a normal part of a trade relationship as large as ours. China also investigates dumping and imposes duties, including on the EU.

在讨论各种逻辑模式时，我们可明显看到关联词语在行文连贯中的重要作用，因此阅读中也要注意观察和积累。表示连贯的关联词语我们已经很熟悉，如 but, yet, because, however, therefore 以及 seeing that…, provided that…, 等等。除此之外，我们还要注意某些对行文连贯不可或缺的词语或表达，如下面几例：

- And linking back to what I said earlier, this relationship is essential because the obstacles to EU-China trade are increasingly intangible—they are non-tariff barriers arising from different traditions and standards.
- As I've highlighted, the EU-China relationship is a partnership based on shared interest and values.
- But, for all that, we face many common challenges in unlocking the potential of renewable energy sources, developing clean energy technologies, and using energy more efficiently.

关于语篇连贯问题，第一篇第一章第三节和第二章第十二节已有较多讨论。不论是文学语篇还是时政语篇，写作的基本要领都是一致的，都必须作到逻辑合理，顺理成章，文气通达。建议汉译英练习和英语写作练习同步安排，比照进行。

本章为阅读英语时政语篇提供了五个可行的切入点，主要聚焦三个方面。一是时政词语的积累（第一节），时政语篇中充斥着大量涉及政治、经济、外交、文化等诸领域的词语，是我们从文学语篇转向时政语篇研读后感到的最大的不同点，也最容易引发我们的关注。二是搭配和句式（第二、三、四节），也就是组词成篇所必不可少的要素。尽量充分地浸入目标语语篇世界中，是获得英语语感，了解和掌握其写作要领的必要途径。三是语篇的衔接和连贯（第五节），这关乎整个语篇的可读性，是英语写作质量的重要评判标准。唯有具备选词、组句、布局谋篇的英文写作能力，方可在汉译英上更有突破。

第二章
双语语篇导读及翻译要略

　　本章是时政语篇双语对照阅读的导读章节。本章的某些小节可看做是对翻译技巧的讲解，但我们更愿意再次强调本章的导读性质：本章所讲的内容只是个引子，大家绝不要就此止步，要沿着这个思路更多、更广泛地阅读，总结自己的体验，悟出翻译的道理。

　　上一章建议阅读英语语篇时可特别留意词语、搭配和结构、语篇连贯三个方面，本章旨在为阅读汉英对照语篇提供指导。阅读双语语篇关注的是汉英差异以及用怎样的英语结构再现汉语的信息。本章从词语（第一节）、主语确立（第二、三、四节）、逻辑安排（第五、六、七节）、词语和句法（第九、十节）等方面进行分析和思考。第八节和拆译相对，简略地讨论了信息的融合或合并问题。

第一节　词　语

　　从文学语篇到时政语篇，不少同学感觉前者翻译起来更有"趣味"，更有"成就感"，时政语篇中好多词语是基本固定的，译者没有更多的自主性。这种说法反映了大家的真实感受，也确实有一定的道理。时政语篇一般不如文学作品那样工于修辞，蕴意悠远，翻译时以准确、达意为准。因此，在阅读汉英对照语篇时，可以特别留意我们耳熟能详的词语在英语中是怎样表达的。比如下面一段谈到我国内外政策，其中就不乏我们常常挂在嘴边的词语：

　　关于中国政府的政策，我愿强调：对内，我们全面深化市场化取向的改革，释放改革的红利，持续发展经济，不断改善民生，促进社会公正，努力使人人享有平等的机会。对外，我们始终不渝走和平发展道路，奉行互利共赢的开放战略，扩大对外开放的领域和空间，特别是扩大服务业对外开放，以开

放促改革、促发展、促转型。

As for the policies of the Chinese government, I just want to emphasize the following: domestically, we will make an all-around effort to deepen market-oriented reform, unleash the dividends of reform, continue to grow the economy, improve people's livelihood, promote social equity and ensure equal opportunities for all. Externally, we will unswervingly follow the path of peaceful development and pursue a win-win strategy of opening-up. We will open up more areas and sectors, the services sector in particular, so as to facilitate China's reform, development and economic transformation.

诸如此类的词语在阅读时政双语语篇时随处可见，尽可信手拈来。比如"中华民族伟大复兴的中国梦"就是 the Chinese dream, namely, the great renewal of the Chinese nation；"冲破制约发展的旧框框"译为 break away from the old confines that fetter development；"力争实现跨越式发展"译为 strive for leap-frog development；"涉及人民群众切身利益的问题"译为 some problems affecting the vital interests of the people；"亟待解决的问题"可以说 problems demanding urgent solution；"把握好以下原则"可以说 act on the following principles；"把扩大国内需求作为促进经济增长的长期战略方针和根本着力点"可以说 make boosting domestic demand a long-term strategic principle and a basic point of departure for stimulating economic growth；"内需在拉动经济增长中的主导作用"译为 the leading role of domestic demand in driving economic growth；"变压力为动力"译为 turn pressure into impetus for growth；"虚拟经济和实体经济"译为 the financial sector and real economy；"扩大内需"可以译为 driving domestic demand in China；"节能减排"译为 to boost energy conservation and reduce emissions；我们还看到，"金融危机对中国实体经济的影响日益显现"中的"影响"一词可以用 fallout 译出：The fallout of the financial crisis on China's real economy is becoming more evident；等等。

下面这些句子也都有值得我们学习和积累的词语。

- 中国要实现富强民主文明和谐的现代化目标，仍然要靠改革开放。
  And to achieve the modernization goal of building a prosperous, democratic, culturally-advanced and harmonious country, we still need to rely on reform and opening-up.

- 让人民生活有基本保障、无后顾之忧，是现代政府的重要职责。

And to meet the essential needs of the people and free them from worries for daily necessities is an important responsibility of modern government.

- 中国的改革已经到了攻坚阶段，必须以更大决心和勇气全面推进各领域改革。
  With China's reform endeavor at a crucial stage, we must advance the reforms in all areas with greater determination and courage.

- 一些人见利忘义，损害公众利益，丧失了道德底线。
  Some people have sacrificed principle and sought profits at the expense of public interests. They have crossed the moral baseline.

- 必须坚持用制度管权管事管人，健全民主集中制，不断推进党的建设制度化、规范化、程序化。
  We must place power, Party affairs, and Party members under institutional safeguards, improve democratic centralism, and promote Party building in an institutionalized and standardized way and through due process.

- 国务院提请全国人大常委会审议了社会保险法、防震减灾法等8件法律议案，制定或修订了30件行政法规。
  Last year, the State Council submitted eight bills, including a draft of the Social Insurance Law and draft amendments to the Law on Protecting Against and Mitigating Earthquake Disasters, to the Standing Committee of the National People's Congress for deliberation. It also formulated or revised 30 administrative laws and regulations.

阅读和分析时政类双语语篇时，也可以按照不同的主题来积累词语和表达。比如谈到改革开放：

- 要使全体中国人民都过上美好生活，我们将坚持改革开放不动摇，牢牢把握转变经济发展方式这条主线，集中精力把自己的事情办好，不断推进社会主义现代化建设。
  We need to make relentless efforts in the years ahead to deliver a better life to all our people. We are unwaveringly committed to reform and opening up, and we will concentrate on the major task of shifting the growth model, focus on running our own affairs well and make continued efforts to boost the socialist

modernization drive.

谈到经济发展：

- 推动发展高新技术产业群，培育新的经济增长点。我们就是要依靠科学技术的重大突破，创造新的社会需求，催生新一轮的经济繁荣。
 We will promote the development of high-tech industrial clusters and cultivate new economic growth areas. All in all, we will rely on major breakthroughs in science and technology to foster new social demand and bring about a new round of economic boom.

- （投资计划）主要投向保障性安居工程、农村民生工程、铁路交通等基础设施、社会事业、生态环保建设和地震灾后恢复重建。中国政府还推出了大规模的减税计划，一年可减轻企业和居民负担约5000亿元。我们还大幅度降息和增加银行体系流动性，出台了一系列金融措施。
 The money will mainly go into government-subsidized housing, projects related to the well-being of rural residents, the construction of railway and other infrastructural projects, social development programs, environmental protection and post-earthquake recovery and reconstruction. The Chinese Government has introduced a massive tax-cut program, which will reduce the tax burdens on businesses and individuals by about RMB 500 billion each year. We have also cut interest rates by a large margin, increased liquidity in the banking system and adopted a range of financial measures.

- 我在达沃斯会议上已重申，应该对国际货币金融体系进行必要的改革，建立公平、公正、包容、有序的国际金融新秩序，努力营造有利于全球经济发展的制度环境。
 As I reiterated at the World Economic Forum Annual Meeting in Davos, necessary reform of the international monetary and financial systems should be carried out to establish a new international financial order that is fair, equitable, inclusive and well-managed. We should create an institutional environment conducive to global economic growth.

谈到对外政策：

- 坚持开放包容，为促进共同发展提供广阔空间。"海纳百川，有容乃大。"我们应该尊重各国自主选择社会制度和发展道路的权利，消除疑虑和隔阂，把世界多样性和各国差异性转化为发展活力和动力。我们要秉持开放精神，积极借鉴其他地区发展经验，共享发展资源，推进区域合作。

We should remain open and inclusive so as to create broad space for enhancing common development. The ocean is vast because it admits hundreds of rivers. We should respect the right of a country to independently choose its social system and development path, remove distrust and misgivings and turn the diversity of our world and difference among countries into dynamism and driving force for development. We should keep an open mind, draw upon development practices of other continents, share development resources and promote regional cooperation.

谈到就业和人才任用：

- 我国劳动力人口近8亿，相当于所有发达国家劳动力资源的总和，每年新进入人力资源市场的劳动力远远超过能够提供的就业岗位，劳动力总量供大于求与结构性用工短缺矛盾并存。

  There are almost 800 million people of working age in China, equivalent to the workforce of all developed countries combined. The annual increase of workforce in the job market far exceeds the number of jobs available. The oversupply of labor and structural labor shortage exist side by side.

- 在新的历史条件下提高党的建设科学化水平，必须坚持五湖四海、任人唯贤，坚持德才兼备、以德为先用人标准，把各方面优秀人才集聚到党和国家事业中来。

  To make Party building more scientific under the new historical conditions, we must recruit people on merits without regard to their origins, adhere to the criterion of evaluating cadres in terms of both political integrity and professional ability with priority given to integrity, and encourage outstanding individuals in all fields to join the cause of the Party and country.

- 我们将把促进就业作为经济社会发展的优先目标，实施更加积极的就业政策，积极开发就业岗位，鼓励自主创业，促进充分就业。

  We will make employment expansion a priority target in economic and social development, implement a more pro-active employment policy, vigorously create new jobs, and encourage self-employment to promote full employment.

谈到解决住房问题：

- 住房问题既是经济问题，更是影响社会稳定的重要民生问题，稳定房价和提供住房保障是各级政府的重要责任。
  The issue of housing is both an economic issue and more importantly, a major issue affecting people's livelihood and social stability. To stabilize the housing price and ensure housing availability is an important responsibility of governments at all levels.

- 我们要进一步规范市场秩序，完善土地、财税、金融政策，加快建立促进房地产市场健康发展的长效机制，抑制投资、投机性需求，引导市场增加普通商品房供给，加快保障性住房建设，发展公共租赁住房，促进形成合理的住房供给结构，满足多层次的住房需求。
  We must further rectify the market order, improve the land, tax and financial policies, accelerate the establishment of a long-term mechanism for the healthy development of the housing market and curb investment and speculative demand. We need to guide the market towards greater supply of ordinary commercial housing, speed up the development of low-income housing and build public rental housing in order to form a rational structure of housing supply and meet the diverse housing needs.

谈到收入分配问题：

- 我们将加快推进收入分配制度改革，努力提高居民收入在国民收入中的比重和劳动报酬在初次分配中的比重，创造条件让更多群众拥有财产性收入，尽快扭转收入差距扩大趋势，促进居民收入和消费可持续增长。
  We will speed up the reform of the income distribution system, and raise the proportion of individual income in the national income and the proportion of the primary distribution that goes to wages and salaries. We will create conditions for more people to earn income from property, reverse the trend of widening income gap as quickly as possible, and boost the sustainable growth of people's income and consumer spending.

谈到医疗和社会保障问题：

- 积极推进医药卫生体制改革，力争用三年时间基本建成覆盖全国城乡的基本医疗卫生制度，初步实现人人享有基本医疗卫生服务。
  We are advancing the reform of the medical and health system and working to put in place a nationwide basic medical and health system covering both urban and rural areas within three years and achieve the goal of everyone having access to basic medical and health service.

- 四是大幅度提高社会保障水平。继续提高企业退休人员基本养老金，提高失业保险金和工伤保险金标准，提高城乡低保、农村五保等保障水平。
  Fourth, significantly raise the level of social security. We will continue to increase basic pension for enterprise retirees and upgrade the standard of unemployment insurance and workers' compensation. We will raise the level of basic cost of living allowances in both urban and rural areas and welfare allowances for those rural residents without family support.

- 启动事业单位基本养老保险制度改革试点。积极探索建立新型农村社会养老保险制度，农民工、被征地农民社会保障工作稳步推进。全面加强城乡居民最低生活保障制度建设，救助人数达到6619万人。
  We launched trials to reform the basic old-age insurance system for employees of government-affiliated institutions. We actively explored ways to establish a new system of old-age insurance for rural residents and made steady progress in making social security available to rural migrant workers in urban areas and farmers whose land has been expropriated. We comprehensively improved the system of cost of living allowances for both urban and rural residents, and provided allowances to 66.19 million residents.

谈到计生政策：

- 农村计划生育家庭奖励扶助制度和少生快富工程实施范围继续扩大。
  We continued to expand the coverage of the reward and assistance system for rural families complying with family planning regulations, and implemented the "lower birthrate equals faster prosperity" program in more places in the countryside.

谈到经贸话题：

- 中国将继续倡导并推动贸易和投资自由化、便利化，加强同各国的双向投资，打造合作新亮点。
  China will continue to champion and promote trade and investment liberalization and facilitation, step up bilateral investment with other countries and boost cooperation in new priority areas.

- 当前和今后一个时期，中国经济将继续保持健康发展势头，国内需求特别是消费需求将持续扩大，对外投资也将大幅增加。据测算，今后5年，中国将进口10万亿美元左右的商品，对外投资规模将达到5000亿美元，出境旅游有可能超过4亿人次。中国越发展，越能给亚洲和世界带来发展机遇。
  Going forward, China will maintain robust growth momentum. Its domestic demand, particularly consumption-driven demand, will continue to grow, and its outbound investment will increase substantially. It is projected that in the coming five years, China's import will reach some 10 trillion US dollars, its outbound investment will reach 500 billion US dollars and the number of its outbound tourists may well exceed 400 million. The more China grows itself, the more development opportunities it will create for the rest of Asia and the world.

- 长期以来，各国各地区在保持稳定、促进发展方面形成了很多好经验好做法。对这些好经验好做法，要继续发扬光大。
  Over the years, many countries and regions have developed a lot of good practices in maintaining stability and promoting growth. We should continue such practices.

- 要加大转变经济发展方式、调整经济结构力度，更加注重发展质量，更加注重改善民生。要稳步推进国际经济金融体系改革，完善全球治理机制，为世界经济健康稳定增长提供保障。
  We should redouble efforts to shift the growth model and adjust the economic structure, raise the quality of development and make life better for the people. We should steadily advance the reform of the international economic and financial systems, improve global governance mechanisms and provide

support to sound and stable global economic growth.

- 坚定不移地保护和发展先进生产力，淘汰落后产能，整合生产要素，拓展发展空间，实现保增长和调结构、增效益相统一，增强国民经济整体素质和发展后劲。
We will unwaveringly protect and develop advanced productive forces, shut down backward production facilities, integrate factors of production and create more room for development. We will balance our efforts to sustain economic growth, adjust the structure and improve economic performance to raise the overall quality of the national economy and strengthen the basis for its further development.

下面长段涉及外商投资的话题：

- 中国巨大的市场容量、完善的基础设施、完备的产业配套能力和稳定公平的市场环境，正在吸引越来越多的跨国企业到中国投资兴业。目前中国是世界上吸引外资最多的国家之一，全球500强企业中已有470多家在中国落户。截至今年7月底，中国已累计吸收外资1.05万亿美元，连续18年居发展中国家首位。今年1—7月我国吸收外商投资同比增长了20.7%。外商投资企业在中国总体运营情况良好，取得丰厚回报，不少企业成为其母公司全球业务增长亮点和利润中心。这些情况说明，中国政府营造良好投资环境的努力得到了投资者的认可，提振了外商投资信心。我们将继续完善涉外经济法律法规和政策，改善外商投资兴业环境。我们真诚地欢迎各国企业积极参与中国改革开放进程，也希望各类企业严格遵守中国的法律法规，在中国依法经营，共享中国繁荣进步带来的机遇和成果。
China's huge market volume, sound infrastructure, strong industrial support ability and stable and fair market environment are attracting more and more multinational enterprises to invest and establish business in China. China is now one of the world's largest foreign investment destinations. More than 470 of the top 500 global companies have established their presence in China. By July this year, China had received 1.05 trillion US dollars of foreign investment in cumulative terms, ranking the first among developing countries for 18 years in a row. In the first seven months this year, foreign

investment in China increased by 20.7 percent over the same period last year. Foreign invested enterprises on the whole enjoy good operation in China and have reaped good returns. Many have become the bright spot and profit center in the global business growth of their parent companies. All of these demonstrate that the efforts of the Chinese government to foster a favorable investment environment have been recognized by the investors and bolstered foreign investors' confidence. We will continue to improve the foreign-related economic laws, regulations and policies, and improve the business environment for foreign investors in China. We sincerely welcome enterprises from all countries to actively participate in China's reform and opening-up process, and hope that all types of enterprises will strictly abide by China's laws and regulations, run businesses in China according to law, and share the opportunities and benefits of China's prosperity and progress.

下面段落涉及外商待遇：

- 在中国境内注册的外资企业都享受国民待遇。同时，中国的政府采购，对外商投资企业和中资企业在中国生产的产品一视同仁、平等对待。
  All foreign invested enterprises registered in China enjoy national treatment. In government procurement, China gives equal treatment to all products produced in China by foreign invested enterprises and Chinese invested enterprises alike.
- 中国始终致力于为外商投资企业创造开放公平的良好环境。中国高度重视知识产权保护，已将保护知识产权提升为国家战略。
  China is committed to creating an open and fair environment for foreign invested enterprises. China gives high priority to intellectual property protection and has already made this a national strategy.

时政语篇涉及诸多领域和话题，纷纷杂杂，现阶段建议大家只作一个概括的了解。对于专业性很强的词语，不必急于完全弄懂，将来可视从事专业的需要再作进一步钻研。比如下面这句话中的划线词语，大家不一定非要记忆，只需收入自己的语料库待查备用即可。

要提倡对主要储备货币发行经济体宏观经济政策和主权信用评级机构的监督。

There should be supervision over the macroeconomic policies of major reserve currency issuing economies and over sovereign credit rating agencies.

除了记忆以上涉及政治、经济、社会民生等各领域的词语以外，对一般常用词语也要加以留心、记忆，并在自己的翻译实践中加以模仿运用。阅读时可着重关注动词（包括短语动词、动词和宾语的搭配等）和形容词的用法。比如：

- 行使权力就必须为人民服务、对人民负责并自觉接受人民监督，……
  In exercising power, we must serve the people, hold ourselves accountable to them, and readily subject ourselves to their oversight.
- 这些都表明，中国经济发展的前景十分广阔，也会给包括瑞士在内的各国发展带来更多机遇。
  All these underscore the enormous prospect of China's economic development and the growth opportunities it will bring to Switzerland and other countries.
- 完善促进就业、以创业带动就业的政策，落实最低工资制度。
  We improved our policy to stimulate and expand employment by encouraging business startups, and enforced the minimum wage system.
- 加大保障性住房建设和棚户区改造力度，低收入群众住房困难问题得到一定程度缓解。
  We intensified efforts to develop low-income housing and renovate shanty towns, thus alleviating some of the housing difficulties of the low-income population.
- 如果腐败得不到有效惩治，党就会丧失人民信任和支持。全党必须警钟长鸣，充分认识反腐败斗争的长期性、复杂性、艰巨性，把反腐倡廉建设摆在更加突出的位置，以更加坚定的信心、更加坚决的态度、更加有力的举措推进惩治和预防腐败体系建设，坚定不移把反腐败斗争进行到底。
  If not effectively curbed, corruption will cost the Party the trust and support of the people. The whole Party must remain vigilant against corruption, be fully aware that fighting corruption will be a protracted, complicated and arduous battle, and give higher priority to combating corruption and upholding

integrity. The Party must demonstrate greater confidence and resolve and take more forceful measures to improve the institutions for punishing and preventing corruption and unswervingly fight corruption.

对时政语篇中出现频率高的动词可以专门收集，比如"推进"一词，可有多种译法：

- 我们全面<u>推进</u>产业结构调整和优化升级。
  We are <u>pushing forward</u> industrial restructuring and upgrading across the board.
- 三是大力<u>推进</u>科技进步和创新。
  Third, <u>make energetic efforts for</u> progress and innovation in science and technology.

再比如"应对"一词：

- 我认为，<u>应对</u>全球性危机，需要增进合作。
  I believe that closer cooperation is needed to <u>meet</u> the global crisis.
- 这里我想谈一谈中国是如何<u>应对</u>这场金融危机的。
  Let me talk briefly about how China has been <u>responding to</u> the crisis.
- 有效<u>应对</u>这场危机，还必须高度重视道德的作用。
  To effectively <u>meet</u> the crisis, we must fully recognize the role of morality.

阅读双语语篇时，我们也经常看到"是"译为行为动词的情况，如李克强总理2012年5月3日在中欧城镇化伙伴关系高层会议开幕式上的讲话中，一连三段的首句都用同样的句式阐述我国城镇化的内涵，译文则将"是"译为aim to。

中国的城镇化，<u>是</u>扩大内需、可持续发展的城镇化。
中国的城镇化，<u>是</u>与工业化、农业现代化协同推进的城镇化。
中国的城镇化，<u>是</u>以人为本、公平共享的城镇化。

China's urbanization <u>aims to</u> expand domestic demand and promote sustainable development.
China's urbanization <u>aims to</u> ensure coordinated development of industrialization and agricultural modernization.
China's urbanization is people-oriented and <u>aims to</u> deliver equitable benefits to all.

除动词外，还要注意形容词的英译，如：

- 日程很充实也很有收获。
  The visit was both substantive and rewarding.
- 中华传统文化底蕴深厚、博大精深。
  The traditional Chinese culture is rich, extensive and profound.
- 到本世纪中叶建成富强民主文明和谐的社会主义现代化国家，实现中华民族伟大复兴的中国梦。展望未来，我们充满信心。
  By the mid-21st century, China will be turned into a modern socialist country that is prosperous, democratic, culturally advanced and harmonious.

除了从话题和常用词语的角度关注汉英转换的规律以外，还可以留心时政语篇中某些独具特色的表达方式。这类词语我们在第一章中曾提过，在双语对照阅读时，可特别关注有关数字增减的表达。建议阅读时聚焦以下几方面：

首先是表示"增加"类别的词语和表达，比如：

- 参加新型农村合作医疗的人口8.14亿，参合率91.5%。城镇居民基本医疗保险试点城市由上年的88个增加到317个，参保人数增加7359万，总计达到1.17亿。
  A total of 814 million people, accounting for 91.5% of the rural population, now benefit from the new type of rural cooperative medical care system. The number of selected cities participating in trials of the basic medical insurance system for urban residents increased from 88 to 317, and the number of participating individuals increased by 73.59 million to 117 million.

而"翻番"可以这样表达：

- 到2020年国内生产总值和城乡居民人均收入在2010年的基础上翻一番。
  By 2020, China's GDP and per capita incomes for urban and rural residents will double the 2010 figures.
- 2012年中国的GDP按可比价算是2000年的3.2倍，翻了一番还多；到2020年通过努力在2010年的基础上再翻一番，需年均增长7%左右。
  China's 2012 GDP, in comparable terms, more than doubled that of 2000, registering an increase of 3.2 times. To double the GDP of 2010 by 2020, China will need to sustain an annual growth rate of around 7 percent.

还要关注下面这类表示"减少"的词语：

- 2009年中国实现进口10056亿美元，全年贸易顺差<u>减少了1020亿美元</u>；今年前7个月，中国实现进口7666亿美元，同比大幅增长47.2%，贸易顺差同比<u>减少226亿美元</u>。
  In 2009, China's imports totaled 1.0056 trillion US dollars, and its trade surplus <u>dropped by 102 billion US dollars</u>. In the first seven months of this year, China's imports reached 766.6 billion US dollars, a surge of 47.2 percent year on year, and its trade surplus dropped by 22.6 billion US dollars year on year.

- 单位国内生产总值能耗比上年<u>下降4.59%</u>，化学需氧量、二氧化硫排放量分别<u>减少4.42%和5.95%</u>。近三年累计，单位国内生产总值能耗<u>下降10.08%</u>，化学需氧量、二氧化硫排放量分别<u>减少6.61%和8.95%</u>。
  Energy consumption per unit of GDP <u>fell by 4.59%</u> from the previous year; chemical oxygen demand <u>fell by 4.42%</u>; and sulfur dioxide emissions <u>fell by 5.95%</u>. For the past three years combined, total energy consumption per unit of GDP <u>dropped by 10.08%</u>; chemical oxygen demand <u>dropped by 6.61%</u>; and sulfur dioxide emissions <u>dropped by 8.95%</u>.

除了具体的数字，还可关注表示"大约"概念的一些词语，比如：

- 这两年，我国财政赤字和国债规模分别控制在国内生产总值的<u>3%以内</u>和<u>20%左右</u>；银行资产质量和抵御风险能力提高，目前资本充足率和不良贷款率分别为11.1%和2.8%，都处于安全范围内。
  In the past two years, China's budget deficit and government debt have been kept <u>below 3 percent</u> and <u>around 20 percent</u> of the GDP respectively. The asset quality of banks and their ability to fend off risks have improved. The capital adequacy ratio and NPL ratio now stand at 11.1 percent and 2.8 percent respectively, both in the safe territory.

- 今年国民经济和社会发展的主要预期目标是：国内生产总值增长<u>8%左右</u>，经济结构进一步优化；城镇新增就业<u>900万人以上</u>，城镇登记失业率<u>4.6%以内</u>；城乡居民收入稳定增长；居民消费价格总水平涨幅<u>4%左右</u>。
  We have set the following major targets for this year's national economic and

social development: GDP will grow by about 8%; the economic structure will further improve; urban employment will increase by more than nine million persons; the urban registered unemployment rate will be held under 4.6%, urban and rural incomes will grow steadily; the rise in the CPI will be around 4%.

除了"大约""左右"等词语，还有表示"持平"等概念的词语，比如：

- 两年来，国内需求特别是消费对经济增长的拉动作用持续增强，今年以来这一势头得到延续，上半年实际增速与去年同期基本持平。
  In the past two years, domestic demand, consumption in particular, has played an increasingly strong role in driving economic growth. This good momentum is continuing and retail sales in the first half of this year grew at roughly the same rate as the same period of last year.

- 中国政府推出了以财政支出带动社会投资，总额达4万亿元的两年计划，规模相当于2007年中国GDP的16%。
  The Chinese Government has announced a two-year investment program that will generate, through fiscal spending, a total investment of RMB 4 trillion nationwide, equivalent to 16% of China's GDP in 2007.

阅读中我们还看到，英语中表达数字时常使用同位语结构，如：

- 城镇居民人均可支配收入15781元，农村居民人均纯收入4761元，实际增长8.4%和8%。
  Urban per capita annual disposable income reached 15,781 yuan, an increase of 8.4% in real terms, and rural per capita net income reached 4,761 yuan, up by 8% in real terms.

- 2009年社会消费品零售总额实际增长16.9%，为1986年以来最高增速。
  Total retail sales in 2009 rose by 16.9 percent in real terms, the fastest since 1986.

- 国民经济继续保持平稳较快增长。国内生产总值超过30万亿元，比上年增长9%；物价总水平涨幅得到控制；财政收入6.13万亿元，增长19.5%；粮食连续五年增产，总产量52850万吨，创历史最高水平。
  The national economy continued to maintain steady and rapid growth. GDP topped 30 trillion yuan, an increase of 9% over the previous year. Overall

price rises were held in check. Government revenue was 6.13 trillion yuan, <u>an increase of 19.5%</u>. Grain output rose for the fifth consecutive year and totaled 528.5 million tons, <u>a record high</u>.

- 改革开放深入推进。财税、金融、价格、行政管理等重点领域和关键环节的改革取得新突破。进出口贸易总额 2.56 万亿美元，增长 17.8%。实际利用外商直接投资 924 亿美元。

  Reform and opening up were further deepened. New breakthroughs were made in reforms in key areas and crucial links, such as the fiscal, taxation, financial and pricing systems and administration. Imports and exports totaled 2.56 trillion US dollars, <u>an increase of 17.8%</u>. Paid-in foreign direct investment reached 92.4 billion US dollars.

- 全年中央财政用于"三农"的投入 5955 亿元，比上年增加 1637 亿元，增长 37.9%，其中粮食直补、农资综合补贴、良种补贴、农机具购置补贴资金达 1030 亿元，比上年增长一倍。

  Central government budgetary spending on agriculture, rural areas and farmers was 595.5 billion yuan for the whole year, <u>a year-on-year increase of 163.7 billion yuan or 37.9%</u>. This included 103 billion yuan, <u>twice the figure for the previous year</u>, in direct subsidies to grain producers, general subsidies for agricultural production supplies, and subsidies for superior crop varieties and the purchase of agricultural machinery and tools.

第一章的第一节和本章的第一节都关注了政治、经济等领域的时政词汇，有些属于我国特色词语，需要确定首创性的译文，但国外流行的类似英文表达仍不失为有益的参照。比如王平兴曾举过一个军队核心价值观的译例（见《中国翻译》2010：1）：

我国当代革命军人价值观是：

忠诚于党，热爱人民，报效国家，献身使命，崇高荣誉。

原译文是：

Being loyal to the Party, deeply cherishing the people, serving the country, showing devotion to missions and upholding honor.

目标语参照：

Loyalty, Duty, Respect, Selfless-service, Honor, Integrity, Personal courage.（美国陆军的核心价值观）

Honor, Courage and Commitment.（美国海军的核心价值观）

因此，建议将原译文改为：

Loyalty, Love, Service, Commitment, Honor.

第二节 主语的确立

英语小句的基本构架是"主语+谓语+宾语"，而汉语的主谓宾结构并不像英语那样明确、彰显，所以汉译英中主语的确立十分重要。主语作为一句之始，引领着谓语和其他句子成分的安排，同时也与谓语等成分相互配合。汉译英过程中，主语的确立常有以下几种情况：

1. 添加主语

汉语中主语常常省略，英译时自然要根据具体的语境，加以补充。比如：

- 稳步扩大服务业对外开放，加强对外商投资方向的引导。
  We steadily opened service industries wider to the outside world and provided more guidance to orient foreign investment in China.

- 回顾90年中国的发展进步，可以得出一个基本结论：办好中国的事情，关键在党。
  Looking back at China's development and progress over the past 90 years, we have naturally come to this basic conclusion: Success in China hinges on the Party.

- 坚定不移地推进自主创新和经济结构调整。实施16个国家重大科技专项。在信息、生物、环保等领域新建一批国家工程中心、重点实验室和企业技术中心。成功研发支线飞机、新能源汽车、高速铁路等一批关键技术和重大装备。
  We unswervingly promoted independent innovation and economic restructuring. We launched 16 major national science and technology projects, and established

a number of new national engineering centers, key laboratories and enterprise technology centers in such fields as information technology, biotechnology and environmental protection. We successfully developed a number of key technologies and major equipment in the areas of regional aircraft, automobiles powered by new energy sources and high-speed railways.

2. 用被动语态翻译汉语无主句
- 全面夺取抗击特大自然灾害的重大胜利。成功举办北京奥运会、残奥会。圆满完成神舟七号载人航天飞行。
  Great victorias <u>were won</u> in the fight against massive natural disasters. The Beijing Olympics and Paralympics <u>were held</u> successfully, and the Shenzhou VII manned space mission <u>was</u> a complete success.
- 向中等职业学校中来自城市经济困难家庭和农村的学生提供助学金，每人每年1500元，惠及90%的在校生。
  Grants of 1500 yuan per student per annum <u>were given</u> to secondary vocational school students from rural areas or needy urban families, benefiting 90% of the current student population in these vocational schools.

3. 加字组成主语
- 国强必霸，不适合中国。
  <u>The argument</u> that a big power is bound to seek hegemony does not apply to China.
- 中国改革开放，最重要的是解放思想，最根本、最具有长远意义的是体制创新。
  The key <u>element</u> of China's reform and opening-up is to free people's mind and the most fundamental and significant <u>component</u> is institutional innovation.
- 农业、农村、农民问题，始终是中国面临的重大挑战。
  <u>Resolving</u> issues related to agriculture, rural areas and farmers will remain a major challenge for China.

4. 原句中抽出某词语作译文主语
- 我对三年前作为中国国务院副总理访瑞记忆犹新。
  <u>My last visit to Switzerland</u> three years ago as China's vice premier remains fresh in my memory.

- 不同国家、不同民族的文化，需要相互尊重、相互包容和相互学习。
  Different countries and nations need to respect, tolerate and learn from each other's culture.
- 90年来，中国社会发生的变革，中国人民命运发生的变化，其广度和深度，其政治影响和社会意义，在人类发展史上都是十分罕见的。
  The profundity and the political and social impact of the changes that have taken place in Chinese society and in the destiny of the Chinese people over the past 90 years are rare in the history of human development.
- 争取民族独立、人民解放，实现国家富强、人民富裕，成为中国人民必须完成的历史任务。
  And the Chinese people faced the historic tasks of winning independence and liberation, and making China strong and prosperous.
- 太平天国运动，戊戌变法，义和团运动，不甘屈服的中国人民一次次抗争，但又一次次失败。
  Not resigned to fate, the Chinese people launched one struggle after another, such as the Taiping Heavenly Kingdom Movement, the Reform Movement of 1898, and the Yihetuan Movement, but all these struggles ended in failure.

以上各汉语原文中的划线部分被抽出重立为英译文的主语，并依此构建全句。

5. 将主谓结构转换为名词短语作主语（参阅本章第十节名物化）

- 我们党旗帜鲜明、一以贯之反对腐败，反腐倡廉建设不断取得新的明显进展，为推进改革开放和社会主义现代化建设提供了重要保障。
  The Party's unequivocal and consistent opposition to corruption and the steady, notable new progress made in fighting corruption and upholding integrity provide an important guarantee for advancing reform, opening up, and socialist modernization.

6. 将动宾短语或名词短语转换成动名词短语、不定式短语作主语

- 实现各国共同发展，依然任重而道远。
  Achieving common development for all countries remains an uphill battle.
- 与瑞方加强金融监管、宏观政策和完善资本市场体系等方面的合作，是中国开放型经济发展的客观需要。
  Enhancing cooperation with Switzerland in financial regulation, macroeconomic

policy making, capital market development and other areas is consistent with China's need for further development of its open economy.

- 在我们这样一个13亿人口的发展中国家，要扩大城乡就业，增加居民收入，维护社会稳定，就必须保持一定的经济增长速度。
  In China, a developing country with a population of 1.3 billion, <u>maintaining a certain growth rate for the economy</u> is essential for expanding employment for both urban and rural residents, increasing people's incomes and ensuring social stability.

- 合作应对、共渡难关，是我们的首要任务。
  <u>To work together and tide over the difficulties</u> has become our top priority.

- 救亡图存的民族使命迫在眉睫。
  <u>To salvage China from subjugation</u> was an urgent mission for the Chinese nation.

- 亲仁善邻，是中国自古以来的传统。
  <u>Promoting good neighborliness</u> is a time-honored tradition of China.

- 充分挖掘市场潜力，有效释放国内需求，是促进中国经济长期稳定发展的关键所在，也是解决经济运行中突出矛盾的重要途径。
  <u>To fully tap the potential and effectively unleash the domestic demand</u> holds the key to long-term and steady development of China's economy, and represents an important means to meet the prominent challenges in the economy.

- 源源不断培养造就大批优秀年轻干部，是关系党和人民事业继往开来、薪火相传的根本大计。
  <u>To continuously train a large number of outstanding young cadres</u> is of fundamental importance for carrying on the cause of the Party and the people from generation to generation.

以上译例中，汉语动宾短语的信息成分正好可纳入英文动名词短语或不定式短语结构中。下面译例中，原文的主谓词组被译为不定式作主语，主谓词组后的信息在译文中有所调整。

- 亚洲和世界和平发展、合作共赢的事业没有终点，只有一个接一个的新起点。

To enhance peaceful development and win-win cooperation in Asia and the world is a race that has one starting point after another and knows no finishing line.

7. 使用形式主语 it

- 这里要着重说明，提出8%左右的国内生产总值增长目标，综合考虑了发展的需要和可能。

  It needs to be stressed that in projecting the GDP growth target at about 8%, we have taken into consideration both our need and ability to sustain development.

8. 使用主语从句

英语中，除了动名词短语和不定式短语可作主语外，从句也可充当主语，即主语从句。主语从句的使用一般有两种情况：一是原文中有较长的主谓结构，英译有可能处理为主语从句；二是某些固定的汉语句式，比如"关键是……""重要的是……""事实证明……"等，可译为主语从句。例如：

- 中瑞关系和务实合作能够达到什么高度，既取决于能否抓住新的机遇，更取决于能否提高双方互信和理解的层次。

  How high we can go in developing our relations and our practical cooperation hinges on our ability to seize new opportunities, and more importantly, on whether or not we can reach a higher level of mutual trust and understanding.

- 关键是要坚持通过对话协商与和平谈判，妥善解决矛盾分歧，维护相互关系发展大局。

  What is important is that they should resolve differences through dialogue, consultation and peaceful negotiations in the larger interest of the sound growth of their relations.

- 事实充分证明，在近代以来中国社会发展进步的壮阔进程中，历史和人民选择了中国共产党，选择了马克思主义，选择了社会主义道路，选择了改革开放。

  What has happened shows that in the great cause of China's social development and progress since modern times, history and the people have chosen the CPC, Marxism, the socialist road, and the reform and opening up policy.

- 一个国家、一个民族对人类文化贡献的大小，越来越取决于她吸收外来文化的能力和自我更新的能力。

How much a country or a nation contributes to the culture of humanity is increasingly determined by her ability to absorb foreign cultures and renew herself.

- 北京奥运会向世界展示的，就是这样一个古老、多彩和现代的中国。
  What the Beijing Olympic Games showcased is a colorful China, both ancient and modern.
- 协调各方面利益诉求、形成能够保障互利共赢的机制需要更好增进理解、凝聚共识、充实内容、深化合作。
  What we need to do is to enhance mutual understanding, build consensus, and enrich and deepen cooperation so as to strike a balance among the interests of various parties and build mechanisms that bring benefits to all.
- 中国特色社会主义道路能不能越走越宽广，中华民族能不能实现伟大复兴，要看能不能不断培养造就大批优秀人才，更要看能不能让各方面优秀人才脱颖而出、施展才华。
  Whether the path of socialism with Chinese characteristics can become wider and whether the Chinese nation can achieve its great rejuvenation depend on our success in training and fostering a large number of outstanding personnel, and particularly, in bringing outstanding personnel in all fields to the fore and bringing out their best.

第三节　拆译和主语安排

　　汉语的时政文件、官方讲话多长句，逗号叠用，分句依次推进延伸，直至一个小话题结束。这样的长句单用英语中的一个主谓宾结构是无法顺畅表达的，必须对长句加以切分，将其化为一个个以主谓小句为基本结构的语段，这便是拆译。

　　有些时候，汉语长句中的分句各有自己的主谓，英译时自可顺势为之，大致按原文的主谓信息确立英语中的主谓便可。比如：

- 瑞士是首批与新中国建交的西方国家之一，中国改革开放后第一家工业性合资企业就是与瑞士合作成立的，瑞士又在欧洲国家中较早承认了中国市场经济地位。

Switzerland is among the first Western countries to have established diplomatic relations with New China. The very first industrial joint venture China entered into after the beginning of reform and opening up was one with Switzerland. Switzerland is also one of the first group of European countries that recognize China's market economy status.

- 世界各国相互联系日益紧密、相互依存日益加深，遍布全球的众多发展中国家、几十亿人口正在努力走向现代化，和平、发展、合作、共赢的时代潮流更加强劲。

Countries have become increasingly inter-connected and inter-dependent. Several billion people in a large number of developing countries are embracing modernization. The trend of the times, namely, peace, development, cooperation and mutual benefit, is gaining momentum.

有时，语义关系紧密的小句可以构成一个并列句，各个分句的主语仍沿用汉语原文的主语。比如下面的汉语句子译为英语时，被拆成两个句子（双斜线表示），而每个句子里又包含了几个并列分句（单斜线表示），分别以汉语中划线词语作主语。

- 鸦片战争以后，中国逐步成为半殖民地半封建社会，/ 列强对中国的侵略步步进逼，// 封建统治日益腐败，/ 祖国山河破碎、战乱不已，/ 人民饥寒交迫、备受奴役。

Following the Opium War, China gradually became a semi-colonial and semi-feudal society, and foreign powers stepped up their aggression against China. The feudal rule became increasingly corrupt, the country was devastated by incessant wars and turbulence, and the Chinese people suffered from hunger, cold, and oppression.

- 同时，天下仍很不太平，// 发展问题依然突出，// 世界经济进入深度调整期，/ 整体复苏艰难曲折，// 国际金融领域仍然存在较多风险，/ 各种形式的保护主义上升，/ 各国调整经济结构面临不少困难，/ 全球治理机制有待进一步完善。

On the other hand, our world is far from peaceful. Development remains a major challenge; the global economy has entered a period of profound readjustment, and its recovery remains elusive. The international financial sector is fraught with risks, protectionism of various forms is on the rise, countries still face many difficulties in adjusting economic structure, and the global governance mechanisms call for improvement.

以上译例中，英译文基本照搬汉语原文的主语。

还有一种情况，汉语中的主语承前省略了，英译文就要补上。增补的主语可重复原文主语（一般是名词），也可用代词复指。比如，下面译例中汉语原句被拆译为两句，后一句沿用第一句的主语，基本重复了同一个名词。

- 孙中山先生领导的<u>辛亥革命</u>，结束了统治中国几千年的君主专制制度，对推动中国社会进步具有重大意义，但也未能改变中国半殖民地半封建的社会性质和中国人民的悲惨命运。

<u>The Revolution of 1911</u> led by Dr. Sun Yat-sen put an end to the autocratic rule that had existed in China for several thousand years. <u>This revolution</u> greatly boosted China's social progress, but it did not change the country's nature as a semi-colonial and semi-feudal society or end the misery of the Chinese people.

- 改革开放的<u>实质</u>，就是坚持以人为本，通过解放和发展生产力满足人们日益增长的物质文化需求，在公正的条件下促进人的全面发展；就是保障人民的民主权利，让国家政通人和、兴旺发达。

<u>The essence</u> of China's reform and opening-up is to put people first and meet their ever growing material and cultural needs through releasing and developing productive forces. <u>It</u> aims to give everyone equal opportunities for all-round development. <u>It</u> aims to protect the democratic rights of the people and promote stability, harmony and prosperity across the land.

这个汉语长句的主语是"实质"，对译为 the essence，译文拆译出的句子均以 it 加以承接。

下面一句的原文拆译为两句，后一句用代词 they 承接第一句的主语 these achievements。

这些成就，标志着我们在中国特色社会主义道路上迈出新的坚实步伐，极大地增强了全国各族人民战胜困难的勇气和力量，必将激励我们在新的历史征程上继续奋勇前进。

These achievements signify that we have taken new and solid steps along the path of socialism with Chinese characteristics. They have greatly fortified the courage and strength of the people of all our ethnic groups to surmount difficulties and will definitely encourage us to bravely forge ahead on the new historical course.

下面译例，原文的主语即是代词，英译文中随后拆出的两个句子自然都补上了同样的代词 we。

（9月份后，国际经济形势急转直下，对我国的不利影响明显加重，）我们又果断地把宏观调控的着力点转到防止经济增速过快下滑上来，实施积极的财政政策和适度宽松的货币政策，三次提高出口退税率，五次下调金融机构存贷款基准利率，四次下调存款准备金率，暂免储蓄存款利息个人所得税，下调证券交易印花税，降低住房交易税费，加大对中小企业信贷支持。

(In September, the international economic situation started to deteriorate sharply and its negative impact became increasingly felt in China.) We again resolutely shifted the focus of macro control to preventing economic growth from slowing down too quickly. We implemented a proactive fiscal policy and a moderately easy monetary policy. We raised export rebate rates three times, lowered the benchmark interest rates on savings and loans for financial institutions on five occasions, reduced required reserve ratios four times, suspended the individual income tax on interest earnings from savings, reduced securities transaction stamp tax rates, cut taxes and fees on housing transactions, and increased credit support to small and medium-sized enterprises.

还有第三种情况：补充主语的操作更加灵活，译文中形成多样化的主语链。如下面译例：

各级干部都要自重、自省、自警、自励，讲党性、重品行、作表率，做到立身不忘做人之本、为政不移公仆之心、用权不谋一己之私，永葆共产党人政治本色。

Officials at all levels must have a keen sense of living up to the people's trust, guarding against wrong doing, and holding themselves to higher standards. We must act in the true Party spirit, ensure integrity, and play an exemplary role in society. One should not forget his origin when in prominent position; he should not abandon the role of public servants once in public post, or use power for personal gains. We must preserve the political integrity of Communists.

  此例原文的主语是"各级干部",英译时被断为五个句子,后四句要补充的主语当然都是"各级干部",可以用代词 they 或 we 复指。但译文行文灵活,将第三句和第四句的主语变为 one 和 he,形成 officials—we—one—he—we 主语链,泛指各级官员,文气连贯,句式多变。

  下面译例原文的主语是"世界各国",通贯全句。而英译构建了主语链 all countries—they—a country—countries,同样将"世界各国"这一信息以主语的形式贯穿整个段落。

  世界各国联系紧密、利益交融,要互通有无、优势互补,在追求本国利益时兼顾他国合理关切,在谋求自身发展中促进各国共同发展,不断扩大共同利益汇合点。

  All countries in the world are closely linked and share converging interests. They should both pool and share their strengths. While pursuing its own interests, a country should accommodate the legitimate concerns of others. In pursuing their own development, countries should promote the common development of all and expand common interests among them.

  下面译例的原文有两句话,第二句是个长句,其主语承接第一句的宾语,统辖各个分句。英译文将原文第一句单独译为一个句子,将第二句拆成三句,形成主语链 this—it—the system of theories of socialism with Chinese characteristics,有复指,有重复,构成连贯的语段。

  另一大理论成果是中国特色社会主义理论体系。中国特色社会主义理论体系是包括邓小平理论、"三个代表"重要思想以及科学发展观等重大战略思想在内的科学理论体系,系统回答了在中国这样一个十几亿人口的发展中大国建设什么样的社会主义、怎样建设社会主义,建设什么样的党、怎样建设党、实现什么样的发展、怎样发展等一系列重大问题,是对毛泽东思想的继承和发展。

  The other theoretical achievement is the system of theories of socialism with Chinese characteristics. This is a scientific theoretical system consisting of Deng Xiaoping Theory, the important thought of Three Represents, the Scientific Outlook on Development and other major strategic thoughts. It has systematically addressed a series of significant issues, such as what kind of socialism China, a large developing country of over one billion people, should build and how to build it; what kind of party we should build and how to build it; and what kind of development China should achieve and how to achieve it. <u>The system of theories of socialism with Chinese characteristics</u> represents the continuation and development of Mao Zedong Thought.

下面一句汉语拆译成四个句子，译文的主语链是：our four countries—this—it—our endeavor，前两句沿用汉语主语，第三句的主语 it 复指前句的 this，第四句主语 our endeavor 则是根据全句的语境添加的。

我们四国政治体制、发展方式、宗教信仰、文化传统不尽相同，却能成为好朋友、好伙伴，这充分证明了不同社会制度可以相互包容，不同发展模式可以相互合作，不同历史文明可以相互借鉴，不同文化传统可以相互交流，顺应了和平与发展的时代潮流，体现了合作共赢的时代特点。

<u>Our four countries</u> differ in political system, development model, religious belief and cultural tradition, but we have become good friends and partners. <u>This</u> shows that countries with different social systems can be inclusive toward each other and countries with different development models can engage in cooperation. <u>It</u> also shows that different civilizations can learn from each other and different cultures can have exchanges. <u>Our endeavor</u> is in keeping with the trend towards peace and development and answers the call of our time for cooperation and mutual benefit.

下面译例，汉语的后一个分句指的是前面分句的内容，也就是说，第一个分句的主语是"增速"，但后面分句所省略的主语显然并非"增速"，而是"增速出现回落"这一事实。英译确立主语时必须注意到这种语义的衔接和连贯。因此，译文以 this 复指前一句话，形成连贯的语段。

二季度后一些主要经济指标增速出现回落，主要是基数影响和主动调控的结果。

Growth of some major economic indicators moderated in the second quarter of this year. <u>This</u> is mainly due to the high level of the base figures and our proactive macro-control measures.

下面原文被拆译为两句，第二句译文的主语 this 复指前句的内容。

全党同志必须牢记，做到权为民所用、情为民所系、利为民所谋，使我们的工作获得最广泛最可靠最牢固的群众基础和力量源泉。

All the comrades in the Party must bear in mind that we must exercise power for the people, identify ourselves with them and work for their interests. This will win us the most extensive, reliable, and solid popular support, which will serve the source of strength for our work.

除上所述，还有更加灵活的拆译方式。比如下面一句被拆译为三句话，译文第一个断句点并不以标点为界，而是断在原文句子中间（双斜线表示）。英译的第一句将原文动宾词组转换成动名词短语作主语，第二句和三句均以代词 it 回指第一句的主语。

以人为本、执政为民是我们党的性质 // 和全心全意为人民服务根本宗旨的集中体现，是指引、评价、检验我们党一切执政活动的最高标准。

Putting people first and governing for the people is what the Party is all about. It fully embodies the Party's fundamental purpose of serving the people wholeheartedly. It is the ultimate yardstick to guide, assess, and test all governance activities of the Party.

下面汉语原句被拆译为三句，前两句沿用汉语原有主语，后一句根据全句语境将主语定为 we。

在党中央、国务院坚强领导下，全国各族人民特别是灾区人民万众一心、众志成城，人民子弟兵舍生忘死、冲锋在前，展开了我国历史上救援速度最快、动员范围最广、投入力量最大的抗震救灾斗争。

Under the firm leadership of the CPC Central Committee and the State Council, people of all ethnic groups in China, especially in the quake zone, worked as one and fought in unison against the earthquake disaster. The people's army rushed to the frontlines without thinking of their own safety. We launched an earthquake rescue and relief operation that accomplished its work faster, mobilized more personnel and committed more resources than ever before in China's history.

下面的英译文也是根据原文全句的语境，在第三句添加了主语 we。

今年是实施"十一五"规划的关键之年，也是进入新世纪以来我国经济发展最为困难的一年，改革发展稳定的任务十分繁重。

This year is crucial for the implementation of the Eleventh Five-Year Plan. It will also be the most difficult year for China's economic development since the beginning of the 21st century. We face arduous tasks in promoting reform, development and stability.

有时候，原文的信息经过了较大的调整，英译文中主语的确立就更需要从英语写作的角度通篇考虑译文的连贯性。比如：

经过 90 年的奋斗、创造、积累，党和人民必须倍加珍惜、长期坚持、不断发展的成就是：开辟了中国特色社会主义道路，形成了中国特色社会主义理论体系，确立了中国特色社会主义制度。

We have embarked on the path of socialism with Chinese characteristics, formed a system of theories of socialism with Chinese characteristics and established a socialist system with Chinese characteristics. These achievements made over 90 years of endeavors, innovation, and enrichment, should be valued, upheld on a long-term basis and continuously built upon by our Party and people.

可以看到，译文将原句冒号后的内容译为第一个句子，主语确立为 we，然后用 these achievements 复指上句，达到了译文自身的连贯。

总之，拆译后各个句子或分句的主语的确立，要从语篇视角整体考虑，统筹兼顾，这样才能构建出主语衔接合理、句与句之间语义连贯的语段。拆译法在汉译英中的应用十分普遍。我们必须通过大量阅读双语语篇，用心体会，勤于实践，切实掌握这一翻译技巧。

第四节　行文视角的变化

上一节我们学习了拆译后的主语安排。主语标示着句子的起始信息，有了主语再确立了谓语，信息的结构走向便明确了。可以说，主语在很大程度上确立了表达信息的视角（即行文视角），决定了句子的信息流向。

本节从信息表达视角出发，考察译文对原文信息进行重新安排或对原文行文方式加以转换的情况。阅读汉英对照语篇时必须细心观察汉英行文的差异，体会英语构句谋篇的规律，并结合自己的翻译实践作进一步的思考和运用。

比如下面汉语原句就以"我们"起始，作为话题，后面都是"我们"要推动各方做的事情。英译文把它拆为两句，第一句仍以第一人称 we 为主语，第二句则换了视角，改为一种客观陈述的句式。

我们要推动各方增强责任感和道义感，努力实现全球平衡发展，既增加发展投入、保障发展资源，又尊重各国基于国情的发展模式和政策空间。

<u>We</u> should encourage all parties to embrace a stronger sense of responsibility and morality and work for balanced global development. <u>It</u> is important to scale up input in development and ensure development resources and at the same time respect each other's development model chosen in the light of national conditions and policy space.

译文视角转换的情况十分常见，不妨再举一个类似的例子：

我们要推动各方努力解决全球经济治理结构不平衡问题，按时完成二十国集团领导人匹兹堡峰会确定的国际金融机构量化改革目标，增加新兴市场国家和发展中国家的代表性和发言权。

<u>We</u> should encourage all parties to address imbalances in the global economic governance structure. <u>It</u> is important to achieve on schedule the quantified reform targets of international financial institutions set by the G20 Pittsburgh Summit and increase the representation and voice of emerging markets and developing countries.

再看下面一例。汉语原文有两句，主语都是"我们"，第二句承前省略了主语。英译文的第一句沿用主语 we，第二句则转换视角，以"多哈回合谈判主要各方"为起始点构句。

我们要推动各方继续推进贸易自由化、便利化，妥善处理贸易纠纷，抵制保护主义。推动多哈回合谈判主要各方展现诚意、显示灵活，尽早达成全面均衡的成果，促进建立开放共赢的多边贸易体制。

We should encourage all parties to continue to promote trade liberalization and facilitation, properly handle trade disputes and reject protectionism. <u>The main parties to the Doha Round negotiations</u> should demonstrate sincerity and flexibility to reach comprehensive and balanced outcomes at an early date and facilitate the establishment of an open and mutually-beneficial multilateral trade regime.

下面译例原文被拆译为两句，第一句添加主语 we，第二句转换叙述角度，将原句"使……理想变为现实"变为被动，译为"理想被变为现实"。

九年免费义务教育的推行，农村合作医疗制度的建立，社会保障体系的完善，使学有所教、病有所医、老有所养的理想，正在变为现实。

We have introduced free nine-year compulsory education throughout the country, established the cooperative medical system in the rural areas and improved the social safety net. The age-old dream of the Chinese nation is being turned into reality, a dream to see the young educated, the sick treated and the old cared for.

下面译例中原文为"传媒在介绍某事",而译文转成"介绍某事是传媒的特色"。

我们的电视、广播、出版等新闻传媒,天天都在介绍世界各地的文化艺术。
The cultures and arts of various parts of the world are featured daily on China's television, radio and print media.

下面汉语长句中,"新中国的成立"作为话题统辖全句,行文视角均从这个话题出发。英译文将原文拆成五句,每句的构句视角都有所转化。

新中国的成立,使人民成为国家、社会和自己命运的主人,实现了中国从几千年封建专制制度向人民民主制度的伟大跨越,实现了中国高度统一和各民族空前团结,彻底结束了旧中国半殖民地半封建社会的历史,彻底结束了旧中国一盘散沙的局面,彻底废除了列强强加给中国的不平等条约和帝国主义在中国的一切特权。

With the founding of New China, the Chinese people became masters of their country and society and determined their own destiny. China achieved a great transition from a feudal autocracy that was several thousand years old to a people's democracy. Great unity and unprecedented solidarity of all ethnic groups were realized in China. The history of old China being a semi-colonial and semi-feudal society which was like a heap of loose sand was brought to an end once and for all. The unequal treaties imposed on China by imperialist powers and all the privileges they had in China were abolished.

我们看到,英译文第一句中把"使人民……"换个角度译成"人民成为……"(the Chinese people became…),第二句"实现了中国……"转译为"中国实现……"(China achieved…),第三句"实现了中国……"转译为被动语态,第四句中的两个"彻底结束……"也转为被动视角,最后第五句,"彻底废除……"也是从被动的角度翻译的。

下面汉语句子是复合句,英译文未改变其逻辑安排,只是译文主句的主语变为了 we——原文说"……不能变",译文说"我们要恪守……"

无论国际形势如何变化、国际体系如何变革,互利共赢的目标不能变,民主公平的原则不能变,相互尊重的方向不能变,同舟共济的精神不能变。

No matter how the international situation may evolve and what changes the international system may experience, <u>we</u> should remain firmly committed to the goal of mutual benefit, the principle of democracy and equity, the approach of mutual respect and the spirit of solidarity and cooperation.

下面译例原文有两句话,译文为两句话,译者没有进行拆译,但同样转换了译文的行文视角。

中国共产党的诞生,是近现代中国历史发展的必然产物,是中国人民在救亡图存斗争中顽强求索的必然产物。从此,中国革命有了正确前进方向,中国人民有了强大精神力量,中国命运有了光明发展前景。

<u>The birth of the CPC</u> was a natural product of the development of modern and contemporary Chinese history as well as the indomitable exploration of the Chinese people for survival of the nation. <u>The birth of the CPC</u> put the Chinese revolution on the right course, gave the Chinese people a powerful motivation and created bright prospects for China's future development.

我们看到,第一句的主语在英译文中保留,第二句三个小句的主语分别是"中国革命……中国人民……中国命运……",英译构句视角变为"中国共产党的诞生……"(重复了汉语第一句的主语),即按照"什么使什么如何如何"的信息走向构句的。

下面一段由一短一长两个句子组成,英译有拆译也有合译。

这些问题内容十分广泛。曾有议员要求延长图书馆的开放时间,亦有议员要求减收非繁忙时间公众泳池入场费,询问有关防治肝炎蔓延的措施,和在新发展地区提供垃圾收集服务以及管制垃圾收集承办商的问题。

<u>These questions</u> touched on a wide arrange of subjects ranging from the extension of library services to cater to the needs of students to the introduction of concessionary charges for swimmers using public swimming pools during off-peak hours. <u>Questions</u> were also asked on the measures taken by the Council to prevent the spread of hepatitis, refuse collection for newly developed areas and the control of private refuse collection contractors.

译文将原文议员要求或询问的信息走向转换为以 questions… 作为起始点的语流。"议员"被隐去未译,但这一意义已经在上文中交代清楚了。

下面的原句省略了主语"我们",全句被拆译为三个句子。

必须始终把制度建设贯穿党的思想建设、组织建设、作风建设和反腐倡廉建设之中,坚持突出重点、整体推进、继承传统、大胆创新,构建内容协调、程序严密、配套完备、有效管用的制度体系。

<u>Institutional building</u> must be fully integrated with our efforts to strengthen the Party ideologically and organizationally, improve its style of work, combat corruption and ensure the integrity of the Party. In improving Party institutions, <u>we</u> must set out clear priorities, take a holistic approach, carry on fine traditions while innovating boldly. <u>Our goal</u> is to establish a system of Party institutions which are well coordinated in terms of scope, comprehensive and effective and are governed by rigorous procedures.

英译文的第一句并未添加主语 we,而是转换视角以原文宾语中的"制度建设"作为起始点,构成被动句;第二句添加了主语 we;而第三句则根据原文的行文逻辑,添加了主语 our goal,以引出上文所述行为的目的。这一视角变化的依据是原文内在的逻辑走向。

下面长句以"中国特色社会主义道路"为主语,并以此为话题展开全句,具体阐明"社会主义道路"的内涵。

中国特色社会主义道路,就是在中国共产党领导下,立足基本国情,以经济建设为中心,坚持四项基本原则,坚持改革开放,解放和发展社会生产力,巩固和完善社会主义制度,建设社会主义市场经济、社会主义民主政治、社会主义先进文化、社会主义和谐社会,建设富强民主文明和谐的社会主义现代化国家。

In taking the path of socialism with Chinese characteristics, <u>we</u> should, under the leadership of the CPC and bearing China's basic national conditions in mind, pursue economic development as the central task, uphold the Four Cardinal Principles, be committed to the reform and opening up policy, free and develop the productive forces, strengthen and improve the socialist system, promote the socialist market economy, socialist democracy, an advanced socialist culture, and a harmonious socialist society, and make China a prosperous, strong, democratic, culturally advanced and harmonious modern socialist country.

汉语原句主语"中国特色社会主义道路"被译为状语,其后由数个动宾谓语并列排开,英译时这些谓语结构的主语需补充完整。译文加上 we,英语句子得以建构。句子的起始点已转换为人,而不是原句以一个概念为起点的构句思路。

以上几个例子都涉及从逻辑安排入手对原文信息进行重组的问题。关于译文的逻辑安排问题可参见本章第五节逻辑显性化。

转换行文的视角,会导致表达方式的较大变化:说的是同一个意思,但说法不同了。比如,下面句子以"贫困人口"起始,说它"减少了"多少人。而译文以人数起句,说"这么多的人脱贫了"。

30 年来,中国贫困人口减少了 2 亿多。

Over the past three decades, more than 200 million Chinese have been lifted out of poverty.

叙事角度的变化在汉译英中更为常见。比如下面的例子,汉语说"乡亲们"如何,而译文则转换角度,说"我看到乡亲们如何"。

可是,时隔 10 天,当我第二次来到这里时,乡亲们已在废墟上搭起了板房教室。

But only 10 days after the earthquake, when I went there for the second time, I had before my eyes new classrooms built on debris by local villagers with planks.

叙述时,汉语从正面说,英语可以从反面说。下面一句汉语呈肯定形式,英语则改译成双重否定形式。

每一次经济的复苏,都离不开技术创新。

No economic recovery is possible without technological innovation.

下面译例由"有多少人吃饭"转换为"要供养多少人":

农业方面,我国有 13 亿人口要吃饭,土地资源有限,粮食安全始终是最大的隐忧。

China's agriculture needs to feed the country's population of 1.3 billion, but our land resources are limited and food security has always been our biggest unspoken worry.

下面译例中的"把风险留给世界"变为"世界面临风险":

在获取高额利润的同时,把巨大的风险留给整个世界。

While they reaped huge profits, the world was exposed to enormous risks.

下面列出更多的译例，大家可自行分析。

- 过去一年的成就来之不易。
  None of the achievements we made last year came easily.
- 解决 4800 多万农村人口的饮水安全问题。
  An additional of more than 48 million rural people gained access to safe drinking water.
- 全面实行城乡免费义务教育，对所有农村义务教育阶段学生免费提供教科书。
  Free compulsory education became available to all students, urban or rural, throughout the country, and all rural students receiving compulsory education obtained free textbooks.
- 城镇新增就业 1113 万人。
  A total of 11.13 million more urban residents entered the workforce.
- 对外开放水平继续提高。
  The country opened wider to the outside world.
- 2008 年 5 月 12 日，我国发生震惊世界的汶川特大地震。
  A massive earthquake that shocked the world struck Wenchuan on May 12, 2008.

行文视角的转换也就是思维走向的转换、写作思路的转换。汉译英过程所体现的，归根结底是从汉语思维取向到英语思维取向的转换。只有通过大量地阅读英语原创语篇，我们才有可能将自己的思维拉近母语为英语人士的行文思路和表达习惯。

第五节　逻辑显性化

逻辑连贯是构句谋篇的重要准则。有些情况下，汉语本身能为英译者提供明确的逻辑标识和导向，比如下面汉语原文中的"在……的情况下"和"针对……"

已经标明这一部分是句子的状语，只是在转换为英语状语的具体类型上可能有所变化。

年中，在国际能源和粮食价格处于高位、世界经济增长放缓的情况下，针对沿海地区出现出口和经济增速下滑苗头，及时把宏观调控的首要任务调整为"保持经济平稳较快发展，控制物价过快上涨"，并采取了一些有针对性的财税金融措施。

In the middle of the year, when energy and grain prices on the international market were high, world economic growth slowed, and exports from and economic growth in China's coastal regions began to decline, we promptly shifted the priority of macro control to maintaining steady and rapid economic development and controlling price hikes, and adopted relevant fiscal, taxation and financial measures.

但更多时候，汉语行文的逻辑关系不如英语那样彰显，英语的词语、句式安排也有别于汉语，英译时需要将汉语原文信息的顺序和逻辑关系进行调整和显性化。阅读双语对照语篇时，要细心观察和思考，总结出可供自己翻译时所能借鉴的规律和技巧。

比如"亲望亲好，邻望邻好"一句没有表示逻辑关系的连接词语，英译时却要分析这两个小句间可能存在的逻辑关系，并将其形式化。比如译为："As a Chinese saying goes, neighbors wish each other well, just as loved ones do to each other." 这样，两个小句间的比照关系就被显性化了。

再比如"中国社会面貌焕然一新，人民生活水平不断提高"，汉语中的两个小句在形式上并无联系，但如果译为"China's society took on a new look, people's living standards keep rising."则不合英语构句规范。将汉语分句间的逻辑显性化则可使英译文的文气顺畅起来，如改译为："China's society has taken on a brand-new look, as the living standards of the people keep improving."

下面一句汉语用逗号分为四个分句，流水般展开。

扩内需、保增长，调结构、上水平，抓改革、增活力，重民生、促和谐。

英译时加上主语，按动宾结构排开，可出现这样的译文：

We must boost domestic demand, maintain economic growth, carry out economic restructuring, raise the overall quality of economic growth, implement reforms, make the economy more vibrant, stress the people's well-being and promote harmony.

但其实每个分句中的两部分是有着内在的逻辑关系的：后者是前者的目的。把这一逻辑彰显出来可改译为：

We must boost domestic demand <u>to sustain economic growth</u>, adjust the economic structure to raise it to a <u>higher level of development</u>, press ahead with reform <u>to make the economy more vigorous</u>, and give priority to ensuring the people's well-being <u>to promote harmony</u>.

译文中的四个不定式目的状语使译文的逻辑有了清晰的层次。

事实上，目的状语在英译中使用最频繁。比如下面的例子：

- 勇于变革创新，<u>为促进共同发展提供不竭动力</u>。
  We should boldly break new ground <u>so as to create an inexhaustible source of power for boosting common development</u>.

- 改革开放的实质，就是维护人的尊严和自由，<u>让每个人的智慧和力量得以迸发，成功地追求自己的幸福生活</u>。
  The essence of China's reform and opening-up is to safeguard the dignity and freedom of everyone <u>so that he or she may pursue happiness with ingenuity and hard work</u>.

- 中国将坚定支持亚洲地区对其他地区的开放合作，<u>更好促进本地区和世界其他地区共同发展</u>。
  China firmly supports Asia's opening up to and cooperation with other regions <u>so as to promote their common development</u>.

- 同时，中瑞可以在国际货币基金组织、世界银行等国际金融机构中携手合作，<u>为维护国际金融稳定和促进世界经济增长发挥"1＋1＞2"的作用</u>。
  At the same time, China and Switzerland can work together at the International Monetary Fund, the World Bank and other international financial institutions, <u>so as to make greater contribution to maintaining international financial stability and promoting world economic growth</u>.

- 我们一定要深刻认识国际国内经济形势的严峻性和复杂性，增强危机意识和忧患意识，充分利用有利条件，积极应对各种挑战，<u>努力做好各项工作，绝不辜负人民的期望和重托</u>。
  We need to thoroughly appreciate how serious and complex the international

and domestic economic situations are, be more mindful of potential perils and crises, fully exploit favorable conditions and actively respond to all challenges so that we can successfully accomplish all our tasks and prove worthy of the great expectations and trust conferred on us by the people.

- 我们必须按照建设马克思主义学习型政党的要求，抓紧学习人类社会创造的一切科学的新思想新知识。
  To build a Marxist political party committed to learning, we must lose no time in studying all scientific, new ideas and new knowledge in human society.

- 我们要准确把握世界发展大势，准确把握社会主义初级阶段基本国情，深入研究我国发展的阶段性特征，及时总结党领导人民创造的新鲜经验，重点抓住经济社会发展重大问题，作出新的理论概括，永葆科学理论的旺盛生命力。
  We should have a correct understanding of the global development trend and China's basic condition of being in the primary stage of socialism, find out more about the features of China's development at the current stage, review the new experience gained in a timely manner by the people led by the Party, and create new theories with the focus on major issues concerning economic and social development, so as to ensure the vitality of scientific theories.

- 我们将把短期调控政策和长期发展政策有机结合起来，把深化改革开放和推动科学发展有机结合起来，切实解决这些深层次、结构性问题。
  To effectively address these deep-seated and structural problems, we will take an integrated approach that balances near-term macro control with long-term development and advances reform and opening-up in the broader context of scientific development.

- 在新的历史条件下提高党的建设科学化水平，必须坚持解放思想、实事求是、与时俱进，大力推进马克思主义中国化、时代化、大众化，提高全党思想政治水平。
  To make Party building more scientific under the new historical conditions, we must continue to free up our minds, seek truth from facts, advance with the times, adapt Marxism both to China's conditions and to the current times,

and make it known to the general public <u>so as to raise the ideological and political awareness of the whole Party.</u>

我们看到，以上各例中英译文都使用了目的状语，状语构成形式有不定式也有从句。

除了目的状语，我们还常常看到结果状语、方式状语、条件状语、伴随状语等，状语的构成形式有从句、不定式短语、分词短语和介词短语等。比如：

- 中国正在积极稳妥地推进城镇化，数亿农民转化为城镇人口会<u>释放更大的市场需求</u>。
  <u>By vigorously advancing urbanization in a steady manner,</u> China will see hundreds of millions of its rural population turn into urban residents, <u>unleashing increasing market demand along the way.</u>

- 希望这次访问不仅能深化领导人之间的了解和互信，而且能提高彼此国家在对方民众中的认知度，<u>在民间交往的广阔天地播下更多友好的种子</u>。
  I hope my visit here will not only deepen the understanding and trust at the leadership level, but also increase the awareness and recognition at the public level of our respective countries, <u>thus planting more seeds of friendship for exchanges between the two peoples.</u>

- 这场艰苦卓绝的抗震救灾斗争，涌现出无数感天动地、可歌可泣的英雄事迹，充分展现了中国人民不屈不挠、自强不息的伟大民族精神，<u>谱写了气壮山河的壮丽篇章</u>。
  This hard struggle against the earthquake produced uncountable touching and brave exploits and fully demonstrated the great indomitable and unyielding spirit of the Chinese people, <u>thus writing a heroic chapter in the history of the nation.</u>

- 我们要推动各方完善国际金融监管体系，<u>扩大监管范围，明确监管职责，制定普遍接受的国际金融监管标准和规范，健全监管机制</u>。
  We should encourage all parties to improve the international financial supervisory and regulatory regime <u>by expanding its scope, specifying responsibilities, adopting universally accepted standards and norms and strengthening mechanisms.</u>

- 在那浩瀚的沙漠中，生长着一种稀有的树种，叫胡杨。<u>它扎根地下50多米</u>，抗干旱、斗风沙、耐盐碱，生命力极其顽强。
  There, in the boundless desert, grows a rare variety of tree called euphrates poplar. <u>Rooted over 50 meters down the ground</u>, they thrive in hostile environments, defying droughts, sandstorms and salinization.
- 第一件大事，我们党紧紧依靠人民完成了新民主主义革命，<u>实现了民族独立、人民解放</u>。
  The first is that our Party, <u>firmly relying on the people</u>, completed the new-democratic revolution, <u>winning national independence and liberation of the people</u>.
- <u>中国是个人口大国</u>，即使城镇人口比例达到相当高的水平，还会有几亿人口在农村生产生活。
  <u>Given its huge population</u>, even when China's urbanization rate reaches a fairly high level, several hundred million Chinese will still live in the countryside.
- <u>各国交往频繁</u>，磕磕碰碰在所难免。
  <u>With growing interaction among countries</u>, it is inevitable that they encounter frictions here and there.
- 我们实施积极的财政政策和适度宽松的货币政策，<u>刺激力度前所未有</u>，同时又比较好地控制了财政金融风险。
  We have implemented a proactive fiscal policy and a moderately easy monetary policy <u>with an unprecedented intensity</u>, and at the same time successfully kept fiscal and financial risks under control.
- 中国人民对战争和动荡带来的苦难有着刻骨铭心的记忆，对和平有着孜孜不倦的追求。
  Knowing too well the agonizing sufferings inflicted by war and turbulence, the Chinese people deeply cherish peace.
- 到本世纪中叶，中国要基本实现现代化，面临三大历史任务：既要努力实现欧洲早已完成的工业化，又要追赶新科技革命的浪潮；既要不断提高经济发展水平，又要实现社会公平正义；既要实现国内的可持续发展，又要承担相应的国际责任。

To basically achieve modernization by the middle of this century, we must accomplish three major tasks: first, achieve industrialization, which Europe has long completed, while keeping abreast of the latest trends of the scientific and technological revolution; second, promote economic growth while ensuring social equity and justice; and third, pursue sustainable development at home while accepting our share of international responsibilities.

- 各项社会保险覆盖面继续扩大，城镇职工基本养老保险、基本医疗保险参保人数分别增加1753万和2028万，失业、工伤、生育保险参保人数继续增加。

  The coverage of all social security schemes continued to expand, with 17.53 million more urban workers subscribing to basic old-age insurance, 20.28 million more subscribing to basic medical insurance, and the unemployment, workers' compensation and maternity insurance steadily expanding to cover more workers.

- 解决这个问题别无他途，必须依靠高科技改造传统农业，培育优质、高产、安全的农作物新品种和健康、专用的动物新品种，大幅度提高农业综合生产能力。

  There is no other way to resolve this issue but to rely on high technology to transform traditional agriculture by cultivating new, safe and high-yield superior crop varieties and healthy, special-purpose new animal breeds to greatly raise our overall agricultural production capacity.

- 我们将坚持统筹城乡区域协调发展，积极稳妥地推进城镇化，因地制宜地把符合条件的农民工逐步转为城镇居民。

  With a commitment to coordinated development between urban and rural areas and between different regions, we will take active and prudent steps to advance urbanization, and allow eligible rural migrant workers to gradually become urban residents in line with the local conditions.

- 我们推进社会主义制度自我完善和发展，在经济、政治、文化、社会等各个领域形成一整套相互衔接、相互联系的制度体系。

  In the course of promoting the self-improvement and self-development of the socialist system, we have put in place a complete set of integrated,

interconnected systems in the economic, political, cultural, and social fields.

除了状语，也可以运用定语实现译文逻辑关系的显性化。

比如下面译例中，原文的谓语由两个"是……"结构组成，形式上是并列的。但译文将其分出主从关系，第一个谓语被纳入定语从句中。

<u>扩大内需特别是消费需求是我国经济长期平稳较快发展的根本立足点</u>，是今年工作的重点。

Expanding domestic demand, particularly consumer demand, <u>which is essential to ensuring China's long-term, steady, and robust economic development</u>, is the focus of our economic work this year.

再比如下面一句汉语中，有两部分信息，②是①的结果，但英译文并未使用结果状语，而是将其处理为定语从句。

①食品安全事件和安全生产重特大事故接连发生，②<u>给人民群众生命财产造成重大损失，教训十分深刻</u>。

A number of serious and major incidents concerning food and workplace safety have occurred, <u>which have inflicted serious loss of life and property on the people and taught us a sobering lesson</u>.

下面句子分三个小句，①是主语，②和③都是谓语，并无明确的主从关系，英译文将③处理成定语。

①中国特色社会主义制度，②是当代中国发展进步的根本制度保障，③<u>集中体现了中国特色社会主义的特点和优势</u>。

The socialist system with Chinese characteristics, <u>which fully embodies the distinctive features and strengths of socialism with Chinese characteristics</u>, is a fundamental institutional guarantee for development and progress of contemporary China.

下面汉语中划线部分可理解为是其前半句"28年浴血奋战"的结果，但译文将其处理为定语从句。

经过北伐战争、土地革命战争、抗日战争、解放战争，党和人民进行了28年的浴血奋战，<u>打败日本帝国主义侵略，推翻国民党反动统治，建立了中华人民共和国</u>。

The Party and the people fought through the Northern Expedition, the Agrarian Revolutionary War, the War of Resistance Against Japanese Aggression and the War of Liberation in 28 years, during which they defeated Japanese imperialist aggressors, overthrew the Kuomintang reactionary rule and established the People's Republic of China.

下面译例中原文的主语是"国家助学制度",后面带有三个谓语结构("……完善,资助……,基本保障……"),译文并未按此结构组句,而是将后两个谓语部分译为定语从句。

国家助学制度不断完善,资助学生2871万人,基本保障了困难家庭的孩子不因贫困而失学。

We constantly improved the national student financial aid system, which benefited 28.71 million students and basically ensured that no children from poor families were denied schooling due to financial difficulties.

下面译例的英译文将原文划线部分(系原文中定语的一部分,注意并不是连续的)的信息提出,纳入了定语从句中。

我们将着力增强政府提供公共服务的能力,逐步形成比较完整、覆盖城乡、可持续的基本公共服务体系,提高社会保障、基本医疗卫生等领域的均等化水平。

We will enhance the government's capability in providing public services, gradually establish a fairly complete and sustainable system of basic public services that covers both urban and rural areas, and promote equal access to social security and basic medical and health care services.

下面一句的英译也使用了定语从句,不过是"同位语+定语从句"的形式。原文划线部分是谓语,译文将其处理成插入结构 an area that…,这也是一种使原文信息分出层次,有主有从地安排句式的方法。

长江中下游地区在中国经济社会发展中具有举足轻重的战略地位,搞好当前的抗旱救灾工作,对于促进粮食和农业稳定发展、保持经济平稳较快发展、管理好通胀预期意义重大。

The success of the ongoing drought-relief campaign on the land along the middle and lower reaches of the Yangtze River—an area that plays a strategically decisive role in China's economic and social development—is key to boosting steady growth of agriculture, especially grain production, to maintaining the smooth and rapid development of economy and to managing inflation expectation properly.

汉英语篇翻译

译文结构除了定语从句，也可以用分词短语作定语成分。如下面译例：

90年来，我们党团结带领人民在中国这片古老的土地上，书写了人类发展史上惊天地、泣鬼神的壮丽史诗，<u>集中体现为完成和推进了三件大事</u>。

Over the past 90 years, our Party has united with and led the Chinese people in writing a grand epic in the history of human development on this ancient land of China, <u>evidenced in three earthshaking events</u>.

分析原文语句中的隐性逻辑关系后，运用英语的各种形式和类型的结构将逻辑关系加以形式上的显化，这是汉译英中必须掌握的技能。逻辑显性化操作基于对原文的逻辑分析，要从形散意合、看似随意实则严谨的汉语语句中识别出英语行文所需要的逻辑关系。不同译者对原文逻辑分析的视角和结果可能不完全相同，他们构建译文的思路、使用的搭配结构和句式也会有所不同。阅读双语对照语篇时要细心分析，领悟译者的逻辑思路和构句意图，结合自己的实践进行思考，持之以恒就会将他人的经验学到手。

下面译例中译者将原文信息分为两部分，将①译作②的目的。

①我们有序推进城镇化、破解资源环境难题，②需要立足国情走自己的路，需要学习和借鉴欧洲相关先进理念、技术与管理经验。

We need to pursue a path of urbanization suited to our own national conditions and draw on Europe's advanced ideas, technologies and managerial expertise <u>to advance urbanization in an orderly way and tackle resources and environmental challenges</u>.

下面一段汉语，原文划线部分是定语，但如此长的定语，这么多的信息，用英语定语结构恐怕难以容纳。于是译者将其转化为由if引导的条件状语从句，译文句子的建构也变得自然连贯了。

我们要坚持创新驱动解释性，着力推动科技进步和产业结构优化升级。<u>这是从根本上解决我国资源环境约束，适应国际需求结构调整和国内消费升级新变化，全面提升国民经济发展质量、效益和国家竞争力，促进经济可持续发展</u>的战略重点。

We will spur economic development through innovation and promote scientific and technological advances and upgrading of the industrial structure. This is a strategic priority <u>if we are to fundamentally ease the resources and environmental constraints, adapt ourselves to the adjustments in the international demand structure and new changes brought by the upgrading of domestic consumption, raise the quality and efficiency of our economic development and national competitiveness across the board, and promote sustainable economic development.

下面原文第一句中的划线部分①是小句的谓语部分，译者将其译为定语，以避免整个句子的英译出现两个并列谓语（如：…is…and serves the interests…）；原文第二句划线部分②也是主谓结构，译者将其视为状语，用介词短语形式译出。

共同发展①是持续发展的重要基础，符合各国人民长远利益和根本利益。②我们生活在同一个地球村，应该牢固树立命运共同体意识，顺应时代潮流，把握正确方向，坚持同舟共济，推动亚洲和世界发展不断迈上新台阶。

Common development, which is the very foundation of sustainable development, serves the long-term and fundamental interests of all the people in the world. As members of the same global village, we should foster a sense of community of common destiny, follow the trend of the times, keep to the right direction, stick together in time of difficulty and ensure that development in Asia and the rest of the world reaches new highs.

下面一句的划线部分则被认为是"维护多边贸易体制"的目的，被译为分词状语。

这充分说明，中国对外开放的步伐不会停顿，中国坚持维护多边贸易体制、积极推动区域贸易自由化、加快实施自由贸易区战略的决心坚定不移。

It fully demonstrates that China will not stall in its opening-up and that it is firmly committed to upholding the multilateral trading regime, vigorously promoting regional trade liberalization, and accelerating the implementation of the FTA strategy.

下面译例原文有三句，对应译为三句。第一句中，译者认定划线部分为从属信息，译为状语。第二句中划线部分是结果状语，译为分词短语。此例中的三个定语的翻译也值得注意：①仍然译为前置定语，②译为定语从句，③译为同位语中的介词短语作后置定语。

第二件大事，我们党紧紧依靠人民完成了社会主义革命，确立了社会主义基本制度。我们创造性地实现由新民主主义到社会主义的转变，使占世界人口四分之一的东方大国进入社会主义社会，实现了中国历史上①最广泛、最深刻的社会变革。我们建立起②独立的、比较完整的工业体系和国民经济体系，积累了在中国这样一个③社会生产力水平十分落后的东方大国进行社会主义建设的重要经验。

The second is that, firmly relying on the people, our Party completed the socialist revolution and established the basic socialist system. We creatively achieved the transition from New Democracy to socialism, therefore creating a socialist society for a quarter of the world's population in this large country in the East, and brought about the most extensive and profound social changes in Chinese history. We established industrial and economic systems that were independent and fairly complete, and we gained important experience of building socialism in China, a country with backward productive forces.

下面译例对原文逻辑关系的分析十分细致、严谨，翻译方法也相当灵活。原文被分号分割为五个部分，译文依次译为五个句子。各句都以划线部分为从属信息，分别用介词短语、不定式短语等形式构建为译文的状语。

我们要以政治互信为基石，坦诚相待，相互尊重，相互理解，相互支持；以务实合作为抓手，重在行动，为合作注入新动力；以机制建设为保障，加大合作力度，拓宽合作领域；以互利共赢为目标，优势互补，最大程度分享合作成果；以开放透明为前提，增进同各方沟通和交流，体现合作的开放性。

We should base our cooperation on political mutual trust, and treat each other with sincerity, mutual respect, mutual understanding and mutual support. We should focus on practical cooperation and make our cooperation more dynamic through concrete actions. We should strengthen institutional building to support increased cooperation in broader areas. We should aim for mutual benefit by combining our respective strengths and sharing the fruits of cooperation to the fullest extent. We should view openness and transparency as the prerequisite of our cooperation and strengthen communication and exchanges to make our cooperation an open process.

译者所掌握的语言资源或手段，对译文的逻辑建构会起到关键作用。比如下面汉语原文，划线部分是一个长定语，译者将其处理为分词状语，而使这种构句成为可能则是对 feature 一词的运用。

当前中国经济运行呈现增长速度较快、结构逐步优化、就业持续增加、价格基本稳定的良好格局。

China's economy is now in good shape, featuring fast growth, structural improvement, rising employment and basic price stability.

此外，英语中还可以用标点符号表示某种逻辑关系。比如下面译例中用冒号引出对上文的解释，相当于原文中的原因状语。

我选择瑞士并非偶然，因为有几件重要的事情要做。

My choice of Switzerland is in no way haphazard: we have got a few important things to do here.

总之，英语的行文逻辑不同于汉语，英译时要按照英语构句谋篇的需要重新对原文信息进行安排。要获得这种技能，阅读双语语篇，细细体会逻辑重组规律，是一条行之有效的途径。

第六节　拆句和逻辑安排

上一节我们观察了在没有拆译的情况下英语行文逻辑安排的方法。如果发生了拆译，行文逻辑就需从更宏观的角度加以考虑，在译文构建的大语境下，确立译文中各句内部和各句之间的逻辑关系。这种逻辑关系，有的在原文中已有所显示，有的则在原文中呈隐性，需要在译文构建过程中加以彰显、调整或确立。

比如下面汉语句子被拆译成三句（双斜线表示），第一句中的"经过……"已表明这是状语，第三句的"但"已表明了转折的逻辑走向，译文的逻辑关系基本照此处理。

经过半个多世纪的艰苦奋斗，中国有了比较大的发展，// 经济总量跃居世界前列，// 但我们仍然是一个发展中国家，同发达国家相比还有很大的差距。

With hard work over the past half century and more, China has achieved great progress. Its total economic output is now one of the largest in the world. However, we remain a developing country and we are keenly aware of the big gap that we have with the developed countries.

再比如下面译例，在拆译出的第二句中，依汉语标识"在……同时"，译文将其处理为 while 引导的状语。

汉英语篇翻译

要巩固和扩大应对国际金融危机冲击成果，// 并统筹考虑当前和长远发展，<u>在继续促进经济复苏的同时</u>，通过经济结构性的改革，为可持续发展创造条件。

We need to cement and build on what we have achieved in countering the financial crisis. We need to take into consideration both the immediate needs and long-term development and, <u>while continuing to energize the recovery</u>, create conditions for sustainable development through structural reform.

又比如下面段落，原文有三个句子，译者译成了五句话，对原文的小句进行了拆译。原文中划线部分已表明，这些是句子的状语，翻译时也基本将其处理为状语。

去年6月，<u>我们在叶卡捷琳堡会晤时</u>，世界经济深受国际金融危机冲击，主要经济体经济纷纷出现衰退，各国民众工作生活受到严重影响。<u>在世界经济一片低迷的气氛中</u>，我们四国共同发出推动世界经济尽快复苏的强烈信号，<u>并进行艰苦努力</u>，率先实现经济恢复增长。<u>经过国际社会携手应对</u>，世界经济形势已出现回暖迹象，有望逐步走出国际金融危机的阴霾。

<u>When we met in Yekaterinburg last June</u>, the world economy was in the quagmire of the international financial crisis. Major economies ran into recession, and the work and life of people around the world were seriously affected. <u>In the face of a gloomy economic picture</u>, the four BRIC countries came together and sent a strong message that we would work for the early recovery of the world economy. <u>Through hard efforts</u>, we became the first to achieve an economic turnaround. And <u>thanks to the concerted efforts of the international community</u>, the world economy has shown signs of recovery and is expected to gradually emerge from the financial crisis.

更常见的情况是，原文并没有明显的逻辑标示，译者需要根据英语行文的需要，重建译文的逻辑。此时，建议把观察的重点仍然放在状语的运用上（参见本章第五节逻辑显性化）。

比如下面译例中，译文在两处添加了 because，表明了原文所暗含的逻辑。原文引用了《胡杨礼赞》中的诗句，译文将后两个"而"字彰显出来，译为 even after...从句。

它"生而一千年不死，死而一千年不倒，倒而一千年不朽"，世人称为英雄树。我非常喜欢胡杨，它是中华民族坚韧不拔精神的象征。

They are known as the "hero tree", <u>because</u> a euphrates poplar can live for a thousand years. <u>Even after it dies</u>, it stands upright for a thousand years, and <u>even after it falls</u>, it stays intact for another thousand years. I like euphrates poplar <u>because</u> they symbolize the resilience of the Chinese nation.

下面几例译文分别运用了状语从句、不定式、分词或介词短语构成的各种状语结构，彰显了原文表层并不明显的逻辑关系，请大家阅读分析。

- 我们将把提高科技创新能力与完善现代产业体系有机统一起来，用先进技术改造传统产业，培育一批有自主知识产权和知名品牌、国际竞争力强的优势企业，建设一批具有国际水平和带动能力的现代产业集群，<u>促进我国由制造大国转变为制造强国</u>。
  We will integrate our efforts in strengthening the capacity for scientific and technological innovation with those for improving the modern industrial system. We will upgrade the traditional industries with advanced technologies, nurture a number of internationally competitive enterprises with their own intellectual property and well-known brands, and build a number of world-class modern industry clusters which can serve as growth drivers, <u>so that China can move from a big manufacturing country to a strong manufacturing country</u>.

- 我们将坚持把处理好保持经济平稳较快发展、调整经济结构和管理通胀预期的关系作为<u>宏观调控</u>的核心，把稳定政策作为宏观调控的主基调，<u>保持政策的连续性</u>、<u>稳定性</u>，增强调控的针对性、灵活性，<u>进一步巩固和发展好的势头</u>。
  In exercising macro-control, we will take it as a central task to appropriately handle the relationship between maintaining steady and rapid economic development, adjusting the economic structure and managing inflation expectations, and we will take policy stability as the main focus. <u>While maintaining the continuity and stability of our policies</u>, we will make macro-control measures more targeted and flexible to <u>consolidate and strengthen the sound momentum of development</u>.

上面汉语原句被拆译为两个英语句子。第一句将原文中重复出现的"作为宏观调控"抽出,译为句首的介词短语。第二句则将"保持政策的连续性、稳定性"和"进一步巩固和发展好的势头"一头一尾两部分处理为状语,将"增强……"译为主句。

阅读下面译例请注意介词短语 with special emphasis on 所引出的状语。

- 我们加快实施国家中长期科学和技术发展规划,<u>特别是核心电子器件、核能开发利用、高档数控机床等 16 个重大专项</u>,突破一批核心技术和关键共性技术,<u>为中国经济在更高水平上实现可持续发展提供科技支撑</u>。

  We are stepping up the implementation of the National Program for Medium- and Long-Term Scientific and Technological Development, <u>with special emphasis on 16 major projects including core electronic devices, development and use of nuclear energy and advanced numerically controlled machine tools</u>. We will strive to make breakthroughs in a host of core technologies and key generic technologies <u>to support sustainable economic growth at a higher level</u>.

注意下面译例中 for sb. to do sth. 介词短语作状语的使用。

- 面对风云变幻的国际形势,面对艰巨繁重的国内改革发展稳定任务,<u>我们党要团结带领人民继续前进,开创工作新局面,赢得事业新胜利</u>,最根本的就是要高举中国特色社会主义伟大旗帜,坚持和拓展中国特色社会主义道路,坚持和丰富中国特色社会主义理论体系,坚持和完善中国特色社会主义制度。

  We are facing drastic changes in the world and arduous tasks of promoting reform and development and maintaining stability in China. <u>For our Party to unite with and lead the people in forging ahead, make new progress in its work and win new victories for its cause</u>, it must hold high the great banner of socialism with Chinese characteristics, keep to and expand the path of socialism with Chinese characteristics, uphold and enrich the system of theories of socialism with Chinese characteristics, and adhere to and improve the socialist system with Chinese characteristics.

- 在新的历史条件下提高党的建设科学化水平,必须坚持标本兼治、综合治理、惩防并举、注重预防的方针,深入开展党风廉政建设和反腐败斗争,<u>始终保持马克思主义政党的先进性和纯洁性</u>。

To make Party building more scientific under the new historical conditions, we must follow the principle of fighting corruption in a comprehensive way, addressing both its symptoms and root causes, and combining punishment with prevention with emphasis on prevention. We must intensify efforts to improve Party conduct, uphold integrity and combat corruption <u>so as to maintain the advanced nature and integrity of the Party as a Marxist political party</u>.

- 亚洲稳定面临着新的挑战，<u>热点问题此起彼伏，传统安全威胁和非传统安全威胁都有所表现</u>，<u>实现本地区长治久安需要地区国家增强互信、携手努力</u>。
Stability in Asia now faces new challenges, <u>as hotspot issues keep emerging, and both traditional and non-traditional security threats exist</u>. The Asian countries need to increase mutual trust and work together <u>to ensure durable peace and stability in our region</u>.

- 亚洲发展需要乘势而上、转型升级。对亚洲来说，发展仍是头等大事，发展仍是解决面临的突出矛盾和问题的关键，迫切需要转变经济发展方式、调整经济结构、提高经济发展质量和效益，在此基础上不断提高人民生活水平。
Asia needs to transform and upgrade its development model in keeping with the trend of the times. Sustaining development is still of paramount importance to Asia, because only development holds the key to solving <u>major problems and difficulties it faces</u>. It is important that we should shift the growth model, adjust the economic structure, make development more cost effective and make life better for our people.

以上我们观察的是拆译后英语各个句子内部的逻辑重组。下面请大家注意英语语篇构建中各个句子之间的逻辑衔接问题。比如：

中国发展离不开亚洲和世界，亚洲和世界繁荣稳定也需要中国。

China cannot develop itself in isolation from the rest of Asia and the world. <u>On their part</u>, the rest of Asia and the world cannot enjoy prosperity and stability without China.

原文拆译成两句。第二句开头加上了 on their part，增强了译文的连贯性。

下面译例中，原文被拆译为两句，第二句用 but 表示转折关系。

和平犹如空气和阳光，受益而不觉，失之则难存。

Peace, like air and sunshine, is hardly noticed when people are benefiting from it. But none of us can live without it.

下面一句拆译为三句，译文第二句句首加上 yet，彰显了转折的逻辑走向。

面对突如其来的国际金融危机冲击，我们采取超常规的政策措施是必要的，这些政策措施在发挥积极作用的同时，难以避免会带来一些负面影响，关键是要把这些影响控制在可以承受的范围内。

In the face of the sudden international financial crisis, the extraordinary policy measures that we have adopted are necessary and these measure have played a positive role. Yet some negative impacts are hardly avoidable. What's important is to keep those negative impacts within a scope that we can manage.

下面一句拆译为两句后则加上状语 in this way，以和前句形成更明确的衔接。

各级党政机关和干部要坚持工作重心下移，经常深入实际、深入基层、深入群众，作到知民情、解民忧、暖民心。

Party and government offices at all levels and their officials should be more community-focused in their work, regularly visit communities, and stay close with the people. In this way, we can learn more about the actual conditions of the people, address their concerns, and give them a warm feeling that we care about them.

下面译例有所不同。被拆译出的最后一句并未添加与上述译例类似的逻辑状语，而是从重新确立主语的角度用 all these steps 重复和概括了前句提到的种种举措，用以引出后半句信息。这也不失为一种强化译文逻辑性的做法。

中国将不断创新发展理念，建设和谐宜居的现代城市，推进农村转移人口真正融入城市，促进就业、教育、医疗卫生、社会保障等基本公共服务均等化，加强保障性住房建设，使广大居民共享发展成果和城市文明。

China is pursuing urbanization in an innovative way. We are endeavoring to build harmonious and livable modern cities, promote rural migrant population's integration into cities, deliver equal basic public services, including employment, education, medical care and health and social security, and we also give priority to building government subsidized housing. All these steps are taken to ensure that development benefits and urban civilization are enjoyed by all.

有时还会见到并未发生拆译而添加逻辑词语的情况，这也值得我们注意。比如下面译例中，原文是两句，译为英语也是两句，但在译文第二句的句首添加了逻辑词语，以使前后两句衔接更为紧密。

目前资本充足率和不良贷款率分别为 11.1% 和 2.8%，都处于安全范围内。我们清醒地看到财政金融领域的潜在风险，特别是地方政府融资平台的债务风险。

The capital adequacy ratio and NPL ratio now stand at 11.1 percent and 2.8 percent respectively, both in the safe territory. This being said, we are keenly aware of the latent fiscal and financial risks, especially the debt risks of the financing platforms of local governments.

下面译例中，原文两句话，译为三句。第一句拆译为两句，第二句未拆译，但句首添加表示渐进的逻辑短语 what is more，强化了译文逻辑。

亚洲与世界其他地区共克时艰，合作应对国际金融危机，成为拉动世界经济复苏和增长的重要引擎，近年来对世界经济增长的贡献率已超过 50%，给世界带来了信心。亚洲同世界其他地区的区域次区域合作展现出勃勃生机和美好前景。

Working side by side with the rest of the world in time of difficulty to tackle the international financial crisis, Asia has emerged as an important engine driving world economic recovery and growth. In recent years, Asia has contributed to over 50% of global growth, instilling much needed confidence in the world. What is more, Asia's cooperation with other regions of the world at regional and sub-regional levels has great vitality and promising prospects.

下面译例和上例类似，整段多有拆译，最后一句很短，没有拆译，但在句首添加了表示概括的词语 in short。

同时，我们必须看到，当前世界经济复苏的基础并不牢固，复苏并不均衡，还存在很多不确定因素。近期一些国家主权债务风险上升，国际金融市场出现波动，各种形式的保护主义抬头，一些国家就业形势严峻，气候变化、粮食安全、能源资源安全、公共卫生安全、重大自然灾害等全球性问题相互交织，世界经济治理结构深层次问题仍未解决。实现世界经济可持续增长还有很长的路要走。

At the same time, we must realize that the world economic recovery is not yet firmly established or balanced, and there are still many uncertainties down the road. We have seen recently the rise of sovereign debt risks in some countries, fluctuations in international financial markets, surging protectionism of various forms and grave employment situation in some parts of the world. Global challenges such as climate change, food security, energy and resource security, public health security and major natural disasters are intertwined, and the deep-seated problems in world economic governance structure are yet to be addressed. <u>In short</u>, there is still a long way to go before the world economy can achieve sustainable growth.

下面译例中，译文将原文第一句译为复合句，划线部分译为状语从句；第二句译为并列句，且在句首加上关联词 therefore，逻辑关系凸显。

全党同志必须牢记，密切联系群众是我们党的最大政治优势，<u>脱离群众是我们党执政后的最大危险</u>。我们必须始终把人民利益放在第一位，把实现好、维护好、发展好最广大人民根本利益作为一切工作的出发点和落脚点。

All the comrades in the Party must bear in mind that maintaining close ties with the people gives the Party its biggest political asset <u>while alienation from the people poses the greatest risk to the Party after it has gained political power</u>. <u>Therefore</u>, we must always place the people's interests before everything else, and make sure that the aim and outcome of all our work is to realize, uphold and expand the fundamental interests of the overwhelming majority of the people.

总之，不论有无拆译，逻辑连贯都是构建译文语篇的重要原则。所谓连贯，一指译文的写作要文从字顺，句子内部的词语、小句之间，句子和句子之间都须衔接得体、层次清楚，段落和段落间也需上下文气贯通。其次，连贯还关乎与读者的沟通问题。英译文的目标读者与我们所处社会文化背景有异，知识结构自然也会有所不同，这些因素译者必须充分考虑。这一点在下面的第十节将作进一步阐释。

第七节　信息的衍化：意译和释义

上面两节关注了英译文的逻辑重建，也就是语篇的连贯问题。而语篇连贯除了与语篇自身的信息安排有关以外，还有一个重要的考虑，那就是译文读者的接受度。译文必须考虑到读者的接受习惯和对有关背景知识的了解程度。

原文的信息用译语重新表达，总会发生这样那样的变化：它已经不是原来的信息，却又与原文十分切近——切近原文的表达意图，切近译文读者的接受语境。在追求最大化传递原文信息过程中，译者有时会采用意译和释义的翻译方法。阅读时政语篇译文时，常常见到意译和释义在翻译中运用的例子。

翻译总是存在着形和义的矛盾。汉英两种语言形式上区别很大，而译者必须尽最大努力再现原文的义，于是就在形和义之间纠结和选择。意译是在无法或不宜保留原文形式的时候采取的趋向于达意的选择，而释义就更进了一步，要在达意上作出更多的努力，有点像"拆开了，揉碎了说"的味道。

比如下面译例中的"两只手"的译法，就采取了两种变通译法。

要充分发挥政府调控和市场调节"两只手"的作用。

译文 1：We will make full use of both the control function of government regulation and adjustment function of the market.

译文 2：We will make full use of both the control function of government regulation as the visible hand and market forces as the invisible hand.

第一种译文译出其意，可谓意译；第二种译文试图保留比喻形象，更有释义或阐释的味道。

下面译例借助释义，对"首届"所指的具体年份作了补充。

首届免费师范生全部到中小学任教，90% 以上在中西部。

All the graduates of 2011 who received tuition-free education in teachers' colleges and universities went to teach in primary and secondary schools, with over 90% of them working in central and western China.

下面译例对"五保户"等特定词语进行了释义。

进一步提高城乡低保补助水平以及部分优抚对象抚恤和生活补助标准，对全国城乡低保对象、农村五保供养对象等8600多万名困难群众发放一次性生活补贴；建立社会救助和保障标准与物价上涨挂钩的联动机制。

We further increased subsistence allowances for rural and urban residents and subsidies and living allowances for some entitled groups, and granted lump-sum living allowances to more than 86 million people in need, including subsistence allowance recipients in urban and rural areas and <u>childless and infirm rural residents who are entitled to five forms of support (food, clothing, medical care, housing, and burial expenses)</u>. We instituted a mechanism to increase social aid and social security benefits when consumer prices rise.

下面译例则对"两基"加以具体化。

经过 25 年坚持不懈的努力，全面实现"两基"目标。

Thanks to tireless efforts over the past 25 years, we have fully attained the goals of <u>making nine-year compulsory education universally available and basically eliminating illiteracy among young and middle-aged adults</u>.

再比如下面一句汉语中的下划线部分，在译文中为"不同文化共同存在并相互影响，没有哪一种文化能一枝独秀"的意思。这和原文基本精神相符，但已是一种释义。

进入 21 世纪，经济全球化、信息网络化，已经把世界连成一体，<u>文化的发展将不再是各自封闭的，而是在相互影响中多元共存</u>。

In the 21st century, economic globalization and the information network have linked us all together. <u>Different cultures live together and influence each other. No culture can flourish in isolation.</u>

汉语中的一些成语、习语、比喻等在英译文中常常只译出其基本含义，而不必拘泥于其具体的表达方式或修辞手法。

- 还需要爬一道道的坡、过一道道的坎。

    The road ahead remains a bumpy and twisted one.

- 咬定青山不放松，真正做到坚定不移、矢志不渝。

    We should be fully committed to doing so to ensure that we remain firm and faithful in our actions.

- 中国古老的经典——《尚书》就提出"百姓昭明，协和万邦"的理想，主张人民和睦相处，国家友好往来。

    The Book of History, an ancient classic in China for example, advocates amity among people and friendly exchanges among nations.

上面三个译例原文，第一个用了常用的比喻，第二个引用了古诗，第三个例子则引用了经典。译文都是译其意而舍其形，这既考虑到读者的感受，也为了顺应英语的行文习惯和规范。

汉语的成语在英译时往往采取意译的办法。比如：

- 但尺有所短，寸有所长，取长补短方能优势互补。
  Just as a Chinese saying goes, an inch has its length and a foot sometimes falls short. Only through mutual learning can we draw on each other's comparative strength.

- 亚洲合作需要百尺竿头、更进一步。
  We need to build on past success and make new progress in promoting cooperation in Asia.

- 第二，要精诚合作，不搞以邻为壑；第三，要标本兼治，不能头疼医头、脚疼医脚。
  Second, carry out cooperation with full sincerity and avoid pursuing one's own interests at the expense of others; and third, address both the symptoms and the root cause of the problem. A palliative approach will not work. We should not treat only the head when the head aches, and the foot when the foot hurts.

这里需要说明的是，成语"头疼医头，脚疼医脚"既有直译，也有释义（双划线部分）相辅，以充分展示其含义。

- 国家无论大小、强弱、贫富，都应该做和平的维护者和促进者，不能这边搭台、那边拆台，而应该相互补台、好戏连台。
  Countries, whether big or small, strong or weak, rich or poor, should all contribute their share to maintaining and enhancing peace. Rather than undercutting each other's efforts, countries should complement each other and work for joint progress.

- 千百年来，中华民族一次次战胜了天灾人祸，渡过了急流险滩，昂首挺胸地走到今天。
  Over the millennia, the Chinese nation has weathered numerous disasters, both natural and man-made, surmounted all kinds of difficulties and

challenges, and made her way to where she proudly stands today.

对于在我国特有政治、经济语境下经常使用的词语、说法，翻译时须加以释义。

- 开辟就业岗位，缓解就业压力。
  We are endeavoring to create more jobs and lessen the impact of the financial crisis on employment.

很明显，上面的译文根据当时的具体经济背景，对"就业压力"进行了释义。

- 整合建立新的对外经济技术合作专项资金。
  We integrated existing funds and set up new ones designed to promote external economic and technological cooperation.

"建立新的……专项资金"译成"整合已有资金并建立新的资金"。

- 巩固退耕还林还草成果。
  We built on the achievements in returning farmland to forests and restoring livestock pastures to grasslands.

- 积极推进境外能源资源合作，企业"走出去"步伐加快，对外援助进一步扩大。
  We actively promoted energy and resources cooperation overseas, further expanded our assistances to other countries, and the pace of enterprises going global was accelerated.

上面译例中，原文后两个小句的信息在译文中有所颠倒，这是出于译文句法和语义的双重考虑而作的调整。

中央财政安排384亿元救灾款和740亿元恢复重建资金，迅速出台一系列支援灾区的政策措施。积极开展对口支援。
The central government allocated 38.4 billion yuan for quake relief and 74 billion yuan for post-earthquake recovery and reconstruction. We promptly introduced a host of policies and measures to support the quake zone. We energetically organized one-to-one assistance to designated areas affected by the earthquake.

汉语中常用四字词语，读来节奏鲜明，言简意赅。翻译的时候则需用意译或释义的方法将原句信息补充完整。

- 90年来，中国共产党人和全国各族人民前赴后继、顽强奋斗，不断夺取革命、建设、改革的重大胜利。

Over the past 90 years, Chinese Communists and the people of all ethnic groups in China have, through indomitable struggles, achieved major successes in revolution, development and reform.
- 只要政策对头，措施得当，落实有力，就有可能实现这一目标。
  As long as we adopt the right policies and appropriate measures and implement them effectively, we will be able to achieve this target.
- 按照出手要快、出拳要重、措施要准、工作要实的要求，迅速推出进一步扩大内需、促进经济增长的十项措施，争分夺秒地加以落实。
  In accordance with the requirement that we act fast, be forceful, take targeted measures and stress implementation, we promptly introduced ten measures to further boost domestic demand and promote economic growth, and implemented them without delay.

有时，原文的信息在译文中需要换一种表达方法，或原文信息次序在译文中被重新排列。比如下面译例的原文"有多大信任就有多大程度的合作"，英译表达成"合作水平取决于信任水平"。

我认为，应对全球性危机，需要增进合作。有多大程度的相互信任，就可能有多大程度的合作。

I believe that closer cooperation is needed to meet the global crisis, and the level of cooperation hinges upon the level of mutual trust.

下面译例中"……每前进一步……就跟进一步"的表述被译成"每一步都要由……伴随"。

理论创新每前进一步，理论武装就跟进一步，这是我们党加强自身建设的一条重要经验。

Every step forward in theoretical innovation should be accompanied by progress in arming Party members with such new theoretical innovation. This is an important experience the Party has gained in improving itself.

下例的"利益融合达到……广度和深度"被译为"从未和……在广度和深度上如此紧密联系"。

中国同亚洲和世界的利益融合达到前所未有的广度和深度。

China's interests have never been so closely connected with those of the rest of

Asia and the world in both scope and depth.

下面译例的"真正做到……"则换译成"是个……使者"的表述方式。

他带去了中国的茶叶、丝绸、瓷器,还帮助沿途有的国家剿灭海盗,<u>真正做到了播仁爱于友邦</u>。

He took with him Chinese tea, silk and porcelain and helped local people fight pirates as he sailed along. <u>He was truly a messenger of love and friendship</u>.

下面是对原文信息次序进行重新排列的典型译例。

瑞士长于金融,管理经验丰富,被称为银行密度最高的国家。

Switzerland boasts the highest density of banks. It has a strong financial industry and rich regulatory experience.

总之,不论阅读英语还是双语对照语篇,都要随时留意英文构句的关键词语和句式,留意译者是如何转换角度来重新表述原文信息的。这有助于翻译时转变汉语思维,使之尽量贴近以英语作为母语人士的思维方式和构句谋篇的思路,从而译出逻辑清楚、通顺地道的英文。

第八节 合 译

本章的第三节和第六节讨论了拆译。时政语篇英译,拆译的技巧运用很普遍,但也有与之相对的合译的情况。合译,顾名思义,就是将原文中的两个句子的信息合并或融合,从而构建成英语的一个句子。比如:

实施16个国家重大科技专项。在信息、生物、环保等领域新建一批国家工程中心、重点实验室和企业技术中心。

We launched 16 major national science and technology projects, and established a number of new national engineering centers, key laboratories and enterprise technology centers in such fields as information technology, biotechnology and environmental protection.

很明显,由于原文的两句话语义关联紧密,被合译为一句话。

下面译例汉语原文的第二句话被译为定语从句,和前一句合并在一起,构建成英语复合句。

我们推进经济体制改革，建立了社会主义市场经济体制。在政府的宏观调控下，充分发挥市场对资源配置的基础性作用。

Through economic reform, we have built a socialist market economy, where the market plays a primary role in allocating resources under government macro-regulation.

我们看到，某些句子之所以能够合在一起，是因为它们的语义关系特别密切，正好可以纳入英语的某种句法结构之中。

下面译例均可体现出语义上的融合和英语句法构架的容纳作用。

只有我们把群众放在心上，群众才会把我们放在心上；只有我们把群众当亲人，群众才会把我们当亲人。

The people will care about and feel close to the Party only when the Party feels the same toward them.

原文信息"放在心上"和"当亲人"被合在了一起（care about and feel close to），而译文中 feel the same 避免了文字的重复。

下面译例原文有两句话，后一句拆译成两部分，前一部分和第一句合译，后一部分单独译为一句。

中国还有很长很长的路要走，还会遇到许多艰难险阻。但是，任何困难都阻挡不住中国人民前进的步伐，只要我们坚持不懈地努力奋斗，中国现代化的目标就一定能够实现。

The journey ahead will be long and arduous, but no amount of difficulty will stop the Chinese people from marching forward. Through persistent efforts, we will reach our goal of achieving socialist modernization.

下面译例的原文，一长一短两句话，第二句的"面对危机"是对上一句的重复，与前一句合译成一句话（划线部分），其余部分拆译为两句。另外，请注意译文最后一句句首 together 所起的逻辑连贯作用。

中国经济面临着严峻的局面。面对危机，我们果断决策，及时调整宏观经济政策取向，迅速出台扩大国内需求的十项措施，陆续制定了一系列政策，形成了系统完整的促进经济平稳较快发展的一揽子计划。

<u>In the face of the grim situation, we have acted decisively.</u> We have made timely

adjustment to the direction of our macroeconomic policy, promptly introduced ten measures to expand domestic demand, and formulated a series of related policies. Together, they make up a systematic and comprehensive package plan aimed at promoting steady and relatively fast economic growth.

下面译例中，信息重新组合的情况要复杂些。

城镇化是中国经济增长持久的内生动力。<u>人口多、资源相对短缺、环境容量有限，是中国的基本国情。我们推进城镇化，需要走节约集约利用资源、保护自然生态和文化特征、大中小城市和小城镇并举的可持续发展之路</u>。

Urbanization is the ever lasting internal force driving China's economic growth. However, given its large population, shortage of resources and limited carrying capacity of the environment, China must pursue a sustainable path of urbanization. We should conserve and make efficient use of resources, protect natural ecology and distinctive cultural features, and promote coordinated development of large, medium-sized and small cities as well as small towns.

原文划直线部分的信息被合译为一句，其中的"是中国的基本国情"略去未译，而波浪线部分被拆出单独译为一句。

本节关注的是英译文打破汉语句子的界限，对两个或几个句子的信息进行重新组合，并将其纳入一个句子结构中的情况。对于汉语一个句子内部所包含的小句，英译文有时也会对其合并。比如下面译例中，汉语将"永无止境"用了三次，译文简化为一个 know no boundary，从而将三个汉语小句合成了一个英语句子。

实践发展永无止境，认识真理永无止境，理论创新永无止境。

The development of practice, cognition of the truth, and innovation of theories know no boundary.

再比如下面汉语原句出现了两个"必由之路"，英译时也合在了一起。

中国特色社会主义道路，是实现社会主义现代化的必由之路，是创造人民美好生活的必由之路。

The path of socialism with Chinese characteristics is the only way for China to achieve socialist modernization and create decent lives for its people.

第九节　构句的关键词语和句式

本篇第一章的第二、三、四节均涉及英语阅读中对词语用法和句式安排的关注。构建一个句子，常常要依赖某些关键的词语。比如下面译例中，一个短语动词就决定了整个句子的构建。

90年来，我们取得的一切成就，是一代一代中国共产党人同人民一道顽强拼搏、连续奋斗的结果。

We owe all our achievements over the past 90 years to the tenacious struggles waged by Chinese Communists and the people of several generations.

短语动词 owe...to... 构成译文句子的骨架。

有时候，一个介词短语也可在构句中发挥重要作用：将原文的两个小句合并成一句话，决定了句子的结构。比如：

我们实施更加积极的就业政策，重点解决高校毕业生和农民工就业问题。

We are following a more active employment policy with special emphasis on helping college graduates and migrant workers find jobs.

下面译例中，play a key role in doing 在构建译文时显然发挥了关键作用。

这些措施对缓解经济运行中的突出矛盾、增强信心、稳定预期、保持经济平稳较快发展，发挥了至关重要的作用。

Together, these measures have played a crucial role in alleviating serious problems affecting economic performance, enhancing confidence, stabilizing expectations and maintaining steady and rapid economic development.

连接词语在构句中同样起到关键作用。

我们党对长期执政条件下滋生腐败的严重性和危险性，对改革开放和社会主义现代化建设全过程都要反对腐败，认识是清醒的。

The Party is soberly aware of the gravity and danger of corruption that have emerged under the conditions of the Party being long in power as well as the need to combat corruption throughout the course of reform, opening up, and socialist modernization.

上面译文中的 as well as 将原文中由两个"对……"引出的状语所表达的信息，处理为 be aware of 的宾语结构。

事实说明，不触动封建根基的自强运动和改良主义，旧式的农民战争，资产阶级革命派领导的革命，照搬西方资本主义的其他种种方案，都不能完成中华民族救亡图存的民族使命和反帝反封建的历史任务。

Facts have shown that <u>neither</u> the mission of striving for national survival <u>nor</u> the historic task of fighting imperialism and feudalism could be accomplished by reformist self-improvement movements which did not touch the foundation of feudal rule, old-style peasant wars, revolutions led by bourgeois revolutionaries, or other attempts to copy Western capitalism.

上面译例中，译文将原句的宾语部分处理为主语，而在这个主语中，neither…nor… 的结构是起到重要作用的。

下面两句译文中的连接词语也都发挥着关键作用。

- 在这场前所未有的世界金融危机中，中国和包括英国在内的欧洲都受到严重冲击。

  This unprecedented financial crisis has inflicted a severe impact on <u>both</u> China <u>and</u> Britain <u>as well as</u> other European countries.

- 如今的中国，早已不是一百年前封闭落后的旧中国，也不是三十年前贫穷僵化的中国。

  China is no longer the closed and backward society it was 100 years ago, <u>or</u> the poor and ossified society 30 years ago.

决定译文句子结构的还有译者选用的句式。比如下面一个译例：

过去的两年，在极为困难、复杂的情况下，中国在世界率先实现经济回升向好，保持经济平稳较快发展。

The past two years have <u>seen</u> China emerge as one of the first countries to achieve an economic rebound and maintain steady and relatively fast economic development under extremely difficult and complex circumstances.

译者用动词 see 构成"时间/地点+see"句型，形成上述译文。

而下面译例是由于使用了强调句式 It was only by… that… 而形成了现在的译文：

我们党能够依靠自己和人民的力量纠正错误，在挫折中奋起，继续胜利前进，根本原因就在于重新恢复和坚持贯彻了实事求是。

<u>It was only by</u> restoring and upholding the line of seeking truth from facts <u>that</u>

the Party was able to correct its mistakes, overcome its setbacks and forge ahead triumphantly by relying on its own strengths and those of the people.

下面两个译例中，汉语都有"取得……进展"之意，英语都用了同一个句式：…progress was made…。

- 城市社区卫生服务体系建设取得重大进展。
  Significant progress was made in developing a system of community-based health services in urban areas.
- 自由贸易区建设、与主要经贸伙伴的经济对话、同发展中国家的互利合作取得新进展。
  Further progress was made in the development of free trade zones, and in our economic dialogues with major trading partners and mutually beneficial cooperation with other developing countries.

以上两句译文都是被动语态，而被动句也是英文常见的构句结构。下面译文的构句就和以上几个译文相仿。

财税、金融、价格、行政管理等重点领域和关键环节的改革取得新突破。
New breakthroughs were made in reforms in key areas and crucial links, such as the fiscal, taxation, financial and pricing systems and administration.

倒装也是英译文中常见的句式。

- 党和人民的实践是不断前进的，指导这种实践的理论也要不断前进。
  The practice of the Party and the people keeps progressing, so should the theories guiding it.
- 挑战与机遇并存，困难与希望同在。我国经济社会发展的基本面和长期向好的趋势没有改变。
  Challenges and opportunities coexist, as do hardships and hopes. Neither the fundamentals of China's economic and social development nor its positive long-term trend has changed.
- 既要发挥市场这只看不见的手的作用，又要发挥政府和社会监管这只看得见的手的作用。两手都要硬，两手同时发挥作用，才能实现按照市场规律配置资源，也才能使资源配置合理、协调、平衡、可持续。
  The invisible hand of the market and the visible hand of government and social supervision should both act, and act vigorously. Only in this way

211

can resources be distributed according to market rules and distributed in a reasonable, coordinated, balanced and sustainable manner.

另外,我们熟悉的 there be 句式在英译文中也常常使用。

人口多,底子薄,发展不平衡,这种基本国情还没有从根本上得到改变。

<u>There has been</u> no fundamental change in our basic national condition: a big population, weak economic foundation and uneven development.

此句译文将原句后半部分信息提前,纳入 there be 句式,将原句前半句化为名词结构,用冒号导出。

加强亚洲地区合作的机制和倡议很多,各方面想法和主张丰富多样。

<u>There are</u> many mechanisms and initiatives for enhancing cooperation in Asia, and a lot of ideas on boosting such cooperation are being explored by various parties.

用 it 作形式主语也很常用。

中英关系的美好前景要靠青年去开拓。

<u>It is</u> incumbent upon you to build an even more splendid future of China-Britain relations.

通过对上述译例观察和讨论,我们进一步看到,翻译从某种程度上可以说是一种特定形式的写作。翻译过程中,译者的思维要顺应英语的措辞行文规范,译者从其占有的各种可供选择的搭配模式和句型中判断、筛选——哪一种能最好地容纳原文信息,能最好地承接上下文,就用哪一种。译者所具有的搭配、句式等英语词汇表达和结构模式的储备量,直接决定着译文的写作质量。而语言资源的储备主要靠英语语篇的阅读,双语语篇阅读是一种辅助手段。

第十节 名物化

名物化指将动词结构译为名词结构,这一点我们在第一篇第二章第十一节讨论过。在时政语篇翻译中,名物化也是一个值得关注的常用的翻译方法。比如:

达成一个高水平的中瑞自贸协定,也等于是树立一个好的标杆,不仅会促进两国经贸合作全面升级,而且会向世界发出反对贸易和投资保护主义、倡导贸易自由化和便利化的强有力信号,给中欧经贸关系深化带来新的动力,给两国消费者和企业带来实实在在的好处,也有利于世界贸易振兴和经济复苏。

A high-quality FTA agreement between China and Switzerland will also set a good example. It will not only upgrade our business and investment cooperation but also send a powerful message to the rest of the world that we reject trade and investment protectionism and instead embrace trade liberalization and facilitation. It will inject fresh impetus into China-EU business ties, bring tangible benefits to consumers and businesses in both our countries, and contribute to world trade and economic recovery.

上面英译文将原文主语"达成……协定"译为名词短语,在接下来拆译出的两个句子里又用 it 承前复指,形成了主语链 agreement—it—it—。

下面译例的原文被拆译成两句,第一句将汉语小句译为名词,作主语,第二句用代词作主语复指之,形成主语链 measures—they—。

我们采取这些措施,把扩大国内需求、调整振兴产业、加强科技支撑、强化社会保障结合起来,把拉动经济增长和改善民生、增加就业结合起来,把克服当前困难和促进长远发展结合起来。

The aforementioned measures will help us boost domestic demand, readjust and reinvigorate industries, enhance the support of science and technology and strengthen social security all at the same time. They will drive economic growth while improving people's livelihood and creating more jobs, and see us through current difficulties while also improving the long-term prospect of the Chinese economy.

从以上两例我们看出,英译时通过名物化形成的主语,借助于代词的复指可贯通整个语段。

下面汉语原句被拆译为两句,英译文第二句将动宾结构"形成……城市群"译为名词短语,作主语。

改革开放30多年来,中国工业化、城镇化步伐明显加快,城镇居民从1.7亿人增加到近7亿人,形成了一批有重要影响与发展活力的城市群,促进了经济发展和社会进步。

Since the launching of reform and opening-up program over 30 years ago, China has quickened the pace of industrialization and urbanization, with urban population increasing from 170 million to some 700 million. The emergence of a number of city

213

clusters with strong influence and dynamism for development has boosted economic development and social progress.

下面是三个类似的译例：

- 总结 90 年的发展历程，我们党保持和发展马克思主义政党先进性的根本点是：……
  A review of its 90 years of development shows that the following are essential for our Party to preserve and develop its advanced nature as a Marxist political party: …
- 综观国际国内形势，我国仍处于重要战略机遇期。
  An analysis of the overall international and domestic situations shows that China is still in an important period of strategic opportunities.
- 进口用于信息网络传播的音像制品，参照本办法第十四条的规定办理。
  The import of the audio and video products used for information network dissemination shall be handled in reference to the provisions of Article 14 of these Measures.

下面译例中，汉语原文都包含小句作状语的结构，英译文将这些小句转化为名词短语。

- 待辅助设施的配套工程完成后，新业务预期可协同现有的散货装卸业务，强化第二港埠公司的竞争力。
  Upon the completion of installing ancillary equipments, the new line of business is expected to synergize with the existing cargo handling business in enhancing the competitiveness of the Second Stevedoring Company.
- 由于集装箱公司的平均处理费及处理量均有增长，集装箱公司期内的业绩令人鼓舞。
  As a result of both increases in average handling fee and handling capacity, the Container Company has achieved an encouraging result in the period.
- 虽然酿酒市场在 2000 年竞争激烈，唯王朝仍然能够位列中国顶尖酿酒厂之一。由于客户的喜好经常改变，市场竞争亦趋激烈，故在广告及宣传活动方面需花上更多工夫，以提高客户对品牌的认识，从而扩展现有的销售网络。
  Despite keen competition in the winery market in 2000, Dynasty is still able

to manage to be one of the best fine wine sellers in China. Due to <u>the changing customer preference</u> and <u>severe competition</u>, more efforts have been placed on advertising and promotional campaign to arouse the brand awareness among the customers and to expand the existing sales network.

- 区域市政局订立了发牌制度，借以管制上述行业及娱乐场所，务求减少严重传染病以及由食物所引起的疾病发生。

  Through <u>a licensing system</u>, the Council maintains its control over such businesses and places of entertainment as a means of minimizing the outbreak of serious infections and food-related diseases.

- 迈出这一步，瑞士将成为欧洲大陆和世界经济20强中首个与中国达成自贸协定的国家，其意义非同一般。

  With <u>the advent of FTA</u>, Switzerland will become the first country in continental Europe and the first of the world's top 20 economies to reach a FTA with China, the implications of which will be significant.

上面译例中的"迈出这一步"指的是自贸协定（Free Trade Agreement）的签署。

从以上几例可以看出，名物化在句子结构简洁化方面有一定的作用。原文的动宾词组或小句在译文中转换成了名词词组，或直接充当主语，或辅以介词构成状语。

下面译例出现了合译。原文第一句被译作名词短语作主语，取代第二句的主语位置，与其余成分构成主谓宾结构。

这项比赛获得了广泛的宣传。比赛除了令饮食业从业人员了解保持高度卫生水准的重要性以及处理事物的正确方法外，还鼓励市民光顾符合卫生水准的食肆。

<u>The wide publicity given this competition</u> not only made people in the trade realize the importance of maintaining high standards and the right way to handle food but also encouraged customers to patronize restaurants with satisfactory standards.

有时译文也会有"反名物化"现象，即原文的名词结构，特别是"……的……"结构，在英文中被译成了小句。比如：

"和为贵"的文化传统，哺育了中华民族宽广博大的胸怀。

The Chinese cultural tradition values peace as the most precious. This has nurtured the broad mind of the Chinese nation.

215

第三章
翻译试笔和思考

时政语篇翻译试笔以拆译练习为主线展开。拆译是将意合形散、逗号连连的汉语长句转换为主谓突出、逻辑层次分明的英语架构的必然手段。拆译涉及主语的确立、语篇的连贯以及句型运用等多项翻译技能。翻译教学实践表明，以拆译为突破口，逐渐熟悉时政语篇的翻译规律，不失为一条事半功倍的有效途径。本章练习基本围绕拆译安排，第一节训练如何对原文进行拆分，第二节着重训练拆译中主语的确立，第三节侧重思考如何实现译文的逻辑连贯，第四节集中练一练数字增减的表达。

第一节 拆句练习

【练习一】

这三件大事，从根本上改变了中国人民和中华民族的前途命运，不可逆转地结束了近代以后中国内忧外患、积贫积弱的 [1] 悲惨命运，不可逆转地开启了中华民族不断发展壮大、走向伟大复兴的历史进军，使具有五千多年文明历史的 [2] 中国面貌焕然一新，中华民族伟大复兴展现出前所未有的光明前景。[3]

参考译文

These three major events reshaped the future and destiny of the Chinese people and the Chinese nation. They irreversibly ended the misery endured by China in modern times when it suffered from both domestic turmoil and foreign invasion and was poor and weak. They also irreversibly started the Chinese nation's historic march for development, growth, and great rejuvenation. They gave China, a civilization of over 5,000 years, a completely new look and created unimagined prospects for the great rejuvenation of the Chinese nation.

思考

1. 此处为定语，其信息在译文中纳入了状语从句。
2. 此处亦为定语，译文将其处理为同位语。
3. 全文只一句话，按语义群拆译为四句英语，后三句均用代词 they 承接首句主语。

【练习二】

做好今年的政府工作，要高举中国特色社会主义伟大旗帜，以邓小平理论和"三个代表"重要思想为指导，深入贯彻落实科学发展观，把保持经济平稳较快发展作为经济工作的首要任务，加强和改善宏观调控，着力扩大国内需求特别是消费需求，着力转变发展方式、加快经济结构战略性调整，着力深化改革、提高对外开放水平，着力改善民生、促进社会和谐，全面推进社会主义经济建设、政治建设、文化建设、社会建设以及生态文明建设。[1]

参考译文

To carry out the work of the government well this year, we must hold high the great banner of socialism with Chinese characteristics, take Deng Xiaoping Theory and the important thought of Three Represents as our guide, and thoroughly apply the Scientific Outlook on Development. We need to make ensuring steady and rapid economic development the main task of our economic work. We need to strengthen and improve macroeconomic control, vigorously expand domestic demand, particularly consumer demand, change the pattern of development and speed up strategic economic restructuring, and deepen reform and improve our work of opening to the outside world. We need to improve the people's lives, increase social harmony and promote all-round progress in socialist economic, political, cultural, social and ecological development.

思考

1. 原文的一句话拆译成四个英语句子。第一句将原文下划线部分译为状语，并添加 we 作主语，后面拆出的句子均沿用此代词作主语。另外注意原文中四个"着力"在译文中用一个副词 vigorously 译出。

【练习三】

我们将进一步完善法规和标准，强化目标责任考核，推动循环经济发展，全面推进节能、节水、节地、节材和资源综合利用，加强对各种自然资源的节约和管理，加强综合治理，保护与修复生态。我们将大力培育以低碳排放为特征的工业、建筑和交通体系，增加森林碳汇，加快低碳技术研发、示范和产业化，全面增强应对气候变化能力，<u>在"共同但有区别的责任"原则下</u>[1] 积极开展应对气候变化国际合作。[2]

参考译文

We will further improve laws and standards, strengthen accountability evaluation in meeting environmental targets, and advance the development of circular economy. We will make all-round efforts to save energy, water, land and materials and make comprehensive use of all kinds of resources, enhance the conservation and management of all natural resources, and take a holistic approach to protect and repair the eco-environment. We will energetically develop low carbon industrial construction and transport systems, increase the forest carbon sink and speed up the R&D demonstration and industrial application of low carbon technologies. We will comprehensively enhance our capacity for tackling climate change, and actively carry out international cooperation against climate change under the principle of "common but differentiated responsibilities".

思考

1. 原文下划线部分即为状语，英译为介词短语作状语。
2. 原文这一段包括两个长句，各带五个或七个并列小句。如同样译为两个英语句子，各带若干个并列分句,在结构上过于冗长,显然不可取。现参照语义群,共译出四个英语句子,各句所含并列小句不过三个,行文较为流畅。

【练习四】

在肯定成绩的同时,也要清醒地看到,我们正面临前所未有的困难和挑战。
一是国际金融危机还在蔓延、仍未见底。国际市场需求继续萎缩,/全球通货紧缩趋势明显,/贸易保护主义抬头,//外部经济环境更加严峻,/不确定因素显著增多。[1]
二是受国际金融危机影响,经济增速持续下滑,已成为影响全局的主要矛盾。[2] 一些行业产能过剩,部分企业经营困难,就业形势十分严峻,财政减收增支因素增多,农业稳定发展、农民持续增收难度加大。[3]
三是长期制约我国经济健康发展的体制性、结构性矛盾依然存在,有的还很突出。消费需求不足,第三产业发展滞后,自主创新能力不强,能源资源消耗多,环境污染重,城乡、区域发展差距仍在扩大。[4]

参考译文

While acknowledging our achievements, we must be clearly aware that we face unprecedented difficulties and challenges.

First, the global financial crisis continues to spread and get worse. Demand continues to shrink on international markets; the trend toward global deflation is obvious; and trade protectionism is resurging. The external economic environment has become more serious, and uncertainties have increased significantly.

Second, continuous drop in economic growth rate due to the impact of the global financial crisis has become a major problem affecting the overall situation. This has resulted in excess production capacity in some industries, caused some enterprises to experience operating difficulties and exerted severe pressure on employment. Factors leading to decline in government revenues and increase in government expenditures have increased. It has become more difficult to maintain steady agricultural development and keep rural incomes growing.

Third, institutional and structural problems that have long hindered healthy economic development still remain, and some of them are still prominent. Consumption demand is insufficient, and development of tertiary industries is sluggish. Our capacity for independent innovation is weak. Consumption of energy and other resources is high. Environmental pollution is serious. Disparities in development between urban and rural areas and between regions are widening.

思考

1. 原文这一句拆译为两个句子（如双斜线所示），包括了五个小句（如单斜线所示）。每个小句都沿用了原文的主语（下划线所示）。
2. 这个长句的译文主从分明：两个下划线部分，前者译为介词短语，作状语；后者译为分词短语，作后置定语。另外，"经济增速持续下滑"被译为名词短语（名物化）。
3. 这个句子被拆译为三句。第一句添加了 this has resulted in... 凸显出与前一句的逻辑联系；第三句运用了 it 作形式主语的句型。
4. 这一句拆译为五句。各句基本沿用原文主语（下划线所示）。

第二节 确立主语练习

【练习一】

　　国务院机构改革基本完成，地方机构改革稳步推进。农村综合改革继续深化，集体林权制度改革全面推开。国有企业改革不断深化。中国农业银行和国家开发银行股份制改革顺利进行。¹ 实施新的企业所得税法，统一内外资企业和个人房地产税收制度。² 酝酿多年的 ³ 成品油价格和税费改革顺利推出。制定医药卫生体制改革方案并公开征求意见。⁴ 体制机制创新为长远发展奠定了坚实基础。⁵

参考译文

Institutional restructuring of the State Council was basically completed and that of local governments is progressing steadily. Comprehensive rural reforms continued to deepen, and reform of collective forest rights was instituted throughout the country. SOE reform was deepened. The transformation of the Agricultural Bank of China and China Development Bank into joint stock companies proceeded smoothly. The new Law on Corporate Income Tax went into effect, and real estate taxes were unified for domestic and overseas-funded enterprises and Chinese and foreign individuals. After years of deliberation, reform in pricing, taxes and fees for refined petroleum products was smoothly introduced. A plan for reform of the pharmaceutical and health care system was devised and referred to the general public for comments. These innovations in systems and mechanisms have laid a solid foundation for our long-term development.

思考

1. 四个句子的译文都基本沿用了原文主语"改革",但译文用了不同的词语,包括 restructuring, reform, transformation 等。
2. 这两个小句的译文都重新确立了主语,分别为 the new law 和 real estate taxes。
3. 句中定语"酝酿多年的"译为状语。
4. 原句省略了主语,译文重新确立主语 a plan。
5. 译文主语 these innovations 起到了承接上文的连贯作用。

【练习二】

人才是第一资源,是国家发展的战略资源。全党同志和全社会都要坚持尊重劳动、尊重知识、尊重人才、尊重创造的重大方针,牢固树立人人皆可成才的观念[1],敢为事业用人才,让各类人才都拥有广阔的创业平台、发展空间,使每个人都成为对祖国、对人民、对民族的有用之才[2],特别是要抓紧培养造就青年英才,形成人才辈出、人尽其才、才尽其用[3]的生动局面。

参考译文

Talent is the most important resource and a strategic resource for a country's development. All the comrades in the Party and the whole society should adhere to the major principle of respect for work, knowledge, talent, and creation, imbue themselves with the view that everyone has potential talent to develop, and do not hesitate to use talents for the cause of the Party and the people. We should provide broad platforms to talented persons of all types to pursue their career and fully tap their development potential, and make sure that everyone contributes their due share to the country, the people, and the nation. It is particularly important to speed up the training of talented young people and to ensure that capable people emerge in great numbers and put their talents to best use and that everyone can bring out their best.

思考

1. 此处的下划线部分译为同位语;"树立"译为 imbue with。
2. 注意此处译文中宾语从句的运用。
3. 划线处的译文结构为两个并列的宾语从句。

【练习三】

坚定不移地推进自主创新和经济结构调整。实施 16 个国家重大科技专项。在信息、生物、环保等领域新建一批国家工程中心、重点实验室和企业技术中心。成功研发支线飞机、新能源汽车、高速铁路等一批关键技术和重大装备。中央财政科技投入 1163 亿元,增长 16.4%。电信、航空等行业重组迈出重要步伐[1]。继续淘汰落后产能,全年关停小火电 1669 万千瓦[2],关闭小煤矿 1054 处。加大基础设施和基础产业投资力度[3],在能源、交通、水利等方面建成和开工一批重大项目。扎实推进区域发展总战略[4],区域经济发展协调性增强。[5]

参考译文

We unswervingly promoted independent innovation and economic restructuring. We launched 16 major national science and technology projects, and established a number of new national engineering centers, key laboratories and enterprise technology centers in such fields as information technology, biotechnology and environmental protection. We successfully developed a number of key technologies and major equipment in the areas of regional aircraft, automobiles powered by new energy sources and high-speed railways. The central government invested 116.3 billion yuan in science and technology, an increase of 16.4%. Significant steps were taken in reorganization of the telecommunications and civil aviation industries. We continued to eliminate backward production facilities. Last year, we shut down small thermal power plants with a total capacity of 16.69 million kilowatts and closed 1,054 small coalmines. Investment in infrastructure and basic industries was increased, and a number of major projects in energy, transportation and water conservancy were completed or launched. Steady progress was made in implementing the master strategy for regional development, and economic development in different regions became better coordinated.

思考

1. 此处译文以 steps 为主语，构成被动语态。
2. 注意此处"小火电"的英语表达方法。
3. 此句英译以 investment 为主语，译为被动句。
4. 此句译文重新确立主语，译为 Steady progress was made in... 句式。
5. 原文段落包括八个句子，其中的第二、三两句语义密切相关，合译为一句。全段大部分的句子、小句是无主句，可理解为省略了"我们"。译文以补充 we 作主语的方式构句，而后面几个句子则另立主语构成了被动结构。

【练习四】

我们推进社会主义制度自我完善和发展，在经济、政治、文化、社会等各个领域形成一整套相互衔接、相互联系的制度体系。[1] 人民代表大会制度这一根本政治制度，中国共产党领导的多党合作和政治协商制度、民族区域自治制度以及基层群众自治制度等构成的基本政治制度，中国特色社会主义法律体系，公有制

为主体、多种所有制经济共同发展的基本经济制度，以及建立在根本政治制度、基本政治制度、基本经济制度基础上的经济体制、政治体制、文化体制、社会体制等各项具体制度，²符合我国国情，顺应时代潮流，有利于保持党和国家活力、调动广大人民群众和社会各方面的积极性、主动性、创造性，有利于解放和发展社会生产力、推动经济社会全面发展，有利于维护和促进社会公平正义、实现全体人民共同富裕，有利于集中力量办大事、有效应对前进道路上的各种风险挑战，有利于维护民族团结、社会稳定、国家统一。

参考译文

In the course of promoting the self-improvement and self-development of the socialist system, we have put in place a complete set of integrated, interconnected systems in the economic, political, cultural, and social fields. They include the following: the system of people's congresses which is China's fundamental political system; the basic political systems which include the system of multiparty cooperation and political consultation under the leadership of the CPC, the system of regional ethnic autonomy, and the system of community-level self-governance; the socialist system of laws with Chinese characteristics; the basic economic system with public ownership being the leading sector and economic entities under diverse forms of ownership developing together; and specific economic, political, cultural, and social institutions based on the fundamental political system, basic political systems and the basic economic system. These systems and institutions are compatible with China's reality and conform to the trend of the times. They keep the Party and country full of vitality and fully tap the enthusiasm, initiative, and creativity of the people and all sectors of society. They serve to free and develop the productive forces and promote all-around economic and social development. They uphold and promote fairness and justice and aim to bring prosperity to all. They make it possible to pool resources to undertake major national initiatives, and they can effectively defuse risks and meet challenges on our road ahead. They serve to maintain ethnic solidarity, social stability, and national unity.

思考

1. 注意此句译文的主从安排；下划线部分译为状语。
2. 这部分例举了各种制度体系，译文添加 They include the following: … 将原文各分句拆译为一句。随后拆译出的多个英语句子便顺理成章地构建出 These systems and institutions 加多个 they 构成的主语链。

第三节　逻辑连贯练习

【练习一】

　　第三件大事，我们党紧紧依靠人民进行了改革开放新的伟大革命，<u>开创、坚持、发展了中国特色社会主义</u>。¹ 党的十一届三中全会以来，我们总结我国社会主义建设经验，同时借鉴国际经验，<u>以巨大的政治勇气、理论勇气、实践勇气实行改革开放</u>，<u>经过艰辛探索</u>，形成了党在社会主义初级阶段的基本理论、基本路线、基本纲领、基本经验，建立和完善社会主义市场经济体制，坚持全方位对外开放，推动社会主义现代化建设取得举世瞩目的伟大成就。²

参考译文

　　The third is that, firmly relying on the people, our Party carried out a great new revolution of reform and opening up, creating, upholding, and developing socialism with Chinese characteristics. Since the Third Plenary Session of the Eleventh CPC Central Committee, we have reviewed China's practices of building socialism and drawn on the experience of other countries. We have embarked on the path of reform and opening up with tremendous political and theoretical courage and courage in practice. Going through an arduous process of trial and error, we have formed the Party's basic theory, line and platform and gained basic experience in the primary stage of socialism. We have established a socialist market economy and constantly improved it, made China fully open, and made world-renowned progress in the socialist modernization drive.

思考

1. 这句话的英译文对主从信息的处理值得注意，特别是"开创、坚持、发展了中国特色社会主义"这部分被处理为分词状语。
2. 注意整个段落中译为从属结构，特别是译为状语结构（下划线部分）的语句。它们在原文中已有较明确的逻辑标识（如"……以来""以……""经过……"等），英译时基本是顺势为之，译为状语。

【练习二】

全党必须清醒地看到，在世情、国情、党情发生深刻变化的新形势下，提高党的领导水平和执政水平、提高拒腐防变和抵御风险能力，加强党的执政能力建设和先进性建设，面临许多前所未有的新情况新问题新挑战，执政考验、改革开放考验、市场经济考验、外部环境考验是长期的、复杂的、严峻的。[1] 精神懈怠的危险，能力不足的危险，脱离群众的危险，消极腐败的危险，更加尖锐地摆在全党面前[2]，落实党要管党、从严治党的任务比以往任何时候都更为繁重、更为紧迫[3]。

参考译文

The entire Party must be keenly aware that at a time of profound changes in global, national and intra-Party conditions, we are now faced with many new developments, problems, and challenges in our effort to enhance the Party's leadership and governance and its ability to resist corruption and degeneration and to withstand risks, and strengthen its governance capacity and advanced nature. We are facing long-term, complicated and severe tests in governing the country, in implementing reform and opening up and in developing the market economy, as well as tests in the external environment. And the whole Party is confronted with growing danger of lacking in drive, incompetence, divorce from the people, lacking in initiative, and corruption.

It has thus become even more important and urgent than ever before for the Party to police itself and impose strict discipline on its members.

思考

1. 这个长句被拆译为两句，划线部分的信息被译为介词短语，作状语。
2. 译文将"全党"确立为主语，原文的主语部分译为宾语。
3. 此处译文运用了 it 作形式主语的句式。

【练习三】

在全球通胀预期不断增强，国际市场大宗商品价格高位波动，国内要素成本明显上升，部分农产品供给偏紧的严峻形势下，我们把稳定物价总水平作为宏观调控的首要任务，坚持综合施策，合理运用货币政策工具，调节货币信贷增速，大力发展生产，保障供给，搞活流通，加强监管，居民消费价格指数、工业生产者出厂价格指数涨幅从 8 月份起逐月回落，扭转了一度过快上涨势头[1]。

下半年，世界经济不稳定性不确定性上升，国内经济运行出现一些新情况新问题[2]，我们一方面坚持宏观调控的基本取向不变，保持宏观经济政策基本稳定，继续控制通货膨胀；一方面[3]适时适度预调微调，加强信贷政策与产业政策的协调配合，加大结构性减税力度，重点支持实体经济特别是小型微型企业，重点支持民生工程特别是保障性安居工程，重点保证国家重大在建、续建项目的资金需要[4]，有针对性地解决经济运行中的突出矛盾[5]。

我们坚定不移地加强房地产市场调控，确保调控政策落到实处、见到实效。投机、投资性需求得到明显抑制，多数城市房价环比下降，调控效果正在显现。我们高度重视防范和化解财政金融领域的潜在风险隐患，[6]及时对地方政府性债务进行全面审计，摸清了多年形成的地方政府性债务的总规模、形成原因、偿还时限和区域分布。这些债务在经济社会发展中发挥了积极作用，形成了大量优质资产；也存在一些风险隐患，特别是部分偿债能力较弱地区存在局部性风险[7]。

参考译文

Amid worsening inflation expectations worldwide, fluctuating and high prices of major commodities on the world market, significantly higher costs of factors of production at home, and a shortage of some agricultural products, we made ensuring general price stability our top priority in macro-control, pursued policies in an integrated way, rationally used monetary policy tools to regulate the supplies of money and credit, vigorously developed production to ensure supply, boosted distribution, and strengthened supervision. <u>As a result</u>, increases in the consumer price index (CPI) and the producer price index (PPI) began falling in August, thus reversing the trend of rapid inflation.

In the second half of the year, when the global economy faced greater instability and uncertainty and when new developments and problems occurred in China's economy, we kept the basic orientation of macro-control unchanged, maintained the basic continuity of our macroeconomic policies, and continued to curb inflation. <u>In addition</u>, we carried out timely and appropriate anticipatory adjustments and fine-tuning, strengthened coordination between credit and industrial policies, and increased structural tax reductions. We focused on supporting the real economy, especially small and micro businesses; improving the people's well-being, especially by building low-income housing projects; and ensuring funding for key projects that are under construction or expansion. These well-targeted measures were taken to solve major economic problems.

We steadfastly tightened regulation of the real estate market and ensured that control policies were fully carried out and achieved real progress. <u>Consequently</u>, speculative or investment-driven housing demand has been significantly curbed, housing prices in most Chinese cities have fallen month on month, and the results of our control measures are beginning to show. We attached great importance to guarding against and eliminating latent risks which exist in the banking and public finance sectors. We fully audited local government debt in a timely manner, and obtained a clear picture of the total amount, due dates, geographic distribution, and causes of the debts local governments incurred over the years. These debts have played a positive role in promoting economic and social development and produced a large amount of quality assets. <u>However</u>, they also contained risks and hidden dangers, and some localities with poor ability to pay their debts were at risk of default.

思考

1. "居民消费价格指数……上涨势头"拆出译为一句，句前加上 as a result，以显化信息逻辑走向。
2. 这一部分被析为从属信息，译为两个 when... 引导的状语从句。
3. 原文用"一方面……一方面……"标示出行文层次，译文在此处添加 in addition 以实现同样的行文连贯。
4. 原文的三个"重点支持/保证……"译为三个并列的动名词结构。
5. 这一部分的译文添加了主语 these measures，以承接并总括上文语义，这也是一种逻辑安排。
6. 7. 这两个部分各自拆译为一个句子，且分别在句首添加了表示逻辑的连接词语 consequently 和 however，显化了译文的逻辑层次。

【练习四】

这里要着重说明，国内生产总值增长目标略微调低 [1]，主要是要与"十二五"规划目标逐步衔接，引导各方面把工作着力点放到加快转变经济发展方式、切实提高经济发展质量和效益上来，以利于实现更长时期、更高水平、更好质量发展 [2]。提出居民消费价格涨幅控制在 4% 左右 [3]，综合考虑了输入性通胀因素、要素成本上升影响以及居民承受能力，也为价格改革预留一定空间 [4]。

综合考虑各方面情况 [5]，要继续实施积极的财政政策和稳健的货币政策，根据形势变化适时适度预调微调，进一步提高政策的针对性、灵活性和前瞻性。

参考译文

Here I wish to stress that in setting a slightly lower GDP growth rate, we hope to make it fit with targets in the Twelfth Five-Year Plan, and to guide people in all sectors to focus their work on accelerating the transformation of the pattern of economic development and making economic development more sustainable and efficient, so as to achieve higher-level, higher-quality development over a longer period of time. In projecting a CPI increase of around 4%, we have taken into account imported inflation, rising costs of factors of production, and people's ability to absorb the impact of price increases, while leaving room for the effect of price reforms.

Taking into consideration all relevant factors, we will continue to follow a proactive fiscal policy and a prudent monetary policy, carry out timely and appropriate anticipatory adjustments and fine-tuning, and make our policies more targeted, flexible, and anticipatory.

思考

1. 这一部分析为从属信息，译为"介词+动名词"短语，作状语。
2. 从原文自身看，这一部分就是表示目的的状语，译文仍以状语形式译出。
3. 这一部分作为从属信息译为"介词+动名词"短语，作状语。
4. 此处的译文用 while 引导的状语从句体现原文"也为……"的逻辑层次。
5. 此处译为分词状语。

【练习五】

全面做好今年的工作[1]，必须坚持突出主题、贯穿主线[2]、统筹兼顾、协调推进，把稳增长、控物价、调结构、惠民生、抓改革、促和谐更好地结合起来[3]。

稳增长[4]，就是要坚持扩大内需、稳定外需，大力发展实体经济，努力克服国内外各种不稳定不确定因素的影响，及时解决苗头性、倾向性问题[5]，保持经济平稳运行。

控物价，就是要继续采取综合措施，保持物价总水平基本稳定，防止价格走势反弹[6]。

调结构，就是要有扶有控[7]，提高经济增长质量和效益，增强发展的协调性和可持续性。

惠民生，就是要坚持把保障改善民生作为工作的根本出发点和落脚点，把促进社会公平正义放在更加突出的位置，切实办成一些让人民群众得实惠[8]好事实事。

参考译文

To ensure success in all our work this year, we must uphold the theme of scientific development, take transforming the pattern of economic development as the main thread, adopt a holistic approach, and coordinate all our work. We must coordinate efforts to achieve steady growth, control prices, adjust the economic structure, improve the people's well-being, implement reform, and promote harmony.

To achieve steady growth, we will continue to expand domestic demand and keep foreign demand stable, vigorously develop the real economy, work hard to counter the impact of various factors of instability and uncertainty at home and abroad, promptly resolve emerging issues that signal unfavorable trends, and maintain stable economic performance.

To control prices, we will continue to take comprehensive measures to maintain basic overall price stability and prevent a rebound of inflation.

To adjust the economic structure, we will support development in some areas while limiting growth in others, improve the quality and efficiency of economic growth, and make development more coordinated and sustainable.

To improve the people's well-being, we will continue to take ensuring and improving the people's well-being as the fundamental starting point and goal of our work, give higher priority to promoting social fairness and justice, and take a number of initiatives that will bring substantive benefits to the people.

思考

1. 这部分译为目的状语。
2. 这部分的译文对"主题"和"主线"进行了释义。
3. 这部分译为目的状语。
4. 这部分译为目的状语。以下三个自然段的"控物价""调结构""惠民生"也都析为目的状语，译为不定式结构。
5. "倾向性"译作定语，对原文有所释义。
6. 这部分译为目的状语。
7. "有控"译为 while 引导的状语（译文划线部分）。
8. 这部分译为定语从句。

第四节 数字表达练习

【练习一】

多渠道开发就业岗位，全力推动以创业带动就业，加强职业技能培训和公共就业服务体系建设。加大财政、税收、金融等方面支持力度，着力促进高校毕业生、农民工等重点人群就业[1]。高校毕业生初次就业率77.8%，同比提高1.2个百分点[2]。农民工总量2.53亿人，比上年增长4.4%[3]，其中，外出农民工1.59亿人，增长3.4%[4]。

参考译文

We created jobs through a variety of channels, expanded job opportunities through the creation of new businesses, strengthened vocational skills training, and improved the public employment service system. We increased fiscal, taxation, and financial support to promote employment of university graduates, rural migrant workers, and other key groups. The employment rate for college graduates reached 77.8%, an increase of 1.2 percentage points over the previous year. The number of rural workers totaled 253 million, an increase of 4.4% over the previous year, of whom 159 million worked in towns and cities, up 3.4%.

思考

1. 这部分译为目的状语。
2. 3. 4. 注意这三处的译文都采用了同位语形式。

【练习二】

发布实施《"十二五"节能减排综合性工作方案》《控制温室气体排放工作方案》和《加强环境保护重点工作的意见》。清洁能源发电装机达到2.9亿千瓦，比上年增加3356万千瓦。加强重点节能环保工程建设，新增城镇污水日处理能力1100万吨，5000多万千瓦新增燃煤发电机组全部安装脱硫设施。加大对高耗能、高排放和产能过剩¹行业的调控力度，淘汰落后的水泥产能 1.5 亿吨、炼铁产能 3122 万吨、焦炭产能 1925 万吨²。

参考译文

We adopted and implemented the Comprehensive Work Plan for Conserving Energy and Reducing Emissions and the Work Plan for Controlling Greenhouse Gas Emissions for the Twelfth Five-Year Plan period, and the Guidelines on Strengthening Key Environmental Protection Tasks. The installed power capacity using clean energy reached 290 million kilowatts, an increase of 33.56 million kilowatts over the previous year. We strengthened the development of major energy conservation and environmental protection projects. We increased daily sewage treatment capacity by 11 million tons in urban areas, and installed desulphurization systems on all new coal-fired power-generating units with a total capacity of over 50 million kilowatts. We tightened controls over industries that are energy intensive, have high emissions or possess excess production capacity, and closed down outdated production facilities whose production capacity amounted to 150 million tons of cement, 31.22 million tons of iron, and 19.25 million tons of coke.

思考

1. 划线部分译为定语从句，注意体会这三个概念是如何用英语表达的。
2. 汉语直接说"淘汰产能"，注意英语要表达为"淘汰产能达到……吨的生产设施"。

【练习三】

在应对国际金融危机中，我们始终高度重视推动经济发展方式转变和经济结构调整。两年来，国内需求特别是消费对经济增长的拉动作用持续增强，2009 年社会消费品零售总额实际增长 16.9%，为 1986 年以来最高增速，今年以来这一势头得到延续，上半年实际增速与去年同期基本持平。产业结构升级加快，今年前 7 个月，高技术产业增加值同比增长 17.7%，高于规模以上工业增加值增速 0.7 个百分点。基础设施建设得到加强，2008 年 8 月 1 日，我国第一条具有完全自主知识产权、世界一流水平的高速铁路¹——京津城际铁路通车运营，全程运行时间只有30分钟，使两大直辖市形成同城效应；²去年12月26日通车运营的武广高速铁路又成为目前世界上一次建成里程最长、速度最高的高速铁路。节能减排和环境保护扎实推进³，去年关停了小火电机组2610万千瓦，淘汰落后炼钢产能1691万吨、炼铁产能2113万吨、水泥产能7416万吨，今年9月底前将再淘汰落后炼钢产能825万吨、炼铁产能3000万吨、水泥产能9155万吨⁴，"十一五"前四年单位国内生产总值能耗累计下降15.6%。区域发展协调性增强，2009年中部地区、西部地区规模以上工业增加值增速分别比全国快1.1和4.5个百分点，今年上半年中部地区比全国快3.1个百分点，西部地区与全国持平，中西部地区占全国规模以上工业增加值的比重由2008年同期的38.1%上升到38.8%⁵。更为重要的是，我们从全局和战略的高度，对加快经济发展方式转变和经济结构调整作出了全面部署。所有这些都将对我国经济长期稳定健康发展起到重要推动作用。

参考译文

In tackling the international financial crisis, we have always given top priority to transforming the economic development pattern and restructuring the economy. In the past two years, domestic demand, consumption in particular, has played an increasingly strong role in driving economic growth. Total retail sales in 2009 rose by 16.9 percent in real terms, the fastest since 1986. This good momentum is continuing and retail sales in the first half of this year grew at roughly the same rate as the same period of last year. The upgrading of the industrial structure has been accelerated. In the first seven months of this year, the value added of high-tech industries increased by 17.7 percent year on year, 0.7 percentage point higher than that of the industries above a designated level. Infrastructure development has been strengthened. On 1 August 2008, the Beijing-Tianjin Intercity Railway, China's first top-class high-speed rail with full intellectual property, was put into operation, shortening the travel time between Beijing and Tianjin to only 30 minutes and binding the two major municipalities as one. The Wuhan-Guangzhou high-speed railway that went into operation on 26 December 2009 set the world record of the longest and fastest high-speed railway completed on an uninterrupted basis. Solid progress has been made in energy conservation, emissions reduction and environmental protection. Last year, we shut down small thermal power plants with a total capacity of 26.1 million kilowatts and phased out inefficient production capacity of 16.91 million tons of steel, 21.13 million tons of iron and 74.16 million tons of cement. By the end of this month, we will have eliminated an additional amount of inefficient production capacity, including 8.25 million tons of steel, 30 million tons of iron and 91.55 million tons of cement. Energy consumption per unit of GDP has been reduced by 15.6 percent in the first four years of the 11th Five-Year Plan period. Regional development has been more coordinated. In 2009, the growth rates of value added of industries above a designated scale in the central and western regions were 1.1 and 4.5 percentage points higher than the national average respectively. In the first half of this year, such growth in the central region was 3.1 percentage points higher than the national average, and that in the western region on a par with the national average. Also in the first half of this year, the central and western regions' contribution to the value added of industries above a designated level in the national total increased to 38.8 percent from 38.1 percent of the same period in 2008. What is more important is that we have made all-round arrangements for accelerating the transformation of economic development pattern and economic restructuring from a macro and strategic perspective. All these will give a strong boost to the stable and healthy development of China's economy in the long run.

思考

1. 这一部分译为同位语。
2. 这两个小句均译为分词状语。
3. 此处译文运用了 Progress has been made in... 句式。
4. 译文将这一部分信息放在了分词短语 including... 的结构中。
5. 这一部分被拆译出来，句首添加 Also in the first half of this year, 以和前句更好地衔接。

第三篇

旅游语篇：
导游解说词、景点介绍等

› 课时安排建议

旅游语篇的功能不外乎提供信息、提出建议，带有很强的感召意向。翻译学习过程中，要特别注意对原文信息的分析、调整和重写，必须充分考虑读者的知识结构和阅读意向。第三周的训练就是针对旅游语篇的这种诉求功能（appellative function）展开的。当然，不论何种交际功能，总是要依靠词语的选择和句式的运用加以实现，所以第一、二周关注的仍是在前两篇中反复讨论过的词语、句式和原文语句的拆分、组合问题。

周次	内容提要	英语及双语阅读	翻译试笔和思考
1	词语和句式	第一章第一节、第二节；第二章第一节、第二节	第三章第一节练习一
2	从属成分的运用以及句子的重新拆分组合	第一章第三节；第二章第三节、第四节、第五节	第三章第一节练习二
3	语篇连贯：信息的调整和重新表述，以适应读者认知语境	第一章第四节；第二章第六节、第七节	第三章第二节

第一章
目标语语篇导读

本章的旅游语篇包括旅游景点、博物馆、展览会等的介绍，在相关网站或出版物中均可找到此类型语篇。

第一节 词 语

阅读旅游语篇，首先要学习和掌握如何恰当而灵活地运用基本词汇。先说最具活力的动词。比如 feature 作动词在旅游语篇中就十分常见。

- This exhibition <u>features</u> more than sixty paintings as well as ceramics, carved bamboo, lacquerware, metalwork, textiles, and even several contemporary photographs, all drawn from the Metropolitan Museum's permanent collections, that illustrate how garden imagery has remained an abiding source of artistic inspiration and invention.
- The exhibition is drawn from collections in the UK, Japan, Europe and USA and will <u>feature</u> some 170 works including paintings, sets of prints and illustrated books with text.

句中 feature 作谓语，意为"以……为特色"。feature 一词除了作谓语，还常以现在分词形式作定语，比如：

- Opened in 1977, Ocean Park Hong Kong is a marine-life theme park <u>featuring</u> animal exhibits, thrill rides and shows.
- Here you can watch Symbio, a multi-sensory show <u>featuring</u> the world's first 360-degree water screen. You can also embark on a journey of exploration into the Grand Aquarium <u>featuring</u> 5000 fish from over 400 species and other

aquatic wonders.

再比如 enshrine 这个词常见其被动用法。

- History is <u>enshrined</u> in its many museums and art galleries, while modern Sydney comes alive in the more recent developments around Darling Harbour and the restaurant and entertainment area nearby at Cockle Bay and Kings Wharf.
- "In this temple, as in the hearts of the people for whom he saved the Union, the memory of Abraham Lincoln is <u>enshrined</u> forever." Beneath these words, the 16th President of the United States, Abraham Lincoln sits immortalized in marble.

以上两个例句中的 to be enshrined 都是"庄严地记录着或珍藏着"的意思。

再多观察几个动词运用的例子。

- Britain's capital is home to the great art collections of the National Gallery, architectural icons such as Tower Bridge, and a rich Royal heritage, but it also <u>spawns</u> underground design and musical innovation.

动词 spawn 形象地表达出伦敦不仅在艺术、建筑等方面历史源远流长，而且拥有了不起的地下设施和音乐创新传统。

- This red-and-yellow cable-car contraption <u>whisks</u> you on a 1,097m (3,599 ft.) jaunt between two points on the Canadian side of the falls.

动词 whisk 意为 take sb. somewhere quickly，此处指缆车可将游人便捷地带到大瀑布的另一侧，用词简洁而准确。

- Underneath the Big Apple's jagged skyscraper skyline, museums <u>dazzle</u> with the latest collections, celebrity chefs <u>unveil</u> their newest creations, and Broadway continues to <u>stage</u> elaborate, glittering shows.

句中有三个动词，dazzle 一词尤为生动，有"令人眼花缭乱，目不暇接"之意。

旅游语篇中还常常见到几个动词连续使用的情况。

- Marineland also has rides, including a Tivoli wheel (a fancy Ferris wheel), Dragon Boat rides, and Dragon Mountain, a roller coaster that <u>loops</u>, <u>double-loops</u>, and <u>spirals</u> through 305m (1,001 ft.) of tunnels.
- In this lush tropical setting, more than 2,000 butterflies (50 international

species) float and flutter among such nectar-producing flowers as lantanas and *pentas*.

以上两个例句中，loops, double-loops, and spirals 和 float and flutter 两组连续使用的动词，分别惟妙惟肖地表达出过山车翻转扭转和蝴蝶上下飞舞的情景。

另外短语动词以及动词与其他词语的搭配也是必须留心观察和学习的。

- Make sure you drop by Neptune's Restaurant for Hong Kong's first aquarium dining experience!
- Ride the London Eye observation wheel to get to grips with the city's layout.
- This is the site of a famous War of 1812 battle, and you can take a walking tour of the battlefield.
- Sydney's greatest summer experience is on the beaches—and with over 20 strung along the city's oceanfront and dozens more around the harbor, you'll be spoiled for choice.

句中 be spoiled for choice 意为"目不暇接，不知选哪个好"。

The exquisite miniature masterpieces made during the Yongzheng (1723–1735), Qianlong (1736–1795) and Jiaqing (1796–1820) reigns were particularly prized for their technical virtuosity and artistic sophistication.

句中 be prized for 为"因……而十分珍贵"的意思。

我们也可以以话题为视角，观察和积累词汇及其用法。比如谈到一个景点有吸引力时可以说：

Lovers of soul head to Harlem's Apollo Theatre. The legendary Blue Note and Village Vanguard pack in jazz fans, while cutting-edge bars and clubs in Meatpacking District lure the beautiful people.

描写商业区时可以说：

Couture designer shops line Madison Avenue, while the major department stores like Saks Fifth Avenue and Bloomingdale's anchor Fifth Avenue in Midtown. Cutting-edge designers show their wares in the Meatpacking District, while high-fashion boutiques and cool housewares peak out behind the cast-iron facades of SoHo. Rummage through vintage clothing boutiques on the Lower East Side or sift through knockoff sunglasses, purses, and watches on crammed Canal Street in Chinatown. Head to Greenwich Village to browse music stores and boutique food shops.

以上例句中请特别留意 anchor 的用法，其本义为"下锚"，此处是"稳固地设立于"的意思。还有 rummage, sift, browse 三个动词，大体上都指在商店挑选商品，但用词分寸各有区别。

谈到美食又可以这么说：

Start in Chinatown for Cantonese noodles or indulge in a juicy steak at a Midtown steak house. Mix with celebrities at a fusion spot in Chelsea or tuck into a steaming bowl of mussels at a cozy Greenwich Village bistro. If you're on the go, grab a slice of pizza or a bagel with a schmear of cream cheese. For cheap, good, ethnic eats, hop the subway to Queens, Brooklyn or the Bronx.

上面段落中可以关注的有动词也有名词，fusion spot 指各种风格的美食聚集的地方，ethnic eats 则是不同民族的美食。

除动词之外，名词也是值得留意的。有的是属于术语或类似术语之类的词汇，比如：

- The Canadian falls has carved a plunge basin （瀑布潭）192 feet (59 meters) deep.
- Her home contains a fine collection of Upper Canada furniture from the period, plus artifacts recovered from an archaeological dig （考古挖掘）.

还有更多的名词，或言简意赅表达力强，或具有修辞效果，或是一种固定的说法，也都值得我们留心和记忆。比如：

- Los Angeles is an international atlas of exotic cuisines: Armenian, Chinese, Japanese, Lebanese, Persian, Peruvian, Thai, Vietnamese? and more. Like everything else in the city, much of L.A.'s dining culture revolves around celebrity-spotting, and places like The Ivy at lunch and Koi for dinner are usually safe bets. But in SoCal, sometimes it's the chefs themselves that are the real celebrities. Wolfgang Puck makes the rounds at Spago and his other fine-dining restaurants when he is in town.

这一段中，celebrity-spotting 意为"邂逅名人"，而 safe bets 则是说在那两个地方用餐是"选对了地方"。

- At Darling Harbour you'll find the world-class Sydney Aquarium. You can

- also start your gourmet tour of Sydney's Modern Australian cooking style, which encompasses the best of freshness with spices from Asia and flavors from the Mediterranean.

句中的 gourmet tour 当然是美食游，freshness 则是"新鲜美味"的意思。

- Yellowstone National Park does have cell service, just not everywhere. Cell service is currently limited to areas of Canyon, Grant Village, Mammoth Hot Springs, and Old Faithful.

句中的 cell service 即"手机信号服务区"的意思。

- Be aware of road construction delays during the spring/summer/fall months. Road construction can take hours out of your day. Be prepared to travel around these delays and still get to your destination.

句中的 construction delays 即道路施工引起的延误。

- This is a city with something for every taste or budget, and best buys remain collectables, vintage fashions, and accessories.

句中 something for every taste or budget 即"各种不同的口味和消费层次"，best buys 即"物有所值的商品"，vintage fashions 即"时装"。

- Nightlife in Los Angeles is hopping. Specifically, Hollywood is the happening place to be for drinking and dancing. Storied live music venues like the Roxy, the Troubadour, and the Whisky A Go-Go continue to build new legacies nightly. Hotel bars across the city, from the Standard Downtown to the Skybar, still lure locals along with regular guests.

句中 happening place 即"热闹的地方"，此处说好莱坞是畅饮和欢舞的最佳去处。legacies 本指"遗产"，此处指那些歌舞表演的场所夜夜都产生着新的传奇。regular guests 即"常客"。

下面例句既有值得注意的名词也有值得仿效的动词。

- Hong Kong is such a feast for the senses, it reminds me of a movie set. Maybe I'm an incurable romantic, but when I stand at the railing of the famous Star Ferry as it glides across the harbor, ride a rickety old tram as it winds its way across Hong Kong Island, or marvel at the stunning views afforded from atop Victoria Peak, I can't help but think I must have somehow landed in the middle of an epic drama where the past has melted into the present.

句中的 a feast for the senses（感官盛宴）, a movie set（电影场景）, an epic drama（史诗剧）等名词词组用盛宴、影剧作为喻体，描绘旅游景观的绚丽多彩和古今融合，以 glide, marvel at, melt into 来捕捉物或人的动态、事物的变迁等。这些都是我们在翻译类似语篇时可以模仿的，而这样的词语，只要留心，俯拾皆是。比如我们说某某东西"贵得让人不敢问津"，英语怎么说好呢？下面这个句子不就很有参考价值吗：Food and public transport are cheap, and attractions are generally not prohibitively expensive.

第二节 句 式

旅游语篇，尤其是电视短片或小册子里的解说文字，大都风格简约，多用小词，句子结构也不复杂。比如：

- National Parks are worth a visit. It is our country's legacy. There's no better way to bond with the family and enjoy the great outdoors. Most National Parks have something unique to become a designated National Park. Yellowstone is beyond special, it is the world's first national park. It is over 2.2 million acres packed inside an ancient caldera. Geysers, waterfalls, wildlife and scenic beauty. All these wonders are at every turn.

请特别注意划线的部分，这个句子其实只罗列了四个名词（组），信息简明、好听、易记。

阅读中要留心句子结构的灵活多变，将常见句式熟记心中，以备在翻译时模仿。建议注意以下几类句式：

1. 祈使句

由于旅游语篇要具有感召功能，因此会有不少的祈使句贯穿其中。比如：

- For those that prefer to wing it, you're probably not reading this or just looking for reservations, in that case have a great journey and go for it.

再观察以下选自不同景点介绍的三个段落，其中颇多祈使句，而祈使句句首

动词的选择很重要，要传神而有力。

- When you're planning your activities, <u>think on your feet</u>. Do what New Yorkers do: walk. Wander the angled tree-lined streets of Greenwich Village or the avenues of million-dollar townhouses on the Upper East Side. Art lovers should not miss the Warhols and Pollocks at MoMA, or the comprehensive and essential Metropolitan Museum of Art. Outdoors, mingle with joggers and skaters in Central Park or smell the blooming flowers at the Brooklyn Botanic Garden. Head to Battery Park for sunset views over the Hudson River, or watch the world below from the top of the Empire State Building.

上面段落中的 think on your feet 意为 to think and react to something quickly，即"赶快拿定主意吧"。

- Old Hong Kong brings the unique culture of Hong Kong in the 1950s, 1960s and 1970s back to life. <u>Savour</u> the sights and sounds of yesteryear aboard the Heritage Tram! Be mesmerised by the colour and buzz of life in accurate recreations of old streets and scenes. Take a trip into nostalgia and take home some antique souvenirs to keep the memories alive!

- <u>Hop</u> aboard a raft and become immersed in the exotic sounds of a tropical rainforest. On this journey, you'll encounter some of the most fascinating animals in the world! Catch the antics of the world's smallest monkey, the Pygmy Marmoset; or see weirdly wonderful critters, including the Capybara, the world's largest rodent, and Kinkajou; as well as the Green Aracari, the world's smallest toucan.

还有一种构成祈使句的句式："动词……, and you will…"。比如：

<u>Add to all this</u> the side trips to the gorges and cliffs of the Blue Mountains, the wineries of the Hunter Valley, and the dolphin- and whale-watching around Port Stephens, <u>and you'll see</u> why Sydney gets so much praise.

这句话的意思是说：除了游览悉尼还可以做周边游，那你就会明白为什么人们对悉尼如此赞赏了。

2. 倒装

倒装也是常见的句式，它有助于和上文更好地衔接，也可以达到简练的效果。

- Among their early products were glass and metal bottles with painted enamel colors that were inspired by European art and, in fact, made under the supervision of European artists.
- As London's center of gravity moves east, so does the dining scene: Nuno Mendes' Viajante is the most creative eatery to grace an eastside hotel.
- Beyond the bustle, though, is a diverse population, taking the city in stride and friendlier than you were led to believe.

3. 插入成分

插入语能够在叙述主流中恰当引入信息，以补充细节或作进一步说明。

- The "Emerald City" is one of the most attractive on earth. Some people compare it to San Francisco—it certainly has that relaxed feel—but the gateway to Australia is very much its own unique city.
- The old always sits alongside the new here—nowhere more so than at Wren's great baroque dome of St. Paul's Cathedral, framed by 21st-century skyscrapers—and London is rightly famed for its museums and galleries.
- And indeed it was an engineer, Gustave Eiffel, who drew—not on paper but on the surface of the sky itself—these extraordinary lines of metal, which soar above the Parisian skyline and seem to triumph over all the older monuments of the city.
- Production continued for the next two centuries or so, and the variety of bottles expanded to include almost all mediums of art—stone, porcelain, ivory, lacquer, metalwork, and even painting and calligraphy—and to reflect artistic developments over five millennia of Chinese civilization.

4. 平行结构

平行结构使语义分明，便于阅读，有助记忆，在旅游语篇中常见。

- If the symbol of Rome is the Colosseum, then Paris's symbol is without doubt the Eiffel Tower: both are monuments unique in planning and construction, both stir admiration by their extraordinary dimensions, and both bear witness to man's inborn will to build something capable of demonstrating the measure of his genius.

句中三个 both 引出三个结构相似的小句，清楚地说明了罗马竞技场和巴黎埃菲尔铁塔的相似之处。

- So many images float by—wooden boats bobbing up and down in the harbor beside huge ocean liners; crumbling tenements next to ultramodern high-rises; squalid alleys behind luxury hotels; elderly people pushing wheelbarrows as Rolls-Royces glide by; market vendors selling chicken feet and dried squid while talking on cellphones.

此句用五个平行结构将传统的和现代的人与事物进行了鲜明的对照。

5. 用 you 作主语或用 it 作形式主语的句式

旅游语篇多是面对读者娓娓而谈，较常用 you 作句子的主语或宾语，比如：

- There's so much to do in Sydney that <u>you</u> could easily spend a week here and still find yourself crashing into bed at night exhausted by trying to see all the main attractions.

另外，it 作形式主语的句式也很常见。

- <u>It</u>'s great chance to get the family all in one spot, nuke some popcorn, then plan and enjoy your next vacation together.
- <u>It</u> is true that official life in this period was governed by strict Confucian laws, but private life was less controlled.

6. 标点的构句作用

标点并不是句式，但我们常常见到英语中运用冒号或分号的句子。冒号可用于引出对某些事物的例举，或进一步解释、阐发。比如：

- Architecture also underwent radical changes: glass, iron and steel were the new construction materials, the most suitable ones to make buildings lighter, more dynamic and more modern.

在例举诸多事物时，常常用分号将其分开，既便于排列，也使读者一目了然。如下面两例：

- *Whales* features more than 20 skulls and skeletons from various whale species and showcases many rare specimens, including the real skeleton of a male sperm whale measuring 58 feet long (or about 18 feet longer than a school bus); life-size and scale models of whales common in the South Pacific; and

ancient and contemporary objects made from whale bone and other materials such as weapons, chiefly adornments, and jewelry.
- The exhibition also includes rarely-viewed specimens and artifacts from the American Museum of Natural History's world-class collections, such as the massive skull of *Andrewsarchus*, a land-dwelling relative of whales; cultural objects depicting the power, majesty, and importance of whales to humans; and a log book from a whaling ship that sailed out of New Bedford, Massachusetts, in 1830.

除了上面举例说明的各类句式外，阅读中还要留意可在我们自己的翻译或英语写作中仿效的句式。比如下面这样将信息重心放在最后，画龙点睛式的段落：

- The best time to return is in the early evening, when the lights of the skyscrapers around Circular Quay streak like rainbows across the water of the harbor, and the sails of the Opera House and the girders of the Harbour Bridge are lit up—it's magical.

段落最后用破折号引出的短句，简明突出地概括了悉尼夜景的美妙。

再比如下面 not only... but also... 句式，由于插入了 as 引导的状语从句，paintings of gardens 后面又带有宾语从句，而变得相当复杂。这也值得我们注意观察和学习。

- Artists were called upon not only to design gardens but also, as gardens came to be identified with the tastes and personalities of their residents, to create idealized paintings of gardens that served as symbolic portraits reflective of the character of the owner.

7. 套话

英语语篇阅读中还要注意积累一些常用说法，即套话，可供翻译实践中随手取用。比如：

谈到门票价格和开放时间可以说：

- Tours run every half-hour. Admission is C$4.75 adults, C$3.65 children 6 to 12, free for children age 5 and under. It's open summer daily 11am to 5pm, fall to spring Wednesday to Sunday 11am to 5pm.
- Admission is C$8.75 adults, C$5.15 children 6 to 12, free for children 5 and

under. Open daily from 9am to 5pm (closes at 7 or 8pm from mid-May till Labour Day).

- Admission is C$40 adults and children 10 and over, C$33 children 5 to 9, free for children 4 and under. It's open daily mid-May to June and September to mid-October 10am to 5pm, July and August 9am to 6pm; it's closed mid-October through mid-May.
- Open daily May to the third Sunday in October. Hours are from 10am to 5pm (closes at 7 or 8pm from mid-May till Labour Day).
- It is open June to October daily from 10am to 6pm, November through May, Monday through Saturday from 10am to 5pm.
- Open from the first Saturday in May to mid-September daily from 10am to 5pm, and weekends only mid-September to Canadian Thanksgiving (U.S. Columbus Day).
- Senior and student prices are almost always available if you have identification.

谈到泊车可说：

- Park Rangers are on only duty from 9:30 am to 11:30 pm daily.
- General visitor parking is available along Ohio Drive between the Lincoln and Jefferson Memorials. Bus parking is primarily available along Ohio Drive near the Lincoln and Jefferson Memorials.

而涉及信息的变化时又可说：

- This information was accurate when it was published, but can change without notice. Please be sure to confirm all rates and details directly with the companies in question before planning your trip.

第三节　从属成分的运用

构建从句是英语写作中要着重训练的，在汉译英过程中当然也是不可缺少的技能。阅读时要仔细观察英语中怎样使用从句，特别是定语从句和状语从句。比如下面这样的从句：
- From here a "must do" is the 3.2km (2-mile) coastal path <u>that</u> leads off across the cliff tops, via cozy Tamarama Beach (dubbed "Glamourama" for its chic sun worshippers), to glorious Bronte Beach, <u>where</u> you can cool down in the crashing waves of the Pacific.
- The ateliers of the imperial household, <u>which</u> were established on the palace grounds by order of the emperor, began manufacturing snuff bottles for court use during the reign of the Kangxi emperor (1662–1722).
- This was very different from the situation in contemporary Europe, <u>where</u> religious bans and prevailing morality enforced an absolute division between "art" and "pornography".
- <u>While</u> the older buildings symbolize the past, the Eiffel Tower anticipates the future and the conquests which man will achieve.
- <u>As</u> the water plunges from the brink of the falls, it fills the air with a silvery mist, <u>which</u> under the sunlight displays many rainbows.
- <u>While</u> bottles were used as domestic ornaments, personal adornments, expensive gifts, or rewards, they also came to manifest social standing and refined taste.

阅读旅游语篇时，以下几种句式结构需要格外留意。

1. 分词短语

分词短语作状语或定语，运用频繁而灵活。
- Turning to the eighteenth century, key works by Luis Paret y Alcázar and Francisco de Goya and their contemporaries demonstrate how drawing greatly increased during the period, forever <u>changing</u> the artistic landscape of Spain.
- Just before <u>flowing</u> over the ledge, the American stream is only about $3^{1}/2$ feet (1 meter) deep.
- <u>Situated</u> between the state of New York and the province of Ontario, Niagara Falls is one of the most spectacular natural wonders on the North American continent.
- Pick up some fish and chips and head for the main beach, <u>flanked</u> by a row of

giant pines that chatter with hundreds of colorful lorikeets at dusk.
- Lavishly illustrated, this volume will feature new research and previously unpublished material from major public and private collections.

2. 同位语

阅读英语旅游语篇，我们发现同位语使用频繁，因为它像插入语一样，可以补充更多更具体的信息。

有些同位语结构比较单一，就是一个名词词组，比如：

- An enduring symbol of freedom for all, the Lincoln Memorial attracts anyone who seeks inspiration and hope.
- Ocean Park's newest attraction, Polar adventure lets you explore the North and South poles from the exhilaration of a bob sled ride, to the wonder of meeting king penguins up close.
- The preferred site for hosting literary gatherings, theatrical performances, and imaginary outings, gardens were often designed according to the same compositional principles used in painting.

以上三个例句中的同位语都位于句首，景点（主语部分）最突出的特点一目了然，十分醒目。

而更多的情况是将同位语置于名词（许多是景点名、器物名）后，因而多半是在句末。比如：

- First, of course, there's the Sydney Opera House, one of the most recognized buildings in the world.
- The most famous is Bondi, a strip of golden sand legendary for its Speedo-clad Lifesavers and surfboard riders.
- In 2012, its impressive ability to offer guests a world-class experience that blends entertainment with education and conservation was confirmed when it became the first Asian winner of the biannual Applause Award, the most prestigious award in the amusement and theme park industry.
- Snuff, a mixture of finely ground tobacco leaves and aromatic herbs and spices, was introduced to China by European missionaries, envoys, and merchants in the second half of the seventeenth century.

有些同位语结构要复杂些，名词短语后带有定语从句或作定语的分词短语。
- This exhibition presents, for the first time outside the United Kingdom, master drawings by Spanish artists from the British Museum, <u>a collection regarded as one of the finest in the world</u>.
- The increasing use of snuff led to the making of snuff bottles, <u>small containers with a corked stopper that were easily portable and airtight to preserve freshness and flavor</u>.
- Part of an American chain of family resorts known for <u>the quality of services, rooms, and activities</u>, Great Wolf is probably best known for its massive indoor water park.

以上同位语都是说明被修饰部分的性质或特点的，而下面例子中的同位语是对所修饰部分的例举，这在旅游语篇写作中很有用。
- They are followed by drawings by the most important artists from Spain's Golden Age, <u>among them, Diego Velázquez, Vicente Carducho, Alonso Cano and Francisco Rizi in Madrid, Francisco Pacheco, Bartolomé Murillo, and Francisco de Zubarán in Seville, and José de Ribera in Spanish Naples</u>.

句中的 among them 实则相当于分词短语 including...。

3. 介词短语作状语

介词短语的应用是我们要特别留心学习的，它可以简化句子结构。比如：
- <u>With its medicinal and stimulating effects</u>, it soon caught on with officials and even the emperor at the Qing Dynasty court.
- <u>With its vast curtain of glass and 40,000 square-metre aluminium roof sculpted to echo a seabird soaring in flight</u>, the striking Hong Kong Convention and Exhibition Centre is a major landmark on the Hong Kong Island skyline.

以上两句都含有由 with 组成的介词短语，第二句中的短语结构由于带有分词短语而显得复杂一些。下面的 from...to... 和 through... 等也都是在旅游语篇中常见的介词短语。
- <u>From</u> the traditions of New Zealand's Maori whale riders and the Kwakwaka'wakw peoples of the Pacific Northwest <u>to</u> the international

whaling industry and the rise of laws protecting whales from commercial hunting, the exhibition traces the close connections humans and whales have shared for centuries.

- <u>Through a variety of interactive exhibits</u>, visitors will experience a re-created dive to the depths of the sea.
- <u>In conjunction with</u> the exhibition, British Museum Press will publish a catalogue with contributions from more than thirty authors worldwide.

4. 连串形容词作前置定语

这种结构在旅游语篇以及文学语篇中都常见。

- <u>Sunny, sexy, and sophisticated</u>, Sydney (pop. 4.1 million) basks in its worldwide recognition as the shining star of the Southern Hemisphere.
- <u>Iconic, hip, trendsetting, and ever-changing</u>, New York City lives up to its superlatives.

第四节 连 贯

连贯是前两篇中都讨论过的老话题。第一篇第一章第三节列出了英语说明语篇常见的逻辑模式，第二章第十二节关注的是汉译英过程中由于语言差异和语境信息的缺失给译文读者造成的连贯问题；第二篇第一章第五节则从英语语篇阅读角度提醒大家注意衔接和逻辑模式的运用。连贯在旅游类实用语篇中也是很重要的，尤其在篇幅较长的介绍性文字中。下面从三个方面提醒大家留心观察，看旅游语篇的行文连贯是如何实现的。

首先，要注意观察逻辑模式的构建。比如下面一个段落：

In fact, one of the most striking characteristics of Hong Kong is this interweaving of seeming contradictions and the interplay of the exotic and the technically advanced. There are as many skyscrapers here as you're likely to see anywhere, <u>but</u> they're built with bamboo scaffolding and in accordance with the principles of feng shui. Historic trams rumble through Central, <u>while</u> below ground is one of the most efficient subways in the world, complete with the world's first "contactless" tickets, cards that can be waved over a scanner without even taking them out of your purse or wallet. The city has some of the best and most sophisticated restaurants in the world, but it also has *da pai dang,* street-side food stalls. Hong Kong is home to one of the world's largest shopping malls, but lively makeshift street markets are virtually everywhere.

本段首句点出全段主题：在香港传统和现代交织成趣。然后用 but…while…but…but… 几个连词构成的对照模式将主题层层展开。

其次，要留意词语的衔接作用。比如：

Landscape in China has always had a human dimension. Consequently, architectural elements, particularly pavilions, are a quintessential feature of both Chinese landscape paintings and gardens. In gardens, pavilions identify prime vantage points from which to view the scenery; they also serve as focal points within landscape settings. In painting, meticulous "ruled-line" renderings of pavilions celebrate historical or literary structures or indicate the fabled dwelling of the immortals—particularly when set within an archaic blue-and-green landscape meant to evoke a so-called golden age. In Chinese lore, such paradises were imagined as the dwelling place of Daoist immortals. Mortals might stumble upon such magical habitations by losing their way, passing through a grotto, or crossing a stream. In such "lost horizons," time stands still and residents cease to age, while generations might pass in the human realm. In the garden, a moon gate or concealed passage might signal a similar entry point into an alternative universe.

显然，consequently 以及 in gardens, … in painting, … in Chinese lore, … in the garden 等位于句首的词语，起到了相互比照、层层推进的作用。作者将园林、绘画、传说的相通之处一一道来，条理十分清晰。

第三，在旅游语篇中，常见到用一系列祈使句提出建议或指示的段落（本章第二节讨论过祈使句），这又是旅游语篇的一个特色。比如：

At the Amazing Asian Animals exhibit you can visit some of Asia's rarest animals. Take an interactive journey of discovery at the Giant Panda Adventure where you'll get to know some of Asia's most precious native animals, including giant pandas, red pandas, Chinese giant salamanders and Chinese alligators. Admire the spectacular

display of goldfish at the Goldfish Treasures exhibit, or visit the colourful birds and playful Asian small-clawed otters at Panda Village.

这类段落有很强的指令功能,一定要时序清晰、方位准确,以确保读者得到连贯信息,参照实行。比如:

Taking the left-hand fork is easier traveling. It continues east and passes large rock domes on the flats below. After passing the domes, the trail soon drops into a wash. It will be necessary to cross the wash and approach the slickrock ridge to the east of the wash. Continue to the east, up and over the slickrock ridge. Once on top, work down the east side (backside) of the ridge, but start bearing to the south (hikers right), and stay as high as it is comfortable, on the steep slopes of the ridge on the right.

第二章
双语语篇导读及翻译要略

第一章从词语、句式、句子结构等方面关注了英语旅游语篇的阅读。无论是词语的选用还是句子的构建，都服务于旅游语篇的两个主要交际功能：提供信息，吸引游客，即语篇的信息功能和行事功能。汉译英当然也要从遣词造句入手，努力实现这两个功能。

第一节 词语和句式

双语语篇对照阅读，首先要关注词语和句式的使用，特别是动词的翻译、名词的翻译以及某些可供套用的句式。

1. 动词的翻译

- 通过互动展品<u>激发</u>公众的兴趣、好奇心和想象力。
  <u>Captivate</u> the public's interest, curiosity and imagination through interactive exhibits.
- 每当能量穿梭机启动时，均为观众<u>带来</u>目不暇给的视听效果。
  When activated, the Machine will <u>trigger</u> a series of fascinating and spectacular audio and visual effects.

以上两例中的"激发"和"带来"分别译作了 captivate 和 trigger。请对照我们自己可能会采用的译法，比如你会不会用更为"对应"的 stimulate, arouse 等动词？请大家体会翻译不是"译词"而是"译意"的道理。阅读中要留心积累词语和搭配，并在自己的翻译实践中灵活使用。

再看几个实例。

香港理工大学纺织及制衣学系的教员专诚为此次展览设计及制作旗袍作

品，显示培育新时代时装设计师的学府如何演绎这种传统服装。

For this exhibition, we have invited teaching staff of the Institute of Textiles & Clothing at the Hong Kong Polytechnic University to design *qipao* to be showcased in this exhibition, to give new perspectives on how a contemporary training institute of fashion design interprets the *qipao* tradition.

此句的"演绎"为"阐释"之意，译作 interpret，而与"归纳""演绎"中的词义无关。这是译其语境意义而非字面意义。

为进一步扩展博物馆的服务，香港美术博物馆于 1975 年 7 月一分为二，成立了香港艺术馆及香港博物馆。

To further enhance museum service, the Hong Kong Art Gallery and Museum was split into the Hong Kong Museum of Art and the Hong Kong Museum of History in July 1975.

句中的"一分为二，成立了"的意义融入了短语动词 was split into 之中。

而为配合上述展览，香港历史博物馆更编制了精美的展览图录及图册，介绍秦人的历史、秦始皇帝陵的建造和相关出土文物，以及国家对秦文化遗迹进行大遗址保护的概况。

To tie in with the exhibition, the Hong Kong Museum of History has produced exhibition catalogue and booklet to introduce the history of Qin, the construction and cultural relics of the Mausoleum of Qin Shihuang as well as China's policy on the conservation of national large-scale sites of Qin Culture.

上例中的"配合"一词译为短语动词 to tie in with。

随着碑刻风化剥落，这些历史资料亦会就此流失。

As the inscriptions faded with time, the historical information they contained was gradually lost.

"风化剥落"虚译成"随时间而褪色"，而不是更"实在"的 weather away 或 peel off 等。此类翻译操作也是值得关注的。

2. 名词的翻译

20 世纪 20 年代的香港，已有学界师生、大家闺秀和歌影名人穿着长衫。40、50 年代，随着大量上海裁缝师傅来港，令长衫在香港盛极一时。

It was in the 1920s that the cheongsam first became all the rage, as students, teachers, ladies from wealthy families, singers and movie stars in Hong Kong began wearing the dress, and the vogue then experienced a surge in the 1940s and 1950s after a large number of tailors from Shanghai emigrated to Hong Kong.

此句中的"长衫"即粤语中对"旗袍"的称谓，属于约定俗成的译法，现在也有根据汉语拼音译作 *qipao* 的。这类词语的译法一般多年沿用，有的甚至已经进入英语词典，比如"功夫"（kung fu）、"馄饨"（wonton）等。

这展览是庆祝香港特区成立十五周年的亮点节目之一。
This exhibition is one of the highlight programmes to commemorate the 15th anniversary of the establishment of the Hong Kong Special Administrative Region.

这里的"亮点节目"是汉语中常用的说法，译为英语注意要达意、地道。

3. 行业常用套话的翻译

旅游语篇中常见一些行业套话，要注意积累。比如，我们常看到展览介绍中有这样的套语："本展览展出文物丰富，包括……"，那就可以借鉴下面译文中的句式：

- 此次展览包罗不同类型的文物，除了展示不同年代的香港硬币和纸币外，亦包括试铸的样币、硬币铸模、纪念金币的石膏模型、纸币的设计图、版票、印钞用的钢版，以及未经切割的连张钞票，等等。
  This exhibition showcased a wide range of exhibits, including Hong Kong coinage and notes from different time periods, trial coins, tools for minting circulated coins, plaster models of commemorative coins, design drawings of banknotes, trial notes, plates for printing banknotes, uncut sheets of banknotes and more.

- 若有疑问或建议请与当值职员联络或电邮至 enquiries@hk.science.museum。
  For enquiries or suggestions, please approach our staff on duty or email to enquiries@hk.science.museum.

- 对于学校或团体的参观或导游服务申请，我们会在七个工作日内办理。
  We will process all requests for visits and guided tours from schools and organizations within 7 working days upon receiving them.

- 整个展览占地 7000 平方米，共有 8 个展区，分布于两层展厅。
  Occupying an area of 7,000 m^2, the Hong Kong Story comprises 8 galleries located on two floors.

257

- 香港科学馆占地12000平方米，楼高四层，与香港历史馆博物馆毗邻。科学馆楼面面积为13500平方米，而永久展览厅总面积为6500平方米。

  The four-storey museum, adjacent to the Hong Kong Museum of History, occupies a site of 12,000 square metres. The total gross floor area of the museum is 13,500 square metres with the permanent exhibition halls alone covering a floor area of 6,500 square metres.

4. 常见句式在旅游语篇翻译中的应用

我们平时英语学习中耳熟能详的一些句式也是有用武之地的，比如：

- 一袭袭不同式样的秀丽长衫，为你诉说一段段香港女性的成长故事，呈现百年来香港社会和女性地位的变迁。

  Display after display of elegant cheongsam not only tells the story of how Hong Kong women grew up with this elegant dress, but also illustrates the changes in their status in particular and Hong Kong society in general.

- 时至今天，邮票已超越了缴付邮资的基本功能，成为社会各界乐于收藏和欣赏的艺术品；然而一直没有改变的是，邮票始终扮演着亲善大使的角色，是世界各地人士与香港初次接触的一个有形媒介。

  Today, stamps are not only used for the pre-payment of postage, but are collected and treasured by people from all walks of life as valuable works of art, while they continue to play the role of cultural ambassadors, serving as an elegant medium through which people around the world first come into contact with Hong Kong.

- 1962年，香港大会堂落成启用，并于高座设立"大会堂美术博物馆"，标志着现代博物馆服务在香港正式开展。

  It was not until the opening of the Hong Kong City Hall in 1962 that a "City Hall Art Gallery and Museum" made its way to the City Hall's High Block, marking the beginning of modern museum service in Hong Kong.

- 香港科学馆自1991年4月启用至今，已成为大众探求科学知识的理想地方。

  Since its opening in April 1991, the Hong Kong Science Museum has proven itself to be an ideal and unique place for learning science.

- 它有别于传统的博物馆，<u>鼓励</u>参观者通过操作展品来发现当中的科学原理，让他们从中体验探索和学习科学的乐趣。
  In contrast to traditional museums, visitors at the Science Museum <u>are encouraged to</u> explore exhibits in their own way and thus experience the fun of discovery learning.

第二节　主语的确立

　　确立主语是构建英语句子的关键，是汉译英必须掌握的技巧。这方面在第二篇第二章第二节中有专门讨论，第一篇各章节中虽无专立标题，但实际上第一篇第二章的第六、七、八、十诸节中都涉及汉英在主语上的差异以及由此而引发的翻译问题。因此，本节只想就此问题再略加提示。

　　旅游语篇中最常见的情况是依据上文补充主语。

　　"香港故事"常设展是博物馆多年来辛勤努力搜集、保存及研究工作的总展示。通过逾4000件展品、750块文字说明、多个立体造景及多媒体剧场，配以声和光的特殊效果，栩栩如生地介绍香港的自然生态、民间风俗及历史发展。

The Hong Kong Story permanent exhibition is a showcase of the dedicated hard work done by the Museum staff in the past years in collecting, preserving and researching the history and development of Hong Kong. Through the display of over 4,000 exhibits with the use of 750 graphic panels, a number of dioramas and multi-media programmes, and enhanced with special audio-visual and lighting effects, <u>the Hong Kong Story</u> outlines the natural environment, folk culture and historical development of Hong Kong vividly.

　　此例原文第一句话的主语是"香港故事常设展"，第二句的主语承前省略，译文则需将其补齐（划线部分）。

　　除依据上文补充主语外，还可以根据语境补充主语。

　　参观"香港故事"展览一般需时两小时，如欲细心观赏展览内的53项多媒体节目，包括影片及电脑互动节目，则至少要预留三至四小时。

You may visit The Hong Kong Story in about 2 hours. However, if <u>you</u> would like to enjoy the 53 multimedia programmes featured in The Hong Kong Story, including theatre shows and interactive booths, <u>you</u> are advised to spare 3 to 4 hours.

这是对展览馆的介绍，面对的是参观者，所以译文便补充了主语 you。

在很对多情况下，译文在句式和结构上与原文发生了很大变化，这就需要根据行文的要求重新确立译文主语。

1959年，随着人民自主意识的崛起，新加坡成立自治政府并首次举行立法议会选举。

In 1959, <u>the growth of nationalism</u> led to self-government, and the country's first general election.

译文没有沿用原文的"状语 + 主谓"结构，而是将状语"随着……意识的崛起"译为主语，然后用 led to 作谓语构建了一个新的句式。

人口多元化和国际化是新加坡一大特色，这也是其得天独厚的地理位置与商业成就所赋予的特质。1819年1月29日，史丹福·莱佛士爵士（Sir Stamford Raffles）决定在新加坡这个小渔村设立贸易站，随即吸引了来自中国、印度次大陆、印度尼西亚、马来半岛和中东的移民和商人纷至沓来。

<u>One of the more remarkable aspects of Singapore</u> is the truly cosmopolitan nature of her population, a natural result of the country's geographical position and commercial success. Established by Thomas Stamford Raffles as a trading post on 29 January 1819, the small sea town of Singapore soon attracted migrants and merchants from China, the Indian sub-continent, Indonesia, the Malay Peninsula and the Middle East.

这个译例的情况更为复杂些，因为重写（见本章第七节）的痕迹更为明显。首先，译文第一句将原文的"新加坡一大特色"译为主语（划线部分），而原文下半句因为译成同位语，其主语"这"便被化掉了。其次，译文第二句将原文的"新加坡这个小渔村"译为主语，而原文的主语"史丹福·莱佛士爵士"被纳入分词短语中。

将动宾结构通过名物化的手段译为主语，也是常见的翻译手法。

过去曾经举办过多次香港历史图片展，皆大受欢迎。

The exhibitions on old photos staged over the past decades were all very well received.

此例中英译文通过将原文的动宾结构（"举办过……图片展"）变为"名词短语+分词定语"的方式，重立主语。

第三节　主从的识别

由于英语组句较汉语更注重形式结构，而汉语中常出现连用几个逗号的长句的情况，因此，将汉语译为英语，要特别强调对汉语长句以英语为参照进行逻辑分析，看哪个部分译作英语中的主句，哪些可以构成从属成分，构成什么样的从属成分。这一点，我们在第二篇第二章的第五节以"逻辑的显性化"为题进行过讨论。就旅游语篇的翻译而言，提醒大家注意以下方面：

第一，最简练的从属形式是由介词短语构成的从属结构。

举办富启发性的活动，加强公众对大自然的欣赏，以及唤起他们的好奇心。

Provide enlightening programmes for a better understanding and a greater appreciation of nature while promoting inquisitiveness.

这句将原文的目的状语部分译为由 for 引导的介词短语。

19 世纪末，新加坡已成为亚洲的国际大都会，国民人口主要由华族、马来族、印度族和欧亚裔组成。

By the end of the 19th century, Singapore had become one of the most cosmopolitan cities in Asia, with major ethnic groups in the country being the Chinese, Malays, Indians, and Eurasians.

上句中原文划线部分被译为"with+名词+being"结构作状语。

女性长衫线条分明、款式多姿，以轻柔舒适的面料与极尽合身的剪裁，充分展现女性体态与曲线美，突显女士的绰约丰姿与妩媚典雅。

With its well-defined lines and myriad designs, the cheongsam combines light and soft fabric with a tight-fitting cut to show off the beauty of the female silhouette and highlight a woman's graceful manners and elegant charm.

汉英语篇翻译

汉语的划线部分在译文中以 with 引导的短语再现，而原文的"充分展现……"部分则译为不定式短语，作状语（to show off...）。

第二，译文中使用同位语结构，也很简练。下面译例中划线部分就被译为同位语。

<u>它（新加坡式英语）是许多新加坡人的身份标记</u>，也代表了一种融汇马来语、华语和印度语的独特混合语。

<u>A badge of identity for many Singaporeans</u>, it represents a hybrid form of the language that includes words from Malay, as well as Chinese and Indian languages.

同位语与定语从句连用，结构会稍显复杂。比如：

展览介绍秦代的历史、文化和人物，<u>以及中国大一统局面形成的过程，见证岭南包括香港正式列入中央政府的管治之内</u>。

The exhibition features the history, culture and relics of the Qin Dynasty, <u>an epoch-making era that witnessed the unification of China and the formal integration of the southern regions, including Hong Kong, into the empire.</u>

原文的主干结构是："展览介绍……，见证……"，即"主语+谓语1+谓语2"。译文将原文下划线部分视做从属信息，译为"同位语+定语从句"结构。

第三，更加复杂的从属结构是各种从句以及分词短语和不定式短语构成的从属成分。比如：

新加坡历史上另一重要时期是公元19世纪，<u>近代新加坡的建立始于此时</u>。

The next important period in the history of Singapore was during the 19th century, <u>when modern Singapore was founded</u>.

原文的一个小句（划线部分）译为 when 引导的状语从句。

2000年1月，康乐及文化事务署成立，<u>代替了市政局及区域市政局接手管理香港科学馆和所有政府博物馆，将香港博物馆的发展带进一个新纪元</u>。

In January 2000, Leisure and Cultural Services Department is set up <u>to replace</u> the Urban Council and the Regional Council <u>to oversee</u> the operation of the Hong Kong Science Museum and all the government museums, <u>taking</u> the development of Hong Kong's museums into a new era.

上面译例中原文的划线部分译为两个不定式短语和一个分词短语。

碑铭文字有助于历史研究，// 最著名的例子要数1799年拿破仑远征军在埃及发现的罗塞达石碑，专家把其中的古文字互相对照释读，终破解古埃及象形文字的内容，为埃及学奠定基础。

Stele inscriptions are a highly valuable resource for historical research. Perhaps the most renowned example is the Rosetta Stone: discovered in Egypt by the army of Napoleon in 1799, it was inscribed with an ancient text that, after it was studied and translated, gave experts the key to deciphering Egyptian hieroglyphics.

原文在双斜线处被拆译为两个句子。译文第二句对原文的信息进行了重组：先是将"最著名的是罗赛达石碑"译为一个小句，然后将"石碑"作为主语（用代词 it）构成主句，以分词短语 (discovered...) 和定语从句 (that...)、状语从句 (after...) 为从属结构，构建出一个复合长句。

下面各句，原文的划线部分在译文中被译为分词短语、不定式短语，作状语。

- 这个由香港历史博物馆为"香港周 2013 @台北"重新策划的展览，<u>特别展出约 130 组清末、民初至现今具有香港时代特色的长衫精品</u>。
  Showcasing around 130 exhibits, including a range of cheongsam from the late Qing and early Republican periods to the present day, this brand new exhibition has been specially created by the Hong Kong Museum of History for "Hong Kong Week 2013@Taipei".

- 梦周文教基金会的藏品包括不少非常珍贵的历史影像，<u>除一般街景、城市面貌外，尚有关于民生、娱乐及商业活动的真实记录，见证了香港从 19 世纪中叶至 20 世纪初的发展历程</u>。
  The collection of Monnchu Foundation captures precious historical scenes, covering streets and everyday life, leisure and commercial activities of the city, vividly illustrating the social development of Hong Kong from the mid-nineteenth to the early twentieth century.

- <u>适逢 30 周年</u>，我们会与大家重温博物馆的变迁。
  To celebrate the Museum's 30th anniversary, we will share with you the changes the Museum has undergone over the years.

- 适值香港邮票诞生 150 周年，本馆与香港邮政携手合作，<u>通过精选的 300 多枚邮票，辅以历史图片，从另一个角度向大家诉说"香港故事"</u>。
  To celebrate the 150th anniversary of the birth of Hong Kong stamps, the Hong Kong Museum of History has joined hands with Hong Kong Post to

stage this exhibition <u>that</u>, through the selection of some 300 pieces of Hong Kong stamps supplemented by historical photographs, <u>tells visitors another fascinating chapter in "The Hong Kong Story"</u>.

上一句的译文除了用不定式短语译出原文的状语外，还将原文的划线部分译作了定语从句。

以上译例表明，翻译过程就是将汉语信息重新纳入英语语言框架的逻辑分析过程，双语对照阅读时，要注意观察译文是如何围绕主句，灵活运用英语的各种从属结构，建构起连贯语篇的。

第四，要仔细观察从属成分运用较多的段落，思考译者是如何将原文理出条理，又如何将原文信息纳入英语的主从构架的。

在新加坡，几乎人人至少会说两种语言，有些人甚至会说三至四种语言。<u>大多数儿童自小就在双语环境中成长</u>，当他们长大后，又学会了其他的语言。受过教育的新加坡人大多数都通晓双语，并以<u>英语和华语为日常生活中最常用的两种语言</u>。英语是学校里的主要教学用语，为了确保语言文化的传承，<u>孩子们也会学习各自的母语</u>。

Almost everyone in Singapore speaks more than one language, with some speaking as many as three or four. Most children grow up bilingual from infancy, learning other languages as they become older. With the majority of the literate population bilingual, English and Mandarin are the most commonly used languages in daily life. While English is the main language taught in schools, children also learn their mother tongues to ensure that they stay in touch with their traditional roots.

上面译例中汉语原文共有四句话，译为英语也是四句话。原文各句中，译为英语主句的部分加了下划线。先观察译文的主句，我们看到第三句主句的主语从原文的"人"变为了"物"（English and Mandarin），其他各句都沿用了原文的主语。再看译文各句从属成分的情况：第一句用了介词结构，第二句是分词短语，第三句是介词短语，第四句是从句和不定式短语作状语。

通过展出约280件旗袍，<u>介绍旗袍的渊源、20世纪20至60年代社会及文化的转变与旗袍发展的关系</u>；也展示<u>70年代末后，旗袍虽在日常服装的领域走向衰微，但如何仍以不同的形式持续地存在</u>；展览亦有分析旗袍从服装走向文化象征的建构过程，以及当代的时装设计师如何将之时装化、现代化，使其得以持续地发展。

Showcasing some 280 *qipao*, this exhibition illustrated the origins of the *qipao* and its transformation between the 1920s and 1960s, evolving along with the changing social and cultural societies. Despite retirement in the late 1970s from its role as daily garment for women, the *qipao* continued to exist in many different ways. This exhibition analysed how the *qipao* has constructed a cultural symbol from a piece of clothing, and how contemporary fashion designers have injected fashion and modern elements into it, making it transforming continuously.

原文的划线部分被析出构建成译文的主句，其他部分的信息则以分词短语（showcasing..., evolving..., making...）和宾语从句（how..., how...）的形式附属于主句。

此次展览通过馆藏和梦周文教基金会的历史图片，并与香港高等科技教育学院合作，以先进科技和创新手法制作多媒体节目，把香港旧貌重现观众眼前。

In collaboration with the Technological and Higher Education Institute of Hong Kong (THEI), the exhibition will employ advanced technology and creative skills for producing a series of multimedia programmes, in which the scenes of old Hong Kong will be reconstructed through utilizing the old photos offered by Moonchu Foundation and the museum's old photo collection.

原句划线部分译成英语的主句（直线部分），原文的波浪线部分的信息放在了译文由 in which 引导的定语从句中，而原文的两个方式状语"通过……"和"与……合作"被拆开，分别以介词短语 in collaboration... 和 through utilizing... 的形式再现。

第四节 拆　句

拆句是前两篇讨论过的老话题了。汉语中有不少由逗号分割而成的小句组成的长句，将其信息纳入以主谓结构为基础的英语句式，往往要把一个长句拆散，译成两个或更多句子。

汉英语篇翻译

旅游语篇中常见将汉语的并列句依势拆开,译为两句。比如下面译例中都是将并列部分(双斜线所示)拆译成两个英语句子的。

- 香港市政局在1976年构思兴建科学馆,// 并在20世纪80年代进行策划和设计。大楼的建造工程在1988年3月展开,1990年9月完成,// 并在翌年4月18日开幕。

  The Urban Council of Hong Kong first conceived the Hong Kong Science Museum in 1976. In the 1980s, the Council proceeded with the design and development of the museum. Construction of the building started in March 1988 and was completed in September 1990. The Museum had its grand opening on 18 April 1991.

- 我们承诺本馆在任何时间最少有500件展品,其中七成为可供操作展品(即350件),// 并保持最少百分之九十的可供操作展品(即315件)正常运作。

  We pledge to provide at least 500 exhibits at all times, of which 70% are hands-on exhibits (350 exhibits). We will keep at least 90% of hands-on exhibits (315 exhibits) in the Museum in working order.

- 这些年来,博物馆一直致力搜集、保存、整理、研究及展览与香港及华南地区有关的文物,// 并通过举办各种教育及推广活动,以提高广大市民对香港历史文化的兴趣及认识。

  Over the years, the Museum has been committed to collecting, preserving, processing, studying and displaying cultural objects related to Hong Kong and the South China area. In order to enhance public interest in and awareness of the local history and culture, we have been organizing a wide range of education and extension activities.

- 1998年,一座现代化的博物馆落成启用,总面积约17500平方米,其中展厅面积达8000平方米,分为长期展览厅及专题展览厅,// 并设有演讲厅、活动室、参考资料室、餐厅及礼品店等,为市民提供更多元化的博物馆服务。

  Completed in 1998, the modern museum building has a gloss floor area of 17,500m², with 8,000m² reserved for permanent and special exhibition galleries. Other facilities include lecture hall, activity rooms, resource centre, café and museum shop, providing a wider range of museum services to the public.

除了并列句可能被拆译，原文的关联词语也可能对拆译起导向作用，逻辑上的推进、转折和因果就成了拆分的依据。比如：

当时，新加坡已是马六甲海峡极具发展潜力的海上贸易站，// 而英国也开始意识到在此设立港口的必要性，// 因为英国需要为日益壮大的帝国商船队寻找战略据点，以及遏制荷兰在本区域扩张势力。

At this time, Singapore was already an up and coming trading post along the Malacca Straits. It was also then when Great Britain started to see the need for a port of call in the region. In particular, British traders needed a strategic venue to base the merchant fleet of the growing empire, and to forestall any advance made by the Dutch in the region.

更多的情况下，拆译要基于对汉语原文的语义、逻辑分析。下面译例后半句是前半句的例证，英译时就将其拆出自立成句了。

我国碑铭文字多不胜数，// 司马迁（公元前145—前90年）写《史记》时就已经注意收集秦代（公元前221—前206年）石刻资料，以述说秦始皇（公元前259—前210年）的史事。

China, too, possesses a wealth of stele inscriptions. While writing his *magnum opus Shi Ji* (*Records of the Grand Historian*), Sima Qian (145 B.C.–90 B.C.) collected information on Qin Dynasty (221 B.C.–206 B.C.) stone carvings in order to document historical events relating to the First Emperor (259 B.C.–210 B.C.) of the Qin Dynasty.

如果后文为前文提供补充信息，自然也可能拆出，单独译为一句。比如：

- 科学馆另设有一745平方米的特备展览厅、295座位的演讲厅、课室、电脑室、实验室及资源中心，// 其他相关设施包括礼品店及书店。
  The Museum also has a 745 sq.m. Special Exhibition Hall, a 295-seat Lecture Hall, a Classroom, a Computer Classroom, a Laboratory and a Resource Centre. Other ancillary facilities include a Gift Shop and a Book Shop.
- 1866年至1868年港府曾成立香港铸钱局，// 一度在港自铸硬币，但只维持了两年。
  Between 1866 and 1868, the Hong Kong Government had set up the Hong Kong Mint. Coins were minted in Hong Kong at one time, but only for a

period of two years.

如后文和前文是时间上的承接关系，当然也可拆译出来，自成一句。比如：

- 在新加坡，多种语言特别是各式马来语和华语方言的存在和并用，明显对英语的使用造成了影响，// 逐渐形成掺杂着其他语言词汇的非正式英语——新加坡式英语 Singlish。

  The presence of other languages, especially the varieties of Malay and the Chinese dialects, has obviously had an influence on the type of English that is used in Singapore. The influence is especially apparent in informal English, an English-based creole that is commonly known as Singlish.

- "香港故事"民俗展览现正展出一块由麻石打制的石碑，是 1988 年在港岛铜锣湾一带修路时被发现，// 后移交香港历史博物馆，所以未收录于《香港碑铭汇编》内。

  The Folk Culture Gallery of The Hong Kong Story exhibition is currently showcasing a granite stele that was discovered in Causeway Bay during road works in the district in 1988. It was not included in *Historical Inscriptions of Hong Kong* but was later handed over to the Hong Kong Museum of History.

- 1863 年，港府从英国运送辅币来港，// 翌年开始在市面流通，成为香港首批硬币。

  In 1863, the Hong Kong Government imported coins from Britain. They went into circulation in the following year and became Hong Kong's first coins.

有时后文是对前文信息的强调或进一步阐发，这也就有了拆译的可能性。比如：

- 香港历史博物馆馆藏品种类繁多，数目庞大，// 其中尤以历史照片最负盛名，相关藏品已经超过 14000 件。

  The Hong Kong Museum of History has established a sizable collection comprising a great variety of historical artefacts. Among them, the old photo collection with 14,000 prints and other related items is the most significant hoard of the museum.

- 香港乡村学校最早可追溯到新界传统的私塾，// 村校的创立、发展、式微和转化，正反映本地乡村教育的发展。

  The earliest village schools can be traced back to *sishu* (private schools) in the New Territories. Their establishment, development, decline and transformation reflect the development of rural education in Hong Kong.

- 时至今天，长衫在香港社会经历传承和转化，// 依然历久不衰，成为不少女性出席重要场合的礼服。

  As the tradition of wearing the cheongsam has been passed from generation to generation, the garment has undergone several changes. It remains hugely popular in Hong Kong today and continues to be worn by many women to important occasions.

- 为了彰显多元种族特色，新加坡分别以四大民族的一种代表性语言为官方用语，// 在宪法中把英语、华语、马来语和淡米尔语定为国家的四种官方语文。

  As a reflection of its collage of cultures, Singapore has adopted one representative language for each of the four major ethnic or "racial" groups. The four official languages in Singapore's constitution are English, Chinese, Malay and Tamil.

拆句和分辨信息的主从关系紧密相关，下面译例就体现了拆译和从属成分综合运用的技巧。句中下划线部分译为从属成分（介词短语或分词短语）。

- 1942 年 2 月 15 日，新加坡沦陷，<u>这个一度被视为坚不可摧的堡垒被日本占领</u>，// 长达三年半之久。

  <u>Once regarded as an impregnable fortress</u>, Singapore fell under the Japanese invasion on 15 February 1942. It remained occupied for the next three and half years.

- 展出的文物超过 700 件，<u>辅以精彩的历史图片和录像</u>，道出香港各种货币出现的时代背景，// 以及货币的购买力转变，<u>与港人的日常生活息息相关</u>。

  Over 700 artefacts, <u>along with fascinating historical images and videos</u>, present visitors with pictures of the eras in which different types of currency emerged in Hong Kong. The exhibits, <u>intricately related to Hong Kong people's everyday lives</u>, showed how the purchasing power of currencies have changed over the years.

- <u>由于当时独特的政治情势</u>，早期不少外国来华摄影师都是取道香港

269

而进入内地，// 他们拍下不少香港风光的照片，<u>有些甚至在这里开业，专门替人拍摄人像照片，并以出售华南风光图片为生</u>，// 这些作品都成为今日研究中国近代史及中国摄影史的珍贵资料。

<u>Owing to the special political circumstances</u>, Hong Kong then became a natural stopover for foreign photographers on their way to the Mainland. These photographers took many pictures on the early development of Hong Kong, <u>while some of them even established studios in Hong Kong specializing in taking portraits and selling scenery pictures of South China.</u> These pictures are all invaluable research materials for studying the history of modern China and the history of photography in China.

第五节 合 句

除了上一节所讲的使用频繁的拆句技巧，我们也会看到将两个汉语句子的信息合并在一个英语句子结构中的情况，也就是合句。

合译的操作首先要依英语句法结构的信息容量而定。比如：

①科学馆常设展览厅的总面积为6500平方米。②馆藏展品逾500件，// ③当中70%是互动展品，老幼咸宜。

Occupying a permanent exhibition area of 6,500 square metres, the Museum houses over 500 exhibits. Nearly 70 percent of them are interactive and suitable for visitors of all ages.

原句可分为三个信息单位：①讲面积，②讲展品数量，③讲互动产品。译文将①和②合在一起，③则另立一句。合译部分将"面积"信息纳入分词短语结构，将"展品"信息设为主句。

此外，当后一句的代词或名词重复了前一句的某个名词时，译文中可用定语从句的形式将后一句纳入前句中，从而合二而一。比如：

而<u>DC-3客机</u>可算是科学馆的另一珍藏。<u>它</u>是香港首架客机，也是馆内第一件安装的展品。

Another attraction is the DC-3 airplane <u>which is the first local airliner and the first exhibit moved into the Museum building</u>.

当后句和前句有着某种时间上的关联的时候，也可用状语形式将后句纳入前句。比如：

- 香港的<u>博物馆服务原来有百多年的历史</u>。<u>第一所"博物院"可追溯至 1870 年</u>，设于昔日的大会堂内，主要收藏书籍图册及动植物标本。
  Museum service in Hong Kong has a history of over a hundred years, <u>dating back to the 1870s</u> when the first "museum" came into existence in the then City Hall, collecting mainly books, pictures as well as plant and animal specimens.
- 在第二次世界大战中，战火无情地摧毁了新加坡的和平与繁荣。1941 年 12 月 8 日，新加坡遭到日军空袭。
  But the peace and prosperity of the country suffered a major blow during World War II, when it was attacked by the Japanese on 8 December 1941.

总之，不论拆译还是合译，都是为了适应英语的句法模式而对汉语进行的重新解析和组合。与其说这是翻译技巧，不如说这体现了译者的英语写作能力。而这种技能只能来自于对英语同类语篇的研读、领悟和模仿。

第六节　信息的调整

信息的调整包括对原文信息的增（包括阐发、细化等）、删、简化、迁移和变通等，下面分别举例。

发展至清代 (1644—1911)，金石学大盛，<u>热潮至 20 世纪 30 年代仍未衰减</u>。
Reaching the height of its popularity in the Qing Dynasty (1644–1911), the discipline still exerted an influence on the study of Chinese antiquities in the 1930s.

译文的划线部分是对"热潮……仍未衰减"的阐发和具体化。

来自中国、印度、阿拉伯和布吉的帆船以及葡萄牙的战舰等，都曾途经此地。
The city served as a flourishing trading post for a wide variety of sea vessels,

including Chinese junks, Indian vessels, Arab dhows, Portuguese battleships, and Buginese schooners.

  译文的划线部分详细说出了 junk，vessel 和 dhow 等不同类型的船只，是对原文信息的细化。

  "林荫下的学校"展览是将研究计划的<u>成果</u>，通过文字、历史图片、声音影像及相关的文物，介绍本地乡村学校的发展概况及它们对香港社会的贡献。

Based on <u>the information and materials</u> collected from the research project, the exhibition "Under The Trees" introduces the development of village schools as well as their contribution to Hong Kong society through the display of panels, old photos, audio-visual materials and historical objects.

  原文中"成果"一词的语义更细致具体地表达为 the information and materials。

  石碑经凿打后，<u>主体部分低陷，两边形成突起的框线</u>，中间列出 32 个善信的名字，其中两人被列做"福首"。

The body of the stele <u>has borders</u>, and the names of 32 donors are listed in the centre, two of which are referred to as *fushou* (literally "first in benevolence").

  译文的下划线部分未对"主体部分低陷，两边形成突起的框线"等信息细节一一纳入，而是笼统地译为 has borders。如果说这是一种简化，那么下面译例就是完全的删除了。

  馆内共有展品约 500 件，<u>分布在大小不同的展览厅</u>。70% 的展品可让参观者亲自操作，适合不同年龄的参观者。

The Museum has about 500 exhibits with 70 per cent of hands-on items for visitors of all ages.

  原文划线部分的信息译文中已删去，原因可能是此信息近乎冗余，删去无关大局。

  <u>新加坡华人之间大多以华语（普通话）交谈</u>。自 20 世纪 80 年代，政府推行"讲华语运动"以来，华语已替代福建话、潮州话、广东话、客家话、海南话和福州话等方言，成为新加坡华人的第二大通用语。到了 20 世纪 90 年代，"讲华语运动"则转向受英文教育的华人。

<u>For the Chinese majority, Mandarin is the main language instead of dialects like Hokkien, Teochew, Cantonese, Hakka, Hainanese and Foochow.</u> Mandarin became

the second most commonly spoken language among the Singaporean Chinese after the start of the Speak Mandarin campaign during 1980 that targeted the Chinese. In 1990s, efforts were undertaken to target the English-educated Chinese.

原文划线的两部分信息在译文中被合在一起（译文下划线部分）。

为保存香港境内的碑铭文字资料，香港博物馆（"香港历史博物馆"旧称）早在 1986 年出版了 // 一套三册的《香港碑铭汇编》，该书共收录 585 项华文碑铭文字，由科大卫、陆鸿基、吴伦霓霞和他们的研究助理在 1978 年至 1984 年间所收集，// 原则上以 1945 年为下限，当中又以祠堂、庙宇和慈善团体所藏的碑刻占大多数，<u>是香港首本碑刻资料汇编</u>。

To preserve the valuable historical information provided by inscriptions in Hong Kong, the Hong Kong Museum of History published its own record back in 1986. The three volumes of *Historical Inscriptions of Hong Kong*, <u>the city's first compilation of this kind</u>, contain 585 Chinese inscriptions collected by Dr. David Faure, Dr. Bernard Hung-kay Luk, Dr. Alice Ngai-ha Ng Lun and their research assistants between 1978 and 1984. The majority of the inscriptions came before 1945 and were found in ancestral halls, temples and charitable institutions.

此译例涉及信息迁移问题。原文全句被拆译成三个英语句子，我们用"//"号大致标出了拆句的节点。可以看到，原文最后一个小句的信息（下划线部分）被前移到了译文第二句的同位语部分（下划线部分）。这里的信息前移显然是由拆译导致的信息重组。

下面译例涉及原文信息的变通。

"路漫漫其修远兮，吾将上下以求索"，这是我们在 1995 年庆祝博物馆成立 20 周年时的<u>心声</u>。

"Long as the journey is, we will keep on searching". This was the <u>mission</u> we set in 1995 when we were celebrating the 20th anniversary of the Museum.

原文中"心声"译为 mission，这是一种以上下文为依据的语义变通。

为谋求更美好的前景，外来移民不断涌入，同时也带来了他们的语言、文化、风俗与节庆。异族通婚及融合<u>不仅造就了新加坡社会的多元化</u>，更赋予了它生机勃勃、丰富多彩的文化传承。

Drawn by the lure of better prospects, the immigrants brought with them their own culture, languages, customs and festivals. Intermarriage and integration helped <u>knit</u>

these diverse influences into the fabric of Singapore's multi-faceted society, giving it a vibrant and diverse cultural heritage.

"造就……多元文化"的信息变通为 knit...into the fabric... 的比喻。

第七节 重 写

上一节讨论了对原文信息的重组和变通，本节探讨译文对原文信息的重新表达，也就是重写。重写对原文信息的处理更为灵活，更能发挥英语的"优势"，使译文更合乎英语表达习惯，更地道。这里所谓的英语"优势"主要指对此类英语文本的行文、文体、修辞习惯的顺应和模仿。看下面的译例。

理想

科学馆通过先进、创新和多学科的展览、展品、活动、表演及外展计划，带领学生和公众以非正式的途径学习科学。

就品质和多样性而言，科学馆是一所世界级博物馆。

在筹办实体和虚拟活动及传播科技和天文学资讯方面，科学馆是东南亚——尤其是泛珠江三角洲——同类型机构、天文馆和科学中心的焦点。

科学馆提供一个平台，展示富启发性——特别是来自内地——的展览和展品，以及本地和亚洲科学家及天文学家的成就。

Vision

We are local leaders in informal science learning for students and the general public using state-of-the-art, innovative and multi-disciplinary exhibitions, exhibits, activities, shows, and outreach programmes.

We are a museum of world-class standard in terms of quality and diversity.

We are a focal point among similar institutes, planetariums and science centres in Southeast Asia, particularly the Greater Pearl River Delta, in the organization of physical and virtual programmes and the dissemination of information on science, technology, and astronomy.

We provide a platform that showcases stimulating exhibitions and exhibits, in particular from the Mainland, as well as achievements of inspiring local and Asian scientists and astronomers.

以上译例摘自香港科学馆的介绍文字，文中提到办馆的理念，分四点以四句话加以概括。译文将原文第三人称的叙述方式改为第一人称 we，并对原文信息调整以将其纳入英语的句法结构。整篇译文似为重写，但又紧扣原文信息。

下面再择取几个译例，具体分析一下译者对原文信息进行重新表述的做法。

科学馆和传统博物馆的分别在于所展出的展品以可操作展品为主，<u>强调操作时参观者的各个感官互相配合</u>，从而体验科学的奥妙。

In contrast to traditional museums, the Science Museum encourages visitors to <u>put their hands on, eyes on, ears on and minds on while they are operating the interactive exhibits</u>.

对比汉英两种文字可以看出，划线部分的信息大体是一样的，但用词和表达方式却大不一样。put their hands on, eyes on, ears on and minds on 是对英语表达"优势"这一概念的很好发挥。

新加坡被誉为繁荣的国际大都市，多元文化、语言、艺术和建筑在此巧妙地融合。<u>不断兼收并蓄、发展新风貌，是这个活力之都的特点，这里提供的独特旅游组合、正是她与众不同之处</u>。

<u>在现今瞬息变化的数字化时代，游客已能更轻易地按个人喜好和需要编排行程、谱写自己的旅行故事</u>。

Singapore has been described as a thriving cosmopolitan city that's brimming with diversity, with a fascinating mix of culture, language, arts and architecture. She is a dynamic city that inspires; constantly innovating to offer fresh experiences. It is her own blend of offerings that sets her apart from other destinations.

However, we live in an ever-changing environment, with the digital age enabling travellers to actively shape and define their own travel stories.

上例的重写主要体现在原文划线部分在英译中的重新表达。译文第二段段首添加的连接词 however 也体现了译者对原文逻辑关系的重新确立。"谱写"译为 shape and define 是对文义的变通。

展览中观众可以看到邮票上标准英皇头像式样，在沿用百年后，到 20 世纪 60 年代才出现转变。随着本地华人参与邮票设计，本地邮票出现更多中国文化和香港元素。

Chronicling the images of British monarchs that were depicted on early Hong Kong stamps, the exhibition traces how the stamp designs featuring royal portraits that had been adopted as standard for over a century were gradually replaced from the 1960s onwards, and it also showcases the various elements drawn from Chinese culture and Hong Kong life that have been used as motifs since local Chinese were first commissioned to design the territory's stamps.

整个汉语句子英译时都有信息调整和变通，表达方式也与原文不同。

不妨花些时间，好好探索<u>这里的精彩纷呈</u>。新加坡体验虽然不断演变，但您仍能<u>自由规划专属自己的美妙假日</u>。

So take your time to explore and discover <u>what awaits you here</u>. While the Singapore experience is constantly evolving, <u>you can decide how and what you want your Singapore holiday to be</u>.

上面译例中，原文下划线部分的译文都是运用疑问词引导的宾语从句来重写的。

下面是比较长的两个段落，我们将信息群标上号，以便进行观察和分析。

①科举制度把教育与选士任官制度合而为一，// ②具有自由报名、公开考试、平等竞争、择优取录的特征，为出身寒门的知识分子进入仕途，提供了一个公平竞争的平台。③此次展览以清代科举考试为主线，通过约100件（组）来自上海市嘉定博物馆，// ④以及从本地征集所得的相关文物，辅以互动教育环节，// ⑤介绍科举考试制度的内容及沿革，剖析科举制度没落原因、以及对中国社会文化的影响，让观众认识在中国推行长达1300年的科举制度，领会这制度所包含的文化内涵。

① The imperial examination was <u>a pioneering system developed in China</u> that combined education with recruitment for the state bureaucracy. ② Upholding the principle of fairness through open participation, public examination, equal competition and selection on merit, it provided the masses with access to social mobility. ③ Showcasing over 100 sets of artefacts selected from the collections of the Shanghai Jiading Museum and the Hong Kong Museum of History, <u>the exhibition took us back to the Qing Dynasty to revisit the imperial examination, its history and its significance</u>. ④ Also featured were a host of artefacts provided by local sources and a series of interactive displays that presented the subject in a dynamic and playful manner. ⑤ By tracing the development, the demise and the legacy of the system, the exhibition provided us with a better understanding of the instrumental role that the imperial examination played in shaping Chinese society and culture over a period of 1,300 years.

　　以上译例的重写体现在如下方面：①添加了信息（译文划线部分）；②拆译独立成句，呈主从分明的句式；③添加了信息，语义也有所调整；④呈倒装句式，信息亦有添加和衍伸；⑤对原文划线部分的信息有所删减。

　　①在新加坡，游客绝对能随心所欲，设计个性化行程，踏上心中向往的旅程。②当然，每趟行程都会是独特的，这也是旅行的魅力所在。③透过世界各地旅客的视角和本地居民的观点，述说或感人或另类的体验，汇集成形形色色的新加坡故事。每个截然不同的故事，无不彰显"我行由我新加坡"的独到之处。

　　① Thus Singapore enables travellers to design their own journeys—stories they can call their very own. ② Undoubtedly, each account will be different, but that is what makes them intriguing and enduring. ③ A multitude of stories told through the eyes of people from all over the world and the local residents themselves. Some intimate, others adventurous. Each story is unique to call one's own.

　　上面译例的重写体现在：①以 enable 为谓语动词重写；②"魅力所在"被释义为 intriguing and enduring；③更是以全新的句式概括出原文信息。

第三章
翻译试笔和思考

第一节　信息功能——词语、句式练习

【练习一】

玉 器 展

中国人历来酷爱玉石，甚至胜过金银。自古以来，这种清澈而坚硬的石头就被制成各种饰物和礼仪用品。多地发掘出土的文物，不仅揭示出玉石雕琢的源远流长，而且展示了当时就已经达到的极高雕琢水平。

玉石是王公贵族生前的饰物、死后的随葬品，玉便成了皇权和高贵的象征。据说，玉还有防止尸体腐烂的神奇功效[1]。后来，这些神奇的功效渐被淡化，人们更看重的是它在制作精美饰品、器具上以及考古上的价值[2]。明清两代，玉石制品的形状和装饰图案常常仿效古代，于是，将远古和近古联系了起来[3]。

本展览是从大约公元前5000年到现代的玉器发展史，玉石色泽、纹理的细微差别以及各种类型的雕琢技艺均有展示[4]。

一般以为，中华文明起源于黄河流域，但现在我们知道，黄河流域以北和以南地区都曾存在过更早期的文化。公元前约3000年至公元前2700年，在现今东北地区的辽宁和内蒙古存在过一个新石器时期聚落，即红山文化[5]。红山先民创立了高度发达的社会，留给今人许多令人赞叹的遗址[6]。红山先民十分推崇玉石，有时候玉器是人们死后的唯一陪葬品。

玉玦是最早出现的精打细磨的玉器之一，主要作为耳饰。最早的玉玦形状更

像是有缺口的圆筒而非环状，出土于东北地区的兴隆洼文化（约公元前 5000 年）和查海文化（约公元前 4500 年），比红山文化（约公元前 3000—前 2700 年）还要早。[7] 玉玦的制作从北方传到东南方的浙江省一带，在河姆渡有发掘[8]，在马家浜—崧泽文化（公元前 5000—前 3000 年）中存在。早期的玉玦相对来说都比较厚实，呈圆形。

玉琮呈圆筒状，截面为方形，中间有一圆孔，是所有玉器中最出彩、也最神秘的。它们的功能和寓意仍不为人知。尽管知道制作于新石器时代的不同时期，但直到最近三十年人们才认定琮起源于东南部的新石器文化。玉琮是江苏省太湖地区良渚文化（约公元前 3000—前 2000 年）的主要玉器之一，在所有主要考古发掘地都有精品出土[9]。玉琮大多内圆外方，呈方柱状，尽管也有扁镯形状的。良渚文化玉琮的主要纹饰是神人兽面纹，大概象征着某种神灵。在方形玉琮上，纹饰位于四角，而扁镯形玉琮的纹饰则出现在方形的侧面，这些纹饰是人和神兽脸部图案的结合。

参考译文

Chinese Jade

Jade has always been the material most highly prized by the Chinese, above silver and gold. From ancient times, this extremely tough translucent stone has been worked into ornaments and ritual objects. Recent archaeological finds in many parts of China have revealed not only the antiquity of the skill of jade carving, but also the extraordinary levels of development it achieved at a very early date.

Jade was worn by kings and nobles and after death placed with them in the tomb. As a result, the material became associated with royalty and high status. It also came to be regarded as powerful in death, protecting the body from decay. In later times these magical properties were perhaps less explicitly recognised, jade being valued more for its use in exquisite ornaments and vessels, and for its links with antiquity. In the Ming and Qing periods ancient jade shapes and decorative patterns were often copied, thereby bringing the associations of the distant past to the Chinese peoples of later times.

      This tour illustrates examples showing the development of Chinese jade from around 5000 BC to the modern period. The subtle variety of colours and textures of this exotic stone can be seen, as well as the many different types of carving.

      It was long believed that Chinese civilization began in the Yellow River valley, but we now know that there were many earlier cultures both to the north and south of this area. From about 3000 B.C. to 2700 B.C. a group of Neolithic peoples known now as the Hongshan culture lived in the far north-east, in what is today Liaoning province and Inner Mongolia. The Hongshan were a sophisticated society that built impressive ceremonial sites. Jade was obviously highly valued by the Hongshan; artefacts made of jade were sometimes the only items placed in tombs along with the body of the diseased.

      Jue, or slit rings, are among the earliest of all ornaments to be made in fine polished jade. They were worn as earrings. The earliest *jue*, which are more like slit tubes than slit rings, are found in the north-east in the Xinglongwa (about 5000 B.C.) and Chahai cultures (about 4500 B.C.), which preceded the Hongshan (about 3800 B.C.–2700 B.C.). The manufacture of *jue* probably spread from the north to the south-east to Zhejiang province, where they are found at Hemudu, and they remained in use in the south-east in the Majiabang and Songze cultures (5000 B.C.–3000 B.C.). Many of these early *jue* are relatively thick and modelled in the round.

      Cong, essentially tubes with a square cross-section and a circular hole, are among the most impressive yet most enigmatic of all ancient Chinese jade artefacts. Their function and meaning are completely unknown. Although they were known to be made at many stages of the Neolithic period, the origin of the *cong* in the Neolithic cultures of south-east China has only been recognised in the last thirty years. The *cong* is one of the principal types of jade artefact of the Liangzhu culture (about 3000 B.C.–2000 B.C.) around Lake Tai in Jiangsu province. Spectacular examples have been found at all the major archaeological sites. The main types of *cong* have a square outer section around a circular inner part, and a circular hole, though jades of a bracelet shape also display some of the characteristics of *cong*. The principal decoration on *cong* of the Liangzhu period was the face pattern, which may refer to spirits or deities. On the square-sectioned pieces, like this example, the face pattern is placed across the corners, whereas on the bracelet form it appears in square panels. These faces are derived from a combination of a man-like figure and a mysterious beast.

思考

1. 此句的译文为分词短语，作状语。
2. 注意译文中独立主格结构的运用。
3. 这部分译为分词短语，作状语。
4. 此句拆译为两句，后一句译为被动语态。
5. 这句的译文运用了 known as…, in what is… 等从属成分。
6. 这部分译作了定语从句。
7. 此句译文有两处译为定语从句。
8. 这一部分译为定语从句。
9. 此句拆译为被动句。

【练习二】

上 海 滩

全球的主要城市都拥有著名的地标做代表。要感受上海风情，只消到外滩走一趟。位于滚滚黄浦江畔的¹两公里长的黄埔滩，是观光客与游人的必然首选。外滩这个国家级保护地标²，现正踏进复兴时代。

外滩最具特色的建筑物，要算位于20号的和平饭店。饭店在1929年开设，前身是华懋饭店³，多年来虽经修葺，但改变甚微。外貌呈现哥特式的美国芝加哥学派风格，楼高77米，铜色金字塔尖顶，奶白色花岗石墙，加上六人乐队在充满传奇的爵士吧夜夜笙歌，不禁勾起对喧嚣的20年代的记忆。⁴ 著名的沙逊套房位于和平饭店10楼，是上海商人及和平饭店创始人维克托·沙逊曾居住的房间。在1945年至1946年美军进驻和平饭店时，将军艾伯特·魏德迈也曾住在这里。⁵

位于2号曾一度是私人会所的上海总会，白色圆柱，巴洛克式顶楼，是一幢英国文艺复兴风格建筑⁶。上海总会建于1911年，长达110英尺的酒吧，尤令它

声名鹊起。当年商贾们会根据自己的地位入座，但妇女和华人却被禁止入内。[7] 酒吧末端的大窗座位，正可观赏外滩景色，是当年那些长江航运船长、企业或银行总裁和经理们的专享位置。当年财大气粗的英国洋行大班，常在午后来到三楼的阳台，一边呷着苦味杜松子酒，一边看着那些中国帆船把他们的货物运向黄浦江上游。上海总会在1879年曾为到访的美国前总统、南北战争时期的英雄格兰特举行了一场豪华舞会。

汇丰银行大楼（位于12号，现为上海浦东发展银行）建于1923年，被视为一幢古典欧洲文艺复兴风格的建筑物。穿过宏伟的旋转门，可看到经过修复的圆拱顶和大堂，在外滩建筑群中可算最为富丽堂皇。银行的拱顶由八根大理石柱支撑着，装饰着八幅马赛克壁画，每幅壁画都代表着一个国际金融中心[8]，包括曼谷、香港、东京、纽约、伦敦、巴黎、加尔各答，当然还有上海。

也许外滩的最大资产并非其建筑物或步行街，而是其生生不息的港口。无论日夜的任何时段，当你驾车由南京东路来到黄浦江畔，都会看到庞大的货轮或商船缓缓驶过，拉着汽笛向小船示警，为这座历史悠久、生机勃勃的商业大都会添上了浓墨重彩的一笔[9]。

参考译文

Shanghai's Bund

All of the world's major cities are defined by their best-known landmarks. To feel at the heart of Shanghai, you need only to take a turn along the Bund. Set beside the swift-flowing waters of the Huangpu River, the two-kilometer-long Bund is first and foremost a magnet for sightseers and strollers. Today, the Bund, an officially preserved national monument, is undergoing magnificent renaissance.

One of the most charismatic buildings along the Bund remains the Peace Hotel at No. 20. Raised in 1929 and originally called the Cathay, it has altered but little over the years. The "Gothic Chicago" exterior, with its hallmark 77-meter high, copper-sheathed pyramid roof and milky-yellow granite walls, together with the six-piece band that thumps out numbers nightly in the legendary Jazz Bar, are all powerfully reminiscent of the roaring 20s. On the 10th floor is the famous Sassoon Room where Shanghai businessman and Peace Hotel owner Victor Sassoon lived. It was the same room that General Albert C. Wedemeyer stayed in when the US military occupied the hotel from 1945 to 1946.

At No. 2 lies the once exclusive Shanghai Club, an English Renaissance structure with elaborate white columns and Baroque attic windows. The Club, which was established in 1911, was famous for its 110-foot Long Bar where businessmen would seat themselves by rank, while women and Chinese were excluded. The window end of the bar—where the Club's bay windows looked out onto the Bund—was the private domain of daring Yangtze River pilots and the directors and managers of the large trading houses and banks. From the third floor balcony, the taipans of the powerful British trading companies could sip their "pink gins" under the afternoon sun while watching Chinese junks ferry their goods up the Huangpu River. The Club hosted a lavish dance for former US president and Civil War hero Ulysses S. Grant when he visited China in 1879.

Hongkong and Shanghai Bank Building (No. 12, now the Shanghai Pudong Development Bank), built in 1923, is considered a classic European Renaissance building. Inside its massive revolving doors, the restored dome and lobby are among the most magnificent on the Bund. Its dome, supported by eight marble columns, is decorated with an eight-panelled mosaic, each panel a salute to one of the world's financial capitals (Bangkok, Hong Kong, Tokyo, New York, London, Paris, Calcutta and of course, Shanghai).

Perhaps the Bund's greatest asset lies not in its buildings or its walkways, but the fact that it lines the approach to a thriving port. At any hour of the day or night, as you drive along Nanjing Donglu toward the river, you may be confronted by the sight of a majestic tanker or merchant ship steaming past, blasting its horn to warn smaller craft of its approach, slotting just one more colorful piece into the gargantuan commercial jigsaw of China's most historic and dynamic city—Shanghai.

思考

1. 下划线部分译为分词从属成分。

2. 下划线部分译为同位语。
3. 这部分译为分词短语。
4. 注意这个句子英译时主语的安排：The "Gothic Chicago" exterior 为主语，后面跟两个 with... 短语。
5. 注意本段最后这两个句子英译时句型的运用：倒装和强调句式。
6. 注意译文的倒装句式以及同位语的运用。
7. 这两句合译成了一个英语句子，注意句中各类从句的使用。
8. 这部分译为独立主格结构。
9. 此处英文运用了不同的比喻：喻体由"绘画"转为"拼图"。

第二节　行事功能——祈使句练习

北京五日游[1]

第一天：黎明起床，直奔天坛。进入南门，可以看到有500年历史的祈年殿，庭院里、长亭上，老人们在练太极，唱传统歌曲或在地面上练习书法。[2]

走出天坛北门，向西，再沿前门大街向北就是前门和大栅栏，胡同里的药店仍在出售早在清朝就闻名遐迩的中草药；在沿街小店吃上一碗面条，继续向北就是天安门广场，[3] 1949年毛主席就是在这里宣布中华人民共和国成立的。

穿过天安门城楼，就是故宫[4]。走出故宫北门，乘出租到北海公园，如果体力好，也可以步行。漫步北海之后，向北沿鼓楼大街到后海喝个下午茶。无名吧景色怡人，环境优雅，是首选之一。稍事休息，乘出租车去簋街，那里有火锅和各种北京美食，大红灯笼高挑，通宵达旦，选择一家即可尽兴入夜。[5]

第二天：起早去长城。司马台长城尽管比大多数长城景点远一点，但是最清静美丽的地段之一，路上花点时间也值得。如果胆子足够大，可以沿索道飞跃鸳鸯湖回到山脚下。回到市内用晚餐，可以品尝全鸭季的北京烤鸭，然后和同伴到大班健身中心享受足部按摩。

第三天：参观大山子艺术区。先来一杯卡布奇诺咖啡或吃个午餐，然后考虑一下有没有你想看看或买得起的绘画作品。[6]

打车到工体北路的雅秀市场，人虽多但值得一去[7]。服装、DVD，一个比一个便宜，是狂购礼品的好去处[8]。吃过午饭，乘出租车到日坛公园南门[9]。傍晚时分，可见年轻的情侣在幽静的角落里接吻、拥抱。再向北是日坛，日坛北面有小王府日坛店，如果天气暖和，可坐在露台上，边赏美景边品尝各色传统菜肴。

第四天：乘出租或地铁到西城，如果有兴致，可参观军事博物馆，观赏毛主席乘坐过的轿车和明朝的火箭发射器。走出军博，北面便是玉渊潭公园。欣赏了夏日美景之后，可乘游船前往颐和园（由八一湖南码头发船，每小时一班）[10]。下午游览曾是慈禧太后夏日行宫的颐和园美景，最后回城到鼎泰丰品尝享誉京城的小笼包[11]。

第五天：如果恰逢周末，打个车去潘家园旧货市场。一排排地摊兜售古玩、旧书、首饰，还有毛主席纪念品，热闹非凡，你肯定能收获大包大包的纪念品。再打一辆出租去雍和宫，在葡萄院吃过午饭，开始仔细参观。雍和宫是市内最幽静的去处之一[12]，白檀木弥勒大佛是用一根完整的白檀木雕刻而成，堪称世界之最。晚饭可打车去鼓楼东大街的北京大理院，享用来自云南的美食[13]。如果你还有精力，就到亚洲风味的妃思客栈喝上一杯[14]，作为五日行程的完满结尾。

参考译文

Best of Beijing in Five Days

On day one, get up at the crack of dawn and head straight for the Temple of Heaven, starting at the south gate, where as well as seeing the 500-year-old temple itself, you'll get to watch local old folk doing tai chi, singing traditional songs and writing calligraphy on the ground in the Temple's parks and pavilions.

Exit the temple's north gate and head first west, then north up Qianmen Dajie until you hit the clusters of hutongs around Qianmen and Dashila, taking the time to explore and check out the shops still selling the same Chinese medicines they were touting in the Qing Dynasty. Grab some noodles from one of the local stalls before continuing north to Tian'anmen Square. It was from the rostrum on Tian'anmen that Chairman Mao declared the founding of the People's Republic of China in 1949.

Pass through the Tian'anmen gate and into the Forbidden City, the magnificent Imperial Palace of the Ming and Qing Emperors. At the north end, hop in a cab to the beautiful Beihai Park, or walk if you're legs are still up for it. Stroll around this imperial playground for a while before heading north again via Gulou Dajie for a pre-dinner drink on Houhai Lake. Try the No Name bar, one of the first in the area, for pleasant views and a wonderful atmosphere. Rested? Then jump in a cab to Guijie—the 24 hour food street laced with red lanterns—and pick one of the hundreds of restaurants serving hot pot or typical Beijing dishes before settling down to eat and drink your way into the night.

Get up early and head to the Great Wall on the second day. Despite being a little further away than most, the Simatai section of the Wall is one of the most undisturbed and beautiful, and worth the extra time investment. If you've got the guts, swing down on the zip wire over the lake to the bottom again before making your way back to the city. Try some Beijing duck for dinner at the hip new Duck de Chine restaurant, then wind down by getting a foot massage with your companions at Oriental Taipan.

On day three, check out the 798 Art district, where you can relax with a cappuccino or lunch before seeing if there are any paintings you (or your wallet) like the look of.

From here, take a cab back to Gongti Bei Lu (near the Workers' Stadium north gate) and stop off at Yashow Market—yes, we know its full of tourists, but there's a reason. Cheap clothes and even cheaper DVDs make it a great place to stock up on gifts before heading out to dinner. Getting in a taxi again, tell the driver to take you to Ritan Park—the Temple of the Sun—south gate. As the evening draws in, spot the young lovebirds kissing and cuddling in the park's quiet corners, and head north toward the main altar. Continuing northeast you'll stumble across Xiao Wang Fu's restaurant. If it's a warm evening, head straight to the balcony where you can enjoy an array of tasty and typical Chinese dishes overlooking the park.

On the fourth day, taxi or subway to the west of the city and, if it takes your fancy, the Military Museum, where you'll get the chance to marvel at Mao Zedong's limo and Ming Dynasty rocket launchers. Once out, walk north and you'll come across the beautiful Yuyuantan Park—a great place to take in the summer revelry before catching a boat to the Summer Palace (boats go from the southern Bayi lake hourly). Spend the afternoon floating around the vast and beautiful former holiday home of the Empress Dowager Cixi before returning to the city and enjoying the city's best dumpling's at Din Tai Fung.

On the fifth day, particularly if it's a weekend, jump in a taxi to Panjiayuan, Beijing's famous outdoor dirt market. Row after row of locals selling "antiques", books, jewellery and Mao memorabilia create a wonderful hubbub, and you're sure to come away with armfuls of souvenirs. From here, jump in another taxi to the Lama Temple, and, after a spot of lunch at The Vineyard Cafe, pay up and visit the temple proper. One of the most tranquil spots in the city, it also contains the biggest Buddha carved out of a single tree in the world. For dinner, taxi to the nearby Gulou Dong Dajie and find Dali Courtyard, a beautiful courtyard restaurant serving tasty cuisine from Yunnan Province. If you've got the energy, a final drink in the trendy Asian-themed Face Bar isn't a bad way to end your week.

思考

1. 本文是为游客提供的游览方略，多有省略主语的句子，译文多用祈使句式，句中谓语动词的选择也很值得关注，这些不再一一提示。
2. 这个句子很长，译文用了从句和从属成分，注意句子主从结构的安排。
3. 译文的句子较长，注意其中从句和分词短语的运用。
4. 译文添加了有关信息。
5. 注意译文句式和结构的变化："稍事休息"译作问句，"大红灯笼高挑，通宵达旦"译作插入成分。
6. 这两句的译文借助 where 从句合在了一起。
7. 这一句的译文添加了一些有关信息，语气很口语化，有助于读者接受。
8. 思考一下汉语句式和英译句式的差异。
9. 这一句的译文也添加了信息，句首的"吃过午饭"被融进了前面一句。
10. 注意译文在结构上的变化："欣赏了夏日美景之后"译为同位语和前句融合，"可乘游船前往颐和园"译为状语。

11. 这里的译文同上句一样也运用了 before doing 构成的状语，这种对事件时间序列的表达方式值得关注。
12. 13. 这两部分均译为同位语。
14. 这部分译为名词短语作主语，也就是名物化。

新闻语篇编译

› **课时安排建议**

本篇拟对新闻稿的编译作简略介绍。依照本书确立的互文性原则,仍旧从英语语篇的阅读开始(第一章)。唯有多读英语新闻,才会领悟到怎样将汉语新闻编译成可读的英文稿。第二章以实际译例简略说明新闻编译技巧,不安排编译练习。整个附录内容可用一周时间教学,教师可安排学生课下阅读,课上择要讨论即可。

英语新闻语篇导读

带着学习汉译英的目的阅读英语新闻语篇,要特别留意些什么?不妨先看看下面一段新闻:

Meanwhile, China's export rivals, namely Japan and South Korea, are losing the currency race to the bottom. The yen is up 3 per cent against the dollar this year, as is the won, while the renminbi is 3 per cent weaker. In China's defence, some technical factors could be at play such as end of month renminbi sales by oil companies. Most analysts are still sticking to their guns, predicting a return to appreciation in the second half of the year. But questions are already being asked in Washington as to whether this is in fact a stealth operation to boost competitiveness.

第一,我们要注意这是经济新闻,有一些有关货币的术语或表达。比如:"the currency race to the bottom(汇率"向下竞赛")"、"The yen is up 3 per cent against the dollar this year, as is the won, while the renminbi is 3 per cent weaker"(日元今年对美元升值3%,韩元亦然,而人民币贬值3%),以及 "a return to appreciation"(恢复升值)等。第二,要注意常用的词组和搭配。比如:"in China's defence"(为中国辩护)、"at play"(发挥作用)、"stick to their guns"(坚持他们的预测/主张)、"boost competitiveness"(提升竞争力)等。第三,还要留意有用的句式和句子结构。比如:插入语 "namely Japan and South Korea",倒装结构 "as is the won",从句句式 "questions are already being asked in Washington as to whether" 等。

下面我们就这三个方面举例讨论英语新闻语篇阅读的关注要点。

一、涉及某一领域或话题的术语和常用说法

接着上面有关人民币升值的新闻,再举一个例子。

But yesterday the dollar reached RMB 6.26（美元对人民币汇率达到 1 美元兑 6.26 元人民币）—its highest level since October 2012. The weaker daily fix（每日指导价）, around which the currency is allowed to rise or fall by 2 per cent, shows that the People's Bank of China is still nudging the rate down （引导汇率下行）. The it's-only-temporary theory was a bet that those borrowing cheaply in dollars and using fake trade receipts（虚开贸易发票）to change their money into the rising—and higher yielding—renminbi would soon stop if currency appreciation（货币升值）reversed. That might fix China's erratic trade data and remove an unwanted source of currency appreciation.

新闻语篇可以按其内容分成几个大类，如社会、经贸、文化、教育、卫生、科技、体育等。阅读时务必留心有关术语和常用词语的表达方式，持之以恒，不断积累，提高自己针对某一话题的表达能力。大类之下还可根据需要分出若干小类，比如大家熟悉的教育类新闻中，便可按以下小类收集有用的词语：教育理念、考试招生、学校教育、教育改革、家庭教育、社会办学、留学、毕业、就业，等等。每个人可根据自己的阅读兴趣和范围，划定词语类别，编出得心应手的专业词汇手册，可供自己使用，亦可与他人分享。

下面以教育新闻大类中的两个小类——家庭教育和考试招生为例作一个示范，希望大家参照这个思路，建立起自己的语料库。

谈到家庭教育 home schooling，下面这些语句大家是否觉得有用？

- Everything is vested into their one child—they pin all their hopes on the next generation.
- Liu Zifan's parents, both with secondary school education, signed up electronic keyboard class for her when she was five. They want Liu to enter a good college.
- Chinese children face increasing pressures on study. Most Chinese parents believe high academic credentials mean a better school, a brighter future. So they send their children to extracurricular classes like music, English and maths to develop a special talent, which later might be a stepping stone to a good school.
- Some parents make their children study ahead. First graders start to take

- classes for second graders, and so on, therefore they can get an advantage in exams.
- Thanks to China's one-child policy, today's college students are part of a generation of singletons, and their newly affluent parents—and, in all likelihood, both sets of grandparents—are deeply invested in their success.
- There is a natural instinct to protect our children from risk and discomfort, and therefore to urge safe choices.
- Chinese parents tend to push their children a lot. A highly competitive pursuit of higher education routinely forces families to spend fortunes, and children to sacrifice their childhoods.
- Chinese students are put under ever-increasing pressure by their parents to study hard due to the country's highly competitive market for university places and jobs. Study pressure has led to an increase in psychological problems and even tragedy. （学习压力也可说 learning stress/pressure）
- Many parents force their children to spend a considerable amount of spare time and energy trying to learn math of an ever more advanced level to give their kids an edge in these selection tests.
- However, learning math in advance and in their spare time not only robs children of their enthusiasm for the subject, it also robs them of their childhoods and the chance to play and learn social skills mixing with other kids.
- The mantra of success as far as their parents are concerned is: "Don't let your kid lose the race on the starting line".
- As parents keep moving the starting line to an earlier and earlier age—for some it's even become prenatal—it spells doom for any hopes that kids might be able to enjoy their childhoods.
- Due to long school hours and growing pressure from parents to study hard, children are feeling unhappy about a lack of playtime.
- However, not everyone has jumped on the homeschooling bandwagon. Some are skeptical about taking children out of an environment where they are

exposed to a variety of people and situations.
- Other homeschooling parents have harnessed the Internet to connect with each other and share their challenges and successes.

而谈到考试招生，下面一些词语和句子就很值得收集和记忆。
- college-eligible population /college-age population
- The national entrance examinations known as *gaokao* have been the only yardstick for college enrollment for more than three decades. It has become an annual ritual for parents and media alike to judge the performance of the nation's schools according to their students' entrance exam scores, with schools that produce high marks gaining fame and attracting more students.
- Taken across three consecutive days at the beginning of June, the *gaokao* covers three mandatory subjects—Chinese, Mathematics, and a foreign language, usually English—and three other topics drawn from a pool of electives: Physics, Chemistry and Biology for science track students, and History, Geography and Political Education for those on the humanities track.
- During their two day grilling for the college entrance qualification, the students will sit tests in Chinese and English languages, mathematics and science or humanities.
- For Chinese students the two days of exams are viewed as two of the most important days of their lives, because the exam results will determine whether they enter higher education or not, which promises—at least theoretically—a decent job in the future.
- She aced the test, scoring in the top 20 of all students. She was a humanities track person, and usually over 600 is considered a very good score for humanities. For science track, a good score is over 720. It's much harder to get high marks on humanities because so many of the questions are open-ended rather than multiple choice.
- As the number of students sitting the exams has decreased for the fourth straight year, shrinking by 1.4 million since 2008, there are more opportunities for this year's test takers, especially as almost all higher learning institutions

- are offering a bigger enrollment program. But this does not necessarily mean the exams will be a piece of cake.
- For those students who have their sights set on an elite college, it remains a make-or-break deal.
- About 5 percent of students in the language program flunk out before their freshman year.
- The Chinese overwhelmingly want to study in the US, with nearly 80% of Chinese test scores sent to the US, followed by 5% to Hong Kong. US schools grooming the world's future business elite have seen applications from Chinese students spike by as much as 30% in a single application cycle.
- Fully 64% of GMAT exams in China were sat by women, and 77% of exams were taken by test-takers younger than 25.
- Over the past five years, the ranks of Chinese students sitting for the GMAT, the examination typically used to gain entry to management schools around the world, has ballooned by over 200% with young women driving that trend.
- The number of young women taking the test is obviously a relatively new phenomenon. It's because a lot of them are now going into entrepreneurial fields and finding this is a very good way to get an edge on their peer group. In addition to the traditional MBA route, many women seek out specialized masters degrees in finance or accounting.
- To prepare for these exams, the young examinees have to toil for more than 1,000 days during their time at senior middle school. They have to read piles of books, trying to memorize facts, figures, formulae, science laws and alien vocabulary and doing mountains of exercises almost 13 hours a day, 7 days a week. There has been no play, no time—or at the most very little—for indulging in entertainment.
- Confronting plagiarism is near the top of the list. Dr. Stevens remembers how one student memorized four Wikipedia entries so he could regurgitate whichever one seemed most appropriate on an in-class essay—an impressive, if misguided, feat.

- American concepts of intellectual property don't translate readily to students from a country where individualism is anathema.
- You have to decide what track you're on before taking the *gaokao*, because its outcome will, quite literally, determine your fate: There are minimum *gaokao* levels required to attend each of China's 2000 or so colleges, and only about two-thirds as many available admissions slots as test-takers.
- For those who do well, the *gaokao* is life-altering. Being among the 8.5 percent of test-takers who score high enough to qualify for one of China's *yiben*, or tier-one universities, means reasonable assurance of eventual high-paying white-collar employment, thereby securing a stable financial future for generations above and below alike.
- For the past two weeks, Chinese students who took part in this year's *gaokao*, the country's notoriously pressure-packed college entrance exams, have been shuffling around in a state of high anxiety, wringing their hands as they wait for results that may or may not justify the years of toil and struggle they have put into attaining that most prestigious of honors: admission into one of the country's elite universities.

以上例句均摘自外报外刊报道或评论中国教育的文章，对我们编译教育新闻无疑是很好的参照和借鉴。阅读英语新闻时，不妨多关注国外媒体对我国时事的报道用语及其表达方式。

阅读英语报刊时可以特别注意和汉语表达方式相近/似的词语，这对汉英翻译具有指导与借鉴意义，也颇具趣味性。比如"It has elements of the FBI, US Treasury Department, Secret Service and GAO [Government Accountability Office] all rolled into one"一句，这其中的"have… all rolled into one"就可以表达汉语"集……于一身"的意思。而"The popularity of Apple's iPhones will play a big role in achieving that goal"中的"popularity"可以传达汉语"人气"的意思。再有，像"Facebook has always had the question of what's private and what's public at its core"中的"have the question of …"不就是汉语的"有……问题"的意思？

另外，还可多注意汉语的一些成语、习语、常用说法在英语中是如何表达的。比如，"To forge iron, you yourself must be strong"是汉语成语"打铁还须自身硬"的可行译文。"President Xi has vowed to take down powerful 'tigers' as well as lowly 'flies'"就是"'老虎''苍蝇'都要打"的英译。

一些常用的套语也是值得注意的。比如,"拒绝评论"的英译,可在下面句子中找到参照:"Heathrow airport in London declined to comment on the new security measures." "Virgin Atlantic said: 'We don't comment on operational security matters.'" "British Airways could not be reached for comment."

二、词语的选择和搭配

英语新闻语篇有其用词特点,阅读时可特别留意以下几方面:

第一是用词简约,尤其一些由名词转化而来或名动兼用的动词,既生动又简练。英语中有许多名动兼用的词语,例如:

有关自然界的名词如 cloud(云)和 bog(沼泽):

- Unconscious biases may cloud your judgment. 无意的偏见会影响你的判断力。
- They got bogged down in the Middle East. 他们陷入中东的泥淖中。

植物名称如 beaver(海狸)和 fleece(羊毛):

- Cranes and bulldozers beaver away throughout the territory. 吊车和推土机在那片土地上忙碌着。
- Private transporters fleece tourists on Delhi-McLeodganj route. 个体车主在德里－麦克劳德根杰线上大宰游客。

人体部位名词如 back(背)和 muscle(肌肉):

- This newspaper backed him for a second term. 本报支持他连任。
- Anyone trying to muscle in on the gang's territory would get his face smashed in. 谁要想挤进这帮家伙的地盘,谁就会挨揍。

工具、器具、物品名称如 jack(千斤顶)、rein(缰绳)、zip(拉链):

- None of this is to say that the Fed should jack up rates without warning. 所有这些并不是说,美联储应在不提出任何警告的情况下加息。
- It took just 20 seconds for him to zip up to the top of the 25-storey building. 他仅仅花了20秒钟的时间,就登上了25层楼的楼顶。
- Faced with complaints, officials took steps last fall to rein in prices. 面对民

众的抱怨，政府官员去年秋天开始采取措施平抑价格。

建筑、场所的名称如 harbor（港口）、doorstep（门口）：

- We must confront regimes that continue to harbor terrorists and pursue weapons of mass murder. 我们必须与继续为恐怖分子提供庇护和谋求大规模毁灭性武器的政权作斗争。
- The newspaper contacted his grandmother to trace his present address, and later doorstepped him at his home. 报社记者联系了他祖母，查到了他现在的住址后便前往登门采访。

职业、身份名称如 soldier（士兵）、engineer（工程师）：

- Faced with the dilemma, he opted for soldiering on. 面临着进退两难的困境，他决定顽强地坚持下去。
- This boom has been engineered by the Chancellor for short-term political reasons. 这片繁荣景象是总理为了短期政治利益而精心安排的。

下面是更多从报刊阅读中摘取的例子：

- The number of Chinese tourists swelled by 140 per cent in spite of political tensions between Tokyo and Beijing over wartime history and maritime territory.
- Washington now has a major opportunity to achieve what sanctions could not—namely, compelling Putin to distance Russia from the separatists in Ukraine.
- However, there's still one fundamental fact: the company is raking in hundreds of millions of dollars selling ads based on the user data it's harvesting.
- A female doctor has been axed to death by a patient in the northern Chinese city of Tianjin in the latest act of violence in the country's hospitals.
- The death shattered a 72-hour cease-fire in Gaza that many US and UN diplomats had viewed as the best chance to bring the conflict to an end.
- As Israel showed signs of scaling back its ground offensive in Gaza, its war from the skies continued Sunday, as an airstrike outside a U.N. school in southern Gaza killed at least 10 people. The bloodshed sparked some of the harshest US criticism of Israel since the war began.

第二，英语的搭配一直是写作和汉译英实践中的难题，而要解决这个难题只能靠大量的英语阅读和用心的积累。这一点我们在第二篇第一章第二节等章节中已有较多讨论，这里只是结合新闻语篇的特点再强调一下。请看下面新闻片段：

The government has confirmed that <u>security is being tightened</u> at UK airports after US officials <u>raised fears</u> about terrorists in Syria and Yemen developing explosives that could be smuggled on to planes.

The Department for Transport (DfT) said on Wednesday night it would "<u>step up some of our aviation security measures</u>" following the warning from US security chiefs.

The transport secretary, Patrick McLoughlin, said: "We constantly <u>keep the whole issue of aviation under constant review</u> along with our international partners and also the aviation industry and obviously we have <u>acted on</u> advice and information that we have received."

"I would like to reassure <u>the travelling public</u> that we have one of <u>the toughest security regimes</u> in the world, along with the US."

如果为了获取新闻信息而阅读，我们可以一扫而过。但为了学习汉译英或提高英语写作能力，就必须留心有没有需要熟悉和记忆的搭配或词语。阅读上面的译例需要注意以下搭配结构：① tighten+security；raise+fears；step up+measures；keep…under constant review；② act on…；③ the travelling public；the toughest security regimes 等三组常见的搭配形式。第一组是动宾搭配，第二组是短语动词，第三组是名词词组。阅读中可以以这三类结构作为观察的重点，兼顾其他，慢慢积累。

动宾搭配的例子如：

- On Sunday, it said a Palestinian rocket had crippled a power line to Gaza from Israel and it would not endanger engineers by sending them to <u>conduct repairs</u>.
- He added that the hospital had <u>increased its security</u> this year, in line with new directives from the health ministry.
- "The hope is that the majority of travellers will not be unduly disrupted but I hope also that people will understand that we have to work together across the world to deal with people who want to <u>inflict harm</u>."

观察动词和宾语，也要留意其后的介词或副词的搭配情况，比如：

- On Tuesday, US and European privacy advocates sent a letter to the Federal Trade Commission and the Irish Data Protection Commission, which <u>has oversight over</u> Facebook's operations in Europe.
- But the company has lately been trying to <u>win trust from</u> users by revamping what it shows users about their privacy options.
- Ministers are hoping to <u>get more clarity from</u> Mr. Li during his visit <u>on</u> whether and how China intends to invest in key UK infrastructure projects, such as nuclear power and the HS2 high-speed rail line.

短语动词结构如：

- This week, a New Economics Foundation working paper also <u>set out</u> alternatives to the marketisation of public services.
- Yet privatisation is touted as a panacea and clichés are <u>trotted out</u> about the evils of the "nanny state".
- Beijing's brinkmanship <u>is redolent of</u> the hard negotiating tactics employed by the Chinese in the run-up to Mr. Cameron's visit last year.
- President Obama said Friday that US intelligence indicates that a Russian-made missile downed the plane from rebel territory, but he <u>stopped short of</u> saying who pulled the trigger.
- This strategy is <u>playing out</u> in a few ways, most notably with Facebook's recent plan to <u>break out</u> its functions <u>into</u> several apps to serve particular, often more personal functions.
- Wang Hongdong, the hospital's chief spokesman, said the man had <u>smuggled in</u> the axe after lunch, when security guards and doctors were on a break.
- When Facebook first <u>came onto the scene</u> over a decade ago, he said, people pretty much had the option to either post their thoughts publicly in blogs or privately in e-mail—with no middle ground.

名词词组如：

- More recently, the company upset users after researchers published a paper on <u>a mood manipulation study</u> of its users.
- This would promote public ownership as the <u>default option</u> for public services

and give the public a say in whether services are privatised.

三、句式和句子结构

句式和句子结构也是前面章节中关注较多的话题，这里结合新闻语篇的特点特别提醒大家注意如下句式和结构。

1. It 作形式主语

- <u>It is far from unheard of</u> for senior world leaders to have a meeting with the Queen.
- <u>It is thought that</u> the extra measures at UK airports could include increased random screening of passengers and tighter scrutiny of footwear, mobile phones and computers.
- Rather, they said, <u>it was a recognition that</u> ground troops had accomplished their mission and other goals can be more easily achieved from afar.

2. 主语从句或动名词短语作主语

- <u>What makes all this heartening</u> is that new social forms of ownership are emerging in which public utilities are run by coalitions of workers and service users.
- <u>Downing Street's willingness to acquiesce to such requests</u> shows how much importance the UK is giving to the bilateral relationship, which it sees as key to helping boost British exports and foreign investment in British companies.

3. 倒装结构

- The US did not specify which airports or countries would be affected, <u>nor did it say</u> what triggered the extra precautions.
- <u>So effectively has the coalition rebranded an economic crisis</u> caused by private greed as the consequence of public ownership, that nationalisation has come to be seen as a universally discredited hangover from bad old Labour.
- We will play our part <u>as will other countries</u> to make sure where security checks can be tightened up, they will be.

4. 同位语结构

- Israel has shown no indication <u>it will pause its campaign of fire from the air</u>

and the sea, as evidenced by Sunday's attack near the U.N. school. Hamas, too, has given little indication <u>it will yield</u>, firing at least 55 rockets toward Israel on Sunday.

5. 长后置结构

按照英语的句法，常常是先构建主句，然后在其后依次叠加更多的信息，这就形成了所谓的"右分支"（right-branching）结构，即一条长长的后置成分链条。比如：

Li Keqiang will fly to London for a three-day visit next week <u>as the two countries seek to finalise the thaw in relations that has occurred in the past few months after a difficult period following Mr. Cameron's decision to meet the Dalai Lama in 2012.</u>

我们看到，主句后出现了由 as（状语从句）… that（定语从句）… after（介词短语作状语）… following（分词短语作定语）四部分组成的后置长链。这样的结构在英语新闻中很常见，我们必须熟悉，并学会使用。

新闻语篇中最具特色的是由同位语或同位语从句引出的后置长链，或用同位语重复上文的旧信息，然后根据行文需要续以新信息；或用同位语从句将上文信息具体化。如：

- But China Mobile is only now building its 4G network—<u>a task that necessitates spending RMB 75 billion this year, which would bring total capital expenditure up by a fifth to RMB 225.2 billion.</u>

- But now Japan has earned its first "tourism surplus" in 44 years—<u>a testament to the transformation of Asia's economies that has turned once prohibitively expensive Japanese cities into affordable destinations for many middle-class Chinese, Thais and Indonesians.</u>

- "I live in fear expecting death. I no longer know what's more difficult—to die or to await death," said Ali Mahmoud, <u>a 40-year-old resident of the northern Gaza town of Beit Hanoun from where the Israeli ground action could be heard just 800 meters (yards) away.</u>

- Zuckerberg's reply revealed his unique view of privacy—<u>one that's not concerned primarily between what users share with companies but with what users share with one another.</u>

- Presumably, the three militants Israel had targeted died, too. A U.N. employee was among those killed, said Adnan Abu Hasna, <u>a spokesman for the U.N. Relief and Works Agency, which is assisting more than 200,000 Palestinian evacuees at 90 schools in Gaza.</u>

常见的还有由从句或分词短语引出的长后置结构：
- Asia's broader tourism shift has been under way for a number of years but it has accelerated since 2012, <u>when the yen began a 20 per cent decline against other leading currencies, further lowering the cost of everything from hotels to meals to shopping expeditions for foreigners.</u>
- The Israeli military confirmed the incident near central Gaza, <u>saying it killed one militant, repelled the rest, and four soldiers were wounded.</u>
- Sunday's bloodshed came <u>as Israel said it had withdrawn most of its ground forces from Gaza but would continue its military operation in the coastal strip.</u>
- The campaign is meant to clean up the party's image—<u>so soiled by graft that some leaders fear public contempt could threaten their grip on power.</u>

介词短语也可以引出长后置结构：
- For the moment, that investment has yet to pay off, <u>with data services not as profitable as SMS texting, and only 1.34 million of its 775 million customers using 4G services.</u>

6. 插入结构

插入结构是在信息主流中加入某些必要信息的常用手段，常见的有以下几种类型：

（1）插入定语从句、分词短语或同位语，以提供详情、添加解释。
- The fate of the airplane's black-box data recorders, <u>which could give crucial information about the plane's final moments,</u> was unclear, with neither side acknowledging possession.
- The mobile operator also cited the subsidies it provides for Apple's iPhones—<u>which it began selling on its network for the first time in January</u>—as a factor for its lower earnings.
- Consumer Dialogue—<u>a collection of consumer groups from the US and</u>

Europe that focus on a number of social policy issues, including information policy—have argued that this dramatically increases the amount of data Facebook holds and that users were not properly notified about the change.
- Gaza officials said that at least 325 Palestinians, including 70 children, have been killed in the 12-day conflict.

（2）插入句子，指明信息来源。
- Japan's aggregate tourism-related revenues exceeded expenditures by Y17.7 billion ($172 million) in April, current account data released by the Finance Ministry yesterday showed, the largest such surplus on record and the first since July 1970.

（3）插入状语，表明伴随情况、叙述者语气、态度等。
- He also indicated, however, that Israeli forces would reassess their mission after destroying Hamas's tunnel networks.
- If, as now seems likely, Russian-supported Ukrainian separatists used a surface-to-air missile to shoot down a civilian airliner killing nearly 300 innocent people, Washington now has a major opportunity to achieve what sanctions could not—namely, compelling Putin to distance Russia from the separatists in Ukraine.

新闻编译

新闻稿件的对外传播一般采取编译的形式，即将一篇或几篇汉语新闻稿编辑整理，用英语重新写出。新华社网站双语新闻稿件下加有这样的注解："Note: The above is the same story reported in English and Chinese respectively, and is not literal translation." 这很清楚地说明了新闻语篇英译的"写作"性质。编译就是用英语重新报道同一个新闻事件，以国际通行的格式、用词规范、表述句式，以外国读者喜闻乐见的方式将中国新闻有效地传播出去。

如本书开篇所言，新闻编译需要以一门课的形式专门加以训练，这里只通过几段新闻编译的实例，对新闻编译的要领作简略的介绍。

新闻稿由导语和新闻主体组成。导语以简明的文字概括新闻全文，引导读者阅读正文。新闻主体部分按新闻事件重要性大小依序排列，有实事、有数据、有引语，既简练又充实。

编译新闻往往要对原文所提供的信息素材进行适当的删减、添加、重新组排，或对某些内容进行归化操作，使其更符合西方读者的知识结构。

下面提供几个编译实例，并对编译方法作简略提示。

【译例一】

习近平会见马来西亚最高元首哈利姆

新华网北京9月4日电【1】 国家主席习近平4日在人民大会堂会见马来西亚最高元首哈利姆。

【2】 习近平强调，中马两国友好交往源远流长。建交40年来，两国关系发展良好。去年10月我访问马来西亚，受到哈利姆最高元首热情、隆重接待，

给我留下深刻、美好印象。你是中马关系发展的重要推动者和见证者。40年前,你首次担任马来西亚最高元首期间,中马建立外交关系。在两国建交40周年之际,你再次访华,我们对此表示赞赏,相信你的这次访问将进一步促进两国友谊与合作。

【3】 哈利姆表示,习近平主席去年对马来西亚的访问取得圆满成功,有力推动了两国关系发展。今年5月,纳吉布总理访华,马中双方就加强全面战略伙伴关系达成新的重要共识,我对此感到高兴。我期待着通过这次访问,增加对中国的了解,深化两国传统友谊。

【4】 会见前,习近平在人民大会堂东门外广场为哈利姆举行欢迎仪式。习近平主席夫人彭丽媛、全国人大常委会副委员长沈跃跃、国务委员杨洁篪、全国政协副主席马培华等出席。

Chinese President Meets Malaysian Supreme Head of State

BEIJING, Sept. 4 (Xinhua)—[1] Chinese President Xi Jinping met with Malaysian Supreme Head of State Abdul Halim Mu'adzam Shah on Thursday at the Great Hall of the People in downtown Beijing.

[2] Hailing the traditional China-Malaysia friendship, Xi said the bilateral relationship has developed smoothly over the past 40 years.

[3] The two countries established their diplomatic ties in 1974, when Halim visited China, also as Supreme Head of State of Malaysia, for the first time.

[4] Xi said he appreciates Halim's visit to China as the two sides observe the 40th anniversary of their diplomatic relationship and that he believes the visit will further cement the friendship and boost cooperation between the two countries.

[5] Xi also expressed his gratitude to Halim for the warm reception last October as the Chinese leader paid a state visit to Malaysia.

[6] Halim said Xi's successful visit has boosted the bilateral ties and that he is happy to see Malaysia and China reach new consensus on strengthening their comprehensive strategic partnership in May this year as Malaysian Prime Minister Najib Razak visited China.

[7] Halim said he hopes his visit will help to further enhance the traditional friendship between the two countries.

[8] Halim is paying a state visit to China at Xi's invitation from Sept. 3 to 8.

编译方法提示：

【1】：首段导语照译。

【2】：一段译为四段，原文划线部分在译文中被放在第[5]段。

【3】：引语在译文中分为两段。

【4】：此段未译。译文中最后一段传达了哈利姆从何日至何日在中国访问的信息。

【译例二】

中国—东盟自贸区：地球三分之一人口的共同期待

新华网南宁 10 月 23 日电【1】 第六届中国—东盟博览会上，印度尼西亚场馆内一家食品公司的展位前贴着大大的标语：寻求中国经销商。出口部经理阿凡提·塔鲁纳说："我们很着急，打算明年打入中国市场。"

【2】"这是我们第一次参加博览会，既要推销产品，也要找到合作伙伴。自贸区一成立，就可以向中国出口免税产品了。"阿凡提说。

【3】 中国—东盟博览会成功举办五届以来，一直是中国与东盟经贸交流合作的黄金平台之一。而本届博览会距离中国—东盟自由贸易区全面建成仅余两个多月，东盟国家的参展商正把握最后的机会，为 2010 年进军中国市场造势。

【4】 中国国务院副总理李克强在与博览会同期举办的中国—东盟商务与投资峰会开幕式上说，自贸区建成后，双方 90% 的贸易产品将实现零关税，并实质性开放服务贸易市场。

【5】"现在向中国出口要征收一定的关税，到明年再出口就不征税了，价格一降低，进入市场更容易，中国消费者也会喜欢。"阿凡提说。

【6】 阿凡提所在的公司主营椰果、果冻、芦荟、亚答子等消闲小食，计划明年尝试将芦荟、亚答子等中国不太常见的食品销往北京、上海等地。

【7】 中国与东盟经贸往来日益密切,不仅大量的东盟客商开始瞄准或继续深入中国市场,中国客商也纷纷调整出口战略、转战东盟挖掘新商机。

【8】 广西三环企业集团股份有限公司近20年来一直从事餐具、陶瓷出口生意,目前90%的商品都销往欧美市场,东盟仅占出口业务的1%都不到。公司业务主管梁立强在博览会上告诉记者,自贸区建成后,他们计划向东盟国家大量出口中低档产品。

【9】 "中国和东盟贸易往来前景大好,自贸区优惠政策对我们也很有吸引力,我们打算以东盟各国旅游宾馆、星级酒店为突破口。"梁立强说。

【10】 "中国瓷器举世闻名,公司总部在广西,有很大的地缘优势。唯一的问题是东盟一些国家交通运输相对落后,物流水平有限。"他说。

【11】 本届博览会及同期举行的高端论坛上,东盟多国高层领导纷纷表示要着力解决中国与东盟互联互通问题,加快公路、铁路等基础设施建设,更好地为自贸区服务。

【12】 近年来,中国和东盟双边贸易发展迅速。据海关统计,2004年中国与东盟贸易额约为1059亿美元,2008年已突破2310亿美元,年均增长率高达21.6%。自贸区的建成有利于中国和东盟联手抵抗金融危机余威,给百姓带来大实惠。

【13】 李克强说,自贸区建成是区域经济一体化进程中具有里程碑意义的一件大事,标志着双方经贸关系站在了一个新的起点上。

【14】 据悉,中国与东盟关于自贸区协定的主要谈判均已完成,一个惠及19亿人口、接近6万亿美元GDP、4.5万亿美元贸易总额、由发展中国家组成的最大自贸区指日可待。

【15】 中国社会科学院亚太所研究员陆建人说:"通常南北型自贸区容易成功,而中国—东盟自贸区属于南南型。虽然没有发达国家参与,但中国市场巨大、产业结构层次多,新加坡等国也是新兴经济体。东盟自贸区很可能打破传统理论,创立新的模式。"

【16】 博览会期间,官员、学者纷纷表示,中国和东盟国家应当充分利用地区资源和经济结构的互补性,实现区域大繁荣。

【17】 马来西亚中国经济贸易总商会会长杨天培说,中马经济"唇齿相依",中国需要向马来西亚进口石油化工、橡胶、棕榈油等产品,马来西亚十分青睐中

国的日用品以及电视机、计算机等高新技术产品。

【18】"我们希望有更多的高科技产品进入马来西亚市场,中国制造的电子信息产品、家电、机械设备等都有非常可观的市场。"杨天培说。

【19】当然,中国和东盟各国一些同质化行业在自贸区建成后将不得不同台公平竞争,压力和危机扑面而来。中国一些专家提出,自贸区建成后,东盟出口到中国的农产品将对中国南方地区的农产品形成较大冲击。

【20】"来自东盟各国的热带水果、谷物等很有竞争力,中国南方的许多农产品都将面临严峻挑战。"广西社会科学院东南亚研究所副所长刘建文说。

【21】博览会上的东盟客商告诉记者,他们已经开始研究策略应对2010年后来自中国同行的竞争。

【22】阿凡提说:"中国生产的果冻、椰果产品价格已经很便宜了,自贸区建成后只会更加便宜。我们只好不断寻找降低成本、提高效率的办法。"阿凡提本人很迷恋中国货,最热衷中国生产的手机和美的牌小家电。

【23】"我们不喜欢竞争,但竞争对公司的长远发展有益无害。自贸区建成后,中国和东盟国家的消费者都能花更少的钱,买到质量更好的商品。"阿凡提说。

A Free Trade Area for World's One Third Population

NANNING, Oct. 22 (Xinhua)—[1] Effendi Taruna, the export manager of an Indonesia-based company, could not wait to find a Chinese import partner before the year 2010.

[2] "Seeking an agent in China," said a poster at the booth of PT. Niramas Utama Food & Beverages Industry at the 6th China-ASEAN Expo held from Oct. 20 to 24 in Nanning, south China's Guangxi Zhuang Autonomous Region.

[3] "It's our first time to join the expo for promotions and seeking partnership. We want to export tariff-free products to China as soon as next year when the Free Trade Area is realized," Effendi said.

[4] Under a series of agreements between China and ASEAN (Association of Southeast Asian Nations), the China-ASEAN Free Trade Area (CAFTA) is due to be established on Jan. 1, 2010.

[5] It will provide zero tariff on 90 percent of products traded between China and ASEAN and other favorable policies on trade and investment.

[6] "We have to pay 10 percent of the price in tariffs if export products to China now, but next year with zero-tariff treatment, things will be much better," Effendi said.

[7] His company planned to explore markets first in Beijing or Shanghai with products of palm seeds and aloe vera, which, unlike coco or jelly, are rare in the Chinese market.

[8] As more and more businessmen from ASEAN are paving the way for entering Chinese market, those from China also start targeting ASEAN markets.

[9] Liang Liqiang, sales supervisor of a Guangxi-based tableware and chinaware export company with a history of almost 20 years, told Xinhua at the expo they would export low and middle-end products to ASEAN countries right after the establishment of CAFTA.

[10] "China-ASEAN partnership looks promising, and CAFTA is a great temptation to us," Liang said, adding that over 90 percent of their products were now exported to the US and European markets.

[11] "Chinaware is special and world-famous, and our company also has a geographic advantage in exporting to Southeast Asian countries. The only problem is logistics, due to underdeveloped transportation in some ASEAN countries," Liang said.

[12] Several officials from ASEAN countries have vowed to improve infrastructure and speed up transportation projects to better serve the China-ASEAN trade cooperation.

[13] China and ASEAN have been deepening mutual economic cooperation over the past few years. The trade volume between the two sides reached 231 billion US dollars in 2008, up 21.6 percent from that in 2004.

[14] CAFTA is highly expected to further boost trade and investment cooperation between China and ASEAN, so as to combat the lingering global economic downtown and bring benefits to both peoples in the long run.

[15] The free trade area will cover 1.9 billion population in China and ten ASEAN members including Brunei, Cambodia, Indonesia, Laos, Malaysia, Myanmar, the

Philippines, Singapore, Thailand and Vietnam.

[16] "CAFTA sets up a significant milestone in regional economic cooperation and it marks that trade ties between China and ASEAN are to enter a new stage," said Chinese Vice Premier Li Keqiang at Tuesday's opening of the 6th China-ASEAN Business and Investment Summit held simultaneously with the expo.

[17] CAFTA is set to create a combined GDP of nearly 6 trillion US dollars to become the third largest FTA in the world, only next to the North American FTA and European FTA.

[18] "Unlike American FTA or European FTA, CAFTA belongs to south-south regional economic integration. Even without the participation of developed countries, China can still serve as a huge emerging market in the area, and Singapore is also a rising economy," said Lu Jianren, a researcher from Asian and Pacific Studies Institution under the Chinese Academy of Social Sciences.

[19] "CAFTA has the potential to break the rules of north-south integration and set up a new mode," Lu said.

[20] Experts agreed that China and ASEAN should take full advantage of complementary resources and economic structures to make regional prosperity come true.

[21] Yang Tianpei, chairman of Malaysia-China Chamber of Commerce, said China and Malaysia were dependent on each other and FTA would work for sure.

[22] "China wants raw materials from Malaysia, especially petrochemical materials for its industrial development, and Malaysia wants a variety of goods from China," Yang said.

[23] Yang also said high-tech products made in China would be desirable in Malaysia, such as household electrical appliances, mechanical equipment and IT products.

[24] Still, some industries in China and ASEAN already feel the pressure from each other, as their products will have to compete on the same stage after FTA is fully realized.

[25] Chinese experts said FTA would have an evident impact on domestic

agricultural products, especially those grown in southern part of the country.

[26] "Tropical fruits and grain from ASEAN countries are quite competitive. It's going to be a tough time for our domestic products," said Liu Jianwen, vice director of Southeast Asia Studies Institution under Guangxi Academy of Social Sciences.

[27] Businessmen from ASEAN countries even started to think about strategies to resist future competition with Chinese counterparts from 2010.

[28] "Chinese jelly and coco products are already very cheap and will be cheaper when FTA is established, and we have to increase efficiency and cut prices from now on," Effendi said, who himself often bought items made in China, including cellphones and cooking machines.

[29] "We hate competition, but it's good for the company's long-term development. After FTA is realized, people in the region will get stuff with higher quality but lower prices," he said.

编译方法提示：

【1】、【2】：两段对应译文 [1]、[2]、[3] 三段，信息出现顺序、引语的形式都有所调整。

【3】：这段未出现在英译文中，而译文第 [4] 段是原文没有的信息。

【4】：原文后半句信息放入译文第 [5] 段。

【5】：引语中信息在译文第 [6] 段里有所调整。

【6】：对应译文第 [7] 段，基本照译，信息有调整。

【7】：对应译文第 [8] 段，信息有所简化。

【8】：对应译文第 [9] 段，信息有所精简。

【9】：对应译文第 [10] 段，原文中划线部分译文省去，且略有补充其他信息。

【10】：对应译文第 [11] 段，引语稍有简化。

【11】：对应译文第 [12] 段，信息有所精简。

【12】：对应译文第 [13] 段，信息简化，包括略去一个数字。译文第 [14]、[15] 段部分信息是添加的。

【13】：对应译文第 [16] 段，此段的译文添加了信息，引用了李克强总理原话的英译。

【14】：对应译文第 [17] 段，原文中划线部分在译文中有所删减，译文中最后部分为添加信息。

【15】：对应译文第 [18]、[19] 两段，原文引语被拆分。

【16】：对应译文第 [20] 段，信息有所精简。

【17】、【18】：原文两段对应译文第 [21]、[22]、[23] 段，引语有所调整，利于突出主要信息。

【19】、【20】：原文两段对应译文第 [24]、[25]、[26] 段，信息有所调整。

【21】：对应译文第 [27] 段，基本照译。

【22】：对应译文第 [28] 段，大体照译。

【23】：对应译文第 [29] 段，基本照译。

【译例三】

手牵手一起向前走

新华网北京 11 月 16 日电【1】一群来自世界各地的孩子，任着命运的安排，相聚在遍布全球的国际学校。在这些至真至纯的童心里，种族和肤色的不同，语言与文化的差异，从来都不会是什么障碍。

【2】伸出你的手，伸出我的手，伸出他的手……
只要手牵手，就是好朋友。

【3】国际学校是个"小联合国"，语言和文化的多样是靓丽的风景。校园里，既有饺子、咖喱饭和通心粉的五味杂陈；有和服、丽纱和长衫的色彩纷呈；也有空竹、呼啦圈和芭比娃娃的争奇斗艳；二胡、小提琴和风笛的共鸣合奏。

【4】国际学校更是个大熔炉，不同肤色、不同种族的孩子们亲密共处，相互拥抱与温暖，彼此理解和包容。在这里，热爱和平、追求平等、尊重与和谐是共同的语言。正如联合国国际学校高中部负责人拉达·拉赞所说："你穿什么不重要，外表也不重要，说什么语言也不重要。我们都是一样的。"

【5】当然，在这个被全球化重新涂抹的大千世界，国际学校只不过是其中一个小小的画卷。不是所有的孩子，都有机会在国际学校感受世界的多元。但在这个越变越小的"地球村"，几乎每一个孩子，都可以通过笔会、互联网等各种

各样的方式,"牵手"世界各地的同龄人,交流情感,分享快乐,建立友谊,感受关爱。

【6】一个孩子的手虽小,但千千万万双小手牵在一起,就有一种奇特的力量,让世界瞩目和倾听。

【7】今年7月,在联合国儿童基金会发起并主办的第五届"青少年八国峰会"上,来自13个国家的54名青少年就气候变化和非洲发展等议题展开讨论,向与会国家领导人建言献策。

【8】今年9月,在联合国气候变化峰会开始之前,世界各地的孩子通过视频,共同"拷问"全球领导人:"我们将从你们手中继承什么样的世界?"

【9】作为人类未来的主人,孩子们今天的牵手,让我们看到了明天世界的希望。孩子们也用实际行动来提醒我们:在人类命运休戚与共的时代,需要牵手的,不应仅仅是孩子,更应是正在塑造世界的大人们。

【10】近年来,在东盟峰会、中日韩领导人会议等国际会议上,与会领导人往往会手牵手地合影留念。各国领导人双臂交叉,牵着手一字排开,<u>个个神情放松,活像一群大孩子</u>。如今,这个简单的动作,<u>这个手牵手的场景</u>,已经成为国际社会团结与合作的象征。在这个人类共同挑战越来越多的世界,太需要各国领导人真诚相待、彼此包容和相互信任了!

【11】牵手,是一种信任,更是一种承诺。不管是大人、孩子,不论肤色、种族,伸出你的手,伸出我的手,伸出他的手……

【12】让我们心手相连,一起向前走。

Hand in Hand We Stand

BEIJING, Nov. 16 (Xinhua)—[1] "Hand in hand we stand, all across the land. We can make this world a better place in which to live. Hand in hand we can, start to understand. Breaking all the walls that come between us for all time," the lyrics of the 1988 Olympiad theme song have driven home the great power of joining hands in creating a better world.

[2] Initiated and hosted by UNICEF, the Fifth Junior Eight Summit or the J8 Summit was held in Italy last July. At the summit, 54 teenagers from 13 countries

discussed major international issues such as climate change and development in Africa, and offered their policy suggestions to world leaders.

[3] Prior to the opening of the UN climate change summit in September, children in all parts of the globe raised a question to world leaders via video conferencing: "what kind of a world would we inherit under your stewardship?"

[4] The hands of a single child are weak, but when millions of little hands join together, they create a magic power to attract the eyes of the entire world and get their messages across.

[5] Children joining their little hands and shouting in their tender voice for a common cause fill us with confidence about the future of our world. It should also awaken us to the fact that in today's increasingly interdependent world, adults have all the more reasons to join hands to tackle waves of new forms of common challenges including climate change, terrorism and environmental degradation.

[6] In recent years, world leaders at major international conference would stand in a line and cross their arms to join hands with each other, which has become a symbol of international communication and cooperation. Today when human being is facing tougher common challenges, we need all the more sincerity, tolerance and mutual trust.

[7] In the UN International School in New York City, children of various nationalities are living happily as close friends regardless of their skin color and ethnic background. They understand and tolerate each other. Their vastly diverse cultures combined form the most attractive scene.

[8] Here, children could savor different cuisines ranging from Chinese dumplings, Indian curry rice to Italian macaroni, or enjoy themselves playing with Chinese diabolos, Western hula hoops and Barbie dolls.

[9] "It doesn't matter what kind of clothes you are wearing, what you look like or what language you speak," said Dr. Radha Rajan, its high school principal. "We are just the same."

[10] International schools like this can be found elsewhere around the world. For innocent children everywhere, differences in race, language and culture will never be barriers to making friends with each other.

[11] Adults should follow their suit. Let's join hands to build a harmonious world of lasting peace and common prosperity not only for ourselves but for the generations to come.

编译方法提示：

【1】：对应译文第 [7] 段，可视为此段的重写。

【2】：对应译文第 [1] 段，此处被替换为 1988 年奥运会的主题曲，以迎合国际受众的认知语境，是对原文信息的归化操作。

【3】：原文划线部分在译文中省去。双划线部分融入了译文第 [7] 段。

【4】：引语对应译文中的第 [9] 段。

【5】：对应译文第 [10] 段，可视为此段的重写。

【6】：对应译文第 [4] 段，基本全译。

【7】：对应译文第 [2] 段，添加了"青少年八国峰会"召开时间和地点的信息。

【8】：对应译文第 [3] 段，基本按原句译出。

【9】：对应译文第 [5] 段，添加部分信息（译文划线部分）。

【10】：对应译文第 [6] 段，原文划线部分信息在译文中省略未译。

【11】、【12】：译文 [11] 段可看做是对原文【11】、【12】两段的重写。

通过上述译例可以看到，编译就是对新闻素材的重新编辑和写作。汉语自成一体，英语也是另一个自立的语篇，也要保证语篇结构衔接，语义连贯。由此我们可更清楚地看到阅读英语新闻语篇的导引作用，编译就是用英语读者认可的词语、句式和语篇模式讲好我们自己的新闻。

清华大学出版社　高等学校英语专业系列教材

高级英语视听说教程学生用书（第二版）上　　　　作者：戴劲、刘晶 等
定价：22.00　　　　书号：978-7-302-22869-1

高级英语视听说教程学生用书（第二版）下　　　　作者：戴劲、刘晶 等
定价：29.80　　　　书号：978-7-302-22870-7

高级英语视听说教程教师用书（第二版）全一册　　作者：戴劲、刘晶 等
定价：49.80　　　　书号：978-7-302-22868-4

中级英语视听说教程学生用书（第二版）上　　　　作者：王祥兵、刘晶 等
定价：28.00　　　　书号：978-7-302-23420-3

中级英语视听说教程学生用书（第二版）下　　　　作者：王祥兵、刘晶 等
定价：28.00　　　　书号：978-7-302-23421-0

中级英语视听说教程教师用书（第二版）全一册　　作者：王祥兵、刘晶 等
定价：34.80　　　　书号：978-7-302-23422-7

英语写作实践教程（第二版）　　　　　　　　　　作者：李贵苍 等
定价：32.00　　　　书号：978-7-302-29921-9

《高级英汉翻译理论与实践》（第三版）　　　　　作者：叶子南
定价：35.00　　　　书号：978-7-302-32813-1

汉英比较翻译教程（第二版）（另有配套练习）　　作者：魏志成
定价：39.90　　　　书号：978-7-302-29526-6

英汉比较翻译教程（第二版）（另有配套练习）　　作者：魏志成
定价：38.50　　　　书号：978-7-302-29015-5

英汉互译入门教程　　　　　　　　　　　　　　　作者：许建平
定价：22.00　　　　书号：978-7-302-19772-0

英汉互译实践与技巧（第四版）（另有配套教参）　作者：许建平
定价：39.80　　　　书号：978-7-302-29029-2

《英汉互译实践与技巧》辅导备考教程	作者：许建平
定价：39.90　书号：978-7-302-32898-8	
英汉语篇翻译（第三版）	作者：李运兴
定价：35.00　书号：978-7-302-26652-5	
汉英语篇翻译	作者：李运兴
定价：49.00　书号：978-7-302-41666-1	
高级汉英语篇翻译（修订版）	作者：居祖纯
定价：22.00　书号：978-7-302-27569-5	
中西翻译理论简明教程	作者：张政
定价：39.00　书号：978-7-302-39601-7	
美国文学学习指南（第二版）——美国文学史及选读综合练习	作者：李正栓 等
定价：33.00　书号：978-7-302-12462-7	
英国文学学习指南（第二版）——英国文学史及选读综合练习	作者：李正栓 等
定价：42.00　书号：978-7-302-12218-0	
英美诗歌教程（第二版）	作者：李正栓 等
定价：48.00　书号：978-7-302-37600-2	
莎士比亚十四行诗导读	作者：李正栓
定价：49.00　书号：978-7-302-40159-9	
英美文学赏析教程（散文与诗歌）	作者：罗选民 等
定价：20.00　书号：978-7-302-05404-7	
英美文学赏析教程（第二版）：小说卷	作者：罗选民 等
定价：55.00　书号：978-7-302-37154-0	
新编简明英语语言学概论	作者：马琰、王峰
定价：49.00　书号：978-7-302-37533-3	
实用大学英语语法新编	作者：曾亚军 等
定价：58.00　书号：978-7-302-36900-4	
高级英语教程：思辨性阅读（上）	作者：杨会兰
定价：35.00　书号：978-7-302-41515-2	